DOLPHIN SQUARE

DOLPHIN SQUARE

The History of a Unique Building

Terry Gourvish

BLOOMSBURY
LONDON • NEW DELHI • NEW YORK • SYDNEY

First published in Great Britain 2014

Bloomsbury Publishing Plc
50 Bedford Square
London
WC1B 3DP

www.bloomsbury.com

Bloomsbury is a trademark of Bloomsbury Publishing Plc

Bloomsbury Publishing
London, New Delhi, New York and Sydney

A CIP record for this book is available from the British Library.

ISBN: 9-781-4729-1109-4

FSC www.fsc.org MIX Paper from responsible sources FSC® C020471

10 9 8 7 6 5 4 3 2 1

Design by Fiona Pike, Pike Design, Winchester
Typeset by Hewer Text UK Ltd, Edinburgh
Printed and bound in Great Britain by CPI Group (UK) Ltd, Croydon CR0 4YY

CONTENTS

LIST OF TABLES

LIST OF ILLUSTRATIONS

LIST OF APPENDICES

LIST OF ABBREVIATIONS

AGM	Annual General Meeting
AIPM	Associate of the Institute of Personnel Management
AMSE	American Society of Mechanical Engineers
ARW&B	Arber, Rutter, Waghorn & Brown
Cdr	Commander (Navy)
CIPFA	Chartered Institute of Public Finance and Accountancy
DSCL	Dolphin Square Caterers Ltd.
DSIR	Department of Scientific and Industrial Research
DST	Dolphin Square Trust Ltd.
DSTA	Dolphin Square Tenants' Association
FCA	Fellow of the Institute of Chartered Accountants (England & Wales)
FIMTA	Fellow of the Institute of Municipal Treasurers and Accountants
FP	Friends Provident
FRICS	Fellow of the Royal Institution of Chartered Surveyors
FRVA	Fellow of the Rating and Valuation Association
GLC	Greater London Council
GRU	Glavnoye Razvedyvatel'noye Upravleniye [Main Intelligence Directorate]
HPM&B	Hillier, Parker, May & Bowden
HSD	Higher Subdivision
LCC	London County Council
LMA	London Metropolitan Archives
LSE	London School of Economics
MJIE	Member of Junior Institution of Engineers
MIPHE	Member of the Institute of Plumbing and Heating Engineering
MOD	Ministry of Defence
MP	Member of Parliament
NCP	National Car Parks

NYPL	New York Public Library
OxDNB	Oxford Dictionary of National Biography
PPS	Parliamentary Private Secretary
R & A	Report & Accounts
RACD	Royal Army Clothing Depot
RPI	Retail Prices Index
SOS	Save Our Square
SoS	Secretary of State
TCC	Town and Country Cars
TGWU	Transport and General Workers Union
TNA	The National Archives
UKPI	United Kingdom Provident Institution
VAT	Value Added Tax
WCA	City of Westminster Archives Centre
WCC	Westminster City Council

PREFACE

Like many people who have spent much of their working life in London, I was aware of Dolphin Square, though I had never been there. My long-serving administrator at LSE's Business History Unit, Sonia Copeland, née Symons, lived in Grenville House when a teenager, and several of my friends and colleagues have since told me that they had relatives who lived in the Square, or have visited - or indeed, still visit - the complex to enjoy its restaurant, social and sporting facilities. So it was with some enthusiasm, and no little curiosity, that I responded to the idea of writing a modern history of the Square, focusing not only on its business, architectural and planning aspects, but also on its social history. In December 2010, Sir Rodney Brooke, then Chairman of the Dolphin Square Trust, asked me if I was interested in writing such a history. An earlier book, by a former general manager, Ken Morris, had been published in 1995. While well written and generally sound, this was not the work of a professional historian and the view was taken that something more authoritative was required. Having agreed to write the book, I was assisted by a steering committee consisting of Rodney Brooke, Deirdre Marshall, Vice Chairman of the Trust, Pam Prebble, a long-serving trustee, and the Trust's last general manager, Adrian Wray. The committee gave me encouragement and assistance, and granted me full access to the Trust's archives. While the surviving documentation was rather patchy in quality - tenancy and staff records in particular were thin on the ground - the administrative material was complete and informative. But the Trust began its work only in 1965, nearly 30 years after the Square began to let flats, and I had to look elsewhere for the early history. Regrettably, the records of Dolphin Square's builders, Costain, have not survived, but I was able to piece the story together from useful information in the London Metropolitan Archives, Westminster City Archives, the National Archives in Kew, the British Library, and London's Guildhall Library. For the early involvement of the American developer, Fred French, in the Square, the manuscript collections in the

New York Public Library, and at Cornell University were invaluable. I also benefited from visits to the Bank of England Archive, Imperial War Museum archives, Institute of Historical Research, Institution of Structural Engineers, the Labour History Archive & Study Centre in the People's Museum, Manchester, the Lloyds Banking Group Archives, London, the Royal Institute of British Architects, the Transport for London Group Archives, and the Women's Library. Committee members also assisted me in resolving some of the trickier research questions. Jan Prebble was particularly helpful. She is recognised as the fount of all knowledge on matters Dolphinesque, and has published a number of pieces on the Square's history. Richard Tovey, Facilities Advisor, Dolphin Square 2005 Ltd., was also helpful and revealed himself to be a not inconsiderable researcher. I should also like to thank those who agreed to be interviewed, in particular, Sir Rodney Brooke, Sir Alan Dawtry, the late Jack Dribbell, Rachel [Ricky] Rees, and Evelyn, Lady Sargant. Many people helped to steer me in the right direction, notably Jenni Adam and Mike Anson from the Bank of England; Amos Barber of Brookhouse Capital Ltd/Westbrook Properties; Toby Cuthbertson, Design and Conservation Officer, Westminster City Council; Judy Faraday, Archivist of the John Lewis Partnership; Steve Hersh from special collections, University of Miami Libraries; Alison Kenney, Archivist of City of Westminster Archives; Steve Logie, Operations Manager, Dolphin Square Foundation; Susan Malsbury of the Manuscripts and Archives Division, New York Public Library; James Mortlock, UK Corporate Archivist, HSBC Holdings; John Pulsford of the Brooklands Museum; Alex Ritchie, Business Archives Advice Manager, The National Archives; Drummond Robson, friend and planner extraordinaire; Karen Sampson, Head of Archives (London), Lloyds Banking Group Archives; Rob Thomas, of the Institution of Structural Engineers Library; and Hilary Dorsch Wong of the Division of Rare and Manuscripts Collections, Cornell University. Last, but certainly not least, I am heavily indebted to Sue Gourvish for making many useful comments on the manuscript, and to Jo Anson for copy-editing the text with her customary skill and patience. Thanks are also due to the Bloomsbury team – Stephen Rutt, Alana Clogan, Lisa Carden and Ellen Grace – for ensuring a smooth publishing process.

I quickly discovered that Dolphin Square was, and still is, an exceptional place. While the list of residents past and present encompasses a wide range of people, it is clear that at every stage there were some remarkable tenants. Nowhere in such a concentrated place have there been so many writers, entertainers, government ministers, recipients of military honours, and public servants of all kinds. I hope I have done justice to this exceptional, indeed unique, housing project in central London.

Terry Gourvish
Norwich, May 2013

ACKNOWLEDGEMENTS

The author and publishers wish to thank the following for kind permission to reproduce material:

A.M. Heath & Co. Ltd, for extracts from *The Sweets of Pimlico* by A.N. Wilson (Copyright A.N. Wilson, 1977); Pami Preller and the British Library, for Illustration no.1; Pan Macmillan, 2; the Museum of London, 3; City of Westminster Archives Centre and Grosvenor, 5 and 6; the *New York Times*, 7 (i); Costain Group Plc, 7 (ii) and (iii); The Governor and Company of the Bank of England, 7 (iv); The New York Public Library, 10 and 11; London Metropolitan Archives, 12 and 13; Dolphin Square Trust, 14–20, 23–29, 33 (ii)-(iv), 34–5, and 38; Harlequin, 21 (i); Norman Dunn, 21 (ii); Getty Images, 21 (iii) and 39 (i); Dolphin Square Trust and Richard Rowan, 21 (iv); H.M. Bateman Designs, 22; City of Westminster Archives Centre, 30 and 31; *Daily Mirror*, 32; National Portrait Gallery, 33 (i); *Mail On Sunday*, 37; mirrorpix, 39 (ii), (iii) and 40; Press Association Images/PA Archive, 39 (iv).

CHAPTER 1

ANTECEDENTS

THOMAS CUBITT

Many of the residents of Dolphin Square are unaware that the 7.5-acre site it occupies played a critical role in the development of Pimlico in the nineteenth century. Pimlico, a large tract of marshy land, 'lying between St. James's Park, the river Thames, the village of Chelsea, Hyde Park Corner and the hamlet of Knightsbridge',[1] was transformed into a desirable residential district thanks to the endeavours of a single speculative builder, Thomas Cubitt (1788–1855). And his activities were organised from offices and workshops which once stood on what is now Dolphin Square.

Thomas Cubitt, the son of a Norfolk carpenter, Jonathan Cubitt of Buxton, near Norwich,[2] was working as a journeyman carpenter when his father died in 1807. He then sailed to India and back as a captain's joiner, returning in 1809 with enough savings to set up as a carpenter in London. Renting a house and workshop in Holborn he quickly gained a reputation as a builder of substance. His first major project was to build a new roof for the Russell Institution in Great Coram Street in Bloomsbury, a work that was completed to the satisfaction of the architect, John Shaw and his client.[3] More ambitious still was the commission to build the London Institution at Finsbury Circus (1815–19), the final bill for which was about £30,000. Since the contract required the work to be completed by a specified date, with a penalty clause for failure to do so, Cubitt took the innovatory step of reducing transaction costs by bringing the various building trades in-house. Instead of contracting separately with independent craftsmen, as was customary, he bought land from Lord Calthorpe on the east side of the Gray's Inn Road, and here he built large workshops for his men – masons, bricklayers, carpenters, smiths, plumbers, plasterers, glaziers, slaters, roofers and general labourers. At the same time he entered into successful business partnerships with his younger brothers William (1791–1863) and Lewis (1799–1883). Together they not only built houses on contract, but also, in order to keep their workforce fully occupied, engaged in speculative building, i.e. acquiring land and building on it ahead of demand. In the mid 1820s the Cubitt brothers developed land in Highbury, Stoke Newington and Barnsbury, then undertook more ambitious work, first on the Calthorpe, Bedford and Southampton estates in Bloomsbury, and then on the Grosvenor Estate in Belgravia in the district known as Five Fields. In Pigot's Directory for 1827 the three brothers are listed as operating from both Gray's Inn Road and 'Grosvenor Basin' in Pimlico.[4] However, this was the year in which the brothers' partnership was dissolved. Thomas Cubitt's biographer, Hermione Hobhouse, found the move 'puzzling'. The most likely explanation is that William preferred the safer business of building on contract, and was worried about the extent of his elder brother's speculative building activities. There was also a personality clash. Thomas was autocratic by nature, something of a control freak in modern parlance. A split with his younger brother gave both of them more freedom.[5]

We know a fair amount about Thomas Cubitt's career thanks to Hobhouse's biography, her contribution to the *Oxford Dictionary of National Biography*, and the efforts of several academic writers, including Ed Cooney and Donald Olsen.[6] It is clear that after the partnership with his brothers was dissolved in 1827 Cubitt concentrated his attention on the development of Five Fields, building Belgrave Square, Lowndes Square, Chesham Place and Eaton Square. He then turned to the marshy land south of Eaton Square, which became known as 'South Belgravia'. The land was raised using spoil taken from the excavation of St. Katherine's Dock. Indeed, such were his efforts over the next three decades that after his death in 1855 South Belgravia was frequently referred to as 'Cubitt's District' or 'Cubittopolis'.[7] Cubitt had found speculative development in Bloomsbury to be risky, and many of the houses that he built in the 1820s were slow to sell. Belgravia and Pimlico proved to be more fertile ground, though even here the period from construction to sale and occupation could be leisurely. Having operated from several locations in Pimlico in the 1820s and 1830s, he eventually settled on a large site close to the Thames and bordered by Lupus Street, the southern extension of Denbigh Street, subsequently named Claverton Street, St. George's Square and the Thames Bank (subsequently Grosvenor Road), the southern portion of which was later to become Dolphin Square. At 'Messrs Cubit's Yard & Workshop', built in 1839–42 on land leased from Robert, Earl Grosvenor, the 1st Marquess of Westminster, Thomas Cubitt employed a workforce of some 1,000 men in a speculative house-building business in Pimlico and elsewhere, and was one of London's, and indeed England's, major building contractors [Illustrations 1, 2, 3]. He obtained capital from insurance companies such as the Guardian Assurance and London Assurance Corporation, and moved in the highest social circles thanks to his relationship with the Marquess of Westminster. He also enjoyed royal patronage, rebuilding Osborne House and Gardens for Queen Victoria and Prince Albert in 1845–51 and constructing new state-rooms at Buckingham Palace. Among many achievements, he lobbied successfully for the establishment of a public park at Battersea, which was opened in 1858.[8]

Thomas's brothers forged separate careers. William Cubitt, who is not to be confused with Sir William Cubitt, the canal and agricultural engineer, remained in Gray's Inn Road, employing about 700 men and specialising in building on contract. He was MP for Andover (1847–61, 1862–3) and served as Lord Mayor of London from 1860 to 1862. Lewis Cubitt worked with Thomas in Pimlico until 1831, whereupon he returned to work with William at Gray's Inn Road. Later he established a sound reputation as architect and contractor for the emerging railway industry, designing the Bricklayers Arms and Dover stations for the South Eastern Railway in 1844, and the Great Northern Railway's King's Cross station and hotel in the early 1850s.[9] By contrast, Thomas was ambivalent towards the coming of the railways. Although his brothers had carried out significant work at Euston and Camden for the London & Birmingham Railway from 1835, he opposed the intrusive effect of railway construction on the urban landscape. A paternalistic employer, he was a campaigner for good drainage, public health, and smoke abatement.[10]

Hobhouse devoted a whole chapter of her biography of Cubitt to the Pimlico works. Leased from the Marquess of Westminster when completed in February 1842, the works occupied 11 acres. There were three rows of buildings: 'a long symmetrical workshop building consisting of three square portions joined by two long ranges of buildings down the central portion of the site'. There was also a substantial stable block, 200 feet by 25 feet, extended in the following year by 20–30 feet, and another workshop block housing a steam engine with an impressive circular chimney 105 feet high. Highly mechanised in comparison with the majority of building firms, Cubitt's works used steam power for a variety of purposes, including sawing timber, polishing marble, pumping water and clipping iron bars. Cubitt, having spent £40,000 on the site and more in improving the surrounding land, asked for generous terms: a 99-year lease from Michaelmas 1838 with a peppercorn rent for the first 10½ years and £100 per annum thereafter. This was accepted by the Grosvenor Estate Trustees.[11] Further extensions included a workshop block built on what is now Claverton Street and Chichester Street.[12]

Cubitt's final years were not without difficulty, and his Pimlico business did not survive his death intact. In August 1854, a serious fire destroyed a large part of the Pimlico works, and it emerged that he was underinsured to a significant extent. Insurances on the works and stock amounted to only £10,000, but as early as 1842 he had sought a loan of £40,000 on the security of the works, which he claimed were worth at least £50,000–60,000. Newspapers speculated that Cubitt had lost up to £150,000 in the fire, but since his workforce had fallen from 1,000 to 600 by this time, and since only around 20 per cent of the premises had been damaged, the loss he experienced was probably nearer to £50,000, though still a substantial sum.[13] At his death on 20 December 1855, Cubitt's reputation was secure. As the architectural historian John Summerson has noted, 'whatever the Cubitts did was done in magnificent style. The land drainage, the sewerage, the road-surfaces, the lighting, the planting, as well as the construction of the houses and mews – everything was accurately thought out and superbly constructed'.[14] However, there remained much to be done in the area. Several of the larger houses were unoccupied, and building in the smaller streets continued into the 1870s.[15] Cubitt's heir, George, later Lord Ashcombe of Dorking, did not share his father's appetite for the building industry. Enjoying much inherited wealth, he devoted himself to politics (representing a Surrey constituency from 1860 to 1892), philanthropy and evangelicalism.[16] Only part of the works continued in operation after 1855, and these premises were run by Thomas Cubitt's former general foreman, George Dines, until 1876. Most of the site was acquired by the army for a clothing depot, to which we now turn.[17]

THE ROYAL ARMY CLOTHING DEPOT

The War Office acquired a lease of part of Cubitt's works from Thomas's executors and trustees, Mary Cubitt, George Cubitt and Andrew Cuthell, from Christmas Day 1858, for a rental of £2,120 10s a year (Table 1.1). The decision to manufacture army clothing in Pimlico was a response to mounting criticism of the manner in which clothing and other army supplies had been procured. The Crimean War had exposed a number of inefficiencies in the army's operations, not least the supply of clothing and equipment, which had been left to the colonel of each regiment to provide. Not only was there little attempt to control the prices charged, but the colonels also received a fixed annual allowance to supply their men. They found that they could save £500–700 a year in the procurement process, a 'profit' known as the 'off-reckoning', which was shared with regimental quartermasters who used the money to maintain themselves as non-commissioned officers in lieu of pay. As a result, the soldiers fighting in the Crimea were found to have been supplied with substandard clothing at high prices. Furthermore, since the colonels were receiving money for an established force of 245,000 men, a figure much higher than the 196,000 actually in service, the public was effectively paying them to clothe men who did not exist.[18] In 1854–5 the system was quickly reformed, first by Sidney Herbert, Secretary at War, then by Lord Panmure, the first Secretary of State for War in the newly-created War Department (from 1857 the War Office). The colonels lost their off-reckonings and instead were paid a fixed emolument.[19] They were then relieved of the responsibility for clothing their regiments, the procurement process passing to the War Department, which created an army clothing department. A new army store was established at Weedon, in Northamptonshire, in November 1855, which inspected and stored cloth, and then inspected and stored clothing made up by contractors.[20]

It was not long before this hastily-introduced reform was also found wanting. Insufficient thought had been given to the logistics of the new system, and very soon serious problems were discovered, especially at the new Weedon depot. In 1858, a Royal Commission that had been appointed to inquire into the workings of the new system found evidence of inefficiency, extravagance, waste, accounting irregularities, and inadequate supervision from the top.[21] One of the Commission's major findings was that it had been a mistake to locate the major stores at Weedon, so far from Army Headquarters in London. The error was rectified by abandoning Weedon as a clothing depot and creating a new clothing store in Pimlico, initially in Bloomberg Terrace, Vauxhall Bridge Road. Larger premises were immediately required, and the packing of army clothing began at the old Cubitt factory premises in 1859.[22] At the same time, the Government decided that in order to benchmark the contracting process, part of the clothing required should be manufactured directly. The decision had come from more modest beginnings in Woolwich, Chatham and Westminster. At Woolwich and Chatham, clothing for the Artillery and Engineers had been made up by military tailors instead of contracting with the clothing trade. In Westminster, the 'putting-out' system was used for the Foot Guards, with the clothing made by local workers in their own homes. This latter operation was quickly transferred to Pimlico when the new store opened. The system of direct manufacture proved so successful that General Jonathan Peel, Secretary of State for War, 1858–9, decided that army production be increased, and 20 regiments were supplied. The introduction of sewing machinery made mass production possible. After a visit to Godillot's factory in Paris, Lord (Sidney) Herbert, Peel's successor, decided that the army should build a clothing factory on the Pimlico site.

The decision to manufacture clothing required the development of land adjacent to that already leased and which was occupied by George Dines. This in turn necessitated a revision of the leasehold arrangements with the Grosvenor Estate. In October 1861, the Cubitt Trustees applied to surrender the 1842 lease of the workshop site and to take out new leases and carry out a building plan.[23] At the same time, the War Office entered into an agreement with George Dines, whereby the latter would erect a factory and stores on the land to the west of the premises already leased, and then lease this property to the War Office at a rent of £2,906 per annum. When the new buildings were completed in 1863, there was accommodation for 1,200 female workers.[24] In fact,

Table 1.1 Army Clothing Depot head leases and underleases, 1861–75

Date	*Term*	*Parties*	*Rental*	*Expiry Date*	*Date of Surrender*
1. Head leases					
29 November 1861	76 years Michaelmas 1861	Grosvenor Estate + Cubitt Trustees	£40	29 September 1937	19 May 1920
20 March 1862	75 years Michaelmas 1863	Grosvenor Estate + Cubitt Trustees	£24	29 September 1938	19 May 1920
10 July 1862	76 years Michaelmas 1862	Grosvenor Estate + Cubitt Trustees	£30	29 September 1938	19 May 1920
2 November 1861	76 years Michaelmas 1861	Grosvenor Estate + Cubitt Trustees	£2	29 September 1937	19 May 1920
2. Underleases					
9 May 1862	78¾ years less 1 Day Christmas 1858	Cubitt Trustees + War Office	£2,120 10s.	28 September 1937	29 September 1933
7 April 1863	74½ years less 1 Day Lady Day 1863	Cubitt Trustees + George Dines then War Office	£350	29 September 1937	29 September 1933
10 July 1862	75¼ years less 3 Days Midsummer 1862	Cubitt Trustees + George Dines then War Office	£356	28 September 1937	29 September 1933
10 August 1875	62 years less 3 Days Michaelmas 1875	Cubitt Trustees + George Dines	£550	26 September 1937	23 May 1932
16 August 1875	61½ years less 10 Days Lady Day 1876	George Dines + War Office	£850	20 September 1937	29 September 1933

Source: Supplemental Abstract of the Title of the Duke of Westminster to Freehold Land in Grosvenor Road Pimlico formerly known as the Royal Army Clothing Depot, 1934, Grosvenor Estate records, WCA 2260/239.

the War Office exercised its option under the contract to buy Dines's leases for about £40,000,[25] and new underleases were then signed with the Grosvenor Estate in 1862–3. There were four headleases, two in November 1861, one in July 1862 and one in March 1863 from the Estate to Cubitt's Trustees, each expiring on 29 September 1937; and three underleases, in May and July 1862 and April 1863 from the Cubitt Trustees, expiring on 28 and 29 September 1937 (Table 1.1). Then in August 1875, shortly before Dines gave up his business, the War Office acquired the final part of the property via an underlease with Dines for £850 a year, expiring on 20 September 1937. The rental paid by the War Office on its four leases amounted to £3,676 10s.[26]

Thus a clothing depot and factory were established on the site of Cubitt's building works. Here, army employees inspected the clothing supplied by independent manufacturers on contract and made a substantial portion of the army's requirements. By 1864, it was reported that the clothing for the brigade of foot guards, for about half of the army outside India, and for the militia, Post Office workers, mounted police and dockyard police was being made at the Pimlico factory. In 1870, the production at Woolwich was transferred to Pimlico.[27] By 1882/3 employment at the factory and store amounted to 2,129 comprised as follows: Factory – females 1,394, males 228; Inspection 180; Clerical 66; and Stores 261. Annual expenditure averaged £1.2–1.3 million in the ten years to 1882/3, with a high of £1.6 million in 1877/8.[28] By this time the factory was also making clothing for the Irish constabulary, Dublin police, Metropolitan police, Board of Customs and the Board of Trade.[29] A contemporary observer noted that a large block on one side was used for the stores, while the factory took up the large block on the other side. The main feature of the latter was an impressive glass-roofed central hall, about 220 feet by 94 feet, three storeys high with galleries on each floor [Illustration 4]. Housing one of the largest factories utilising female workers, particular attention was paid to ventilation and the temperature of the working environment. It was noted that there were 527 female workers in the central hall, with 500 women and 200 men working in the side rooms. Competition for jobs was intense. It was noted that:

> very vigorous rules have been obliged to be made to guard against unworthy admissions . . . all candidates must first of all appear

> before a committee, consisting of the matron, the foreman cutter, the foreman viewer, and the instructor, who are held responsible for the selection of proper persons. In-door candidates as needlewomen must be healthy and strong, and, if single, between the ages of seventeen and thirty; if married or widows, they must have no children at home young enough to demand their care. These points being settled, the candidates are examined as to any previous training or fitness for army work, and are required to show what they can do.[30]

Pride in the establishment remained evident at the turn of the century, when the depot, now known as the Royal Army Clothing Depot, boasted of its effective production at low cost and, according to the Director of Clothing, was 'universally recognized as a model factory'.[31] Army historians such as Fortescue have confirmed the view that the reforms benefited the British soldier, providing better military clothing than ever before.[32]

Given the changes experienced by the British economy between 1860 and the 1930s, including the watershed represented by the First World War, it is perhaps surprising that the Royal Army Clothing Depot continued to supply and inspect army clothing for over 70 years. However, evidence of the need for change appeared in the 1920s. First of all, the Army Council was fully aware that the leases on the factory premises were due to expire in September 1937, and it began to look at alternative uses for the site, including barracks for two infantry battalions.[33] There was also some pressure from the freeholder, the Duke of Westminster, whose personal secretary, Detmar Blow, was becoming increasingly dissatisfied with the falling real value of rents, and was recommending that he buy out existing leases to facilitate rebuilding or reletting.[34] The army factory was such a case, and its rentals were well below the estimated market value of £8,500. In 1923, Colonel Teape from the War Office asked the Grosvenor Estate whether it would be willing to extend the existing leases, or, failing that, what it would offer for their early surrender. When the Estate replied that it was unwilling to offer a new lease, the War Office suggested that a surrender would be worth some £50,000–60,000. Hiller, Parker, May & Bowden, surveyors advising the Estate, observed that while the premises were well built and in a good state of repair, they were unsuitable for industrial purposes. However, development for residential use was certainly feasible, 'either for the erection of small up-to-date bijou residences or medium-sized residential flats suitable for the "middle man"'.[35] In this case a surrender price of no more than £20,000–25,000 was deemed appropriate.[36]

In April 1925 the War Office looked at three options: 1) to stay at Pimlico and replace the lease; 2) to postpone the issue until nearer the expiration date; and 3) to surrender the lease and go elsewhere. A committee had raised the possibility of building at Didcot, but at this stage nothing was decided. In December, an Army Council committee chaired by Commodore Douglas King reported that it was in favour of maintaining the factory, but that if it were to be moved to another site, it should be operated with half the number of pieceworkers (500 instead of 950). It would then specialise in the manufacture of full dress uniforms, which the committee felt should not be left to the private sector to provide. Costings were presented which purported to show that there was little difference in cost between using the private sector and operating a factory with either 160, 500 or 950 pieceworkers.[37] However, rumblings of discontent with the Pimlico factory surfaced in the House of Commons, where questions were raised, also in December 1925, suggesting that the stores were overstocked and that the clothing made in Pimlico was more expensive than that produced by the private sector.[38] For a time the factory was used as a political football in a battle between the army and the Air Ministry for resources. The army had acquired a large, 267-acre property at Chilwell, near Nottingham during the First World War, but this had been unused since 1923 and in 1925 the Air Ministry suggested that they should acquire it.[39] The army at first resisted the idea, and used the possibility of moving the clothing factory from Pimlico to Chilwell as a key argument in its defence. In 1927 an Army Council committee chaired by Commodore Douglas King was also asked to examine three options: 1) to remain in Pimlico 'indefinitely'; 2) to postpone a decision until nearer the end of the Pimlico lease; and 3) to surrender the lease and transfer the factory and store to Chilwell. At the request of the Secretary of State for War, Sir Laming Worthington-Evans, the committee undertook a cost-benefit exercise and found the arguments for and against a move to Chilwell to be 'evenly balanced', though it also expressed the view that there was 'a good deal to be said for the policy of sticking provisionally to Pimlico and awaiting developments'. The assumption was made that after 1937 the rent on the Pimlico premises would be doubled to £8,000 a year, while surrendering the lease would produce £9,000. It was estimated that transfer costs would exceed savings by £45,000, while the operating costs of Chilwell would be about £9,000 higher than those of Pimlico (and the ordnance depots at York and Selby, which were also to be transferred). Weighing up the options, the Army Council took the view that Chilwell should be retained.[40]

The clothing factory issue was quickly overtaken by the possibility of using Chilwell for another, more pressing, purpose: to house the Territorial Army's mechanised transport. However, the Treasury was unhappy with this idea also, and by February 1930 the army had accepted that Chilwell should be handed over to the Air Ministry.[41] Nevertheless, some telling criticisms of the existing state of Pimlico had emerged in the course of the debate. In particular, a letter sent to the Treasury Secretary from Sir Herbert Creedy, Permanent Secretary in the War Office, in November 1926, contained the following candid assessment of the clothing factory:

> The desiderata for a clothing depôt and factory for the Army are that the site should be outside the danger area for hostile aircraft; that it should afford ample room for expansion in war; that it should be a good railway centre for external communication; that it should possess internal railway sidings for the avoidance of double handling and road transport; and that it should be within easy reach of the manufacturing district. In each of these respects Pimlico . . . is signally lacking. It is situated within the aircraft danger zone; its location involves difficulty and delay in external conveyance by rail; there is no area for expansion; it possesses no internal railway sidings; it is far removed from the Midlands where the cloth is manufactured; and in addition the old-fashioned construction of its buildings prevents the work from being organised on modern lines and leads to heavy expense. The particular disadvantage of lack of space for expansion caused great trouble and delay during the [First World] war.[42]

This rather disparaging view of the Pimlico operation was shared with the Treasury and did nothing to ensure its survival. In any case, the 1927 committee had found that the cost of providing a factory and store on a new site would be around £500,000, and with the onset of the Great Depression in 1929 there was considerable pressure on Britain's public expenditure, with all areas subjected to intense scrutiny. In fact, the demand for clothing had fallen with the reduction in the army establishment (from 247,000 in 1913 to a low point of 188,500 in 1930, a cut of 24 per cent) and with the growing preference for plain khaki instead of full dress uniforms.[43] Higher overheads, old-fashioned methods of manufacture, and the constraints imposed by the factory layout, little changed since the nineteenth century, were also evident. During the Labour administration (1929–31) the future of the factory was certainly questioned. When Labour's Secretary of State for War, Thomas Shaw, was asked in the Commons how the average per capita cost of army clothing had changed from 1913 to 1930, he replied that the cost for an infantryman had risen from £7 12s. to £9 3s. 4d., an increase of 21 per cent.[44] Towards the end of the factory's life, efforts were made to introduce more economical working. In 1928, a staff reorganisation scheme was introduced to save £1,000 a year. And in December 1929, an experimental scheme to manufacture clothing with more subdivision of labour – the 'HSD' or higher subdivision system – was tried in an attempt to 'determine whether a closer approach to methods of manufacture in the outside trade will conduce to the public interest'. The initial results were promising. In the year to 26 December 1930 savings amounted to about £1,780 on an expenditure of £25,000.[45] But it was clear that the antiquated layout of the factory precluded a wider application of the new methods, and the incoming National Government of 1931, formed in the wake of a severe financial crisis, announced that while the experiment had had some success, the improvement was not sufficient to make the clothing cheaper than that offered by the private sector.[46]

By this time rationalisation and closure were clearly on the Government's agenda, part of a more general programme of cuts in public expenditure, including a reduction of nearly £4 million in the army's budget for 1932–3 alone.[47] The Duke and Duchess of York may have visited the factory in December 1930, but this had no impact on the decision to abandon

Pimlico, and in November 1931 the War Office announced that a shortage of orders would necessitate a reduction in the number of pieceworkers.[48] In the following month a committee appointed to consider the matter under the chairmanship of Alfred Duff Cooper, Financial Secretary to the War Office and MP for St. George's Westminster, reported that savings of £25,000 a year could be made if the army's clothing requirements were obtained from the trade. It was accepted that in the existing economic climate, capital for a new factory could not be justified. The committee included a comparison of prices quoted by the clothing factory and the private sector for a range of clothing, finding that the latter was some 10–30 per cent cheaper, though the differential was narrower with dress uniforms made by the HSD method (4–13 per cent). The committee concluded that the army should use the private sector for its requirements, with the exception of full dress clothing, which would be transferred to Woolwich if an experiment to obtain these items from the trade proved unsuccessful. The Pimlico site was to be given up, with the residual functions (stores and inspection) transferred to Didcot. Arrangements were then made to vacate the premises on Michaelmas Day, 29 September 1933.[49] Civil servants then entered into serious negotiations with the ground landlords, the Grosvenor Estate. By this time the War Office was pushing on an open door. The Estate, while fully aware of the army's vacillation, had been expecting it to quit for some time, not least in February 1927, when the *Daily Mail* leaked the story (erroneous as it turned out) that the Pimlico Depot 'was moving to the Midlands'.[50] The estate agents and surveyors, Hillier Parker, reporting in November 1928, had advised it to make the War Office a definite offer for the leases and press ahead with redevelopment. There had been a number of enquiries about the future of the site, notably from Sir Robert McAlpine and St. George's Hospital.[51] Finally, the Estate had acquired the leasehold interest of the Cubitt Trustees in 1920, and only a small portion of the factory site was leased to another party, the Trustees of George Dines.[52] Colonel H.C. Cole, the War Office's chief land agent and valuer, was able to obtain relatively attractive terms for the early surrender of the leases: a sum of £5,000, and an acceptance by the Estate that the army would have no liability for dilapidations.[53] After endorsement by the Treasury, the closure proposal was put to the Cabinet, which accepted the recommendation of Lord Hailsham, the Secretary of State for War, at its meeting on 22 January 1932. No discussion was reported.[54]

The decision was made public in February. Substantial economies were realised, with the workforce of 1,030 planned to fall to about 200. Only 160 people were to be transferred from London to Didcot, where total employment was planned to increase by about 360.[55] Redundancies at Pimlico were to be effected over the course of 1932, at a time when unemployment was at an extremely high level as a result of the Great Depression - about 3.75 million at its peak.[56] Duff Cooper, the junior minister charged with announcing the decision in the Commons, expressed some regret at the closure. 'It is always unpleasant to close down a factory, and put a number of people out of work, and I may say, for my own part, that the fact that this factory was in my own constituency did not make me the more eager to recommend, as I did, this decision to the Secretary of State'. Asked whether another factory could be opened, he claimed there was 'nowhere else where we can get a factory site in that part of London. We have had a very careful search made all over the Pimlico district, and that is the case'.[57] However, St. George's Westminster was one of the safest Conservative seats in the country, and the evidence suggests that the minister was personally unaffected by the demise of the clothing factory. Best known as a diplomat, *bon viveur*, gambler and womaniser married to the actress and socialite Lady Diana Cooper, née Manners, he had much more exciting events to engage him, and neither his diary nor his authorised biography made any mention of army clothing. 'The Year 1932 has been for me an uneventful one', he wrote on New Year's Day 1933. 'I have continued quietly to function at the War Office, and have only made two speeches in the House of Commons.'[58]

How strong the case for closure was is not clear. The Treasury was usually critical of War Office costings and the arguments it made for resources,[59] and it is not easy to find a candid assessment of the factory that was not concocted for policy reasons. Pimlico certainly had its supporters - in 1926, the Commons Select Committee on Estimates, far from recommending closure or curtailment, found it to be 'well organised' and argued that it should be given more work.[60] King George V expressed concern about the redundancies that would follow the decision,[61] while the closure also provoked protests from the trade union movement with the Workers' Union convening a meeting at Central Hall, Westminster in February 1932, at which W.J. Brown,

General Secretary of the Civil Service Clerical Association, said that the £25,000 the Government would save by closing the factory would be at the expense of making 'the sweaters' den in the East End the standard of wages'.[62] A petition was also sent to the Duke of Westminster by Ida Bould on behalf of her fellow factory workers.[63] By then, of course, it was too late to reverse a decision which was to have significant consequences for Cubitt's old works.

WESTMINSTER AND PIMLICO, 1860–1939

It scarcely needs to be said that London is at once a coherent whole and a collection of smaller centres. Many see the capital, in Michael Thompson's words, as 'nothing much more than a haphazard conglomeration of villages and small towns, more or less articulated by a transport system, and more or less held together by blocks and wedges of routine housing - standard for its particular period - interspersed between the old centres'. But as Thompson has reminded us, this is an extreme view. Central districts such as Westminster, and, within it, Pimlico, possess an individual character but also exemplify the general economic and social forces shaping London since the Industrial Revolution, including social segregation, industrial and technological change, and the competition for space between commercial and residential needs.[64] One of the main changes in the mid Victorian period was a resurgence of railway building, with all the dislocation it brought to working-class inhabitants of the inner districts. In 1858, a railway line from Crystal Palace reached Battersea, but the intention of the promoters had been to cross the Thames. This ambition was in fact realised by a competing scheme, the Victoria Station & Pimlico Railway (VS&PR), a rare example in Britain of a terminus company on the American model. The VS&PR, formed in 1858 with financial support from the London Brighton & South Coast Railway (LB&SCR), which had also acquired the Crystal Palace company, obtained powers to construct a railway along the route of the Grosvenor Canal to a terminus adjacent to the new thoroughfare of Victoria Street, which had opened in 1851. The first passengers used the new Victoria Station in October 1860, and the facility was then shared with another company, the London Chatham & Dover Railway, which opened its own station adjacent to the LB&SCR's in 1862.[65] Further demands on urban space from the railways came with the building of the Metropolitan District's underground line from Brompton to Mansion House via Victoria and Westminster in 1865–70, and the enlargement of Victoria Station, on which £2 million was spent.[66] These constructions had predictable effects on their localities. The historian of the impact of the railways on the Victorian city, John Kellett, puts it thus: 'The main effects of railways in the centre of the Victorian city were to add to the congestion of traffic and the overcrowding of working class housing, and to contribute, both directly and indirectly, to the changes in land use, and the rapid increase in land values.' In the inner districts the effect was 'to compress the areas which were within walking range of the city centre, to interrupt communications between them, to stabilise their land values for residential uses and reduce their improvement prospects'.[67]

Thus we should not be surprised that Westminster and Pimlico were affected by these projects, though railways were as much a response to, as a creator of, commercial development. Stephen Inwood, one of London's historical chroniclers, suggests that Pimlico 'always had a certain social ambiguity'. He draws our attention to Charles Booth's description of the area in 1902, in his book *Life and Labour of the People of London*, as 'depressing', with a 'shabby gentility', conveying a sense of 'gradual decay' and 'grimy dilapidation'.[68] The dense development of the area, the opening of Victoria station, and the existence of the large army factory scarcely encouraged the middle class to choose it for their homes in the later nineteenth century. The area immediately adjacent to the clothing depot was 'seedy', and there were apparently many brothels in Claverton Street from the 1860s. William Carey's encyclopaedic cornucopia of Pimlico provides further documentation. He notes that the railway extensions had the effect of separating Pimlico from Belgravia, and in the quarter-century after the building of Victoria station hundreds of terraced houses had been transformed into a dense network of lodging houses and small 'commercial' hotels.[69] Closer to the clothing factory the streets between Grosvenor Road and Lupus Street became overcrowded and depressed. 'South of Lupus Street the grim streets with tightly packed single storey terraces had their gin parlours, beer shops, public houses, pawn brokers, evangelical halls and street fights . . . The distilleries, gas works, lead works, clothing depot, small arms factory, docks and warehouses provided the industry of Thames-Bank.'[70] Of course, the finer houses and squares of Cubitt's Pimlico always held an attraction for the lesser gentry and retired military families, who coexisted with their lower-middle and working-class neighbours. The area north of Lupus Street was particularly popular with this group, who gave it a genteel quality.[71] At the turn of the century, the maps of Charles Booth and his research assistants showed Pimlico to be a mixed area inhabited by the affluent and the poor, certainly not as poor as the worst slums of Westminster (for example, in Great Peter Street). However, his written descriptions tended to be more damning. The part of Pimlico near the factory, he thought, presented 'an admixture of shabby gentility and vice, hardly less depressing than the low life of the old slums'. He felt the area exemplified the problem where 'if flats are built, but are not well tenanted, there is the danger, almost amounting to certainty, that unsatisfactory characters will get in, as has so largely happened in the adjoining district to the South and West of Vauxhall Bridge Road'. Prostitution was rife, though mainly evident north of Lupus Street. 'The streets near Victoria Station are their home parade; the small hotels in Vauxhall Bridge Road their houses of accommodation; and the pink streets barred with red their dwelling place.'[72]

The popularity of South Pimlico among the better-off declined with the outbreak of the First World War, which saw a competing use of the district for behind-the-lines military establishments: hospitals, hostels and clubs. In the 1920s Pimlico became more polarised, and was, as Carey makes clear,

> a strange mixture of middle class desperation and lodging house enterprise . . . The widows of Pimlico increasingly found it difficult to maintain that terraced isolation which they and their husbands had achieved before the war . . . Many of them sold out, or turned their homes into "private apartments and lodgings for gentlemen and gentle ladies". This was the beginning of the Belgrave Road, Warwick Way, Hugh Street and Saint George's Drive "Bed and Breakfast" establishment. The whole grid was peeling; repairing and painting the stucco facades beyond the financial means of the owners. Many owners lived on the ground floor, using the basement and leaving the upper floors empty.[73]

The neighbourhood close to the clothing factory was generally held in low esteem, and the poverty of the area near the river, particularly in Pulford and Aylesford Streets, around St. George's Square, was commented on by scholars from the London School of Economics researching the area for the new *Survey of London Life and Labour* of 1928. In the same year a serious flood, on 7 January, claimed ten lives, most living in Grosvenor Road, and seriously damaged 450 homes. The deaths revealed the poor housing conditions experienced by many working-class people living close to the river and the factory. For example, the Harding family of 8 Grosvenor Road lost four of their eight children, four daughters who were drowned when the floodwaters inundated the basement kitchen in which they were sleeping.[74] The social scientists from the LSE subsequently noted that Westminster's population had fallen sharply as a result of commercial expansion, from 244,000 in 1831 and 202,000 in 1891 to only 130,000 in 1931.[75] Pressure was also exerted by the expansion of both central and local government from the 1870s, which made Westminster an increasingly important destination for white-collar work, altering the balance between work and residence in the borough. As Peter Hennessy has noted, 'the human requirements of the state machine began to shift irreversibly as did its size'. In 1870, there were about 40,000 civil servants; 30 years later the number had increased almost threefold to 116,000. There was a further substantial rise in employment during the Liberals' welfare reform period (1906–14), and on the eve of the First World War the number of civil servants exceeded 282,000.[76]

Thus, a number of factors established the conditions for the potential development of the army clothing site in the 1930s: growing commercial pressures; an increase in central government and civil service employment; intensifying economic difficulties for local industries during the Great Depression; and a fall in the esteem of the residential housing stock. Charles Booth had long since expressed the wish that South Pimlico should be improved. In 1902, he argued that 'something more complete and far-reaching was needed' for the river front, and looked to the new Metropolitan Borough of Westminster, established in 1899, to encourage its development. He felt that the area occupied by the army factory was a promising candidate for improvement. St. George's Square possessed:

> an out of the way charm which, making little pretence after fashion, seems to defy decay; whilst the river frontage offers many advantages. Thus it may be hoped that some healthy development will check the spread in this direction of the disreputable and decaying condition of the district to the North, and prevent any further influx of squalid poverty and disorder from the evictions in Westminster.

Thirty years after this was written, Booth's aspirations were about to be realised.[77]

NOTES

1 Peter Cunningham, *Hand-Book of London Past and Present* (2nd edn, 1850), p.401. See also K.F. Morris, *A History of Dolphin Square* (1995), p.13ff.

2 On the Cubitt family see Walter Rye, *Collections for a History of the Family of Cubitt of Norfolk* (Norwich, 1873), pp.15–17. Cubitt's great-grandson, Sir Stephen Tallents, said that he was 'the penniless son of a Coltishall farmer': Tallents, *Man and Boy* (1943), p.30.

3 Tallents, *Man and Boy*, p.31; Hermione Hobhouse, *Thomas Cubitt, Master Builder* (1971, rev. edn, Didcot, 1995), pp.4–5.

4 John Summerson, *Georgian London* (1945; new edn, 1988), pp.181–3; Hobhouse, *Thomas Cubitt*, pp.5–9, 16–17; *Pigot & Co.'s Metropolitan New Alphabetical Directory for 1827*, p.105. Cf. the earlier *Post Office London Directory for 1826*, which shows the brothers only at Gray's Inn Road.

5 Hobhouse, *Thomas Cubitt*, pp.96–8.

6 Hobhouse, *Thomas Cubitt*, and 'Cubitt, Thomas (1788–1855)', *Oxford Dictionary of National Biography* (2004–11), henceforth *OxDNB*. See, inter alia, E.W. Cooney, 'The Origins of the Victorian Master Builders', *Economic History Review*, 8:2 (1955), 168–72; Donald J. Olsen, *Town Planning in London: the Eighteenth and Nineteenth Centuries* (2nd edn, New Haven, 1982), pp.57–63; Francis Sheppard, *London 1808–1870: The Infernal Wen* (1971), pp.97–8; and Simon Jenkins, *Landlords to London. The Story of a Capital and its Growth* (1975), pp.76–85.

7 Hobhouse favours 'Cubitt's District', Sheppard 'Cubittopolis'.

8 See Hobhouse, *Thomas Cubitt*, pp.281–4, figure 15, plates 56a and b; William Carey, *William Carey's Pimlico* (1986), pp.63–74, 77–8, 99–100, 158–60; *Morning Post*, 9 March 1853, p.3; *The Times*, 31 May 1856, p.8.

9 Gordon Biddle, *Historic Railway Buildings* (Oxford, 2003), p.734; *Illustrated London News*, 4 May 1844, p.285.

10 Hobhouse, *Thomas Cubitt*, pp.72–3, 189, 253.

11 Grosvenor Estate Trustees' Minutes, 12–26 February 1842, and lease plan, 22 February 1842, City of Westminster Archives Centre (henceforth WCA), 1049/5/12, 1049/10/347.

12 Hobhouse, *Thomas Cubitt*, pp.283–5.

13 Ibid. pp.297–302, 337–8; *Daily News*, 18 August 1854, p.3; *The Builder*, 19 August 1854, p.443, 26 August 1854, p.453; *The Era*, 20 August 1854, p.13. *The Builder* reported that the workforce was increased to 700 after the fire: 23 September 1854, p.501.

14 Summerson, *Georgian London*, p.186.

15 Adam Stout, *Pimlico: Deep Well of Glee* (1997), p.37.

16 Carey, *Pimlico*, p.162; *Who Was Who*.

17 Hobhouse, *Thomas Cubitt*, pp.283, 292, 393, 491. Dines had been first employed by Cubitt on the recommendation of the brewer, Sam Whitbread.

18 Hon. J.W. Fortescue, *A History of the British Army. Vol.XIII: 1852–70* (1930), p.525 (data from Army estimates of 1856).

19 Quartermasters had to wait until 1865 to be paid an allowance: Fortescue, *History*, p.543.

20 See Hayter and Howell, 'Memorandum as to the Past and Present System of Packing the Army Clothing', 26 June 1858, 'Joint Report of the Directors of Contracts and Clothing upon the system pursued in obtaining Supplies of Clothing for the Army', c.1881, and George D. Ramsay, 'Report of the Director of Clothing for 1882–3', 29 November 1883, file of historical memoranda, The National Archives [henceforth TNA], WO377/44.

21 *The Times*, 23 August 1859, p.7, *Daily News*, 24 August 1859, p.4. The performance of the chief storekeeper at Weedon, James Sutton Elliott, which culminated in his absconding

with a French actress, attracted particular criticism: *Caledonian Mercury*, 6 July 1858, *Morning Post*, 16 December 1858, p.2, *Daily News*, 17 December 1858 p.2, *Daily News*, 24 August 1859, p.4.

22 J.R. Godley-Hayter and Howell, 17 February 1858, TNA WO377/44; *The Standard*, 24 August 1859, p.6; Edward Walford, *Old and New London: A Narrative of Its History, Its People and Its Places*, Vol.V (1878), p.40 [address corrected from 1851 census index].

23 Grosvenor Estate Trustees' Minutes, 30 October 1861, WCA 1049/5/14.

24 'Joint Report', c.1881, TNA WO377/44; Agreement between George Dines and Secretary of State for the War Department, 5 October 1861, in *Copy of Agreement between the War Office and Mr Dines, as to Building or Leasing of Premises in Pimlico, for the Clothing Factory*, 11 March 1863, P.P.1863, xxxii (105).

25 The Agreement between Dines and the War Office stipulated that the price for exercising the option to purchase the leases would be £39,600, if notice were given within a month of possession, or failing that, £46,200: Ibid. para.6.

26 Memorandum for A.C.H. Borrer (Boodle Hatfield & Co., solicitors to Grosvenor Estate), n.d. [1933], Grosvenor Estate correspondence on sale of RACD, 1923–35, WCA, 2444/5/19.

27 'Joint Report', c.1881, TNA WO377/44; *Morning Post*, 8 January 1864, p.5.

28 'Report for 1882–3', TNA WO377/44. Expenditure in 1918/19 was £1.3m: *Annual accounts of the Royal Army Clothing Factory, for the year 1918–1919*, 17 March 1920, P.P.1920, xxviii (51).

29 R. Loyd Lindsay (War Office)-Treasury, 14 October 1879, Treasury correspondence and papers, TNA T1/16968.

30 Walford, *Old and New London*, V, pp.40–1.

31 G. Fleetwood Wilson (Director of Clothing), 'Confidential Report on the Royal Army Clothing Depot', June 1897, TNA WO377/44.

32 Fortescue, *History*, p.542.

33 W. Stanley Edgson (Chartered Surveyor, Hillier, Parker, May & Bowden [henceforth HPM&B])-Borrer, 18 February 1926, WCA 2444/5/19.

34 Francis Sheppard (ed.), *The Survey of London. Vol.XXXIX: The Grosvenor Estate in Mayfair, Part 1: General History* (1977), p.76.

35 HPM&B-Boodle Hatfield & Co., 30 July 1923, WCA 2444/5/19.

36 Edgson-Borrer, 19 November 1928, Grosvenor Estate records on Royal Army Clothing Depot, WCA 2305/187, and further correspondence in WCA 2444/5/19.

37 War Office Recommendations and Decisions, April 1925, TNA WO377/44; Report of the Committee on the Maintenance of an Army Clothing Factory, 17 December 1925, TNA WO33/1104. The costings were as follows: no factory £539,327; factory with 160 piece-workers £538,651 + rent, rates; 500 piece-workers £533,631+, 950 piece-workers £529,433+.

38 *Parl. Deb. (Commons)*, 5th ser. (Session 1924–5), 16 December 1925, c.1420, PQs from Sir Frederick Hall (MP for Dulwich), and Lt Col. Sir Joseph Nall (MP for Manchester Hulme) to Capt. Douglas King.

39 B.M. Draper (War Office)-A.P. Waterfield (Treasury), 19 May 1928, Treasury file on 'Army Ordnance Depot, Chilwell: Future of', and C.F.M.N Ryan (Treasury), Minute, 31 March 1932, Treasury file on 'Army Ordnance Depot, Chilwell: Accommodation at', TNA T161/1061.

40 'Report of the Committee on the Future of the Royal Army Clothing Department, Pimlico', 24 September 1927, 'The Acquisition of Chilwell by the War Department [Précis 1301]', Army Council Minutes, 10 October 1927, TNA WO163/33.

41 Report of the Committee on the Utilization of Chilwell, 5 December 1929, Army Council Minutes, 25 February 1930, TNA WO163/36.

42 Sir Herbert J. Creedy (Permanent Under-Secretary, War Office)-Treasury Secretary, 26 November 1926, TNA T161/1061.

43 Richard Holmes (ed.), *The Oxford Companion to Military History* (Oxford, 2001), p.934. Army establishment no.s from *Statistical Abstract for the UK 1913 and 1917 to 1930* (1932), p.128.

44 Thomas Shaw (SoS for War), *Parl. Deb. (Commons)*, 5th ser. (session 1930–1), PQ, 17 February 1931, c.1033. The increase in real terms was probably about the same. See the Sauerbeck-*Statist* index of textile material prices in B.R. Mitchell, *British Historical Statistics* (Cambridge, 1988), p.726.

45 War Office, note to Treasury, 2 May 1928, Creedy-Treasury Secretary, 7 January 1930, A.E. Widdows (Asst. Under-Secretary, War Office)-Treasury Secretary, 13 March 1931, TNA T162/250.

46 Duff Cooper, *Parl. Deb. (Commons)*, 5th ser. (Session 1931–2), 8 March 1932, c.1656–7.

47 Army Council Minutes, 31 August and 2 September 1931, TNA WO33/1273.

48 *The Times*, 9 December 1930, p.11, 20 November 1931, p.11.

49 Report of Committee on Maintenance of an Army Clothing Factory, December 1931, TNA WO377/44.

50 *Daily Mail*, 19 February 1927, cutting in WCA 2444/5/19.

51 Edgson-Borrer, 19 November 1928, WCA 2305/187, John Leaning & Sons (Surveyors)-Detmar Blow (Grosvenor Estate), 10 and 13 January 1930 and other correspondence in Memo. for Borrer, 1933, cit.

52 Supplemental Abstract of the Title of the Duke of Westminster to Freehold Land in Grosvenor Road Pimlico, formerly known as the Royal Army Clothing Depot, 1934, Grosvenor Estate records, WCA 2260/239.

53 Col. H.C. Cole (Chief Land Agent & Valuer, War Office), Minutes, 23 December 1931 and 11 January 1932, TNA WO32/3406; Cole-Lionel Brown (auctioneer, Arber, Rutter, Waghorn & Brown, henceforth ARW&B), 25 January 1932, WCA 2444/5/19.

54 Viscount Hailsham (Secretary of State for War), Memo. on 'Future of the Royal Army Clothing Department', 19 January 1932, Cabinet Conclusions, 22 January 1932, TNA CAB23/70, CAB24/227.

55 *The Times*, 2 February 1932, p.9; *Parl. Deb. (Commons)*, 5th ser. (Session 1931–2), Duff Cooper, PQ, 8 February 1932, c.494–5; Duff Cooper (Financial Secretary, War Office)-Leslie Hore-Belisha (Financial Secretary, Treasury), 5 December 1932, TNA T161/544.

56 Duff Cooper, *Parl. Deb. (Commons)*, 5th ser. (Session 1931–2), 9 and 10 February 1932, c.642–3, 852–3; *Times*, 16 February 1932, p.8, 29 June 1932, p.9; Sidney Pollard, *The Development of the British Economy 1914–1980* (1983), p.155.

57 Duff Cooper, *Parl. Deb. (Commons)*, 5th ser. (Session 1931–2), 8 March 1932, c.1658, 1767.

58 Duff Cooper, Diary, 1 January 1933, in John Julius Norwich (ed.), *The Duff Cooper Diaries 1915–51* (2005), p.219, and see also John Charmley, *Duff Cooper: the Authorized Biography* (1986), pp.63, 69, 72.

59 Cf. W.R. Fraser (Treasury), Minute, 7 December 1926, TNA T161/1061.

60 *Report from the Select Committee on Estimates (Supply and Inspection of Clothing)*, 13 December 1926, P.P.1926, vi, and see also Fraser, minute, 23 December 1926, TNA T161/1061.

61 Major the Hon. A.H.L. Hardinge (Asst Private Secretary to King George V)-Creedy, 20 January 1932, TNA WO32/3406.

62 *The Times*, 16 February 1932, p.8; *Westminster & Pimlico News*, 19 February 1932, WCA.

63 Ida E.M. Bould, Petition, 8 February 1932, WCA 2444/5/19.

64 F.M.L. Thompson, *Hampstead: Building a Borough 1650–1964* (1974), pp.2–3.

65 T.C. Barker and Michael Robbins, *A History of London Transport*, I (1963), pp.141–2; Gordon Biddle, *Britain's Historical Railway Buildings* (Oxford, 2003), pp.59–60.

66 Jack Simmons, *The Railway in England and Wales 1830–1914*, I (Leicester, 1978), p.122; John R. Kellett, *The Impact of the Railways on Victorian Cities* (1969), p.96.

67 Kellett, *Railways*, p.337.

68 Stephen Inwood, *A History of London* (1998), p.575, citing Charles Booth, *Life and Labour of the People in London. Third series: Religious Influences*, III (1902), p.87.

69 Carey, *Pimlico*, pp.122, 130, 133.

70 Ibid. p.102.

71 Ibid. pp.142–3.

72 Booth, *Religious Influences*, pp.74, 79. The areas marked 'pink with red bars' on Booth's map included Warwick, Denbigh, Claverton, Chichester and Bessborough streets.

73 Carey, *Pimlico*, p.183.

74 *The Times*, 11 January 1928, p.7; City of Westminster Council Minutes, 12 January 1928, WCA; *Westminster and Pimlico News*, 13 January 1928, p.6. See also Stout, *Pimlico*, pp.57, 63–4.

75 LSE, *The New Survey of London Life and Labour*, VI (1934), p.389.

76 Peter Hennessy, *Whitehall* (Pimlico, 2001), pp.51, 59.

77 Booth, *Religious Influences*, pp.77, 88; Stout, *Pimlico*, p.61.

CHAPTER 2

THE DEVELOPERS, 1933–8

THE GROSVENOR ESTATE OFFERS THE LAND FOR DEVELOPMENT

When, in 1932, the army announced its intention to surrender its lease on the premises in Pimlico and close its clothing factory, *The Times* suggested that 'the ground will probably be cleared for flats or offices'.[1] Duff Cooper, the Financial Secretary to the War Office, had already announced that he felt that Pimlico was 'not an ideal site for a factory'. He indicated that had another factory been required, it would have made more sense for it to be located in the north of England.[2] But, as we have seen, there was little doubt that the War Office was determined to procure clothing from the private sector, and by December 1932 it decided that full dress uniforms would also in future be obtained 'from the trade'.[3] The Duke of Westminster's Estate lost no time in seeking a buyer. On 4 March 1933 *The Times* included a notice by Arber, Rutter, Waghorn & Brown of Mount Street, near Berkeley Square, for an auction sale on 25 May 1933. The auction details did not give a clear indication of whether the future use would be commercial or residential, though the suggestion was that a commercial use was more likely. Thus, the 'very valuable and unrestricted FREEHOLD BUILDINGS and SITE of about 314,000 SQUARE FEET' [7.2 acres] were held to occupy 'a prominent position in the heart of a populous and favourite neighbourhood and the very centre of a busy hive of industry with a wharf on the river of great benefit for water-borne goods'. The buildings, with a total floor area of nearly 500,000 square feet, were 'well equipped in every respect for the conduct of a large manufacturing business'.[4] A further announcement of sale on 29 April included a sketch of the site, giving visual support to the contention that the frontage on Grosvenor Road amounted to about 466 feet, the depth was 640 feet, and the rear on Chichester Street was 464 feet. This also showed the Thames-side wharf, with a frontage of about 178 feet [Illustrations 5, 6].[5]

*

Vacant possession was promised on 29 September 1933, but with the economy only just beginning to emerge from the Great Depression, this was scarcely a time to attract industrial purchasers to buy over seven acres in the City of Westminster. Nor were the prospects for an alternative use as a housing development immediately apparent. The 1920s had seen a housing boom, but much of it had been initiated by the private sector, and most of the new houses had been built in the suburbs and small towns of south-east England. In London, private builders had been responsible for 71 per cent of the 394,000 houses built in 1920–32. The contribution of the City Corporation and the Metropolitan Boroughs to this total was modest – only 14,000 houses, and Westminster's record was more modest still, having erected or acquired a mere 621 houses for working-class occupation, about four per cent.[6] Of course, land was scarce and the resident population of central London was shrinking, as we have observed. But slum clearance remained a key objective for boroughs such as Westminster, and some fairly substantial schemes were launched, not only by the Council, but also by important charitable institutions. Thus, slum properties were replaced in Great Peter and Tufton Streets, in Horseferry Road, where Peabody Trust flats were built in 1922, while Page and Vincent Streets, which had suffered from the flooding of January 1928 (see Chapter 1, p.18), were enhanced by the 'chequerboard' blocks of flats designed by Edward Lutyens for Westminster Council and opened in 1930.[7] In Pulford Street, close to St. George's Square, which included a redundant gasworks, a group of activists formed the Westminster Housing Association, bought the site from the London County Council (LCC) in 1929 and then established a housing trust to build flats for working-class occupation. This was the forerunner of the seven five-storey blocks of the Tachbrook Estate, a joint venture of the Westminster Housing Trust and the LCC, the first part of which was opened in July 1935.[8] There was no intrinsic reason why interest in the clothing factory site could not have been shown by either the Council or specialists in working-class housing. However, enthusiasm was necessarily dampened by the Great Depression, and although house-building remained historically buoyant, participation by local authorities was more constrained than it was at the height of the housing booms of 1928 and 1938.[9] For example, Westminster Council had been unwilling to develop the Pulford Street site, claiming that it was fully occupied with two large schemes - Grosvenor Road and Ebury Bridge Road.[10] The Duke of Westminster, a man of leisure with a love of travel and outdoor sports, had little interest in the minutiae of Estate affairs, though he had sometimes offered land in support of working-class housing improvement, as he did in Ebury Bridge Road and Pulford Street.[11] However, he ruled out development of the factory site for charitable housing. When a friend, the Marchioness of Londonderry, wrote to him in March 1933 to raise the possibility of reserving two acres for working-class housing, his answer was firmly negative, the reason given being that if the site were split the sale would be jeopardised.[12]

The Duke's advisers favoured development of the site for speculative housing. As we have seen (see Chapter 1, p.13), a report from the estate agents, Hillier Parker, in 1928 revealed that during the negotiations with the War Office in 1923–6 'several schemes were prepared by the Estate Surveyor for the development of the site by the erection of a series of blocks of flats', and there had been some enquiries from building firms about the prospects.[13] On the other hand, this was an exceptionally large central London plot of land. Indeed, Lionel Brown, the auctioneer charged with the sale, told A.C.H. Borrer from the Grosvenor Estate's solicitors, Boodle, Hatfield & Co., that 'no such site as this has during my experience of nearly forty years come onto the market'.[14] The resources required to buy and develop the site were considerable, and only the largest companies and institutions could contemplate taking it on. Exactly how many potential buyers of the factory site came forward in 1933 is difficult to ascertain. We know that there were several enquiries prior to the auction, including some apparently serious negotiations with Holland & Hannen and Cubitts, the firm which had been created when Holland & Hannen merged with William Cubitt's building business in the late nineteenth century.[15] William Stewart, a public works contractor and Belfast MP, inspected the site, but found the existing buildings to be 'quite useless'.[16] It is also evident that the auction itself, on 25 May, proved to be something of a farce. The auctioneers were embarrassed to report to the Estate that having received a bid of £360,000, close to the reserve price they had recommended,[17] the bidder promptly left the auction house without revealing his name. As Lionel Brown explained: 'I must own it was a strange happening but Auctions are always a gamble.'[18] Immediately after the sale Brown received an offer with conditions: £108,000 for a third of the site, together with a proposal to lease the rest for £10,000 a year, plus a five-year option to purchase for £242,000. He advised the Estate to accept this, since many would-be purchasers were being deterred by the fact that they would need to spend a further £200,000–300,000 on development (one potential buyer thought that much more, £2 million, would be required). However, the Duke declined to do so.[19] A further complication was the height restriction insisted upon by the Estate to protect the interests of occupants of adjacent properties in St. George's Square and Claverton Street.[20]

Further enquiries emerged in the months following the auction. Two motor manufacturers are mentioned in the Estate's papers: an undated note identifying Ernest Payton, a director of the Austin Motor Company, whose idea seems to have been to build flats together with an arena – 'a sort of Olympia'; and Ford's recently-launched British subsidiary, which was interested in taking about a third of the property. The Austin proposal had been sufficiently serious to produce a preliminary application to the LCC under the London Building Act of 1930. The Duke's officials also made efforts to encourage the brewers Watneys to move from the Stag Brewery in Victoria, the valuable freehold of which they had acquired from the Estate in 1902 when sales were made to meet taxation arising from the death of the 1st Duke in 1899.[21] By this time the Grosvenor Estate fully accepted the assessment that the existing buildings could not be adapted for an alternative commercial use, and that the site should be cleared in order to attract developers. Fuller, Horsey, Sons & Cassell, auctioneers and valuers of plant and machinery, reported in December 1933 that the army buildings were badly organised and badly lit, with 'considerable variation in the floor levels' and the Greenham Demolition Co., which had offered to clear the site in four months, was then instructed to proceed.[22]

ENTER FRED FRENCH, 1934

At last, as the green shoots of economic recovery began to appear in 1934, a successful bidder for the Army Clothing Depot property emerged. He came from an unexpected quarter, however. It was an American real estate specialist, Frederick Fillmore French, who offered to buy the property from the Duke of Westminster. French was a self-made property developer born in New York's Bronx in 1883. His was very much a rags-to-riches story, though it was often embellished to the extent that it is difficult to separate fact from fiction. An article in London's *Evening News* is a good example. Here he claimed to have been raised in a New York slum, his mother a 'brave woman who was something of a poetess and related to an English titled family. Her husband was a brilliant man, but misguided'. He went on:

> At 13 I got a scholarship to Columbia University. I won another scholarship at Princeton University. After a year there I made my way to Pennsylvania by freight train. I cow-punched in New Mexico, and worked in the mines in Texas, before I went back to Columbia, took an engineering course, and studied law by night. I started the Fred French Company in 1910 with a capital of minus 200 dollars, for the 200 I had saved went in fees to the lawyers.[23]

In fact, we know that although impoverished by the early death of his father, a cigar maker, French was well-connected. His mother was a graduate of the University of Michigan, and he derived his middle name – Fillmore – from his great-uncle, Millard Fillmore, the 13th President of the United States (1850–3). He won a Pulitzer scholarship to the Horace Mann School, and after a year at Princeton and a period 'ranching and mining', he studied engineering at Columbia University New York, followed by work in the construction industry. At the age of 27, he established the Fred F. French Companies, and embarked on a career in property development[24] [Illustration 7 (i)]. In the interwar period his company developed a series of properties in New York, provided architectural design services, and acted as investor, contractor and property manager. Subsidiary companies were established to operate each part of an integrated business. His business strategy – the 'French Plan', first formulated in 1919 – circumvented the conventional financing of projects through the bond market by attracting private investors directly and at lower cost. Separate owning companies were created for each property acquired, and 50 per cent of the acquisition costs were financed by a mortgage. The remaining 50 per cent was obtained through the sale of securities. Investors bought preferred stock paying a cumulative dividend of six per cent, and for each $100 of stock acquired equity in the scheme through the issue of two ordinary shares, one of which was given to the preferred stockholder, the other being retained by the French Company. Profits were used to pay the dividends and redeem the preferred stock, after which subsequent profits were shared between the Company and the stockholders.[25] French is best known for his ambitious development of New York's East Side, notably Tudor City in the 1920s, and Knickerbocker Village in the 1930s. These, along with the art deco Fred F. French Building at 551 Fifth Avenue and 45th Street, built in 1927, remain a legacy to his efforts. He died suddenly, after a heart attack, in August 1936, as Dolphin Square was being built.

What distinguished French from other property developers in New York was his interest in applying Charles Paterno's 'vision of a dense urban suburbia' on a larger scale.[26] To that end he redeveloped entire areas of run-down industrial and slum property for middle-class occupation. As the American planning expert Alexander Garvin points out, 'He believed that only a giant, economy-size, self-contained enclave could survive negative pressures from surrounding areas and provide the necessary critical mass of new residents for community rebirth.'[27] His two giant projects in Manhattan, Tudor City, built in 1926–31, and Knickerbocker Village, built in 1933–4, both had a resonance with what became Dolphin Square, but Tudor City clearly provided the template for what he had in mind in Pimlico.[28]

Tudor City was one of New York's largest speculative housing ventures of the 1920s. In 1925 French bought three large square blocks of what at first sight appeared to be an unpromising collection of slum properties on Prospect Hill, at East 42nd Street, between Second Avenue, the 'El' (elevated railway) and the infamous abattoirs bordering the East River. Here, with some architectural reference to Corbusier's schemes in Europe, he built a high rise, high density residential enclave on the five-acre site between 40th and 43rd Streets and First and Second Avenue which in many ways established a model for apartment enclaves in Manhattan. The risks of failure were high, and critics were sceptical about the prospects of attracting residents to this area. But Grand Central Station was within walking distance, and French's scheme was extremely imaginative. For his 'Tudor City' he built an apartment village consisting of ten redbrick residential blocks. The development was a 'potpourri of apartments, hotels, gardens and garages'.[29] It was dominated by three large 32-storey towers, named Prospect, Tudor and Windsor. The other residential blocks were smaller, each ten storeys high. A fourth 32-storey tower, Woodstock Tower, contained a hotel with 454 rooms. The main development provided 2,800 flats with accommodation for around 4,500 people. The drop in elevation between Second Avenue and First Avenue was put to good use. The complex was built some 30 feet above 42nd Street and First Avenue, and a private road, Tudor City Place, provided access. On the west side, two 15,000 sq. ft. parks were created, with gardens, tennis courts and a miniature golf course. Residents were shielded from the abattoirs by making the flats face west, with no windows to the east side. The buildings, designed by the architect H. Douglas Ives and finally completed in 1932 with the addition of Hotel Tudor, were more neo-Gothic than anything else; the red brick was decorated with a 'hint of Tudor appliqué'. French's promotional literature made his intentions clear: 'Tudor City is for people who spend carefully. Large scale production reduces overhead and cost. Tudor City offers people with modest incomes a home life in beautiful surroundings.' He sought to win back middle-class suburbanites who would value the ability to 'walk to work' and a relatively tranquil environment. The apartments, priced at about $500 a room per year, immediately attracted midtown office workers and other middle-class residents, and by 1936 the 'city within a city' was worth around $100 million.[30] Over time Tudor City has prospered. The district was transformed with the building of the United Nations complex on the site of the old abattoirs in 1947–52, and Tudor City itself was accorded the status of 'historic district' in 1988. Today, with its restaurants, hotel, grocery, deli, convenience stores, hair salon, laundry and dry cleaners, gardens and a children's playground, it provides a self-contained environment[31] [Illustration 8].

Knickerbocker Village anticipated Dolphin Square in another way. This $10 million project, scaled down from an even more ambitious venture, comprised 1,593 apartments for tenants on five acres of a run-down neighbourhood on Manhattan's Lower East Side, just north of the Brooklyn Bridge. It was an early American example of publicly-subsidised urban redevelopment. French built the Village with the help of a 25-year real estate tax exemption and an $8 million loan from the New Deal's Reconstruction Finance Corporation, the first of only two loans it made to a housing project. The terms limited the developers to a six per cent profit and pegged monthly rents to an average of $12.50 per room.[32] Designed by John S. Van Wart and Frederick L. Ackerman, Knickerbocker Village applied the courtyard-apartment design to low-rental housing on a large scale. It replaced slum properties on a site bounded by Cherry, Catherine, Monroe and Market Streets. There were two 12-storey perimeter blocks, each of which anticipated Dolphin Square in its basic shape, divided by a central 'play ground' (park). Like Tudor City, it was aimed at middle-class New Yorkers, and most of the interest came from young, university-educated professionals. However, the development lacked the long-term cachet of its midtown neighbour. The Knickerbocker flats were tiny, ventilation was limited, and the interior courtyards were small in relation to the scale of the buildings. Almost immediately it was criticised for being too large and too bland.[33] Nevertheless, it was a brave venture in slum clearance and another striking example of French's ability to build on an ambitious scale, even during the Great Depression [Illustration 9].

Whatever the strength of French's concept, on this occasion his execution of the scheme left much to be desired. When, in early October 1934, the first tenants moved in, they found a great deal to complain about: elevators were not working, floors had not been finished, and bathrooms and kitchens lacked fixtures and fittings. With French himself busy in London on his Pimlico scheme (see below), the initial response of the Fred F. French Management Company was unsatisfactory, and angry tenants mobilised support. They formed the Knickerbocker Village Tenants' Association, and by the time that French returned to New York, over 600 residents had attended a meeting at which they voted to withhold rental payments until their demands were met. By the end of November the Management Company had agreed to undertake repairs and compensate the tenants for their hardship.[34] The tenants went on to form a permanent tenants association, fought off a rival, management-supported body, and produced a regular newsletter and organised clubs and social activities. An attempt by the French

Management Company to evict some of the leaders of the Association by not renewing their leases was resisted, and although the tenants failed to enforce renewals in court, the battle produced a new group of more radical leaders who expanded the Association's activities, increased the membership to over 1,000, and became advocates of tenant activism and rent control in the city. The Knickerbocker Association gave support to striking building service workers in March 1936 and inspired a City-Wide Tenants Council which lobbied strongly for rent control in New York and encouraged the measures introduced during the Second World War in 1942–3.[35] This example of tenant action anticipated the tenant activism in Dolphin Square (see below, p.322), although in New York there was a more radical tinge to the protest.

The evidence indicates that French had a template for the Pimlico development in Tudor City. Indeed, his few surviving papers on the London project are indexed as 'Tudor City London'.[36] A letter circulated to prospective British investors made it clear that he wished to bring something of New York's 42nd Street to Westminster. He envisaged the City of London fanning out from Blackfriars Bridge, and a 'Grand Central Zone' extending from Waterloo Bridge. Just as at Tudor City, he was anxious to alleviate the commuting hardships of 'government clerks and minor officials' by offering many of them a central London apartment.[37] Although the Depression had made money tight, and there were emerging problems with the completion of Knickerbocker Village, French was enjoying the success of Tudor City, and in October 1934 he visited London with his senior engineering staff and his Personal Secretary, Dorothy Driscoll. Here he made a firm offer for the Pimlico site. A deposit of £35,000 was put down, ten per cent of the agreed sale price of £350,000 (about £27 million in 2012 prices).[38] French and his team, including Charles M. Chuckrow, Chief Executive of the British subsidiary, and the architect of Tudor City, Douglas Ives, then put together a British corporate institution to front their interest - first the 'Chichester Wharf Co.', then the 'Fillmore Construction Co.' - and found an office in 3 Carlos Place, W1, close to the Grosvenor Estate's HQ.[39] The LCC were first told that the Frederick F. French Co. were acting on behalf of Chichester Wharf Co., the British company which had become 'tenants in possession' of the property, with the right to purchase the freehold from the Grosvenor Estate on or before

30 December 1934.[40] However, it was some time before French and his associates were able to submit plans to the LCC's architect's department under the London Building Act of 1930. The outline plans seeking preliminary approval were not sent until 8 November, only seven weeks before the right to purchase was due to expire.[41]

French was anxious to obtain local authority approval for his scheme, not only under the 1930 Act but also under the emerging town planning regulations.[42] Although the LCC had not obtained ministerial approval for an interim development scheme for this area [No.19], the flats represented an ambitious and in many ways novel development. Chuckrow, in his letters seeking preliminary approval, asked the LCC's town planning committee to assess the application as if the building regulations were already in force.[43] What were the Anglo-American developers proposing to build? It is clear that earlier plans conceived in the United States were quite unlike anything seen in Britain.[44] The first sketch was of a densely developed block of ten storeys with a 23-storey skyscraper emerging from its centre (the area currently occupied by Dolphin Square's garden). The second envisaged a more uniform ten-storey development [Illustrations 10, 11]. However, in both cases, the intention was to provide around 6,000 rooms.[45] French thought that the scheme would cost $10 million or £2 million to build. Having taken soundings from estate agents Knight Frank & Rutley, he estimated annual rentals at a relatively conservative $340 or £68 per room.[46] British opposition forced the Americans to modify their ideas, however, and the preliminary plans submitted to the LCC were less radical. They comprised a plot plan, basement floor plan, ground floor ideas, a typical upper floor plan, and longitudinal and cross sections. There was to be a rectangular block comprising basement, ground floor and nine storeys, except on Chichester Street, which was to be limited to seven storeys. A central garden area would be provided [Illustration 12]. The building was to be of steel frame construction with fire resistant floors and walls. All flats would have central heating, and a continuous hot water system. The initial plans as drawn showed a preponderance of 3½ room [bedroom, reception, kitchen + alcove] and 4½ room [two bedrooms, reception, kitchen + alcove] flats. However, Chuckrow promised a modification of the plans to make about half of the flats smaller, as one- and two-room flats. The LCC's advice was sought on the Grosvenor Road property line and the building line either side of the longitudinal dimension. Was the scheme to be regarded as one building or several? Here the applicants pointed out that the entire building would be accessible at basement level via a continuous corridor. A 50-foot carriageway was included, giving access to garages. No shops were to be included, but a restaurant would be installed on the ground floor for the tenants' exclusive use. The buildings on the Thames-side wharf, included in the freehold, were to be demolished and the area converted into a garden or recreational pier. In his preliminary drawings French also included gardens, four bowling greens, a children's playground and tennis courts at ground level; and in the basement a swimming pool and squash courts.[47]

The LCC's architect's department raised issues relating to means of escape, garage ventilation, and staircase lighting, and amendments were promised by the applicants.[48] Chuckrow was also given the views of the Town Planning Committee, which wanted the building to be set back from both Grosvenor Road and Chichester Street and was concerned about the impact on Claverton Street and St. George's Square and about the lack of sunlight in some living rooms to the rear. There were discussions about the Committee's view that the overall height should be reduced to 70 feet, which Chuckrow thought would make the project uneconomic. But the LCC made it clear in early December (1934) that had the town planning regulations been in force, the scheme as submitted would not have been permitted.[49] A revised planning application, made on 12 December, which responded to the Committee's views and modified the type of flat to be built - four 3-room, one 2-room and three 1-room flats in the west wing, and one 3-room, two 2-room and one 1-room flats in the east wing - was then accepted conditionally by the Council on 17 December.[50] Newspaper reports of the scheme then began to emerge. On 19 December *The Times* reported that French and his associates had obtained an option to purchase, exercisable until the end of the year. Reference was made to a scheme for 1,300 flats containing 4,370 rooms. The *New York Times* carried a similar piece, noting that it was 'one of the most ambitious schemes for London in years' and that the flats, 'intended for persons of middle-class incomes', would be 'the last word in modernism'.[51] The fullest account appeared in the *Daily Telegraph*, based on an interview with Fred French. The headline ran: 'TEN-STOREY FLATS FOR LONDON: £1,750,000 SCHEME'. The 'huge block of flats', which was to be named Ormonde Square, would consist of 4,400 rooms, divided into 1,340 suites. The building would be 'one of the largest, if not the largest block of flats in Europe'. If all went well, the flats would be available for occupation in September 1936. French also told the *Telegraph* that on completion a separate company – 'Ormonde Square Ltd' – would be established to manage the building. The facilities were fully described, including the large central garden, and details were given of the type of flats to be provided, and the proposed rentals, which would range from £75 a year for a one-room flat to £275 for the large suites. The large tenants' restaurant would charge reasonable prices, and meals would also be served in the apartments 'at little extra expense'. The promoters' intention, explained the *Telegraph*, was to 'provide for tenants of moderate means'.[52]

On 8 January 1935 the LCC consented to a building which would be higher than that prescribed in the 1930 Act and stipulated that the construction work was to be started within six months and completed within 18 months of 17 December 1934, i.e. by 16 June 1936.[53] The matter was clearly urgent. French was able to obtain relief from his earlier obligation to complete the transaction by the end of December 1934, though the further agreement he made with the Grosvenor Estate still required a speedy resolution of the matter. Effected through an exchange of letters on 28 January 1935, it required completion no later than 25 April 1935, 'time being in this respect the essence of the contract'. If the transaction were not effected by 25 March, the French company was to pay interest until completion on the outstanding balance at the rate of five per cent per annum.[54] The Council's requirement that French give notice of the development produced more newspaper articles in January 1935. The public consultation produced a few complaints from residents in Claverton and Chichester Streets, who were worried about the height of the proposed building, but in general the response seems to have been positive.[55] At the end of the month the *Daily Telegraph* announced that the scheme had been 'successfully concluded', with contracts exchanged and the plans approved by the LCC. Building work would start in early April.[56]

The *Daily Telegraph*'s optimism was somewhat premature, since French still had the task of finding financial backers for his scheme. This proved to be difficult in the aftermath of the Great Depression, and the innovative approach to property financing favoured by French in Manhattan did not win immediate acceptance in Britain. Some respectable British partners were recruited to the Fillmore Construction Co. as directors, viz. Sir Felix Pole, Chairman of Associated Electrical Industries since 1929 and former General Manager of the Great Western Railway (1921–9), and Sir Hardman Lever, a former Financial Secretary to the Treasury (1916–21) with senior experience in the United States. However, it is not clear how enthusiastic they were about the scheme. Pole, for example, had several irons in the fire at this time.[57] French proposed to form a British company, tentatively called 'Tudor City London Ltd.', with a capital of £1 million, organised on the French Plan with ordinary and preference shares. This company would take over the property from the construction company once the building was completed. But there were now questions about French's credit, since having invested considerable sums in Tudor City and Knickerbocker Village he had become financially stretched, and his inability to pay the interest on some of the preferred stock under earlier French Plans was beginning to produce lawsuits from angry investors.[58] The story goes that French went round the major British building firms to see whether he could attract a backer. In the event, with time running out, he turned to the only company that expressed some willingness to take on his obligations. That firm was Richard Costain Ltd.[59]

ENTER COSTAINS, 1935

Costains were a long-established building firm, founded in Liverpool in 1865 as Costain & Kneen. Growing steadily, Richard Costain & Sons widened the area of its activities, building housing for steel workers in Redcar in the north-east and for munitions workers in Sheffield and South Wales. A significant step was taken when William Percy Costain, the second son of the founder, came to London in 1922 to exploit the speculative opportunities offered by housing and construction, which were more evident in the south-east. He was accompanied by a non-family member, George Warren Peachey, who proved to be a most effective estate designer and sales director. The establishment of a

London branch enabled the firm to participate in the housing and construction booms of the mid-late 1920s and mid-late 1930s.[60] In 1923 the private partnership form for the London business was abandoned in favour of a private limited company, Richard Costain & Sons Ltd., and subsidiary companies were established. The death of W.P. Costain in 1929 gave new responsibilities somewhat earlier than envisaged to a third generation: Richard Rylandes [R.R.] Costain (1902–66), who had become joint managing director in 1927 at the age of 25, and became sole managing director on the death of his father; and Albert P. Costain (1910–87), his younger brother, who acted as production director from 1928 [Illustrations 7 (ii) and (iii)]. Growth was rapid. Large housing estates were constructed in Surrey at Kingswood, then at Selsdon, near Croydon (1,000 houses), and estates of c.1,500 houses were built at Brentwater (Cricklewood) in north London, Sudbury Hill in Middlesex, and in Dagenham. The largest was at Elm Park, Hornchurch, where 5,400 houses were built. Nevertheless, the business remained very much a family enterprise – the chairman of the limited company was the younger Costains' uncle, Richard Arthur Costain. In 1933, the London business – by this time operated through three private companies from 18 Upper Woburn Place, WC1 – was converted into a public company, Richard Costain Ltd., with an authorised capital of £600,000. However, the company remained in family control, with four Costains on the board of eight directors, and 290,000 or 64 per cent of its 450,000 ordinary shares held by seven members of the Costain family.[61] Now one of the largest speculative house building firms in Britain,[62] Costain was anxious to diversify in order to spread risks in the aftermath of the Great Depression. It built blocks of flats in Bloomsbury, Highgate and Streatham, sewerage works in Beckton and Hornchurch, and a laboratory for Glaxo at Greenford. One of the earliest of many overseas projects undertaken by the firm was a section of the Trans-Iranian Railway. However, its largest contract in the 1930s was undoubtedly what became Dolphin Square.[63]

Costain's Dolphin Square archives have not survived, and our account is based on the public record, supplemented by the few company documents for the period 1933–63 which have found their way into the archives of the Dolphin Square Trust.[64] However, the circumstances in which Richard Costain Ltd. took over French's project were recalled by

Sir Albert Costain, and his narrative has appeared in several publications.[65] As he remembers it, 'one Friday morning an American gentleman by the name of Frederick French called at the Costain offices in Upper Woborn Place and asked to see my brother, who was Managing Director [R.R. Costain]'. French apparently said that he needed to complete the transaction on the following Tuesday but was having difficulty raising the finance.[66] Albert was called into the meeting, shown some outline drawings, and asked to estimate the development cost; George Peachey, the Sales Director, was asked to assess the rental values. 'With the help of John Whiter, then senior Contracts Manager, and who later joined the Costain Board, and one of our senior agents, Bert Holmes, we spent the weekend trying to estimate from the rough sketch plans . . . There was much speculation as to whether it was a viable proposition to build what would be the largest block of flats in Europe, in an area which was not considered ideal for residential purposes, particularly as there was no bus service.' In addition, the costs, though correctly forecast by the Costain team, were high, and the anticipated rentals relatively modest: five shillings per foot for most of the flats.[67] But the Costain company was not to be deterred. Albert explained: 'Although on these calculations the financial viability of the project did not look very attractive, the Board took the view that as we were heading for a depression in the building industry, it was a risk worth taking in order to keep our best technical staff and skilled artisans together.'[68] Thus, on 16 April 1935 Costain's solicitors, Bracewell & Leaver, informed the Grosvenor Estate's solicitors that by an assignment of the same date between Frederick F. French & Co., Frederick Fillmore French, and Richard Costain Ltd., the latter had assumed French's interest in the property, including the benefit of the £35,000 deposit.[69] There had been some urgency in the matter, since the agreement between French and the Estate had specified completion by 25 April. Costain inherited the obligation to pay the balance of £315,000 in eight instalments, the last payment being £150,000 on 16 April 1936. In addition, interest at five per cent was payable from 25 March 1935 until the balance was paid off.[70] Clearly, Costain was taking a considerable risk in embarking on the project, and its competitors were not slow to point this out. Among the family anecdotes about the degree of financial exposure was Sir Richard Costain's recollection that he had told a colleague, when standing outside the site, that 'in two or three years we'll either drive up to this spot in a Rolls-Royce, or we'll be standing here selling matches'.[71]

Constraining the financial risk was an immediate concern. To take over a project costing over £1 million demonstrated the entrepreneurial boldness of the young Costain brothers, but the company was already being stretched by its earlier policy of diversification. Losses were being made on two contracts in particular – the Trans-Iranian Railway and Beckton sewerage works.[72] With pre-tax profits of £111,000 in 1934, the first full trading year of the new public company, the margin between profit and loss was not large. At its annual general meeting on 27 March 1935, shareholders had agreed to increase the company's capital from £600,000 to £1 million, and £150,000 in six per cent preference shares were then issued.[73] Further resources were needed, but Costain's bankers, Barclays Bank, were unwilling to continue the company's overdraft, and the directors were forced to turn elsewhere. Albert Costain recalled that his brother Richard, who was an accomplished golfer,[74] was playing golf with Brian Parkes, son of one of the joint general managers of Lloyds Bank, and he took the opportunity to mention the company's financial difficulties. Brian arranged a meeting with his father, Sydney Parkes, and after obtaining a report on the company's accounts and outstanding contracts from Peat Marwick Mitchell, Lloyds agreed to offer Costain an overdraft of £450,000 on 14 June. Richard and Albert Costain also obtained personal overdrafts with the Bank, and the transactions marked the beginning of a long-term relationship between Lloyds and Costain.[75] No less important was Costain's early sale of its freehold interest in the property, which also raised cash. In a sale and leaseback arrangement on 13 September 1935, the United Kingdom Temperance and General Provident Institution of 196 Strand in London, a long-established life insurer, secured the freehold of the site, including the Thames-side wharf. It then leased the property back to Costain for a period of 99 years from 24 June 1935 in return for a rental of £20,250 a year, plus insurance costs. The building work was to be completed within 50 months, and there were 14 restrictive covenants, agreements and conditions in all. The covenants established by the Grosvenor Estate respecting frontage to Grosvenor and Chichester Streets and the light to adjacent properties in St. George's Square and Claverton Street were retained.[76]

Having agreed to take over French's obligations, Costain lost no time in taking the scheme forward. The company appointed an architect, Gordon Jeeves of 16 Hanover Square, and with the assistance of Cecil Eve he submitted new drawings to the LCC on 15 June and 12 July 1935.[77] Another significant appointment was that of Oscar Faber of Marsham Street as the consulting engineer, who also made an immediate impact. [Stanley] Gordon Jeeves (1888–1964) was awarded a Military Cross in the First World War. Having founded his own firm in 1924, he became a Fellow of the Royal Institute of British Architects in the following year. He specialised in office buildings and flats, but French's project was much the biggest of his commissions. Prior to this he had designed flats in Claridge House, Davies Street in 1925 and at 20 Chesham Place in 1927, designed Ideal House in Great Marlborough Street for the National Radiator Co., also in 1927, and had been the architect for no fewer than 26 Lilley & Skinner shoe shops in 1930–2.[78] But these contracts were generally small, rarely exceeding £100,000, while the contract for what became Dolphin Square was ten times higher than this.[79] Jeeves was no stranger to the Army Clothing Depot site. On 16 May 1933, nine days before the auction, his name had been mentioned by Lionel Brown, the auctioneer, in correspondence with the Grosvenor Estate's solicitors. Apparently a client of Knight Frank & Rutley had 'appointed an architect to go into the question of development', and since the architect concerned, Gordon Jeeves, had 'made many enquiries as to the restrictions concerning light', this interest was deemed to be serious. We do not know who the client was.

Oscar Faber (1886–1956) was an eminent consulting engineer and acknowledged expert on constructional steelwork, reinforced concrete, and heating and ventilation. The author of several books on these subjects, he was a former Vice-President of the Institution of Civil Engineers (1925), and at the time of his appointment by Costain, he was President of the Institution of Structural Engineers (1935–6). The son of the Danish Commissioner for Agriculture in London, he graduated with an engineering BSc from the City and Guilds Central Technical College (subsequently part of Imperial College). In 1915, he was awarded an engineering DSc from the University of London for his work on reinforced concrete beams. He worked for two important construction firms – Associated Portland Cement Manufacturers, and

Trollope and Colls – before establishing his own consultancy firm in 1921.[80] Having worked with Herbert (later Sir Herbert) Baker on a cantilever grandstand for Lord's Cricket Ground in 1923 he began a successful collaboration with the architect. Together they built India House (1930) and South Africa House (1933) in central London. Their largest joint project was the £5.7 million rebuilding of the Bank of England in 1921–42. Faber was engaged as constructional engineer in 1924, and took over responsibility for the mechanical engineering in the following year. He was responsible for the underpinning of Soane's boundary wall with a reinforced concrete retaining wall, the provision of air-conditioning and ventilation systems, water supply and an independent generating station.[81] He worked on at least two other projects alongside his work for Costain – the Earl's Court Exhibition Centre (1935–7) and Queen's Hotel, Leeds for the LMS Railway (1936–7). His later work included the rebuilding of the House of Commons after bomb damage in 1948–50.[82] Faber was adept at combining the structural and mechanical engineering functions in complex modern buildings. His approach to construction was evident from a lecture he gave to the Institution of Civil Engineers in 1944. There were, he argued, four essential elements for a good engineering structure: 'strength, permanence, reasonable economy and beauty'.[83] He was known to Costain, having designed the Spillers grain silo and warehouse at Avonmouth, a large reinforced concrete building that was 'constructed at low cost and high speed'; he also designed Spillers Tyne Mill flour mills and warehouse in Newcastle, which was built by Costain at the same time as Dolphin Square, in 1936–7.[84] This exceptional engineer, described as 'big and heavy of frame', 'splendidly untidy in appearance' and with 'something of the air of a still untamed Viking', was to become a critical figure in the determination of how exactly Dolphin Square was to be constructed[85] [Illustration 7 (iv)].

DESIGNING 'ORMONDE COURT'/'ORMONDE SQUARE'/'DOLPHIN SQUARE', 1935–9

When Jeeves first began to interact with the LCC's Architect's Department in June 1935, the evidence suggests that both he and Costain were happy to run with the basic scheme that had been drawn up by their predecessors, though there was of course much detailed planning work to be done. The drawings submitted in June and July made no change to the overall height of the proposed building, nor to its basic design - a single rectangular building, divided into distinct blocks of flats, later called 'houses', with basement, ground floor and nine storeys above (though at some stage the seven storeys planned by French for the frontage onto Chichester Street was reduced to six).[86] The new team also inherited the name of the development, although there continued to be some uncertainty about exactly what this was. Both 'Ormonde Court' and 'Ormonde Square' had been used by French, and it was the latter which had been quoted by the *Daily Telegraph* in its articles in December 1934 and January 1935. All the early plans prepared by Messrs Gordon Jeeves, and which have survived in the RIBA archives, referred to 'Ormonde Square', up to and including those of 12 March 1936. Although the names 'Dolphin Square' and 'Dolphin City' were used by A.P. Herbert in his promotional brochure for Costain in September 1935, the first plans to include the name 'Dolphin Square' were those dated 20 July 1936.[87] As late as 21 April 1936 an agreement between Costain and London Relay Wireless referred to 'Ormonde Square', as did a contract note from Jeeves to the LCC three months later, on 20 July.[88] And yet the name 'Ormonde Court' continued to be used, appearing in Faber's correspondence with the LCC until October 1935, and in some of Jeeves's correspondence until July 1936.[89] In fact, another name was introduced before the matter was settled. Costain's advance advertising of the flats in the *The Times* of 3 March 1936 referred to 'Dolphin House', and the same name was used at the company's AGM on 25 March. Eventually 'Dolphin Square' won the day. A piece in the *The Times* on 4 June declared that 'the new estate will be known as 'Dolphin Square', and this ended the confusion, at least outside the architect's office.[90] The reason for making the change was explained by Albert Costain in *Reflections*. Apparently,

> it seemed more appropriate to select a name which had some connection with the river or the sea. At the time we were discussing possible names my uncle, AJ Costain, then headmaster at Rydall [sic] Mount School, Colwyn Bay, happened to be staying with my brother and mentioned that his school magazine was called "The Dolphin", and the old boys' tie had a dolphin motif

> embroidered on it. He suggested Dolphin Court, but because of the layout of the buildings we finally agreed on Dolphin Square, with each house bearing the name of a well known Admiral or other historic figure with maritime connections.[91]

The Jeeves/Faber design differed from that of French in a number of ways, and was regarded by the LCC planners as being 'a considerable improvement on the plans previously submitted'.[92] While the French scheme had envisaged a west wing consisting of two small courts and six large ones, and an east wing made up of ten small courts, the Jeeves/Faber alternative introduced a more symmetrical pattern, with eight identical wings or spurs, four on each side [see Illustrations 12 and 13]. More natural light was introduced into the courtyards, and the setbacks from both Grosvenor Road and Chichester Street were extended. Furthermore, while the French scheme had proposed two main types of flat, two-bedroom and one-bedroom, Costain's Dolphin Square provided much more variation in the design of the flats, introduced guest rooms, and in January 1937 proposed a more commercial element in the development in the form of a 'residential club' (see below). Jeeves and Faber also proposed a more novel method of construction. Faber, an acknowledged expert on building with reinforced concrete, wanted to use the material with brick facings in Dolphin Square. At the time British engineers and builders had generally been cautious about introducing this technology, while the way in which building projects were organised, which left the constructional risk with the builder, also worked against innovation.[93] Faber, however, was certain that for multi-storey buildings, reinforced concrete offered a substantial cost saving over construction with steel, amounting to some 30–40 per cent.[94] And by 1935 there were supporters of the technology within the building trade, notably the firm Holland & Hannen and Cubitts.[95]

In London, the use of concrete was governed by the LCC's reinforced concrete regulations of 1915. While these gained acceptance elsewhere in Britain, they were both conservative and far from comprehensive in scope. For example, they did not include provision for load-bearing concrete wall construction, and so a waiver was required for each project. In 1933, a new code governing the use of reinforced concrete was produced by the DSIR's Building Research Board. This introduced more liberal standards for the use of the material in building, justified by advances in the quality of the product, and modified the method of calculating permissible stresses. However, the regulators continued to base their calculations of allowable stresses on a theoretical approach to the behaviour of the material, called the elastic modular ratio theory.[96] Faber had carried out important experimental research into reinforced concrete beams under stress in which he challenged the established orthodoxy. In 1927, he delivered a pioneering lecture at the Institution of Civil Engineers in which he argued that the behaviour of concrete under stress differed from existing expectations, since both plastic yield ['creep'] and shrinkage had the effect of transferring part of the load from the concrete to the steel. Consequently the existing regulations governing the permissible stress of steel columns were far too conservative. He therefore criticised the prevailing view that the calculation of safe limits should be based on elastic limits, preferring instead to base his calculations on the ultimate strength of the concrete and steel. The 1933 Code was more in line with Faber's thinking, and thus for Dolphin Square he wanted to use its compressive stress limits, which were greater than those permitted by London's 1915 regulations.[97]

In August 1935, Faber applied to the LCC for waivers from the 1915 Regulations; in total 11 specific changes were requested.[98] Three of these were challenged by the Architect's Department and at the suggestion of the superintending architect, E.P. Wheeler, Faber wrote to the DSIR's Building Research Station at Garston, near Watford, for an opinion. The Director of the Research Station, W.A. Glanville, had, like Faber, conducted research into the behaviour of reinforced concrete under stress, and had confirmed some of Faber's views. He concluded that the plan for Dolphin Square would be 'quite safe and conservative in competent hands'.[99] LCC officials continued to drag their feet, however, and asked for more tests. After two meetings with W. Berry, Chairman of the Building Acts Committee, Faber submitted a revised application on 17 September. The waivers he requested were eventually agreed by the LCC, but it took until 17 October before the letter authorising the work to proceed was sent.[100] Here it seems that the LCC was irritated to find that excavation and foundation work had started before the full list of waivers had been granted. Faber, for his part, was infuriated by the delay. On 26 October he wrote to Wheeler, pointing out that as Chairman of the Institution of Structural Engineers he had been asked to help the Council discourage professional engineers from allowing work to proceed in advance of LCC consents. But when engineers acted properly, as with this project, 'we are treated so harshly and with apparently so little consideration that possibly one begins to find the excuse for those people who have, in some cases, in a spirit of exasperation, proceeded without waiting for the consents.' With this project, he noted, his clients (Costain) were bearing the cost of 'ground rent and cognate expenses' amounting to £1,000 per week.[101] The work that had started was covered by the earlier consents, and did not relate to the three waivers which had been referred to the Building Research Station. But Faber was also aghast to find that officials had inserted an additional clause into the waiver dealing with the use of superimposed loads. By amending it to read 'for the purpose of designing the skeleton framework', the LCC had [unintentionally] limited the loads intended for the floor slabs. This, Faber argued, would delay the works by at least ten weeks.[102] It was only after the LCC had sought the advice of Laurence Shiner, the District Surveyor for Westminster South, that Faber's position was accepted and consent was given at the end of October 1935.[103] A further modification of the Reinforced Concrete Regulations was applied for in March 1936, when Jeeves sought permission to use 11-inch external cavity panel walls. This was consented to in May, when building was well under way.[104]

Jeeves and Faber also had battles with the LCC's planners over other issues, extending the process of authorisation and ensuring that while the LCC had given its general planning consent to the building in November 1935,[105] some matters were not decided until the first tenants of Dolphin Square were in occupation. For example, the LCC rejected Jeeves's initial design for the lift gear and tank rooms on the roof, on the grounds that their height was 'excessive'. The architect responded by submitting revised plans which reduced the height from 108 feet to 102 foot 6 inches.[106] The LCC approved the change in December 1935,[107] but by this time it was clear that the timetable had been compromised, and Jeeves asked for an extension of time to complete the building. In October 1935 the LCC consented to a six-month extension, with completion required by 16 December 1936.[108] Some matters were the responsibility of Costain and its professional team. The decision of the developers to complete and let the southern half of the building before completing the rest of the Square and its attendant facilities (see below) meant that the plans for the latter were submitted to the LCC while building work was in progress.[109] The process put added pressure on the timetable. The 'up-to-date social centre' (Jeeves's phrase) was to be a wide-ranging facility, with provision for a swimming pool, squash courts, gymnasium, restaurants and grill room, veterinary department, laundry, registry office and shops. Unsurprisingly, the main components – sports centre, restaurant, winter garden and shops – required the careful attention of both sides. Jeeves submitted a series of applications from January to October 1936 and approval was given by the LCC over the period July-November 1936.[110] Further consents were required in 1937–8 for the 270-seat Dolphin Restaurant, which replaced a temporary restaurant on Grosvenor Road, where the issues raised resulted from Costain's application for a music and dancing licence.[111]

Particular complications arose with Costain's plans for the large underground garage, which included a petrol station, servicing bays and car showrooms as well as parking spaces for 300 cars. The initial planning applications for the garage and petrol station were submitted by Jeeves on 1 January and 26 March 1936, and consent was given under the Petroleum (Consolidation) Act of 1928 instead of the more intrusive London Building Act of 1930. The LCC agreed to do this after receiving an assurance from Costain in February 1936 that both the garage and the petrol station would be for the sole use of the Dolphin Square tenants and patrons of the sports centre. The initial consents were given in May.[112] Shortly afterwards, Costain's request to double the capacity of the petrol store, from 4,000 to 8,000 gallons, and to introduce two service lines at the petrol pumps, was also approved.[113] While LCC officials felt that the garage was a 'borderline' case for closer scrutiny, their further concerns were met by the requirement of the LCC's Public Control Committee that sprinklers and drenchers should be added.[114] However, Shiner, the District Surveyor, expressed doubts as to whether reliance on the 1928 Act was the correct course of action, since, despite Costain's protestations to the contrary, he felt that because the garage included a car showroom, it was in fact a trading establishment, and its size – 940,000 cubic feet – was considerably in excess of the 250,000 cubic feet limit beyond which partition walls were required under the 1930 London Building Act. Shiner put this to Costain in October 1937, after construction had started.[115] The developers were disappointed by this response. First of all, Jeeves told Wheeler that he hoped that the requirements of the 1930 Act would not be enforced, and enclosed a further assurance from Dolphin Square Ltd., Costain's newly-established subsidiary company, that the garage would not be used by the public. Then, after reluctantly agreeing to the reference, he expressed the hope that further conditions would not be imposed. By this time half of the garage was in use, and the other half was nearing completion.[116] In fact, the consent, which was sent to Jeeves in July 1938, contained no fewer than 31 conditions. The most important of these was the insistence on fireproof partitions between the garage and the servicing workshop, and between the garage and the rest of the building. It was not until February 1939 that the process of authorising the required steel shutters was finally completed.[117]

Costain also wished to make changes to the composition of the residential units, after it had completed the southern half of the building (see below). In January 1937 Jeeves asked the LCC to authorise an increase in the number of one-room flats and the addition of a 'residential club'. He explained that in letting the southern section Costain had found a significant demand for small furnished rooms with a bathroom attached, and the company intended to cater for this demand by modifying the internal layout of the northern part and, in particular, the sections facing Chichester Street. The intention was to rearrange four of the houses by increasing the proportion of one-room flats from 14 to 16 per cent, and to provide 98 guest bedrooms.[118] Then, in the four sections fronting Chichester Street, Costain wished to create a residential club of 320 furnished bedrooms, with two lounges and hotel services, including a restaurant. In this way, the 16 houses originally intended would be reduced to 13. The rooms were to be offered at about £2 2s. a week, and no long lets would be permitted.[119] The LCC was unhappy with the latter part of the application, however, and in March 1937 Jeeves wrote to Wheeler pointing out that the proposal for a club might have been misread. While the planned restaurant was to be open to the public, the club and its lounges were for tenants only. This explanation did not change the opinion of the planners. The LCC agreed to the modification of the flat designs, but not to a residential club, which was considered 'inappropriate' for the area.[120] However, the Council did agree to a belated application by Jeeves in February 1937 to revise the building line to Chichester Street, reducing the setback from 8–11 feet to 7 foot six inches (6 feet for the two central features) in order to accommodate an arcade of shops.[121]

There were more disagreements about the use of neon advertising signs. Boro' Electric Signs of Ranelagh Road, SW1 made several signs for Costain, some of them obtaining retrospective planning permission, others falling foul of the LCC. The most important were the larger illuminated signs advertising the new complex. Thus, in July 1936 the signmakers applied for permission for a temporary twelve-foot neon sign they had erected on the roof earlier in the year. This was lettered 'DOLPHIN SQUARE', 'EUROPE'S MOST COMPLETELY EQUIPPED FLATS', 'RICHARD COSTAIN LTD', and 'LETTING OFFICE', with a directional arrow. Officially, the LCC permitted this to be displayed until 1 December 1937, but it was not removed until March 1938.[122] Two large [34 ft. x 3 ft.] 'DOLPHIN SQUARE' signs were also fixed to the top of the building's parapet, and after some debate as to whether they constituted an advertisement or merely an address, were duly authorised by the LCC in 1937. Nine smaller signs followed in 1937–8.[123] However, a 48 foot 6 inch x 12 foot teak-lettered sign reading 'DOLPHIN SQUARE Richard Costain Limited Contractors', which had been placed on the roof in December 1936, was considered to be a 'sky sign' and ordered to be taken down.[124]

The seemingly interminable process of obtaining planning permission from the LCC clearly added to the anxieties of the developers. While some of the disputes arose over the detailed fitting-out of the building, the arguments over the units to be provided in the North Block in March–April 1937 indicated that this half of Dolphin Square had not been completed to the timetable agreed with the LCC in October 1935, which specified completion by December 1936. In April 1937, Jeeves therefore asked for another extension of the time for completion, the reason given being the 'great difficulty of obtaining materials'. The LCC once again agreed to extend the deadline, this time by two years, i.e. to 17 December 1938. This proved sufficient for the company to complete all the elements of the building and its immediate environment.[125]

BUILDING 'DOLPHIN SQUARE', 1935–8

Albert Costain recalled that it was Lloyds Bank who had insisted that the building should be built in two stages, with the amenities left until stage two. However, given the speculative nature of the project it certainly made sense to seek to secure some income before the project was complete. In the absence of Costain archives, our account of the construction timetable must be approximate. Clearance of the site and foundation work began in the summer of 1935. The southern block – comprising eight houses named after the admirals Howard, Nelson, Hawkins, Raleigh, Drake, Grenville, Frobisher and Collingwood, and given the initial code letters E, F, G, H, I, J, K and L – was begun first, in September 1935 and was largely completed by November 1936, when the first tenants moved in [Illustrations 14, 15]. According to John Faber, there were 'tarpaulins over the lift wells, and one or two other scrambled innovations'.[126] At the same time Costain established Dolphin Square Ltd. to manage the property, and a management and letting office was opened. The first four leases were signed on 19 September 1936, and a further 81 agreements had been completed when the first 11 tenants moved in on 16 November. Altogether 178 tenancy agreements had been signed by the end of the year, when 116 flats were occupied.[127] For the initial tenants a temporary restaurant was provided on Grosvenor Road, facing the Thames, but this was converted into flats once the main restaurant, adjoining the swimming pool, was opened.[128] In July 1937, when the South Block was fully operational, tenancy agreements for 491 flats, 76 per cent of the total [645] available for sale, had been signed, and the occupancy rate had reached about 62 per cent.[129] The basic structure of the houses in the northern half – Beatty, Duncan, Rodney, Hood and Keyes, with the code letters D, C, B, A, P, O, M, N [with Rodney House occupying the entire Chichester Street frontage [BAPO]] – was finished by November 1937, but several flats were not ready for occupation until the summer of 1938.[130] The principal amenities – the underground garage, and the sports and leisure facilities, enclosed in a sports centre or pavilion with restaurant, swimming pool, eight squash courts and a gymnasium – followed a similar timetable.[131] The garage, about 100 yards long by about 75 yards wide, was approached by ramps leading down from the service roads on the east and west sides, with the petrol station on the west side near Howard House

[Illustration 16]. Hailed as the longest single storey underground garage in Britain, it was partially opened in 1937 and was fully operational in the following year.[132] The sports and leisure complex was reported to have cost £130,000 to build.[133] The 'Blue Pool' Restaurant drew its inspiration, according to Albert Costain, from the luxurious lido on the Champs Elysées in Paris, which had opened in February 1928. The Blue Pool's aim was to combine fine dining with cabaret and a swimming pool.[134] Dolphin Square's more modest facility opened on 14 December 1937.[135] A shopping arcade had not been included in Frederick French's design. But Costain decided to include one as part of the Chichester Street frontage, and this was opened in February 1938. Eventually, eight shops, including a baker (Barrett & Pomeroy), greengrocer (Freshfruits), grocery and delicatessen (Dolphin Stores), chemist (Victoria Pharmacy) and hairdresser (Kyrle's), were provided, along with a newsagent/tobacconist, a lending library, and a travel agency kiosk (Frames' Tours).[136] A sub-branch of Lloyds Bank was opened in May 1939.[137] Much was also made of the innovative nursery and children's centre, supervised by the resident matron, Evelyn Pantin, and situated on the top floor of Beatty and Duncan Houses. Here, a range of child-care services, including meals, were provided for children from ten days old to ten years. There were many other centrally organised services available by 1938, including room and window cleaning, shoe cleaning, laundry and dry-cleaning, maintenance, parcel delivery, radio and telephone.[138] However, the proposals for the Thames-side wharf did not materialise. The promised terraced garden, café and marina, anticipated with such whimsical enthusiasm by A.P. Herbert in September 1935, and highlighted in artist's drawings in newspaper advertisements until 1937, were never built. Instead, a rather modest tennis court was provided.[139] Nevertheless, this was an impressive example of large-scale urban living. Costain was clearly proud of its achievement, and held its annual general meeting for 1938 in the Chichester Room of Dolphin Square, on 30 March 1939. In their report for the year, the directors announced that the complex had been completed and that '99 per cent' of the flats had been let.[140]

Particular attention was also paid to the 3.5 acres of gardens, which were designed by Richard Sudell, President of the Institute of Landscape Architects. A prolific writer, he had published several books on landscape gardening and the urban garden before he tackled Dolphin

Square.[141] Here he laid out two main lawns, flanking an avenue of chestnut trees. In the centre there was a rose garden, fountain and pool [Illustration 17]. In the building recesses formal flower beds were arranged after the Dutch, Italian, Japanese and Old English styles. Alpines were placed along the paved walks. The sports centre roof gardens were laid out with climbers and pots applying Spanish and Mexican themes. The quantity of materials required was impressive: 2,000 tons of paving and wall-stone, 3,000 tons of soil, 6,000 turves, 16 tons of fertiliser and 10 cwt of grass seed. The initial planting consumed about 10,000 bulbs and 5,000 plants, but Sudell suggested that many more would be needed to complete the job.[142] His conception was that 'a stroll around the Square will, as it were, enable you to make a tour of the whole horticultural world'.[143] Edward Irvine Halliday (1902–84), a school friend of Richard Costain's, was commissioned to design the interior of the swimming pool and restaurant. The 66-foot pool was equipped with modern features, notably filtration and sterilisation with ozone instead of chlorine, to protect the diners.[144] There was also a wave machine and sunray lamps. A major feature was the 90-foot mural in the swimming pool gallery. It was in map form, and depicted historical events on the Thames from Hampton Court to Woolwich. Albert Costain later lamented the fact that the post-Costain management had replaced it with a modern design.[145] Halliday also designed the north side entrance lounge on Chichester Street.[146] He suggested that a dolphin fountain be added as a feature of the swimming pool, and this was designed by John Rattenbury Skeaping (1901–80) and cast in bronze. It depicted a dolphin rising up from an enormous scallop shell.[147] Both Skeaping and Halliday were emerging talents in the mid 1930s who subsequently established national reputations. Jack Skeaping, who studied at Goldsmith's College and the Central School of Arts and Crafts, and was the first husband of Barbara Hepworth, became well known as a sculptor of horses. After the war he was Professor of Sculpture at the Royal College of Art.[148] Halliday was born in Liverpool and studied at the city's School of Art, then at the Atelier Colarossi in Paris and the Royal College of Art in London. He went on to establish himself as a portrait painter; his portraits of Princess Elizabeth and the Duke of Edinburgh in 1948 are part of the National Portrait Gallery's collection.[149]

*

Dolphin Square was a large and complex building project, and the scale of the work was impressive. According to London's *Evening Standard* and the *Morning Post*, it required the excavation of some 200,000 tons of earth, the use of 125,000 tons of concrete and 6,000 tons of steel, 12 million bricks for the external walls, 125 miles of electric cable, 3,080 radiators and 5,300 light bulbs. There were 22 acres of floor space and 6,700 windows. A labour force of 3,000 was deployed.[150] The total cost of the building was put at £1.25 million, which with the price of the freehold made the total £1.6 million. Some estimates appearing in the press put the cost as high as £2 million (about £143 million in today's prices).[151]

It was no mean achievement to complete Dolphin Square in under three years.[152] The Costain team and especially Richard and Albert Costain worked under considerable pressure, as did the architects, engineers, and building workers. John Faber, biographer of his father Oscar, noted that the 'enterprising and speculative development' was extremely demanding, requiring the services not only of Oscar Faber but also of the able lieutenants in his practice, Jim Vaughan and Rob Kell. Design and construction had to proceed in tandem since the first tenancies specified a moving-in date of 16 November 1936. Construction was necessarily swift. It was organised with four separate gangs of workers, who were incentivised with daily bonuses, and apparently one floor was built every ten days.[153] We know very little about the army of workers engaged on the site. However, the 40th anniversary newsletter of the Dolphin Square Tenants' Association refers to a memoir from Jack Curran, who was engaged as a painter and later became a Westminster City councillor and a founding member of the Dolphin Square Trust. Curran confirms the speed of the work: 'we were decorating one floor while they were building the one above . . . the quick-drying cement made an enormous difference'. But it also brought its hazards. Dust was a particular problem, and Costain sprayed the floors with water to keep it down. It appears that 'the combination of water and electric cables leading to hoists and other equipment resulted in more than one fatality on the site'.[154] We know more about the firms engaged on the project. Costain used a veritable army of subcontractors and suppliers on the site, and this required able management. No fewer than 52 firms were listed by the *Builder*, the *Architect & Building News*, and Costain's promotional booklet *The House of Costain*, in 1937–8, and these are reproduced in Table 2.1. The scale and complexity of the work demanded effective project management, and the evidence suggests that this was achieved by sound organisation.

Table 2.1 Subcontractors and suppliers employed on Dolphin Square, 1935–7

Function/product	*Firm*	*Reference*
Excavation	Willment Bros	A, B
Reinforcing steel	United Strip and Bar Mills	A, B
Hoists, elevating plant	Ace Machinery	C
Stonework	Girling's Ferro-Concrete Co.	A, B
Artesian wells	R. Richards & Co.	A, B
Electrical, mechanical and hydraulic engineers	Drake & Gorham	A, B, C
Pumps	K.S.B. Manufacturing Co.	A, B
Sewage pumps	Ralph E. Smart & Co.	A, B
Facing bricks	Middlesex Brick Co.	C
Kontite fittings	Kay & Co.	A
Piers, marble	Fenning & Co.	A, B
Bull motors	E.R. & F. Turner	A
Cork insulation	G. Stephenson	C
Cork tile flooring	Cork Insulation Co.	A
Copper tubes	Yorkshire Copper Works, Leeds	C
Hot water installation	G.N. Haden & Sons	A, B
Joinery	Rippers	A, B
Asphalt	General Asphalte Co.	A, B
Rubber flooring	British Tyre & Rubber Co.	A, B, C
Vitrolite tiling	British Vitrolite Co.	A, B, C
Sanitaryware + piping	Edward Marshall	C
Industrial flooring, partition slabs	E.J. Elgood	A, B, C
Linoleum	Modern Floorings Co.	A, B
Cork flooring	Cork Insulation Co.	A, B
Motor showroom flooring	J. White & Sons	A, B
Painting and decorating	Kings Decorators	A, B, C
Wallpaper	Essex & Co.	C
Tube lamps	Tubelight Sales	A, B
Thermotiles	D. Anderson & Son	A, B
Tiling	Chas. Walker & Co.	A, B
Kitchen appliances	Benham & Sons	A, B, C

Carpets, tables, chairs	Maple & Co.	A, B
Heat insulation products	Moler Products	C
Wallboard, flush doors, water-proofing	MacAndrews & Forbes	A, B, C
Glazing contractors	E.A. Heatherington	A, B, C
Glazing	Haywards	A, B
Grilles, steel shutters	Haskins	A, B, C
Windows and screens	Crittall Manufacturing Co.	A, B
Lifts	Express Lift Co.	A, B
Squash courts	Gradidge Construction Co.	A, B
Lockers	Roneo	A, B
Electric fires	Belling, Enfield	C
Radio installation	Radio Furniture & Fittings	C
Kitchen cabinets	Peerless Kitchen Cabinets	A, B
Swimming pool lighting	Lenscrete	C
Architectural metalwork/brass dolphin	Morris Singer Co.	A, B, C
Cocktail bar counters	Ring's	B
Copper roof (loggia)	Frederick Braby & Co.	A, B
Pool treatment plant	Turn-Over Filter Co.	A, B
Restaurant windows	Mellowes & Co.	A, B
Terrazzo and tiling	Diespeker & Co.	A, B
Sprinklers	Mather & Platt	A, B
Lightning conductor	J.W. Gray & Son	A, B

Source: Richard Costain Ltd., ***House of Costain: Seventy-Three Years of Progress*** (n.d. [1938]), pp.9–29; ***The Builder***, 1 October 1937, p.586; ***Architect & Building News***, 7 January 1938, p.11.

Key: A Architect & Building News; B Builder C House of Costain

In particular, Costain encouraged a close liaison between architect, engineer and builder, and specifically weekly on-site meetings between Albert Costain, John Whiter, responsible for subcontracting operations, Bert Holmes, the on-site agent, and the consulting engineer, Oscar Faber or his representative. This practice was not common at the time, though it rapidly became a fundamental way of organising such projects.[155] The idea emerged from a visit Albert and Arthur Costain had made to New York in 1931 as part of an Institute of Builders study group. Here Albert saw how important the concurrent communication between client, architect and builder was in the construction of the

McGraw-Hill Publishing Co. building, and he applied this knowledge to the construction of Dolphin Square.[156]

How many flats were built, how many were made available for letting, and who were the first tenants? The answers are not entirely straightforward. First of all, the surviving source materials are limited. For the first two decades of Dolphin Square's existence, we have to rely on only two documents: the register of leases for the South Block for 1936–7, and the inventory and valuation of the property conducted by Goddard & Smith for the new owners, Lintang Investments, in February 1959.[157] Westminster's electoral registers and rate books provide an alternative to corporate archives, but they are frustrating to use. The registers certainly give a rough indication of the resident population, but are far from comprehensive since many tenants failed, or chose not, to place their names on the register. Rate books represent an improvement in this regard, but the information they provide is at best rudimentary. The practice of subletting was to create another complication.[158] In July 1937 only 273 or 57 per cent of the 476 tenants who had signed tenancy agreements for the South Block were listed on the electoral register for that year.[159] Second, the calculation of numbers and apartment type is complicated by the actions of the management company, Dolphin Square Ltd., in retaining some of the units for staff and office purposes, offering some flats to firms, and reserving a relatively large number of flats for the company's use, for occupation by clients, family and friends. The first corporate clients of Dolphin Square appeared in April 1937, when the Edwards Glass Co. leased 508 Hawkins House.[160] Mrs M.M. Costain was an early tenant of 603 Drake House, and Costain retained several flats for its own use (both Richard and Albert Costain lived in the Square for some years). When Goddard & Smith surveyed the Square for Lintang in 1959 they found that Richard Costain Ltd. held leases on 21 flats in Rodney House. However, this was clearly an underestimate. Further listings reveal that in 1959 the company had signed 37 seven-year leases, 21 in Rodney House, and 16 elsewhere.[161] Nine Costain subsidiary ventures gave Duncan House as their address in 1964.[162] Elsewhere in the Square, some furnished or unfurnished rooms were made available for wealthier tenants who wished to house their maids separately.[163] Some tenants entered into agreements to lease adjoining flats in order to house employees or to provide additional space, and these agreements were generally considered to be a single let for management purposes. The lease register for the South Block reveals that there were 15 of these double occupancies by July 1937, and the rate books indicate that the total for both blocks was 22 by April 1939.[164] There is also the further matter of guest rooms, i.e. small single and double bedrooms for hire to the friends and relatives of tenants, in much the same way as guest rooms are provided in Oxbridge colleges. The only guest room clearly identified in the 1937 lease register for the South Block was No.1 Raleigh House. For the North Block Costain had made plans for 98 guest rooms, but after the plan for a residential club was turned down the number appears to have been scaled down. War-time conditions disrupted the provision of these rooms, and in the immediate post-war period the rate books suggest that guests were accommodated in Beatty and Duncan houses.[165] In any event, we know that in 1959 there were 30 of them, situated on the ground floor of Keyes House, near the shopping arcade, and on the ground floor of Hood House. Furnished apartments represent yet another complication. Four furnished flats are listed in the South Block's 1937 lease register, with two of them let at £6 6s. a week. They were the forerunner of the 'hotel' style accommodation available in Rodney House from the late 1950s. How many furnished flats were made available in 1938 is impossible to say, but by 1957, when the Dolphin Square management decided to consolidate them in Rodney House, there were about 120 of them, scattered among all 13 houses. It therefore seems safe to assume that the numbers increased once the North Block had opened in 1938, with other flats being converted in the South Block as flats became more difficult to let on an unfurnished basis during the war.[166]

In the planning and construction stages Costain offered several estimates of the total number of flats it was intending to build. These ranged from 1,218, in the 1936 brochure for the South Block, to 1,310, which appeared in the architectural press in 1937–8.[167] Our best estimate of the number by house is set out in Table 2.2, in which we combine the evidence for 1937, 1959, and 1962, when a further sale of the Square was organised. We know that 660 units were built in the South Block, with a further 560 more planned for the North Block.[168]

Table 2.2 Number of Dolphin Square flats by house

House		*Flats*	*Double lets*	*Total less double lets*	*Reserved for staff*	*Total [net]*
South Block 1937						
Grenville		80	1	79	2	77
Drake		45	3	42	2	40
Raleigh		45	1	44	2	42
Hawkins		80	-	80	1	79
Nelson		93	1	92	4	88
Howard		111	5	106	-	106
Collingwood		112	-	112	2	110
Frobisher		94	4	90	2	88
Total		660	15	645	15	630
South + North Blocks 1959/62	*Flats 1959*	*Flats 1962*				
Grenville	80	80	-	80	-	80
Drake	42	45	3	42	-	42
Raleigh	45	47	2	45	-	45
Hawkins	80	82	2	80	3	77
Nelson	89	93	6	87	-	87
Howard	109	112	3	109	-	109
Collingwood	111	112	1	111	-	111
Frobisher	86	94	8	86	2	84
Beatty	110	111	2	109	-	109
Duncan	91	92	1	91	1	90
Rodney	152	152	1	151	-	151
Keyes	96	99	5	94	-	94
Hood	111	111	1	110	1	109
Total	**1,202**	**1,230**	**35**	**1,195**	**7**	**1,188**

Source: South block from 1937 lease register; North block from 1959 inventory and 1962 sale document (corrected).

This would make a total of 1,220 units, before reservation for staff or office use. In 1946, when Dolphin Square Ltd issued debentures, it announced that there were 1,216 flats. Goddard & Smith's inventory for Lintang in 1959 gave a lower figure of 1,202.[169] More detailed information was provided for the 1962–3 sale. Although the sale document referred to a total of 1,196 flats, the accompanying schedule produces a total of 1,195, i.e. 1,230 less 35 double occupancies. If seven staff flats are discounted, the total available for letting was 1,188 (Table 2.2). Turning to the breakdown by the number of rooms (Table 2.3), it is clear that while 2,630 rooms were made available, there were very few spacious apartments, and the vast majority of flats were relatively small.

Table 2.3 Dolphin Square flats, by room (excluding kitchenette and bathroom)

	No. of	*Rooms*						
House	*1*	*2*	*3*	*4*	*5*	*6*	*7*	*Total*
Grenville	19	42	15	1	2		1	80
Drake	10	13	7	10	2	-	-	42
Raleigh	12	14	8	9	1	-	1	45
Hawkins	20	40	17	-	2	-	1	80
Nelson	11	56	17	5	-	-	-	89
Howard	23	56	24	5	-	1	-	109
Collingwood	25	56	25	4	1	-	-	111
Frobisher	14	49	14	6	-	3	-	86
Beatty	23	51	33	3	-	-	-	110
Duncan	10	47	31	2	1	-	-	91
Rodney	30	87	34	1	-	-	-	152
Keyes	13	48	29	1	2	3	-	96
Hood	24	53	32	2	-	-	-	111
Total by flat	234	612	286	49	11	7	3	1,202
Total by room	234	1,224	858	196	55	42	21	2,630
Morris	240	600	284	50	13	10	3	1,200
1962 sale	239	598	283	50	13	10	3	1,196

Source: Goddard & Smith, Inventory and Valuation for Lintang Investments, 28 February 1959, DST; Morris, ***Dolphin Square***, p.37.

Using the data for 1,202 units provided by Goddard & Smith for 1959, only 70 (under six per cent) had more than three rooms, and there were only three 7-room flats. 'Bedsitters' (234) and 1-bed flats (612) predominated, together accounting for 70 per cent of the total (Table 2.3). It seems clear that the target market for the flats was as a central London pied-à-terre for the professional and rentier classes, people who had at least one property elsewhere. There were also single people who chose

Dolphin Square as their sole residence and, like their New York counterparts in Tudor City or Knickerbocker Village, valued both living and working in the centre of the city. Costain's initial advertising revealed its aspirations for the development. In its colour brochure in 1936 it suggested that the Square would 'carry the prestige associated with many residents notable in public life and society. Members of Parliament, people of Title, Government officials and Professional men are amongst those who have been attracted as Residents'.[170] Above all, Dolphin Square was for 'modern people'.[171]

What facilities were provided? The developers boasted that these were luxurious apartments with every modern convenience, and the evidence suggests that they were correct. The flats were served by electric lifts and there were separate entrances to each of the 13 houses, with a clearly understood numbering system for the flats.[172] Residents enjoyed coke-fired central heating and a constant hot water supply. There were 'scientific fitted kitchens'; a free cooker and refrigerator, with a choice of either electric or gas as a fuel. The internal telephones were connected to a central exchange - Victoria 3800 - and provision was made for radio from a central control station.[173] Heating and hot water were provided by four coke-burning boiler houses, but the dust caused nuisance to ground floor tenants, and in 1951 Dolphin Square joined Westminster Council's new housing estate, Churchill Gardens, in deriving its supply from Battersea Power Station in an innovative scheme by which exhaust heat was trunked across the Thames in underground pipes. The fuel savings were put at 10,000 tons per annum.[174] The water supply was taken from four artesian wells on the site, and stored in reservoirs in the gardens, with an additional 80,000 gallons on the roof.[175] Considerable thought was given to the interior design of the flats. In most of them the kitchen and bathroom were positioned next to the same rooms in the adjoining flat, as were the bedrooms.[176] Particular attention was given to sound insulation in Faber's design. The outer walls were of cavity wall construction. Inside, noise was reduced both between floors, using compressed cork insulation, and between flats, using pumice composition blocks. Ventilation shafts in the bathrooms were also fitted with 'special baffles' to reduce noise.[177] The plumbing was probably the least satisfactory aspect of the design. There was no external pipework, and instead internal ducts were used.

This was to present a serious maintenance challenge in later years since many of the ducts, 124 in all, could only be reached through small trapdoors in bathrooms and kitchens.[178] In addition to enjoying their well-appointed flats, residents were promised a range of services which were to be provided either directly to their flats or were available on site, such as shoe cleaning, laundry, valeting, the use of errand boys, and the hire of private rooms for 'music, parties, art studies, etc.' The first Dolphin Square handbook offered access to doctors, vets, massage and an ice cream parlour, sports activities (including 'spotlight golf'), and a restaurant.[179] The first issue of a monthly magazine for residents called *The Dolphin*, published in May 1937, contained a bullish editorial from 'The Dolphin' (Theo Langbehn of 507 Frobisher House). Countering a comment by Lady Rhondda that soulless blocks were springing up all over London 'like gigantic mushrooms', he retorted that Dolphin Square was 'providing its residents with every kind of communal enjoyment and opportunity for social life'.[180]

DOLPHIN SQUARE – 'EUROPE'S GREATEST RESIDENTIAL LANDMARK ON LONDON'S RIVERSIDE DRIVE'[181]

Dolphin Square was formally opened on 25 November 1936 by Lord Amulree, the former Labour politician, patron of the Building Industries National Council, and a campaigner for residential planning in Westminster.[182] Also present were: Lord Clwyd, the former Welsh Liberal MP, who was a director of both Costain and Dolphin Square's freeholder, the UK Temperance and General Provident Institution;[183] and Duff Cooper, the local MP and Secretary of State for War, who, as we have noted, had disposed of the Army Clothing Depot and therefore freed up the land for development. The Children's Centre and Nursery, in Beatty House, was opened by Duff Cooper's wife, Lady Diana, though it was to have a short-lived existence, as it was closed on the outbreak of war[184] [Illustration 18]. Costain was proud of its achievement, the Chairman telling shareholders that 'this magnificent conception' would become 'the most desirable and attractive place of residence in the Metropolitan area'.[185] The public quickly expressed its interest in the property, and the first lettings were arranged before the show flats, furnished by Maples, were fitted out in the South Block.[186] Albert

Costain recalled that the Square attracted attention in the technical press and elsewhere. In 1937 T.C. Campbell, a Vice-President of the Frederick F. French Management Co. who was concerned in the management of Tudor City, visited London and was reported to have been impressed by Costain's work and, in particular, by the communal facilities.[187] An architect from South Africa visited Albert and asked him to advise on the construction of a similar block of flats in Durban.[188]

How did contemporaries view the building? *The Builder*, Britain's long-established journal of architecture, was sober and descriptive in its review, though it noted with approbation that less than a third of the site had been built on, drawing attention to the gardens and the sporting facilities. The 300-car garage was heralded as 'an interesting experiment in underground car-parking', one of the largest in the country. The self-contained nature of the development was also highlighted. 'The shops provide for a great variety of wants, including valeting service, beauty parlour, laundry depot, theatre booking-office, etc., the sports centre covers a wide range of sports and games, and there are a fully equipped nursery and children's centre, a large restaurant, music-room and other social features.'[189] *The Architect & Building News* was equally descriptive. It noted that particular care had been taken with sound insulation and ventilation, and emphasised the comprehensive services (central heating, constant hot water, etc.) and the variety in flat design, ranging from bedsitting-rooms at £75 p.a. to special suites, with five bedrooms and a maid's room, at £455 p.a.[190] Later assessments were more critical. Nikolaus Pevsner was scarcely impressed with the 'gigantic quadrangle', and expressed a preference for the neighbouring Churchill Gardens Estate, built by Westminster Council after the war. According to Simon Bradley, Pevsner's editor in the 2003 edition of *London 6: Westminster*, 'Pevsner thought it made a poor show alongside Churchill Gardens, a huge lump, seven to ten storeys high, relieved only by an occasional striping of brick and stone, and a few motifs of no great vigour.' Bradley himself felt that its affinity with 1930s council housing was its most endearing feature.[191] *The Observer* also offered a scathing comment, dismissing the Square as 'the most spiritually deadening building in Europe'.[192] Support for the concept of Dolphin Square was offered by David Hamilton Eddy, writing on 'Castle Mythology in British Housing' in the journal of the

Royal Institute of British Architects in 1989. It provided a 'perfectly good model for large-scale living environments in the heart of London', he wrote. In turn it was 'inspired by the longstanding myth of the castle, a fortified environment containing all amenities and resistant to siege'. Much of what he had to say was disappointing, however. Full of its own myths about the Square, Eddy's article failed to make the central point that the development owed its origin to an American developer. If it represented the Englishman's love of the castle as a fortified home, then the concept was derived from the neo-Tudor aspirations of a New Yorker. And there is no sound evidence to support the contention, which appears here and elsewhere, that Faber and Jeeves designed the Square 'in response to Prime Minister Stanley Baldwin's dictum that 'the bomber will always get through'. The design may have helped Dolphin Square weather the blitz (see below, p.97), but the major reasons for using reinforced concrete were lower cost, speed of construction and sound insulation properties.[193] The assessment of Edward Jones and Christopher Woodward is more measured. In their 1983 guide to London's architecture they noted that 'the style is a dull neo-Georgian for the base and upper storeys, with a modern striped top floor'. For these critics the comparison with Churchill Gardens (1946–62) was equally striking, but not in the way Pevsner had argued. Dolphin Square was the 'space-making "block"', Churchill Gardens the series of 'isolated slabs standing on lawns'. But while the former had a higher residential density – 1,236 [sic] flats squashed into 7.6 [sic] acres, compared with the latter's 1,661 flats on a 30-acre site – it was the latter that appeared cramped and densely-populated.[194]

This £1–2 million scheme was an impressive project to have been taken on in the capital by young builders from Lancashire (Albert Costain was only 25 when construction began). The competition in housing was fierce. With interest rates low, the 1930s witnessed a move into real estate investment, and substantial numbers of flats were put up. For example, a dozen new or newly-converted blocks were advertised in *The Times* in the first fortnight of 1936 alone.[195] And Dolphin Square severely strained the resources of Costain, as the directors' annual reports to shareholders made clear. In March 1936, Arthur Costain, the Chairman, told the AGM that 'Dolphin House' was its 'most important undertaking . . . The magnitude of this undertaking is such that it will be impossible to complete it during the current year'. In the following year the directors reported a 36 per cent fall in profits – from £110,000 in 1935 to £71,000 in 1936. This, they explained, was 'due largely to the concentration of a considerable part of the activities of the Company on the construction of Dolphin Square'.[196] Subsequent results were even worse. In 1937, profits fell to £62,000, and the ordinary dividend at five per cent was half that paid out in 1934 and 1935. In 1938, no dividend was paid, and the company was forced to dip into its reserves to pay the preference shareholders. The Sudetenland crisis in September was blamed for the slump in profits as much as Costain's exertions in Pimlico, where, the directors reported, Dolphin Square was 'now fully let'. However, any hopes of a recovery were dashed with the onset of war in September 1939. The Square was reported to have fully justified the directors' expectations as a profitable investment in the first nine months of the year, but the company was then forced to abandon the housing market in favour of war work, and profits remained low for some time.[197] Richard and Albert Costain took a brave step in investing so much of the company's resources in speculative housing in Westminster, and they were unlucky that political events prevented them from enjoying earlier returns. This said, Richard Costain Ltd. was a model of the well-managed, multifaceted building firm, something that Thomas Cubitt would surely have applauded.

NOTES

1 *The Times*, 2 August 1932, p.17.

2 *Parl. Deb. (Commons)*, 5th ser. (Session 1931–2), Duff Cooper, 8 March 1932, c.1658.

3 *The Times*, 15 December 1932, p.11.

4 Sale Particulars of the Royal Army Clothing Depot, Grosvenor Road, Key Plan, Grosvenor Estate Records: abstracts of title and other documents re RACD, 1930–5, WCA 2260/239; *The Times*, 4 March 1933, p.22, and also 6 March 1933, p.12.

5 *The Times*, 29 April 1933, p.26.

6 London County Council, *London Statistics, 1932–33*, p.134. Westminster was, however, the first metropolitan borough to provide a block of flats for working-class occupation (Regency Street, 1904): City of Westminster, Churchill Gardens and The Pimlico District Heating Undertaking, July 1951, p.6, Dolphin Square Trust archives [henceforth DST].

7 Isobel Watson, *Westminster and Pimlico Past: a visual history* (1993), p.135.

8 E.M. Stopford (Secretary, Westminster Housing Trust)-Boodle, Hatfield & Co., 8 August 1930; correspondence between the Westminster Housing Association, Westminster Housing Trust and the Grosvenor Estate re Pulford St., 1926–32, WCA 2379/4/50; Westminster Housing Trust Committee of Management Minutes, 28 November 1929, 4 February and 7 May 1930, and 14 January 1931; Stout, *Pimlico*, p.66.

9 Cf. Marian Bowley, *Housing and the State 1919–1944* (1945), p.99; A.E. Holmans, *Housing Policy in Britain: A History* (Beckenham, 1987), pp.66–7.

10 Town Clerk (Westminster City Council [WCC])-Boodle Hatfield & Co., 29 July 1929, WCA 2379/4/50.

11 See correspondence in WCA 2379/4/50 and 2444/5/19.

12 Marchioness of Londonderry-Duke of Westminster, 17 March 1933 and reply, 20 March 1933, WCA 2444/5/19. On the 2nd Duke see *Survey of London, Vol.XXXIX* (1977), pp.67, 75.

13 Edgson (HPM&R)-Borrer (Boodle, Hatfield & Co.), 19 November 1928, Grosvenor Estate records on Royal Army Clothing Depot, WCA 2305/187.

14 Brown (ARW&B)-Borrer, 11 April 1933, WCA 2444/5/19, and see *Westminster & Pimlico News*, 28 April 1933, p.5.

15 Holland & Hannen and Cubitts, *The Inception and Development of a Great Building Firm* (n.d. c.1929), pp.47–9, and *Team*, 1:2 (December 1957), p.5. A single private company was formed to cement the merger in 1909.

16 Brown-Borrer, 16 May 1933, WCA 2260/239. Stewart was Conservative MP for Belfast Ormeau.

17 Brown had recommended a reserve of £365,000, but it is not clear that this figure was accepted, and later the Estate was willing to accept £350,000.

18 Brown (ARW&B)-Denis Hyde (Grosvenor Estate), 29 May 1933, WCA 2260/239.

19 Brown-Borrer, 16 May 1933, and Brown-Hyde, 29 May 1933, WCA 2260/239.

20 Brown-Borrer, 16 May 1933, WCA 2260/239; Jonathon Waldram & Sons (Consulting Engineers & Surveyors, Gray's Inn Sq.), 'The Grosvenor Estate. The Royal Army Clothing Factory Pimlico. Report on Limits of Light on Buildings on the Site to Preserve Reasonable Amenities to Adjoining Lessees', 20 March 1933, WCA 2305/187, and see also copy of Percy J. Waldram-Estate Surveyor, Grosvenor Office, 2 November 1934, LCC Building Act Case file on Dolphin Square, London Metropolitan Archives [henceforth LMA], GLC/AR/BR/06/075760/01.

21 Note [n.d.] pinned to Brown-Hyde, 29 May 1933, Memo. of meeting with Brown and Borrer, 3 November 1933, WCA 2260/239; G. Topham Forrest (Superintending Architect,

LCC), Report, 19 November 1934, LMA GLC/AR/BR/06/075760/01; *Survey of London, Vol. XXXIX*, p.67.

22 Fuller, Horsey, Sons & Cassell-Boodle, Hatfield & Co., 11 December 1933, and subsequent correspondence in WCA 2305/188.

23 *Evening News*, 30 January 1935, p.9, cutting in Grosvenor Estate records, WCA 2260/239. The obituary in *New York Times*, 31 August 1936, p.15, is scarcely more illuminating.

24 The surviving primary material on Fred French and his companies is limited, the main deposits being in the New York Public Library Manuscripts & Archives Division [NYPL], MssCol. #6206, and in Alan Rabinowitz's papers, Cornell University Library, coll. #6708. The most useful secondary sources are: Eugene Rachlis and John Marqusee, *The Landlords* (New York, 1963), pp.164–93; Alan Rabinowitz, *Fred F. French: A centennial history, 1883–1983* (mss, 1983), Cornell coll. #6708; John W. and Fred F. French, *A Vigorous Life: The Story of Fred F. French, Builder of Skyscrapers* (Vantage Press, New York, 1993); James Morrison, 'Who in the World Was Fred F French?', *City Journal* (Manhattan Institute) (Autumn 1998); and Alexander Rayden, *The People's City: A History of the Influence and Contribution of Mass Real Estate Syndication in the Development of New York City* (BookSurge [Amazon], 2007), esp. pp.51–2, 64.

25 Fred. F. French, 'Financing Private Construction', address to the Association of General Contractors of America, 30 January 1934, NYL #6206, Box 2. A copy of the 11th edition of Fred. F. French, *The French Plan* (1929) is in the Alan Rabinowitz papers, Box 4, folder 11, Cornell #6708. See also Rachlis and Marqusee, *The Landlords*, pp.167–8, and Rayden, *People's City*, pp.52–63.

26 Charles Paterno was a physician and property developer who, with French and the architect George Pelham, designed the Tudor-style co-operative housing project called Hudson View Gardens at 182nd Street in Washington Heights (1924): Richard Plunz, *A History of Housing in New York City: Dwelling Type and Social Change in the American Metropolis* (New York, 1990), p.148. Rayden suggests other possible antecedents for Tudor City: *People's City*, pp.90–1.

27 Alexander Garvin, *The American City: What Works, What Doesn't* (New York, 2002), p.254, and see also Robert A.M. Stern et al., *New York 1930* (New York, 1987), p.437ff. and *New York 1960* (New York, 1997), p.279, and Paul Goldberger, *The City Observed: New York* (New York, 1979), pp.133–4.

28 See French, mimeo letter to British investors, 9 October 1934, NYPL MssCol #6206, Box 7.

29 Rachlis and Marqusee, *The Landlords*, p.164.

30 *New York Times*, 6 September 1936, S.11, p.1; Rachlis and Marqusee, *The Landlords*, pp.169–73.

31 Garvin, *American City*, pp.254, 274–5; Stern et al., *New York 1930*, p.438 and *New York 1960*, pp.606–7, 618; Goldberger, *City Observed*, pp.133–4; Rayden, *People's City*, pp.87–97. Tudor City was sold to Walter Hemsley & Associates in 1970.

32 The loan from the Reconstruction Finance Corporation was $8,075,000 @ 6%. The Corporation's work was subsequently taken over by the Public Works Administration. See *New York Times*, 6 September 1936, S.11 p.1; Rachlis and Marqusee, *The Landlords*, pp.175–87; Plunz, *Housing in New York City*, pp.207–8; Rayden, *People's City*, pp.106, 112–16.

33 Cf. Rachlis and Marqusee, *The Landlords*, pp.189–90, Stern, *New York 1930*, p.419, Plunz, *Housing in New York City*, pp.210–11. Goldberger, in his *The City Observed*, omitted it from his compendium of New York buildings.

34 *New York Times*, 1 December 1934, p.27, 10 December 1934, p.35; Rachlis and Marqusee, *The Landlords*, pp.188–9.

35 Garvin, *The American City*, pp.258–60; Stern et al., *New York 1930*, pp.418–19; Mark Naison, 'From Eviction Resistance to Rent Control: Tenant Activism in the Great

Depression', in Ronald Lawson and Mark Naison (eds.), *The Tenant Movement in New York City 1904–1984* (Brunswick, NJ, 1986), pp.116–119, 128–30.

36 NYPL MssCol #6206, Boxes 7 and 10.

37 French, letter to investors, 9 October 1934, NYPL MssCol #6206, Box 7.

38 See reference in 'Agreement between the Duke of Westminster and Frederick F. French & Co. Ltd', 16 April 1935, WCA 2444/5/19.

39 Brown-Borrer, 16 May 1933, WCA 2260/239; Charles M. Chuckrow (Frederick F. French Co.)-Forrest, 8 November 1934, LMA GLC/AR/BR/06/075760/01.

40 There is some doubt about these corporate creations. At one stage Chuckrow told the LCC that the Fillmore Construction Co. were 'architects for Chichester Wharf Ltd': Chuckrow-Forrest, 12 December 1934, LMA GLC/AR/BR/06/075760/01.

41 Chuckrow-Forrest, 8 November 1934, cit.

42 See Town and Country Planning Act, 12 July 1932, 22 & 23 Geo.V c.48.

43 Chuckrow-Forrest, 8 November, cit.; Chuckrow-Clerk of Council, LCC, 8 December 1934, LMA GLC/AR/BR/06/075760/01. On the limited progress with town planning see *Estates Gazette*, 13 June 1936, p.1061; Barry Cullingworth and Vincent Nadin, *Town and Country Planning in the UK* (14th edn, Abingdon, 2006), p.22.

44 Cf. Osborn & Mercer-French, 7 September 1934, NYPL MssCol #6206, Box 7.

45 See bird's-eye drawings, 12 October 1934, in NYPL MssCol #6206, Box 7.

46 French, letter to investors, 9 October 1934, NYPL MssCol #6206, Box 7.

47 Chuckrow-Forrest, 8 November 1934, cit.; Frederick F. French & Co. Ltd., 'preliminary plans', 5 November 1934, LMA GLC/AR/BR/17/075760. The plans also appear to show a continuous corridor on the ground floor [as well as at basement level] connecting all parts of the property.

48 See planning forms, 12 and 14 November 1934, LMA GLC/AR/BR/06/075760/01.

49 Binnie (LCC Architect's Dept.), 'Note to Mr Hobday', 12 November 1934, Clerk of Council, LCC-President, Frederick F. French Co., 7 December 1934, LMA GLC/AR/BR/06/075760/01.

50 Forrest-Chuckrow, 19 December 1934, LMA GLC/AR/BR/06/075760/01. The conditions required there to be a separate application for the garages, and insisted upon no building above roof level.

51 *The Times*, 19 December 1934, p.11; *New York Times*, 19 December 1934, p.20.

52 *Daily Telegraph*, 19 December 1934, p.14.

53 Forrest-Chuckrow, 8 January 1935, LMA GLC/AR/BR/06/075760/01.

54 Agreement of 28 January 1935, referred to in Agreement for Sale of Freehold Land fronting on Grosvenor Road Pimlico . . ., 16 April 1935, WCA 2444/5/19.

55 *The Times*, 12 January 1935, p.22; T. O'Brien, letters to LCC, 14 and 29 January 1935, and E. Tallback for M.R. Morris, letter, 15 February 1935, LMA GLC/AR/BR/06/075760/01.

56 *Daily Telegraph*, 30 January 1935, p.14.

57 Pole and Lever were identified in ibid. There is no mention of the scheme in Pole's privately circulated autobiography: *Felix J.C. Pole: His Book* (1954). At the time of the Fred French scheme Pole was a director of Airports Ltd, a company seeking to develop Gatwick airport: Geoffrey Channon, 'Sir Felix John Clewett Pole', *Dictionary of Business Biography*, IV (1985), p.750.

58 French, letter to investors, 9 October 1934, NYPL MssCol #6206, Box 7; Rabinowitz, 'Fred F. French', Pt.1, pp.6–8, Cornell coll. #6708.

59 Morris, *Dolphin Square*, p.25–6, based on Sir Albert Costain, *Reflections* (Cirencester, 1987), p.46; Interview with Sir Alan Dawtry, 11 February 2011.

60 Costain Group, *Bulletin*, 212 [Centenary Issue] (June 1965), 3–21; David Burrage and David J. Jeremy, 'Sir Richard Rylandes Costain', *Dictionary of Business Biography*, I (1984), pp.792–3; 'Norman Kipping, 'Sir Richard Rylandes Costain', *OxDNB*; Costain, *Reflections*, pp.18–20, 24, 26, 30.

61 Burrage and Jeremy, 'Sir R.R. Costain', p.793.

62 Marian Bowley, *The British Building Industry: Four Studies in Response and Resistance to Change* (Cambridge, 1966), p.210.

63 Richard Costain Ltd., *The House of Costain: Seventy-Three Years of Progress* (n.d., c.1938).

64 Clive L. Franks (Company Secretary, Costain Group plc)-author, 28 April 2011.

65 A.P. Costain, 'Dolphin Square', Dolphin Square Tenants' Association [DSTA] 40th Birthday Newsletter, November 1976, pp.6–11; Costain, *Reflections*, pp.46–51; Morris, *Dolphin Square*, pp.25–9.

66 It is not clear when the Friday meeting took place. The 'Tuesday' referred to does not square with the contracted completion date, 25 April, which was a Thursday. The meeting was probably on 12 April.

67 Costain, *Reflections*, p.46; Morris, *Dolphin Square*, p.26. Albert Costain claimed that the cost estimate was within ½d./cu. foot of the actual cost, and rentals ranged from 4s./ sq. ft. for the relatively unattractive flats to 7s./sq. ft. for the luxury penthouses. Whiter was Albert Costain's brother-in-law.

68 Costain, *Reflections*, p.47; Morris, *Dolphin Square*, p.26.

69 Bracewell & Leaver-Boodle, Hatfield & Co., 16 April 1935, and Agreement, 16 April 1935, WCA 2444/5/19. Frederick F. French & Co. Ltd were now at 27 John St. WC1.

70 Agreement, 16 April 1935, cit.

71 Kipping, 'Sir Richard Rylandes Costain', and also in Richard Tames, *The Westminster & Pimlico Book* (2005), p.45 and cf. a similar anecdote in Costain, *Reflections*, p.47.

72 Costain, *Reflections*, pp.68, 72.

73 Richard Costain Ltd. *Report and Accounts 1934*, Guildhall Library, London [henceforth Costain, *R & A*].

74 R.R. Costain was a member of Walton Heath Golf Club. He was described as 'an eminently sound player and a fine putter', and reached the third round of the English Amateur Championship in 1936: *The Times*, 9 March 1936, p.7, 30 April 1936, p.6.

75 Lloyds Bank Board Minutes, 14 June and 20 September 1935, Lloyds Banking Group Archives, HO/D/Boa/MIN/41; Costain, Reflections, pp.47, 68, 72. Costain recalled that the young accountant sent out to Iran to look at the company's position was [Sir] Ronald Leach, subsequently a partner in Peat Marwick Mitchell: DSTA Newsletter, November 1976, p.8.

76 Schedule attached to Lease between the United Kingdom Temperance and General Provident Institution and Richard Costain Limited, 13 September 1935, contained in Goddard & Smith and Marcus Leaver & Co. (joint sole agents), and Messrs. Walters & Hart (solicitors), Particulars, Plans, Photographs, Conditions of Sale and Forms of Tender of the Long Leasehold Property known as Dolphin Square London, S.W.1 . . ., n.d. [1962], DST. The UK Temperance and General Provident Institution, founded in 1840, began by offering life insurance to teetotallers.

77 Gordon Jeeves-E.P. Wheeler (Superintending Architect, LCC), 15 June and 12 July 1935, LMA GLC/AR/BR/06/075760/01. Cecil Eve (1900–85) joined the firm in 1924 and later became a partner.

78 Stanley Jeeves, biographical file, Royal Institute of British Architects (RIBA) Library.

79 Stanley Jeeves, Order Book, GJ/1, and List of completed contracts, GJ/2, RIBA archives at Victoria & Albert Museum. The contracts for Claridge House and 20 Chesham Place were

£80,000 and £54,000 respectively. Bigger contracts of £372,000 and £385,000 were undertaken contemporaneously with Dolphin Square, at Latymer Court, Hammersmith, and Cranmer Court, Chelsea, in 1936–7.

80 *The Times*, 9 May 1956, p.13; *The Structural Engineer*, 34 (August 1956), pp.302–4; Bowley, *British Building Industry*, pp.37, 96; John Faber, *Oscar Faber: his work, his firm, & afterwards* (1989); J.R. Harrison and Anita McConnell, 'Oscar Faber', *OxDNB*. Note among his books, *Reinforced Concrete Design* (edns, 1912–24), *Reinforced Concrete simply explained* (edns, 1922–6 et seq.), *Constructional Steelwork simply explained* (1927), and (with J.R. Kell) *Heating and Air-conditioning of Buildings* (1936).

81 Oscar Faber contract and correspondence files, Bank of England archive, ref. IA86/12, E5/38. See also Daniel M. Abramson, *Building the Bank of England: money, architecture, society, 1694–1942* (New Haven, 2005), pp.229–31.

82 Faber, *Oscar Faber*, pp.44–54.

83 Oscar Faber, lecture on 'The Aesthetic Aspect of Civil Engineering Design', 19 April 1944, in ICE, *The Aesthetic Aspect of Civil Engineering Design* (1945).

84 Costain, *House of Costain*, p.8; Faber, *Oscar Faber*, p.47; *The Structural Engineer*, 13 (June 1935), pp.265–6 [my thanks to Rob Thomas of the Institution of Structural Engineers Library for this reference]. Faber also worked with Costain on Harringay Arena, and the Pirelli-General cable works in Southampton: Costain, *House of Costain*, p.47.

85 RDC [Richard Charques], obituary note, *The Times*, 9 May 1956, p.13.

86 Seven storeys above ground are shown on French's plan of the elevation of 8 November 1934, while six are shown on Jeeves's elevation plans (No.447) of 26 January 1937: LMA GLC/AR/BR/17/075760.

87 A.P. Herbert, *Dolphin Square* (September 1935); Messrs. Gordon Jeeves, plans for Dolphin Square, RIBA archives, PA 862.

88 Licence granted by Costain to London Relay Wireless Ltd., 21 April 1936, DST.

89 Oscar Faber-Wheeler, 29 August, 17 September and 26 October 1935, refer to 'Ormonde Court'; Jeeves-Wheeler, 20 September 1935 and 8 May 1936 refer to 'Ormonde Square' but the letter and note from Jeeves to Wheeler on 20 July 1936 refer to both 'Ormonde Court' and 'Ormonde Square'! LMA GLC/AR/BR/06/075760.

90 *The Times*, 3 March 1936, p.70, 4 June 1936, p.24; Costain. *R & A, 1935*, Guildhall Library; Jan Prebble, *Square Tales* (2008), p.6.

91 Costain, *Reflections*, p.48, and DSTA Newsletter, November 1976, p.9. The School was Rydal Mount, and is correctly spelt in Morris, *Dolphin Square*, p.27. R.R. Costain was a former pupil.

92 Frank Hunt (valuer) and Wheeler, Report, 25 August 1935, LMA GLC/AR/BR/06/075760.

93 Bowley, *British Building Industry*, pp.15–27, 47–52, 177–80.

94 Faber, quoted in ibid. pp.114–15.

95 Ibid. p.57.

96 S.B. Hamilton, *A Note on the History of Reinforced Concrete in Buildings* (National Building Studies Special Report no.24, HMSO, 1956), pp.21–4; Bowley, *British Building Industry*, p.65; Michael Bussell, 'The Development of Reinforced Concrete Design and Practice', in James Sutherland, Dawn Humm and Mike Chrimes (eds.), *Historic Concrete: Background to Appraisal* (2001), pp.84ff; J.L. Clarke, 'Historical approaches to the design of concrete buildings and structures', *Concrete Society Technical Report no.70* (2009), pp.32–3. The 1915 Regulations emerged from the London County Council (General Powers) Act, 1909.

97 Oscar Faber, 'Plastic Yield, Shrinkage and other Problems of Concrete, and their Effect on Design', 15 November 1927, cit. in Hamilton, *History of Reinforced Concrete*, pp.21–4; Faber, *Oscar Faber*, pp.11–14; Bussell, 'Development of Reinforced Concrete', pp.88–9.

98 Faber-Wheeler, 12 and 19 August 1935, LMA GLC/AR/BR/06/075760.

99 Faber-W.A. Glanville (Director, Building Research Station, Garston), 23 August 1935 and reply, 28 August 1935, Faber-Wheeler, 29 August 1935, LMA GLC/AR/BR/06/075760.

100 Faber-W. Berry (Chairman, Building Acts and Town Planning Committee, LCC), 6 September 1935, Faber-Wheeler, 17 September 1935 and reply, 17 October 1935, LMA GLC/AR/BR/06/075760; LCC Minutes, 29 October 1935, LMA.

101 Faber's figure was an exaggeration: the ground rent on the property was £428 per week.

102 Faber-Wheeler, 26 October 1935, LMA GLC/AR/BR/06/075760. The letter had been intended to go first to Tom Moodie, a more junior official in the Architect's Department, but was sent direct to Wheeler in error.

103 Wheeler-Laurence Shiner (District Surveyor, Westminster South), 17 October 1935, Wheeler-Faber, 31 October 1935, LMA GLC/AR/BR/06/075760.

104 Jeeves-Wheeler, 27 March 1936, N. Elliot (Deputy Superintending Architect, LCC)-Jeeves, 8 May 1936, LMA GLC/AR/BR/06/075760.

105 Jeeves-Wheeler, 20 September 1935, Wheeler- Jeeves, 28 November 1935, LMA GLC/AR/BR/06/075760.

106 Wheeler-Jeeves, 11 September 1935, Jeeves-Wheeler, 14 October 1935, Wheeler, Report, 5 November 1935, LMA GLC/AR/BR/06/075760.

107 LCC Solicitor-Jeeves, 8 December 1935, Wheeler-Jeeves, 19 December 1935, LMA GLC/AR/BR/06/075760.

108 Wheeler-Jeeves, 10 October 1935, LMA GLC/AR/BR/06/075760.

109 Note, for example, the provision of four porters' lodges: Jeeves-Wheeler, 13 November 1936, LMA GLC/AR/BR/06/075760.

110 Jeeves-Wheeler, 29 January, 8 May, 20 July, 25 August, 25 September and 12 October 1936, Clerk of Council, LCC-Jeeves, 8 July, 13 October and 20 November 1936, LMA GLC/AR/BR/06/075760.

111 Jeeves-Wheeler, 29 May 1937, Clerk of Council, LCC-Jeeves, 29 July 1937, Clerk-Secretary, Dolphin Square Ltd., 18 September, 20 October and 8 December 1937, 14 January and 25 February 1938, Bracewell & Leaver (for Costain)-Clerk, 11 November 1937 and 5 January 1938, Clerk-R. Costain Ltd., 4 March 1938, LMA GLC/AR/BR/07/2787. The name 'Blue Pool Restaurant' also appears in the planning file in c.1959.

112 Jeeves-Wheeler, 1 January 1936, Jeeves-Clerk of Council, LCC, 14 February 1936; consent, 19 May 1936, referred to in Jeeves-Wheeler, 28 October 1937, LMA GLC/AR/BR/06/075760.

113 Jeeves-Wheeler, 21 September and 12 October 1936, Clerk of Council, LCC-Jeeves, 20 November 1936, LMA GLC/AR/BR/06/075760.

114 A.H. Toms, Note, 6 March 1936, Wheeler-Chief Officer, Public Control Dept., LCC, 11 March 1936, Wheeler, Report, 27 May 1938, A. Firebrace (Chief Officer, London Fire Brigade), Report, 3 June 1938, LMA GLC/AR/BR/06/075760.

115 Shiner-Richard Costain Ltd., Jeeves and Wheeler, all on 15 October 1937, and see summary in Wheeler, Report, 25 May 1938, LMA GLC/AR/BR/06/075760; London Building Act, 1 August 1930, 20 & 21 Geo.V c.158, s.80–1.

116 Wheeler-Jeeves, 21 December 1937, Jeeves-Wheeler, 28 December 1937, 24 and 25 February 1938, W. Whiter (Dolphin Square Ltd.)-Jeeves, 27 October 1937, R.T. Fenton (LCC), note, 1 December 1937, LMA GLC/AR/BR/06/075760.

117 Jeeves-Wheeler, 25 February, 4 July and 10 August 1938, Wheeler-Jeeves, 11 July 1938, Wheeler-Secretary, Richard Costain Ltd, 19 September 1938 and 25 January 1939, Wheeler-Jeeves, 23 September 1938, Wheeler-Messrs Haskins Rolling Shutters, 17 February 1939, LMA GLC/AR/BR/06/075760.

118 The revised scheme would create 64 1-room, 206 2-room, 107 3-room, nine 4-room, two 5-room and one 6-room flats.

119 Jeeves-Wheeler, 26 January 1937, LMA GLC/AR/BR/06/075760. The 'club' had a similarity, if on a smaller scale, to the hotel block included in the Tudor City complex in New York.

120 Jeeves-Wheeler, 3 March 1937, Clerk of Council, LCC-Jeeves, 15 March 1937 and reply, 30 April 1937, LMA GLC/AR/BR/06/075760.

121 Jeeves-Wheeler, 9 February 1937, Elliot-Jeeves, 18 March 1937, LMA GLC/AR/BR/06/075760.

122 Boro' Electric Signs-Wheeler, LCC, 8 and 27 July 1936, Costain, signed agreements, 17 August and 27 November 1936, Wheeler-Boro', 25 August 1936, Costain-Architect's Dept., LCC, 11 March 1938, Shiner-Wheeler, 12 March 1938, LMA GLC/AR/BR/06/075760.

123 Boro'-Wheeler, 11 December 1936, 19 May 1937 and 28 February 1938, Clerk of Council, LCC-Boro', 11 January 1937 and 11 April 1938, Wheeler-Boro', 2 July 1937, LMA GLC/AR/BR/06/075760.

124 Boro'-Wheeler, 18 December 1936, J. Rawlinson (Chief Engineer and Surveyor)-Wheeler, 30 December 1936, Clerk of Council, LCC-Boro', 25 January 1937, and to Parker Morris (Town Clerk, LCC), 8 February 1937, LMA GLC/AR/BR/06/075760.

125 Jeeves-Wheeler, 22 April 1937 and reply, 3 June 1937, LMA GLC/AR/BR/06/075760.

126 Faber, *Oscar Faber*, p.39. At the end of October 1935 Jeeves noted that the buildings were 'so far advanced that the foundations are already in', while the Costain directors reported in March 1937 that the first half was 'approaching completion': Jeeves-Wheeler, 31 October 1935, LMA GLC/AR/BR/06/075760, Costain, *R & A, 1936*, Guildhall Library. The first edition of *The Dolphin* in May 1937 stated that the 8 houses were 'in full running order': 1 (May 1937), p.2, WCA 2518/17.

127 Dolphin Square Ltd. register of leases, southern section, 1936–7, DST [and see Appendix 1]; Faber, *Oscar Faber*, p.39.

128 DSTA Newsletter, November 1976, p.8.

129 Dolphin Square register of leases, 1936–7, DST, and see Appendix 1. There were 660 flats in the block, of which 645 were available for letting, including four furnished flats [14 were reserved for staff and offices etc., and there was one guest room shown.]; 399 flats were shown as occupied, including two by members of staff. One flat in Nelson and one in Collingwood were recorded as empty in the lease register, but have electoral register entries for 1937: St. George's Westminster register of electors, October 1937, WCA.

130 Costain's directors reported on 22 March 1938 that the second section was 'nearing completion': Costain, *R & A, 1937*, Guildhall Library. The original code letters are from Jeeves, Plans no.379R and 381R, 22 January 1937, LMA GLC/AR/BR/17/075760 and RIBA PA862, also reproduced on the plan shown in *Architect & Building News*, 7 January 1938, p.6. A subsequent revision of the lettering produced ABCDEFOP for Grenville, Drake, Raleigh, Hawkins, Nelson, Howard, Collingwood and Frobisher, and GHIMN for Beatty, Duncan, Rodney, Keyes and Hood.

131 The squash courts opened in May 1937: Dolphin Squash Brochure, May 1937, WCA 2518/8, *The Dolphin*, 1 (May 1937), p.8; *The Times*, 6 May 1937, p.11.

132 *The Dolphin*, 10 (March 1938), p.6, DST. The garage's dimensions were c.70,500 sq. ft. and c.940,000 cu. ft.

133 *Hotel Review*, February 1938, p.158, DST.

134 Costain, *Reflections*, p.48; Jan Prebble, 'The Paris Inspired Restaurant', *A Hotchpotch of Tales from Dolphin Square* (January 2006), p.14; http://www.jazzageclub.com/venues/lido-deschamp.

135 *Daily Mail*, 15 December 1937, p.18; Clerk of Council-Secretary, Dolphin Square Ltd., 14 January 1938, and other correspondence in LCC building file for 'Blue Pool' restaurant, LMA. GLC/AR/BR/07/2787.

136 Kyrle's was replaced by 'Maurice' [Maurice Shaiman] in 1939. The travel agents' kiosk was situated in the restaurant foyer. *The Dolphin*, 5 (October 1937), p.4, 9 (February 1938), pp.4–5, 10 (March 1938), pp.1–2, DST; Dolphin Stores Shopping Guide, n.d., WCA 2518/6; WCC Rate Book No.5, ½-years ending 30 September 1939 and 31 March 1940, WCA.

137 My thanks to Karen Sampson for this information.

138 *Dolphin Square for your especial convenience*, brochure, n.d. [1937] and *Dolphin Square for your especial convenience*, handbook, n.d. [1938], WCA 2518/4 and 5; Dolphin Square, Note on Shoe Cleaning, n.d., Dolphin Laundry service, n.d., WCA 2518/7 and 10; *The Times*, 14 January 1937, p.25.

139 Herbert, *Dolphin Square*; *The Times*, 14 January 1937, p.25. The promised registry office and veterinary department also failed to appear, although the 1938 handbook revealed that a veterinary surgeon was resident in the Square: *Dolphin Square for your especial convenience*, p.12.

140 Costain directors' report, 21 March 1939, Costain, *R & A, 1938*, Guildhall Library.

141 Costain, *Reflections*, p.49; Morris, *Dolphin Square*, p.28; Richard Sudell, *The Town Gardening Handbook* (1927), *The Town Garden* (1930), *Landscape Gardening* (1933), and *The New Garden* (1935). Dozens more titles followed, including *A National Food Production Guide* and *Intensive Culture* (both 1942), *Practical Gardening and Food Production in Pictures* (1948), *The Life-Saving Garden* (1952) and *Garden Planning* (1953).

142 Sudell estimated that a further 30,000 bulbs and plants and 3,000 shrubs would be required. *The Dolphin*, 3 (July 1937), p.5, WCA 2518/18, 5 (October 1937), p.8, DST; Costain, *Development*, 2 (n.d.), WCA 2518/16.

143 *The Dolphin*, 5 (1937), p.9, DST.

144 Oscar Faber, 'Lessons derived from Twenty Years of Heating and Ventilating Experience', presidential address to Institution of Heating and Ventilation Engineers, 14 February 1945, in *Architects' Journal*, 29 March 1945, p.251.

145 *The Times*, 24 January 1938, p.19; *The Dolphin*, 9 (February 1938), pp.3, 6, 9, DST; *Hotel Review*, February 1938, p.159, DST. See also Costain, *Reflections*, p.49, Morris, *Dolphin Square*, p.28, Jan Prebble, 'The Murals', April 1998, reproduced in *Hotchpotch* (2006), p.10.

146 *Architect & Building News*, 23 December 1938 (supplement).

147 Costain, *Reflections*, p.49; Morris, *Dolphin Square*, pp.28–9.

148 *The Dolphin*, 4 (September 1937), WCA 2518/19; John Skeaping, *Drawn from Life: An Autobiography* (1977). Skeaping makes no reference to Dolphin Square.

149 See http://www.npg.org.uk/collections and http://www.lissfineart.com/artistsindex.

150 *Evening Standard* and *Morning Post*, 3 June 1936, cutting in R.R. Costain, Dolphin Square Press Cuttings Book, May-December 1936, DST; Morris, *Dolphin Square*, pp.31, 36.

151 *Builder*, 1 October 1937, p.586. No precise figure was given to Costain shareholders.

152 The period of construction varies according to what exactly is counted, with the facilities taking longer to refine. Albert Costain claimed that each half was completed in under a year [*Reflections*, p.100], but this appears to be an exaggeration.

153 Faber, *Oscar Faber*, pp.39, 53.

154 DSTA, Newsletter, November 1976, p.16, and Morris, *Dolphin Square*, p.36.

155 Cf. J.R. Colclough, *The Construction Industry of Great Britain* (1965), pp.80–1.

156 Costain, *Reflections*, pp.99–102; Morris, *Dolphin Square*, p.31.

157 Dolphin Square register of leases, 1937, Goddard & Smith, Valuation for the Directors, Lintang Investments Ltd., 28 February 1959, DST.

158 Tenancies did not prohibit subletting. Cf. 3-year lease with Mervyn Brecknell on 403 Hood House, 24 November 1938, DST.

159 St. George's Westminster electoral register, October 1937, WCA; Dolphin Square register of leases, 1937, DST. The no. of South Block tenancies = 491, the number of tenants = 476 (15 tenants held leases on two flats).

160 Dolphin Square register of leases, 1937, DST.

161 Goddard & Smith, Valuation, 1959, DST; List of tenancies, n.d. (c. December 1962), and cf. Lt Col. Brian C. Garrard, FCIS, Dolphin Square's General Manager, Initial Report to Dolphin Square Trust Ltd., 11 November 1964, DST.p.10. Costain also occupied basement and/or ground floor space in Beatty, Hawkins, Duncan and Keyes, 1st floor space in Rodney, and 9th floor space in Duncan.

162 Richard Costain Properties, Richard Costain Property Management, Costain Property Investments, Dolphin Development Co., Rank Property Development, Rylandes Estates, Triland (Coalville), Costain Concrete Co., Stahlton Floors: Costain Group, *The Bulletin*, 207 (May 1964), DST.

163 See 'Maids' Rooms' entry in *Dolphin Square for your especial convenience*, Handbook, n.d. [1938], p.5, DST.

164 WCC Rate Book No.5, ½-year ending 30 September 1939, WCA.

165 WCC Rate Book No.5, ½-year ending 30 September 1942, years ending 31 March 1948 and 31 March 1951, WCA.

166 General Manager's Report, November 1964, p.8, DST. The rate books are difficult to use to determine occupancy.

167 Richard Costain Ltd., Dolphin Square: Rentals and Accommodation, n.d. [1936]; *The Builder*, 1 October 1937, p.586; *Architect & Building News*, 7 January 1938, p.6.

168 *The Dolphin*, 5 (October 1937), p.4, DST.

169 *The Economist*, 30 March 1946, p.515; Goddard & Smith, Valuation, 1959, DST.

170 Richard Costain Ltd., *Dolphin Square*, Illustrated brochure, n.d. [1936], p.3.

171 Costain, *Development*, 1, n.d. [1937].

172 The suffix for each flat revealed its floor, e.g. flat 1 or 01 (ground), 101 (1st floor), 201 (2nd floor), 301 (3rd floor), et seq. *The Dolphin*, 1 (May 1937), p.2, WCA 2518/17.

173 Costain, Rentals and Accommodation, 1936; Costain, *Dolphin Square*, 1936; Dolphin Square & Electricity, brochure, n.d., Gas Light & Coke Co., brochure, n.d., WCA 2518/13–14; Morris, *Dolphin Square*, p.37.

174 Agreement between the City of Westminster and Dolphin Square Ltd., 9 August 1950, DST; Westminster CC, Churchill Gardens and Pimlico District heating undertaking, 1951, DST; photograph, 1 August 1950, LMA/4547/25/050.

175 *Architectural Review*, 83 (March 1938), pp.133–4; General Manager's Report, November 1964, p.4, DST; Morris, *Dolphin Square*, pp.32–3. Morris records that Sloane valves were installed for flushing WCs in the North Block: pp.33–4.

176 Morris, *Dolphin Square*, pp.31–2.

177 Costain, Dolphin Square, 1936, pp.13–14.

178 General Manager's Report, November 1964, p 4, DST; Morris, *Dolphin Square*, p.32. Morris also points out that the window frames could only be removed from the outside, while the use of cork on the flat roof produced thermal heat loss markings on the ceilings of the top floor flats.

179 Costain, Dolphin Square, 1936, p.5, *Dolphin Square for your especial convenience*, handbook, n.d. [1938], WCA 2518/5.

180 *The Dolphin*, 1 (May 1937), p.1, WCA 2518/17. Margaret, Viscountess Rhondda, was a writer and editor of *Time and Tide*. Ironically, she subsequently acquired tenancies of two

Dolphin Square flats, 410 and 503 Keyes House, in 1943. These were retained until 1951: WCC Rate Book No.5, half-year ending 31 March 1944, year ending 31 March 1951, WCA. Cecil Theo Langbehn was a journalist, better known as a writer of crime fiction using the name Theo Lang: http://www.crimefictioniv.com/Part_40.

181 As described in Costain, Dolphin Square, 1936.

182 Rodney Lowe, 'Sir William Warrender Mackenzie' [1st Baron Amulree], *OxDNB*; *The Times*, 26 February 1936, p.4. Amulree had written to *The Times* on 10 August 1936 to argue that 'from every point of view Westminster should be regarded as the natural residential adjunct to Central London': *The Times*, 13 August 1936, p.11, and see also his article in *Sunday Times*, 30 August 1936, and other newspaper cuttings in 'Costain, Dolphin Square Cuttings Book', 1936, DST.

183 John Herbert Roberts (1863–1955) had been MP for Denbighshire West, 1892–1918; he was ennobled in 1919 and retired from the Costain board in 1950. *The Times*, 20 July 1951, p.51, 21 December 1955, p.11.

184 On the opening, see (London) *Evening News*, (London) *Star*, 25 November, *Daily Express*, *The Times*, 26 November, *Daily Telegraph*, *Daily Mail*, 27 November 1936, and other cuttings in Costain, Dolphin Square Cuttings Book, 1936, DST; Costain, *Reflections*, p.49.

185 *The Times*, 26 March 1936, p.24, 1 April 1937, p.24.

186 Costain, Dolphin Square, 1936, pp.27–8, 30, and *Development*, 1, n.d. [1937]; DSTA Newsletter, November 1976, p.5. The show flats were at 202 Nelson and 204 Hawkins (electric) and 205 Raleigh and 208 Hawkins (gas).

187 *The Dolphin*, 1 (May 1937), p.5.

188 DSTA Newsletter, 1976, p.10. A search of flats developed in Durban in 1936–45 has failed to identify a similar design.

189 *The Builder*, 1 October 1937, p.586.

190 *The Architect & Building News*, 7 January 1938, p.6.

191 Simon Bradley and Nikolaus Pevsner, *The Buildings of England. London 6: Westminster* (New Haven, CT, 2003), p.781.

192 *The Observer*, 20 January 1963, cutting in DST.

193 David Hamilton Eddy, 'Castle Mythology in British Housing', *RIBA Journal*, 96:12 (December 1989), 28–9. Eddy also repeats the myth that de Gaulle was living in the Square when it was bombed.

194 Edward Jones and Christopher Woodward, *A Guide to the Architecture of London* (1983, rev. edn, 1992), p.338. Jones and Woodward produce densities of 163 flats per acre (Dolphin Sq.) and 55 (Churchill Gdns). Our figures (1,188 flats, 7.2 acres) indicate a density of 165.

195 See *The Times*, 1–17 January 1936. New flats were advertised in Hampstead, St. John's Wood, Curzon Street, Hammersmith, and Putney Hill.

196 Costain, *R & A, 1935* and *1936*, Guildhall Library; *The Times*, 26 March 1936, p.24.

197 Costain, *R & A, 1937–43*, Guildhall Library; *The Times*, 23 March 1938, p.20, 31 March 1938, p.25, 31 March 1939, p.25, 29 March 1940, p.14. The 1938 results were also affected by recession and the uncertainty caused by the Sudetenland crisis in September.

CHAPTER 3

LIVING IN THE SQUARE, 1936–57

THE FIRST RESIDENTS, 1936–43

When the Dolphin Square's flats were first offered to the public in 1936, the South Block was still under construction, and the North Block was a building site. Despite this speculative environment, there was – if Costain is to be believed – a headlong rush to participate. Apparently, more than 200 flats had been let before the show flats were 'anywhere near completion'.[1] The reality of the competitive London market was somewhat different, however. The South Block lease register reveals that at the beginning of 1937 Dolphin Square Ltd. still needed to fill 72 per cent of the block of eight houses, and the decision was taken to reduce prices in order to win tenants. The flats were initially offered on three-year tenancies at prices ranging from £75–130 a year for a bedsit to £455 for a seven-room suite with additional bathroom, maid's bathroom, balcony and pantry (Table 3.1).[2] However, as the market tightened, many of the tenancies agreed in the period January-July 1937 were concluded at discounted prices, usually a rather modest reduction of £10 a year, under ten per cent, though two flats were offered at a discount of £25. The register is not always easy to interpret, but it appears that at least 128 flats were let at a discount.[3] In the absence of a lease register we know less about the North Block, which was filled in 1937–8, but from the clues available in the residents' magazine *The Dolphin* and elsewhere it seems that some initial discounting was also introduced here, particularly for the two-room flats.[4] Advertised prices then held firm over the course of 1938, and the Directors of Costain reported in March 1939 that the Square was 'fully let'. However, the contemporary rate book suggests that by no means all of the flats had been let at this time.[5]

Table 3.1 Dolphin Square south block advertised tenancies, 1936

Flat type	*No. of rooms*	*Rental [£]*	*Flat type*	*No. of rooms*	*Rental [£]*
Henley	1	75	Sunbury	3	145
		80			165
		85			175
		90			195
		95			210
		100			235
		115			260
		120	Chertsey	3+dr	190
		130			210
Marlow	2	115			270
		120	Richmond	4	255
		130			275
		135			280
		140	Oxford	4+dr	295
		145			300
		150			310
		155			350
		165	Kingston	5	400
		200			465
			Windsor	7	455

Source: Dolphin Square schedule of rentals, 1936, DST.

Key:
dr = dining recess

Who, then, moved into the complex? The first 476 tenants are listed in the South Block lease register of July 1937 (Appendix 1). It would be a mammoth task for family historians to research all these individuals, but we may conclude that there was a fairly wide range of middle- and upper middle-class people, since the highest renters were paying nearly ten times more than the lowest, and flats ranged from the compact one-room 'Henley Suite' to the spacious seven-room 'Windsor' [Illustrations 19 (i) and (ii)]. Some were members of the aristocracy, politicians and military figures. Among the earliest tenants was Lord Burghley, the conservative politician and Olympian. He won the 400-metre hurdles in 1928, was president of the Amateur Athletic

Association (1936–76), organised the London games in 1948, and was caricatured in the 1981 film *Chariots of Fire*.[6] Also resident were: Lord Frederick Cambridge;[7] Lord Cottenham, the motor racing driver and MI5 officer who campaigned for driving tests and compulsory insurance;[8] Lord Gifford;[9] the 2nd Earl of Halsbury (see below); the Earl of Listowel, Labour minister and author of *A Critical History of Modern Aesthetics* (1933);[10] Lord Perry, the motor vehicle manufacturer;[11] and Ethel, Viscountess Snowden, the feminist and peace campaigner.[12] In addition, there were a dozen or so minor aristocrats about whom information is more difficult to find.[13] From the beginning there were politicians, past and present: Lord Allen and Violet, Lady Apsley (Conservative),[14] Sir Clement Barlow (Conservative),[15] Eric Errington (Conservative),[16] Arthur Henderson (Labour),[17] Sir Dennis Herbert (Conservative),[18] and Col. Josiah Wedgwood (Independent Labour).[19] The Labour politician and deputy leader of the party, Arthur Greenwood, lived in Dolphin Square, in 202 Keyes House, from 1939. Like Ellen Wilkinson (see below), he was a staunch anti-appeaser, though his effectiveness was limited by heavy drinking.[20] Others who caught the eye were: Ida Cook, the Mills & Boon novelist, patron of the opera and campaigner for Jewish refugees (see below); Stefan Lorant, founding editor of *Lilliput* (1937–40) and *Picture Post* (1938–40);[21] Dr William Summerskill, the father of baroness Edith Summerskill;[22] the film star Margaret Lockwood (see below); Ronald Armstrong-Jones, the father of Antony, the future Lord Snowdon; Lady Frances Ryder, organiser of Dominion services, including hospitality for ANZAC troops during the Second World War;[23] Hon. Arthur Maxwell Stamp (see below), the third son of Sir Josiah Stamp, Baron Stamp, chairman of the LMS Railway;[24] the cartoonist Oscar Berger (see below); Clementine Mabell Freeman-Mitford, cousin of the Mitford sisters;[25] and, later on, Oswald Mosley, who was arrested at his flat in 1940 (see below). Military men were well represented, with nearly 70 commissioned officers, including among the senior ranks Vice-Admiral John Edgell, Major-General Harry Cummins, Brigadier-General Edward Vaughan, Brigadier Hubert Clementi Smith; a number of colonels – Oliver Edgcumbe and Gerald Kinsman; lieutenant-colonels – John Foster, Charles Hordern, David Munro, William Penney and Alexander Richardson; commanders – Hugh Browning, John Cowie, Frank Fowle and Windham Hornby; lieutenant-commanders – Eric Brooks, Ian Elliot, George Fitz-George,

Osman Giddy and Philip Yorke; and wing-commanders - Francis Alford and Harold Lydford. Also prominent were residents with the title 'doctor'. Whether they were medical or not, there were at least 26 of them before the war.[26] Morris, in his Dolphin Square history, makes special mention of Dr Denis Murphy, a friend of Richard Costain, who practised from 04 and 05 Frobisher House, and organised an emergency hospital in the basement of Beatty House during the war.[27]

About a third of the tenants in the South Block - 156 - were women. Of these, 51 were reported to be single, but the status of 39 of them was not recorded.[28] Whether single, widowed or divorced, Dolphin Square offered them a safe and secure environment in London. This protection could also extend to anonymity. Two famous women who were early residents of Dolphin Square do not appear in the existing public listings: the novelist Radclyffe Hall, and the Labour politician Ellen Wilkinson. Both lived in flats in Hood House in the 1940s, though their circumstances were far from happy. Marguerite Radclyffe-Hall, author of *Adam's Breed* (1926) and the scandalous lesbian novel *The Well of Loneliness* in 1928, was a brave campaigner for the rights of homosexuals, but was also an anti-semitic supporter of the extreme right. When she became ill with cancer of the colon in 1943 her partner, Una, Lady Troubridge, moved with her into a furnished flat, 502 Hood House. Hall's stay was brief, and since she required constant nursing she can have seen little of the environment around her. When she died in October she had been in Dolphin Square for only two months.[29] Ellen Wilkinson, the pioneering socialist, anti-fascist and champion of the Jarrow marchers, was something of a political celebrity when she came to the Square, having written *The Town that was Murdered* in 1939 [Illustration 20 (ii)]. It has been said that while living in 902 Hood House she used the anagrammatical pseudonym 'Nellie N.K. Wilson'. She certainly had need of discretion, since she had an enduring relationship with Labour stalwart Herbert Morrison. However, she appears in the Westminster rate books from 1943 in her real name: 'Miss E.C. Wilkinson'.[30] She appears to have chosen Dolphin Square as much for its relative security as its location, having been bombed out of her home twice in 1940.[31] She was Minister of Education in the post-war Labour government until her death from heart failure following an overdose of medication. In February 1947, she was taken to St. Mary's Hospital, Paddington, where she died shortly afterwards.[32] Whether the two women ever met is doubtful, but they could not have presented a greater contrast.

Ida and Louise Cook made a more lasting contribution to the life of Dolphin Square. In their thirties when they first arrived in Howard House, they lived and entertained there for over 50 years.[33] Starting out with her sister as a junior civil servant in the 1920s, Ida Cook made a name for herself first as a journalist, then as a romantic novelist. Both sisters developed a passionate interest in the opera, and became well-known in operatic circles after meeting the American-based Italian soprano, Amelita Galli-Curci. Through her friendship with the Austrian conductor and opera impresario, Clemens Kraus, and his wife, the Romanian soprano Viorica Ursuleac, Ida became a rescuer of Jewish families trapped in Germany as Nazi harassment intensified in the years immediately prior to the Second World War. In 1936, Ida embarked on a highly successful career writing romantic fiction for Mills & Boon, and she used her early royalties to fund several trips to Germany with her sister to help Jews to escape. Using her enthusiasm for operas as a cover, she was able to travel in both Austria and Germany without attracting the attention of the Gestapo, and returned to Britain with valuables which were later used to provide Jewish immigrants with the necessary sureties. The Cooks' main home was in Morella Road, Wandsworth, but their flat in 311 Howard House was used to take in refugees. In her autobiography Ida wrote:

> Soon after we started our refugee work, it became apparent to Louise and me that, apart from our own home, we must have some sort of clearing house or, at least, temporary accommodation, for the people whom we brought into England. And at this time I acquired what I had always hoped to have since I started writing, a small flat of my own. We continued to live at home, but used the flat as the central point of our work. Occasionally, we try to reckon how many people lived in my flat, or at any rate, passed through, on the way to a new life elsewhere, but we have lost count . . . To this day there is an atmosphere of brightness and happiness which most people who enter my flat remark upon. Maybe it is only due to the fact that it is a light, pleasantly furnished place with plenty of windows.[34]

Ida had signed her tenancy agreement in December 1936, and took possession of the flat in March 1937 (Appendix 1). The first of at least 29 Jewish 'cases' she and her sister helped was Else Mayer-Lismann, the daughter of Mitia Mayer-Lismann, official lecturer to the Salzberg music festival. Else was the first refugee to live in Ida's flat, and she later appears, together with Emma, her cousin [?], in the Dolphin Square flat in the electoral registers for 1951–5. Another resident was Friedl Bamberger, a school friend of Else's, who, said Ida, 'lived longest of all in our flat, keeping it beautifully for us'.[35] The flat was also used to house impoverished opera singers.[36] Ida wrote over 120 books for Mills & Boon, under the pen name Helen Burchell, and it is hard to believe that she had no romantic attachments of her own; she was certainly a close friend of both Tito Gobbi and Ezio Pinza. She retained 311 Howard House until her death in 1986; it was then occupied by her sister Louise until she died in 1991. The sisters continued to support refugee charities and the opera, and many fundraising parties were held in Dolphin Square. Maria Callas was a visitor in 1964 [Illustration 20 (i)].[37]

Not all the residents were either respectable or well-behaved. A bankruptcy notice appeared in the *The Times* in March 1938 for A.S. Linney, described as 'lately carrying on a business at 139, Western Road, Brighton, as a motor driving tutor, but at present of no occupation, and now residing at 905, Frobisher House, Dolphin Square, London, SW1'.[38] In October, Mrs Bertha Verrall of Raleigh House was fined 30 shillings plus 15 shillings costs for dangerous horse-riding at the junction of Knightsbridge and Albert Gate.[39] Nor were aristocrats immune. Hardinge Goulburn Giffard, the 2nd Earl of Halsbury, KC, of 602 Nelson House, entertained readers of the *The Times* in 1938 when he unsuccessfully applied to the High Court to overturn an order to pay costs.[40] The son of a famous father – Hardinge Stanley Giffard, the 1st Earl, who had been Lord Chancellor (1885–92 and 1895–1905) – Hardinge Goulburn had been Recorder of Carmarthen from 1923 to 1935. But his involvement in business, including chairmanship of the General Mortgage Society, had not improved a rather precarious financial position, and growing in desperation, he tried to avoid paying the costs of the legal action by falsely claiming that he had never been a party to it. Bankruptcy followed soon afterwards. In May 1938, the Earl was due to appear before the bankruptcy court, but the case was adjourned after he wrote from Paris to say that a medical condition was preventing him from travelling to England. He estimated his debts to be some £6,000–7,000. He never returned to the Square. Remaining in Paris until the German occupation, he died in an internment camp in 1943.[41] And sometimes residents were victims. In December 1938 *The Times* reported that a 17-year old man had been charged with demanding money with menaces from Mrs Margaret Leon, a Dolphin Square resident, better known as the film star Margaret Lockwood.[42]

It was not long before the Square had more than its fair share of letter writers to *The Times*. The first was Margaret Lane Wallace, of 512 Collingwood House, who wrote on 9 March 1937 seeking material for her biography of her father-in-law, the novelist Edgar Wallace.[43] She was followed in 1939 by Mrs Steuart Erskine, of 508 Hood House, on the distress in Newfoundland; Lord Gifford, 603 Raleigh House, on anti-German war propaganda; and Ethel, Viscountess Snowden, 206 Beatty House, on the summary dismissal of Hungarian maids employed in Britain.[44] The first letters to the *Economist* were written after the war. Brigadier John G. Smyth of 302 Drake House wrote in August 1946 and 13 November 1948 on the importance of the Empire for defence; Cdr Stephen King-Hall, of 804 Hood House did so too in July 1947, supporting the policy of requiring MPs to make their sources of income public.[45] The first Court Circular entry for Dolphin Square appeared in *The Times* on 16 April 1937: 'Mrs W.J. Colquhoun has returned from Germany to 604, Grenville House, Dolphin Square, Westminster, S.W.1, which is now her permanent address (Telephone: Victoria 3800)'.[46] Similar entries were posted in 1938 for Viscountess Snowden, Sir Montague and Lady Barlow, who moved from 71 Prince's Gate to 809 Beatty House, and Mrs F.N. Rose and family, of 110 Rodney House.[47]

THE DOLPHIN SQUARE EXPERIENCE, 1936–9

At 75 years' distance it is difficult to capture fully the living experiences of those who enjoyed Dolphin Square for the brief period before the Second World War. We certainly know what the expectations of the developers were, thanks to the several prospectuses and brochures published by Costain. The earliest, somewhat fanciful, expectations appeared in an unusual brochure of September 1935, written by the humorist and satirist A.P. Herbert, with cartoons provided by H.M. Bateman. It was published as building work began, and the author had only 'the announced intentions of those behind the plan' to guide him. Herbert was nevertheless confident that Dolphin Square would prove to be a modern attraction, appealing to those who valued 'horizontal' living [i.e. without stairs] and the use of electricity for both lighting and power – its residents would 'command warmth by pressing a switch'. The residents would 'enjoy at the same time most of the advantages of the separate house and all the advantages of the big communal dwelling-place'. The plans for the sports centre took Herbert's eye. He suggested that Dolphin Square 'in embryo' would have 'Home and Exercise and Health, Swimming and Squash, and, for all I know, a golf-course and a yachting pond, assembled together under the same generous roof'. There would be modern, soundproofed living, with all the conveniences associated with this. The restaurant was seen as a particular boon, 'ready for those wives who forget to buy food, those husbands who forget to say that they are bringing three men home to dinner' [Illustration 21]. Herbert could not resist making the observation that the 'Dolphin lady' might be spoiled by all the modern conveniences at her disposal: 'A little drudgery is good for wives, perhaps'. But he conceded that the modern woman would find easy access to shops and the provision of a nursery invaluable should she wish 'to "live her own life" and run the Cabinet or a business as well as a husband'.[48] Costain's colour brochure of 1936 also contained aspirations about what would now be called 'life style', in which its tenants, experiencing an 'effortless home life', would dress for dinner, 'crèche' their small children at the children's centre, exercise in the gym, and eat in the poolside restaurant. The brochure was illustrated with residents in evening dress, the best furnishings that the famous furniture store Maple & Co. could offer, and expensive motor cars [Illustration 22]. The appeal to busy professionals and the wealthy was as attractive in 1936 as it is to inhabitants of expensive apartments in Mayfair and Canary Wharf today.

> Home life at Dolphin Square, from dawn to midnight, will be as effortless as modern science can make it, leaving free the maximum amount of time in which to enjoy the many amenities of the Sports Centre and Gardens, as well as the fathomless interest

> and recreation afforded by London – lavish in her offerings to sight-seers, shoppers and pleasure-seekers.[49]

The press responded to the development with enthusiasm. From Gloucester to Grimsby, from the *Dorset Daily Echo* to the *Banffshire Advertiser*, journalists took up the themes of luxury and convenience, and were particularly impressed by the children's centre, which the *Daily Telegraph* declared to be the first of its kind in England. There was also much interest in Costain's plans for the Embankment, with the promise of a riverside terrace and a pier for pleasure craft and river taxis.[50]

Of course, estate agents' publications tend to stretch credulity, and while some tenants may have lived in the manner portrayed, the reality for most residents was more prosaic. Costain's brochure conceded that there were 'no bus routes actually running along the front of Dolphin Square' and invited tenants to make an implausibly short 'half a minute's walk' to 'many services connecting with Victoria and the West End'.[51] In fact, for car owners Dolphin Square's relatively quiet location was regarded as an advantage, especially if the journeys they made were westward. Costain noted that Grosvenor Road was 'the quietest part of the great riverside drive', and the least congested route to 'Putney, Richmond, Kew, up-river resorts and . . . beautiful Surrey'. Indeed, it regarded the absence of bus traffic on Grosvenor Road as a positive advantage, reducing noise.[52] For those without a car, there was London Transport's long-standing number 24 bus, which ran from Hampstead Heath to Pimlico, terminating in Grosvenor Road. There was a stop in Claverton St., close to Dolphin Square. The bus service was improved when the 135, which ran from New Barnet to Camden Town and Victoria, was extended to serve Chichester Street every ten minutes in 1938. The change was celebrated on the front cover of *The Dolphin* in May.[53] This made it a little easier to satisfy the developers' promise that the Houses of Parliament could be reached in three minutes, and Piccadilly Circus in ten minutes, though these times doubtless required a taxi.[54] Some of the promised amenities proved to be short-lived. The children's centre enjoyed an all-too-brief existence, while the Thames-side facilities never materialised, the onset of the Second World War putting paid to both. And the artists' impressions of the Thames-side views were also somewhat illusory. Residents who were unaware that both the builder and the consulting engineer of Dolphin Square had also built large industrial structures in the same material, concrete, had only to look across the Thames at the Southern Railway's Nine Elms warehouse, also designed by Faber, and evident in a photograph published in *The Dolphin* in October 1937 [Illustrations 22 (i) and (ii)].[55]

More domestic elements are evident from the surviving documentation. An invoice and receipt from Maple's for carpeting and curtaining the lounge, bedroom and hall of 612 Collingwood House reveals that Mr George L. Taylor paid £53 14s. 1d. – around £3,100 in current prices – to the company.[56] Much more is contained in tenants' agreements. A lease signed in November 1938 made it clear at the outset that the lessee was to pay the cost of outward telephone calls at the rate of 2d. per local call, and for each trunk call 2d. plus the Post Office charge (internal calls were free). A maintenance charge of £4 a year, twice the amount initially envisaged, was made for the use of kitchen equipment (cooker, refrigerator). There were 14 covenants attached to the lease. They required the lessee inter alia: in the last month of the lease, to paint the flat 'with three coats of good oil and lead paint', and 'also to varnish whitewash colour stop and distemper and generally decorate in an appropriate style all the inside parts of the flat', or to pay a month's rent in lieu; to clean the windows at least once a month and to keep any chimneys and flues swept; not to allow any obstruction to passages, stairs, landings &c.; 'not to assign underlet or part with possession of the flat or any part thereof without the written consent of the Landlords, such consent not to be unreasonably withheld in the case of a respectable and responsible tenant'; and to abide by the schedule of rules and regulations (see below). The Landlords undertook 'to pay the water rate and all rates taxes and assessments charged on the building of which the flat forms part other than any charges for gas electric current or wireless relay for which the Lessee is liable'; to light the common areas and keep them cleaned and swept; to supply a constant service of hot water for domestic use and also for heating between 1 October and 30 April each year. There were nine rules and regulations for tenants, covering such things as noise from radio or musical instruments, the hanging of washing, instructions for refuse collection and car parking etiquette (Table 3.2). There is little surprising about these regulations, which were necessary to organise everyday life for 2,000–3,000 people in relatively dense conditions.

Table 3.2 Dolphin Square Schedule of Rules and Regulations for lessees, 1938

1. No piano or other musical instrument to be used or played upon between twelve p.m. and eight a.m. and no piano pianola gramophone wireless loudspeaker or mechanical musical instrument of any kind shall at any time be used so as to cause annoyance to any of the other occupiers of the building...The use of an outdoor aerial of any description or type for wireless television or the like is prohibited.
2. The Lessee shall not place any showboard namebill placard advertisement or notice of any description upon the external parts or in any of the windows of the flat or expose any wearing apparel or domestic linen or washing in or upon any parts of the flat.
3. No bird, dog or other animal shall be kept by the Lessee upon any part of the flat (without the consent in writing of the Landlords which consent may be withdrawn from time to time) which may occasion annoyance to the Landlords or to any of the other occupiers of the said buildings ...
4. The porter (or caretaker) shall be under no obligation to furnish attendance or other use of his services to the lessee for private convenience ...
5. The Lessee shall not allow any mats to be shaken inside the buildings or out of the windows thereon and shall not throw anything out of the windows or place on the outside window sills a flower box flower pot or other object.
6. Each Lessee shall be furnished with two keys of the flat door. The keys will not be transferable and shall be given up to the Landlords or their agents or representatives at the end or determination of the tenancy.
7. Entrance doors of flats shall be kept shut. The Lessee shall each night after 12 p.m. or each morning before 9 a.m. place the refuse container in cupboard receptacle provided by the Landlords.
8. The Lessee shall give immediate notice of any case of infectious or contagious illness in any flat and shall not without the previous consent in writing of the Landlords nurse or permit to be nursed any such case in any flat ...
9. The parking of cars or vehicles on the road approaches or forecourts or lawns of the flats is expressly prohibited and the speed limit of vehicular traffic shall not exceed 15 miles per hour. Vehicles shall be drawn up at the side of the road or approach furthest from the entrances to the flats in order to give room at all times for traffic and pedestrians to pass on side of road nearest the entrances.

Source: Lease of 403 Hood House, 24 November 1938, DST.

Seen through the eyes of Theo Langbehn and his contributors, the monthly magazine *The Dolphin* gives something of the 'Dolphin Square experience', if a rather bowdlerised version. Reporting in October 1937 on the introduction of goldfish to the garden pool, Langbehn reminded residents that the Square's telegraphic address, 'Dorado', signified a golden fish identifiable in English, French and Spanish. There were also pieces on how to 'plan your flat with intelligence', tips for 'Mrs. Dolphin at Home', radio reviews, and advertisements for wine, specialised furniture ('put-u-up' settees and divans, etc.) and vacuum cleaners.[57] Some of the residents were the subjects of feature articles, many of them contributed by Gay Jackson. In the October 1937, issue readers were told about 'Britain's only woman film "doctor"', Julia Wolf. Miss Wolf, who had moved into a one-room flat in Collingwood House (No. 06) in January 1937, was a Wardour Street film editor with responsibility for handling European films. 'Practically every German and French film that comes into this country is cut, edited, and given its English subtitles by this *petite*, vivacious brunette, with large blue eyes and a boyish hair-cut.' Her personal life was also revealed. She enjoyed travelling, 'smart restaurants' and dancing. 'Her constant companion is a small, five-shilling mongrel, called Nipper.' She also had a kitten called Roddy. Her flat was attractively smart, with chalk-white walls and ceiling, deep-cream woodwork, black lino and rugs on the floor, and red corded silk curtains. Her corner divan and a large chair were covered in black satin, 'with a lot of gay cushions in red, white and black stripes'. The small kitchen was white, the bathroom 'a delicate shade of Nile green'. In interview, she said that 'it was a great joy to return to her little flat by the river. As she looked out across the broad peaceful gardens she felt as though she was many miles from the noise and bustle of the West End and the world of films'.[58] In February 1938 there was a piece on 'Mrs Stephen Thomas' of 205 Raleigh House. She was better known as the actress Nadine March, while her husband was a pioneer producer of television programmes for the BBC at Alexandra Palace. With their main home near Bishop's Stortford, they were using their flat as a pied-à-terre. Dolphin Square, they said, was ideal for this purpose, since they had a son called Billy aged 2½. Nevertheless, neither Miss Wolf nor the Thomases became long-term tenants, and we see that new tenants had taken their flats in time to be listed in the electoral register for 1939.[59]

Major Robert and Mrs Thorva Mayo of 806 Hawkins House were the next tenants to be featured in *The Dolphin*, in March 1938. Major Mayo was introduced to readers as the inventor of a new composite, 'piggy-back' aeroplane. He was General Manager (Technical) of Imperial Airways. His invention was a large and lightly loaded plane with a smaller, more heavily loaded, seaplane on its back. The intention was to facilitate more effective long-distance flying and, in particular, to improve the Atlantic route from Ireland to Newfoundland by avoiding the need for take-off fuel for the second plane. Short Brothers built a prototype for the airline and the Air Ministry in 1937: the S20 (upper) and S21 (lower), named *Mercury* and *Maia*. The first flight in which separation was effected was in February 1938. In July, *Mercury* flew non-stop to Montreal in 20 hours 20 minutes, and in October made a record-breaking non-stop flight from Dundee to Orange River, South Africa, a distance of 6,045 miles, in just over 42 hours. However, the composite was 'never more than an expensive experiment', and its shortcomings in commercial terms were immediately apparent. It was not long before more powerful single planes were put into service for transatlantic flights [Illustration 20 (iv)].[60] *The Dolphin* was naturally more interested in the Mayo family flat. They were renting a Windsor Suite, one of the most luxurious flats, and this was fully described by Gay Jackson. The three-bathroom apartment was decorated in off-white, with stone-beige carpeting. The drawing and dining rooms were curtained in an egg-blue, star-patterned satin. The drawing room furniture was upholstered in an off-white tweed with cretonne cushions patterned with maps of the Thames. The dining room had mahogany chairs in the Chippendale style, and Mrs Mayo was engaged in making tapestry seats decorated with the Mayo crest. Their eight-year-old daughter Jennifer had her own suite of bedroom, sitting room and bathroom, with a cabinet containing her 'greatly-prized collection of [over 60] china and glass rabbits'. Full advantage had been taken of the flat's balcony. The Mayos boasted of having grown 16 large tomatoes on it. They were enthusiastic 'Dolphins', using the restaurant for entertaining, and the swimming pool for exercise.[61] Captain Harry and Mrs Winifred Parker, the subject of an article in the May 1938 issue, were also held to be enthusiastic Dolphins. The Parkers had left their house in Westcliff to live in London, and were renting two flats in Raleigh House (Nos. 101 and 102). They had a daughter, Mollie, and Dinkie, a small Pekinese. Gay Jackson found the flat to be 'full of valuable old paintings and etchings, and some very beautiful antiques'. The carpeting was in stone beige, the curtains and pelmets made of heavy brocaded damask in light gold. 'A very lovely painting of Ilfracombe, by John Tennant, R.A., hangs over the electric fireplace.' Antique oak furniture was used in the dining room. Here there was a painting of the 'London and Leicester Royal Mail Coach, by James Pollard'. Captain Parker was managing director of the Parker Gallery in Albemarle Street, a venture founded in 1750. He had written books on naval history and steamships. His daughter was a great traveller, and had decorated her room with 'a fearsome collection of knives and daggers', two Jamaican rumba sticks, a boomerang, and 'a very large Buddha'. Once again the tenants declared themselves to be regular patrons of the restaurant and sports centre.[62] There was a brief anonymous piece about the cartoonist Oscar Berger in September 1937. He was well-known for his advertisements for Shell, London Transport and the Post Office, and for his sketches of film stars in the *Sunday Dispatch*. Berger agreed to provide cartoons for *The Dolphin* [Illustration 24].[63]

Joy Barnett wrote about 'Mrs Llane Morton' in the September 1938 issue. Occupying a flat on the sixth floor of Rodney House (No. 616) with her mother, Lilian Morton was a painter from life of 'the wild animals of the jungle'. A former big-game hunter, she was writing a book on 'Jungle Lands with Brush and Camera' and had decorated her flat with tiger skins, Burmese tapestries and jade figures.[64] Ms Barnett also informed readers about the Hon. Arthur Maxwell Stamp in December 1938. The Stamps had just returned to their newly-furnished flat (206 Collingwood House) from their honeymoon, having been married in the Henry VII Chapel of Westminster Abbey in late October. The couple had met at Cambridge, where Arthur had read economics and his wife Janet modern languages. Concerns about the hairs from their red cocker spaniel Jane had influenced their choice of décor. The fitted carpets and velvet curtains were in dark mushroom tinged with gold, while the chairs and couch were in supple white rawhide. The Stamps were keen television watchers, and were looking for a set in grained walnut to match their table. The bedroom was decorated in cream and peach, the curtains were in quilted peach satin, and the furniture was made of avodire. The study had curtains with a design showing full glasses of champagne and lager. There was no guest room, since the couple intended to make full use of the ones provided by Dolphin Square.[65] A less glamorous contribution marked the presentation of a portrait to Mr A.W. Thomas, the Managing Director of Royal Typewriters, in April 1938. The portrait was unveiled by the Lord Mayor of London, Sir Harry Twyford. The piece seems to have been somewhat tongue-in-cheek: 'The Lord Mayor, in a happy little speech, told his audience that the unveiling was his sixth function that day . . . the portrait is a realistic likeness . . . showers of congratulations, verbal and telegraphic, greeted Mr Thomas'.

The children's centre attracted particular attention in *The Dolphin*. Kathleen Poer wrote about it in the July 1937 issue, and Joan Brook contributed articles in October 1937 and March 1938. Poer emphasised the security of the children. The Matron, Evelyn Pantin, assured readers that 'the most devoted mother can have freedom and at the same time perfect peace of mind during the first seven years of a child's life.' There were descriptions of the play activities, dining, cots and toys. A qualified governess provided two hours' schooling for the older children. A medical examination preceded admittance to the centre in order to reduce the risk of infections, and (weather permitting) there were daily walks to Battersea Park.[66] The facilities offered by the centre reflected contemporary attitudes and the priorities of the wealthy middle classes towards child care. In the first of her articles Brook emphasised the centre's convenience, in this instance in looking after a three-year-old child for two weeks. Very much a 'puff' for the amenity, which at this time was housed in temporary accommodation, the piece referred to the playroom, bathrooms, meals, and emphasis on hygiene.[67] The second article celebrated the opening of the permanent facility. The new nurseries occupied most of the top floor of Beatty and Duncan Houses, the entrance being from Beatty House. As the Matron, Evelyn Pantin, pointed out, with their own kitchens, laundry, store rooms, play rooms and schoolroom, 'we really have a little world up here all to ourselves.' There were balconies on two sides, enabling the children to play outside in safety. Considerable attention had been given to the décor of the inner rooms, using 'pinky peaches' and 'delicate greens'. The bathroom contained six full-sized baths mounted on platforms and four miniature baby baths. Miss Pantin and the Sister also had 'their own little self-contained flats in the children's centre to enable them to be always on the spot'.[68] Children could stay overnight and for weekends. As we have seen the busy Thomases found the centre invaluable, Mrs Thomas remarking: 'I can't think why central nurseries in flats haven't been thought of before. They are an absolute boon for flat-dwellers, especially people like ourselves who work at night at theatre or studio'.[69] And in an article in May 1938, Jennifer Graham asserted that the Square was 'A Children's Paradise', with facilities for all ages. 'Many tenants claim that it is as airy and quiet as living in the country', she wrote. 'I hear there is already a young people's colony who meet for swim and treasure hunts'.[70] The children's centre charged 6s. 6d. for a 12-hour stay, including meals, for babies and young children up to two years of age. A night cost 3s 6d., a weekend £1 5s., and a week £3 3s. For older children, aged from two to ten years, the same periods cost 9s. 6d., 5s., £ 15s., and £3 13s. 6d.[71]

Organised sporting activity was introduced at an early stage. A Dolphin Square squash team secured a narrow win over Wanstead in early 1938. A swimming gala was held on 15 February, with races for men over 88 yards (four lengths) and 44 yards, and for women over 66 and 44 yards.[72] On occasions the portrayal of an idyllic existence gave way to more disturbing news. Langbehn reported that a correspondent had written to him about a conversation overheard in the garden, in which reference was made to the problem of litter. Despite the provision of litter boxes, people had 'thrown their papers and cigarette cartons on the paths and grass'.[73] The early handbooks for residents contain information on what was intended to be 'unobtrusive, comprehensive and economical service'. There was, of course, a price to be paid, but the tariffs seem to have been competitive.[74] The guest rooms provided for residents' guests cost 7s. 6d. a night for a single room, 12s. 6d. for a double. A week's stay was priced at £1 17s. 6d. and £3 15s., a month at £7 10s. and £12 10s. The Matron was available in case of accidents, and charged 5s. to dress a wound in the tenant's flat, 2s 6s. at the Nursery. The cleaning services compared favourably with the alternative of employing and accommodating a maid. The premier service (making beds, vacuuming, dusting and washing up each day) was 10s. a week for a bedsit, rising to 14s. for three rooms and 20s. for a seven-room flat. The standard service (making beds and washing up daily, but vacuuming and dusting three times a week) was 6s. 6d., 10s. 6d. and 16s. respectively. The charge for window-cleaning was described as a 'modest' 3s. a month for a bedsit, inside and out, rising to 6s. for five rooms and more. Shoes were cleaned for 2d. a pair. Laundry charges depended on the type of garment, but men's shirts were priced at 7d.–10d. each, a ladies blouse at 9d–1s. 3d. The price for garaging a car ranged from 7s. 6d. a week for cars of ten horsepower or less, to 15s. for cars of over 30 horsepower. A 1,000-mile service cost 12s. 6d.–17s. 6d., a 5,000-mile service £2 15s.–£4 15s. Connection to the radio service via Radio Furniture & Fittings Ltd. cost 1s. 9d. a week for two stations, rising to 2s. 9d. for four stations. In the restaurant, breakfast cost 2s., and residents paid 2s. 6d. for lunch and 3s. 6d. for dinner (with à la carte prices of 1s. 6d. for Omelette Florentine, 2s. 6d. for Tournedos Niçoise).[75] A season ticket for the swimming pool cost £3 3s., individual swims either 6d. or 1s. Guests paid much more – 2s. 6d. a session. For a 30-minute game of squash residents paid 1s. per person, their guests 2s.[76] It is difficult to assess these charges, given the progressive changes in the standard of living, and a 70-fold increase in prices since the mid 1930s. At a time when a doctor earned about £1,000 a year, a bank clerk £400, and a bus driver £200,[77] Dolphin Square tariffs were certainly affordable for the 'comfortable' middle class and above.

In pre-war Dolphin Square there was naturally the normal ebb and flow of life, of births, marriages and deaths. In *The Times*, the first notifications of a Dolphin Square birth were in September 1937. On 8 September a daughter was born to Naomi and Dale Bourn of 704 Grenville House, followed by a son born on 13 September to Mr and Mrs R.R. Curtis (Ronald and Doris) of 702 Drake House. Both events were recorded in *The Dolphin*. It was pointed out that Dale Bourn was a former amateur golf champion, while his wife was the former actress Naomi Waters.[78] Another eight births were announced in *The Times* before the outbreak of war in September 1939.[79] Several engagements and forthcoming marriages were announced in 1937–9, the first in *The Times* being the engagement of George Gordon, of 702 Collingwood House, to Rosemary Graham, in June 1937. It was followed in October by the marriage, 'shortly to take place', of Mr A.P. Pearson of 604 Collingwood House and Miss Daphne Veitch. *The Dolphin* recorded the marriage in September 1937 of Mr and Mrs E.R. Mort of 207 Howard House.[80] Of the others, the wedding of Bruce Fraser, of 613 Rodney House, to Audrey, stepdaughter of Mrs Florence Crosleigh of 112 Collingwood House, received a lengthy report in *The Times* in May 1939. The wedding took place at St. Michael's Church, Chester Square. The bride 'wore a gown of ivory duchess satin, the front cut in princess lines with a heart-shaped neckline and the flared skirt extended to form a short pointed train'. The reception was held at the Goring Hotel in Grosvenor Gardens and the couple took their honeymoon in Scotland.[81] Also of interest was the forthcoming marriage, also announced in May 1939, of Terence Carothers and Annabel, younger daughter of Lt Col. J.J. Harper-Nelson, CIE OBE MC and Mrs Margaret Harper-Nelson, of Achaban House, Fionnophort, Isle of Mull, and 612 Rodney House. Both Annabel and her mother were on the electoral register for Dolphin Square prior to the marriage.[82] The first publicised death was that of Major Cecil Brownhill of the Irish Guards in June 1938. This was followed by the announcement in December that Caroline Wall, the 81-year-old former nurse to Mrs Gerald Bevan and family, had died at Dolphin Square. Elsa Wall was the tenant of 707 Frobisher House.[83] Most distressing was the death of Miss Pamela Lenney of Beatty House. Due to be married, she was knocked off her bike in August 1939. And the first reported suicide was that of Mrs Violet Wood of Drake House, the widow of a shipping agent, in the following October.[84]

Dolphin Square offered residents the opportunity to live the bourgeois life of the late 1930s, with dinner dances, martinis, games of canasta, and the smoking of exotic cheroots. Equally, it offered privacy for those attracted to a less conventional lifestyle. At a time when the legalisation of homosexual acts was still three decades away, there were a number of same-sex couples in the Square, and the complex doubtless offered some of them a safe refuge from an unforgiving society. There was something undeniably glamorous about Dolphin Square which attracted not only the managerial and administrative classes, but also diverse members of Britain's pre-war ruling elite. Here, in close proximity, if not necessarily close familiarity, were those with right-wing political views such as the Mosleys and Clementine Mitford, and equally ardent supporters of the left, such as Ellen Wilkinson, Viscountess Snowden and Arthur Greenwood. It made for a volatile cocktail.

MANAGING DOLPHIN SQUARE

The management and staff of Costain's Dolphin Square remain something of a mystery. Costain did not maintain its archive, and we must once again piece together the story from occasional scraps of information, or else extrapolate backwards from the material available once the

Dolphin Square Trust had been established in 1964. One thing is quite clear. The first general manager was Henry J.W. Castle, known as 'Harry', who lived in 02 Drake House with his wife Alice. The first issue of *The Dolphin* in May 1937 asserted that he was also Dolphin Square's founding resident, since he had moved in with his family during the building work, in September 1936. The Castles 'gained entrance to their flat through a cut in the hoarding. In the late evening this was locked, and they were prisoners for the night. A temporary water supply and a temporary gas supply were laid on'. Castle was responsible for the entire management of the Square, including staffing (the appointment of the office and domestic staff, management of the office, and the choosing of uniforms, etc.), lettings, engineering and services, the sports centre, including the restaurant, porterage and the children's centre. He was considered to be a sound appointment, since he had been 'manager of a great international company'; in fact he had been London Manager of American Express for the previous 25 years. Castle was also remembered by Albert Costain: he 'was known to several of our directors as a man of great tact, with exceptional flair and experience on dealing with members of the public from all walks of life'.[85] Costain also praised the work of Charles 'Andy' Anderson, the Head Porter, and John A. 'Dobbie' Dobson, MIPHE, MJIE, AMSE, the Chief Engineer, and subsequently Building Superintendent. Porters were required to be at least six feet tall, and Anderson, having served in the Guards, was one of the earliest recruits. 'Dobbie' was remembered for his sterling service during the war. He had been an engineer in the Merchant Navy, and having joined Costain in 1936, worked in Dolphin Square until he retired in 1972.[86] His department contained some long-serving staff: W. Groves, Chief Engineer from 1940; F.J. Bailey, Assistant Chief Engineer, and Harry Bailey, Foreman Plumber, both appointed in 1938. All were still in post in 1964.[87] *The Dolphin* also made passing mention of some of the other staff, including the Matron, Evelyn Pantin; the garage superintendent, Mr E.J. Cooper; Mr T.C. Land, the squash professional, who came to Dolphin Square from the Naval and Military Club; John T. Powell, gymnasium instructor and manager, and a physical training instructor, Mr McCarthy; swimming pool instructors, Mr F. Smith and Mrs Chambers; and Monsieur G. D'Angelo, manager of the restaurant.[88] Here, music was initially provided by Eddie Carroll and his band, an eight-piece ensemble highly regarded by the music paper *Melody Maker*, which ran a short piece on the engagement under the headline 'Swinging at Dolphin Square'.[89]

Underpinning the professional staff was an army of support staff – administrative staff, receptionists, telephonists, housekeepers, nurses, mechanics, porters, gardeners, maintenance and cleaning staff, building labourers, and so on. According to the report of the General Manager in 1964, there were 85 maintenance workers in 1939, 30 of whom were painters (Table 3.3). While we do not know the total number of pre-war employees, it is likely that this was at least as high as 400, since after several bouts of rationalisation, including the outsourcing of lift maintenance and the garage and restaurant facilities to external firms, the staffing complement in 1964 was only just below 200, and there were 42 maintenance workers then, half the number there in 1939.[90]

Table 3.3 Dolphin Square maintenance staff in 1939

Job	*Number*
Administration and Clerical	7
Engineers	8
Drain Cleaners	4
Carpenters	8
Electricians	4
Plumbers	6
Plasterers	4
Bricklayers	4
Labourers	6
Upholsterers	3
Seamstresses	1
Painters	30
Total	**85**

Source: General Manager's Report, November 1964, p.6, DST.

Photographs, handbooks and other memorabilia provide further glimpses into the work of the staff. Three undated photographs of the children's nurses, restaurant staff, porters and page boys were probably taken in 1939 [Illustrations 25 (i), (ii) and (iii)]: the Matron (front row centre, holding a tiny puppy) is shown on the children's centre's protected balcony with six of her nurses; pictured also are eight restaurant staff, three men and five women; and nine porters and three page boys were photographed on one of the lawns. The boys are wearing berets, though an early reference to them in *The Dolphin* – in February 1938 – suggests that they were equipped with pillbox hats: residents were promised that 'pill-box hatted boys will be on the spot to run any errand from exercising your dog to delivering important letters or papers for you'.[91]

Dolphin Square's postal operations are also revealing. An article appeared on the subject in *The Dolphin* for May 1938 under the headline '"Run, Postman Run"', which was apparently an exhortation that anxious residents used to write on their more urgent letters. The postal requirements 'of some 5,000 souls' demanded 'some very snappy work on the part of the carriers of His Majesty's Mails', particularly during the morning rush-hour. At the SW District Post Office, four men were deployed in sorting the daily delivery of about 2,500 letters, cards and packets. Soon after 7.30 a.m. the men were taken by van to the Square.

> Then ensues a rapid perambulation of the various Houses, commencing with a quick rise in the world up to the top storey and a slower descent to the ground . . . When it is realised that in some of the Houses there are as many as 27 flats on one floor,[92] one cannot but appreciate the magnitude of the job.

Productivity was emphasised. The men were allowed an hour to complete the delivery, i.e. by 8.30 a.m., and the process was repeated no fewer than six times a day, at 10.15 a.m., 12.15 p.m., 2.15 p.m., 3.45 p.m., 5.15 p.m., and 8.30 p.m. Thirteen collections were taken from four large post boxes, equipped with stamp machines, at each corner of the Square.[93]

THE SECOND WORLD WAR

War brought an abrupt end to the 'normal' times at Dolphin Square. Managers and tenants had barely a year of full operation before the hostilities began and it was not long before their impact was felt. On 13 September 1939, *The Times* announced that Pilot Officer Anthony St. Croix Rose, aged 29, from 110 Rodney House, had been killed in action two days earlier.[94] By January 1941, four others had shared his fate.[95] The central London rental market was clearly affected even during the phoney war, from September 1939 to April 1940. Costain tried to capitalise on the building's 'ten floors of solid concrete'. In November 1939, the company advertised short-term tenancies in *The Times*, proclaiming that the Square was 'Supreme in the Black-out'. Both furnished and unfurnished flats were available: the unfurnished ones cost from £17 10s. a quarter for one room excluding rates to £23 10s. for two rooms; furnished bedsits were £9 2s. a month inclusive, two rooms from £13 13s. a month, with larger flats priced proportionately.[96] These rates represented a considerable reduction on what had been asked for earlier (see Table 3.1, above). In fact, advertisements placed in *The Times* give a good indication of the direction in which the market was heading. In October 1939, Dolphin Square's letting office advertised as follows: 'Furnished Flat cheap; owner on active service; one of best flats in Dolphin Square'. No price was given, but three months later a tenant offered a furnished two-room flat for £3½ guineas a week, not far short of half the rate Costain was charging for such flats in 1936 (see p.75).[97] Of course, the facilities available at Dolphin Square were almost immediately constrained by the exigencies of war. The underground garage had already been requisitioned for use as one of Westminster's four major casualty depots, when it was visited by the Mayor and Corporation in October 1939. A mobile first-aid unit was attached to the depot, there was a decontamination centre, and Air Raid Precautions [ARP] staff were housed in the basement under Rodney House.[98] But the restaurant remained open, and after December 1940, when it was requisitioned by the Government for use as a canteen for the depot and civil defence staff, a residents' restaurant was opened in the Chichester Room in Rodney House.[99] For a time Costain advertised the Square as a 'tranquil and stately' address where, in spite of the war, shopping, maid service, valeting and other services were still being offered.[100] And life did continue. For example, on 20 April the marriage took place in Kuala Lumpur of James King and Elizabeth Banon, younger daughter of the late Christopher Banon, DL, JP, and Mrs Banon, of Broughall Castle in Ireland and 302 Keyes House. This was followed on 8 June by the marriage at St. Mary's, Cadogan Square of Henry George Nelson and Pamela, 'daughter of the late Mr E. Roy Bird, MP and Mrs Roy Bird of 204 Dolphin Square [sic]'. And on 1 May 1940 Ellice Gifford, Lady Gifford, gave birth to a son in her flat, 603 Raleigh House.[101]

In the autumn of 1940, Pimlico experienced a series of German bombing raids and Dolphin Square was soon affected. The incidents were recorded by ARP Sector 245, Post number 27. The first bomb fell on 22 September, affecting Hawkins House; it was followed by hits or near misses on 27 September, 15, 16 and 25 October, 5 and 6 November 1940, and on 16–17 April and 10–11 May 1941 (Table 3.4). As Jan Prebble points out in her recent booklet, *Wartime in Dolphin Square*,[102] the most serious incident in terms of fatalities and injuries was in fact the first.

Table 3.4 Bombing incidents in and around Dolphin Square, 1940–1

Date	*Location [House]*	*Comments*	*Casualties*
22/9/1940	Hawkins (corner)	Bomb fell through to basement 23.35 hrs	Seven dead, 58 injured
27/9/1940	Grenville (roof); Grosvenor Road opp. Drake		None
15/10/1940	Garage (used as depot)	'engine room between Howard and Beatty'	'a few'
16/10/1940	Outside Drake; centre west drive ramp	01.25 hrs 'One bomb on grass, one on roof'; one on drive ramp	One injured
25/10/1940	Grenville (top)		
5/11/1940	Frobisher (roof and 7th floor), Grenville (6th floor), Collingwood	04.55 hrs	Four dead
6/11/1940	Rodney (outside); West drive ramp opp. Duncan	Several bombs fell in the area	None
16–17/4/1941	Hawkins; road between Raleigh and Drake; tennis court on Embankment opp. Raleigh; Duncan	23.30 hrs, 04.40 hrs 'river wall completely demolished'	One dead [Mr Bregonzi], 4 injured
10-11/5/1941	Grosvenor road opp. Hawkins	23.45 + 00.04 hrs	One dead [Vivian Tidmarsh]

Source: Westminster Civil Defence records: incident forms, WCA CD1; Permanent Record Book of Bombing Incidents, WCA CD3; and Situation Reports, WCA CD17.

On 22 September 1940 at 11.35 p.m. a high explosive bomb caused slight damage to Hawkins House at the main entrance, but in fact the bomb fell through the ten floors to the basement, where people were sheltering in a local authority-built shelter. There were 58 casualties and seven deaths.[103] The *Westminster & Pimlico News* provided a rather sanguine account, observing that the flats had had a narrow escape when a bomb hit the corner of the building. London's *Evening News* was more revealing. Under the headline 'PEOPLE KILLED AS THEY SHELTER UNDER WEST END FLATS', it reported that seven foreign refugees had been killed and a number injured. 'The refugees, of different nationalities, had been sheltering in a basement for only 20 minutes, following the destruction by a delayed action bomb of the house in which they were billeted in a street 100 yards away.'[104] There was another serious incident on 5 November 1940, when Frobisher House was hit by another high explosive bomb. The *Westminster & Pimlico News* reported that two men and two women had been killed by the bomb, which hit the top of the building [Illustrations 26 (i) and (ii)]. The ARP documentation observed that Frobisher's seventh floor sustained considerable damage, with Grenville and Collingwood Houses also being affected.[105] There were two more deaths in April and May 1941. On 16–17 April, there was a heavy bombing raid on Westminster, in which 173 high explosive bombs were dropped, 191 people were killed and many iconic buildings were damaged, including the Houses of Parliament, Admiralty Arch, Law Courts, National Gallery, and the Charing Cross Hotel. Several bombs fell in and around Dolphin Square, where Hawkins House was hit. Mr Bregonzi, Costain's assistant accountant, was killed, and his wife was badly injured. Across Grosvenor Road, the tennis court was destroyed and part of the Embankment wall was demolished.[106] Finally, on 11 May, during another heavy raid, Vivian Tidmarsh, a part-time air-raid warden living at 403 Collingwood House, was killed when a bomb fell close to Hawkins House (Table 3.4).[107] It is impossible to be exact about total numbers, but about 20 bombs fell on or around the property, killing 13 men and women and injuring about 80.[108] This was a tiny proportion of Westminster's wartime casualties – 1,100 persons were killed in 1940–4 and 2,500 were seriously injured – and since so many residents and others had sheltered in the basement during the raids, the low casualty rate was a testimony to Faber's sound method of construction.[109] Tenants were reluctant to leave, but the bombing in 1940–1 had the effect of emptying the Square. Mrs Erskine of Hood House (see above, p.81) is a good example. As *The Times* put it, 'during the 1939–45 war she was living in Dolphin Square and it was only after 11 bombs had been dropped on it that she was persuaded to leave and went to Scotland'.[110]

Other wartime excitements were provided by the activities of Maxwell Knight for MI5 and the operations of General de Gaulle's Free French Movement in Grenville House. Both were shrouded in secrecy, but while Maxwell Knight's work as a spymaster has been documented in several memoirs and official histories, the work of the Free French in Dolphin Square is more of a mystery. Charles Henry Maxwell Knight (1900–86) volunteered for the Royal Navy in 1916, and was briefly a civil servant, preparatory school teacher and hotelier before he was recruited by MI5. Sympathetic to the far right, he had worked for Sir George Makgill's private intelligence agency, the Industrial Intelligence Bureau, in the 1920s, spying on communists. In 1929, he and his agents were recruited to carry out similar work for SIS (MI6), and after a reorganisation of security in 1931, he joined the Security Service (MI5), where he ran section B5b, later known as 'M' section or 'M.S.'.[111] Knight was an eccentric figure, with a penchant for both the occult and the keeping of exotic animals as pets – including a bear. If Joan Miller, his secretary and subsequently an agent, is to be believed, he concealed his homosexuality with a succession of unconsummated marriages, and after his first wife Gwladys committed suicide he married Lois Coplestone in 1937.[112] He then moved his operations from 38 Sloane Street into her brother's flat, 608 Hood House.[113] After Knight separated from Lois (they were divorced in 1943) he apparently took another flat – 10 Collingwood House – and moved Joan Miller into it. Miller remembered sheltering in the hall during the air-raids, watching the docks burning, with Knight, on the roof of Collingwood House, and being advised by Labour MP Arthur Greenwood on how to protect herself against mugging.[114] When MI5 moved from Thames House, first to Wormwood Scrubs and then to Blenheim Palace, a third flat, probably 02 and 03 on the ground floor of Keyes House, was acquired as an office.[115] Knight's biographer suggests that Knight also made use of a flat rented by David Lloyd, 709 Nelson House.[116] Westminster's Rate Books raise further questions about occupancy. In April 1943, Coplestone gave up 608 Hood House and Knight moved into 612. At the same time he took tenancies on 02 and 03 Keyes, and 315 and 316 Rodney. However, the tenancy of 10 Collingwood was held by George and Evelyn Nichols, and Evelyn continued to hold it until 1943. Knight's interest in it cannot be confirmed.[117]

From Dolphin Square Knight conducted important surveillance operations on both the left and the right, and successfully penetrated the Communist Party and the British Union of Fascists. While he recruited a number of male agents, and also obtained information from communist sympathisers such as Tom Driberg, he preferred to use young women as moles, recruiting, in addition to Joan Miller, Olga Gray, Marjorie Mackie and Helène de Munck. During the war he placed three female agents in the Right Club, an anti-semitic, pro-Nazi organisation, and here he achieved one of his major successes by securing the arrest in May 1940 of Tyler Kent, a cipher clerk in the American Embassy, and Anna Wolkoff, a member of the Right Club. They were subsequently sentenced to seven and ten years' imprisonment respectively for breaching the Official Secrets Act.[118] At the same time, Knight was also involved in the arrest and internment of a fellow Dolphin Square resident, Sir Oswald Mosley, who had been living with his wife Diana, née Mitford, on the floor above Knight in 706 and 707 Hood House, since December 1939.[119] Knight generally maintained a discreet presence in the Square. After the war he pursued a successful career as a naturalist and broadcaster, where he was known as 'Uncle Max'. While he wrote two crime thrillers in the 1930s, he is best known for his many books on animals, birds and pets, including *Pets Usual and Unusual* (1951), *Animals after Dark* (1956), *Instructions to Young Naturalists* (1956–8), *Pets and their Problems* (1968) and *How to Keep a Gorilla* (1968).[120] He continued to live in the Square, and was a leaseholder of 612 Hood House until January 1964. His other flats were given up in 1947–50.[121]

The operations of the Free French are more difficult to pin down. After a temporary billet in St. Stephen's House on the Embankment, they were headquartered at No. 4 Carlton Gardens, and as the work expanded, further accommodation was taken up in Westminster House.[122] Other buildings were also used, but almost nowhere in the several memoirs and biographies that have appeared since is there mention of Dolphin Square.[123] However, the Westminster Rate Books reveal that in 1942 Grenville House was transferred to the Government, and was then placed at the disposal of the 'Free French Forces'.[124] Another reference suggests that at least one flat - 05 Grenville House - had been occupied by them earlier, in January 1941.[125] Serge Vaculik, a Czech who joined the Free French as a parachutist-saboteur, recalled with some contempt the desk-bound 'heroes' who were awarded the resistance medal 'for fighting gallantly behind a big desk strongly entrenched on the first floor of some big block of offices in Dolphin Square or some similar place'.[126] Dolphin Square staff and residents remember that security passes labelled 'No Go' were required for workmen entering this part of the building when de Gaulle was present.[127] In fact, the general presence of government intensified, and Dolphin Square was asked to give up more of its space to the war effort. The rate books show that not only Grenville House, but Drake, Hawkins and Raleigh were transferred to the Government in 1942.[128] Government departments moved in, and *The Times* carried some of their notices. In July 1942, the Board of Trade invited enquiries from the public about clothes rationing, giving Raleigh House as its address. In September, the same department offered coupon-free permits to people whose homes had been bombed since the beginning of 1942. In October, the Board of Trade's Industries & Manufactures Department published an announcement from its Hawkins House address imposing restrictions on the manufacture of 'headgear' (hats, caps, bonnets &c.). By 1945, Hawkins House was also home to the Directorate of Office Machinery, part of the Board of Trade's Industrial Supplies Department, and the Department of Overseas Trade.[129]

Further information about the Square in wartime can be obtained from many sources: from Morris's history; Prebble's account; the recollections of Albert Costain, and of Mrs Stella Brecknell, who lived with her husband Mervyn St John Brecknell in 403 Hood House; and a 'blitz memoir' by Marjorie Gallop, who lived with her husband Rodney in 709 Nelson House.[130] Here, we learn that William J. O'Brien lived in Drake House, where he worked on an invention - hyperbolic radio navigation - that was to prove critical to allied success in the Normandy landings. O'Brien was an American engineer who was recruited in 1942 by a fellow American, Harvey Schwarz, chief engineer and director of the Decca Record Co. He and Schwarz invented the Decca Navigator system for ships and aircraft, which was successfully trialled in 1942–4, and was used to guide ships during the D-Day invasion. Transmitting stations were built in secret, and O'Brien kept a prototype receiver in his flat, and was therefore aware when transmission began in June 1944 and the invasion was under way. After the war a subsidiary, Decca Navigator Co. Ltd., was formed, and the system was deployed over a substantial part of the world's shipping routes until it was superseded by GPS satellites in the present century.[131] Also important to the war effort was the work of 692 General Construction Company of the Royal Engineers. This was made up of Costain staff, who volunteered to build landing strips in France. The unit, led by Col. Albert G. Bonn, was seriously depleted after the early fighting in France and was evacuated from Dunkirk.[132] Reference was also made to the existence of an emergency hospital (in the gymnasium), rifle range, decontamination centre and mortuary, to the regular sheltering of tenants and other Pimlico residents in the basement, and the bombing of Palmolive's soap factory in nearby Claverton Street, which released particles of soap over the whole of the Square. Marjorie Gallop's wartime memoir is revealing. She was shaken by the death of the refugees sheltering in Hawkins House in September 1940, and as a consequence decided to volunteer as an air-raid warden. In Post 27 she worked with a 'motley crowd' – a brigadier, taxi driver, journalist, Army & Navy Stores packer, newspaper seller, department store manager, and the father of the film star Dennis Price. Sheltering was tense, and both snoring and the crying of babies caused annoyance. In the Dolphin Square basement some segregation was organised, but in the St. George's Square shelters this was not done. However,

> there was always a stir of pleasure at the arrival of a charming, fair-haired lady who descended quite unofficially every night wearing a tin hat and a row of pearls over her expensive jumper, and dispensed tea all round, conversing in tones that made one feel one was attending an exclusive social function. Her effect on the shelters was magical.[133]

Josiah Wedgwood MP was living in 903 Howard House during the war. He was a fervent anti-Nazi who made several attempts to get the United

States to join Britain in 1940–1. On 19 October 1940, at 10 p.m., he wrote to his children while sheltering from the bombing in Lady Snowden's flat, 206 Beatty House. His own flat had already suffered some damage and was more exposed. A copy of the letter is included in his correspondence deposited in the archives of the Imperial War Museum, and is worth reproducing at length.

> Dear Children, this is for Helen, Rosamund and Charles, a story of adventure . . . So far tonight they have not hit us; but we have had nine bombs in six weeks and are getting perfectly callous. Three on the roof burst on that superb bit of concrete and only wrecked the rooms just underneath; one got the shelter by accident and killed six.[134] Otherwise only an ambulance driver has been killed.[135] On Friday 13th a second bomb dropped in on the soap factory 100 yards away and, like a volcano, all the stone and steel flew into the air over Dolphin Square. It was at 3pm and I had only just gone down. An iron pipe entered No 903 and smashed the back of the armchair and hurled it about the room. So that the balcony window is boarded up. A 2 ton iron girder wandered over the roof and sat up in the middle of the garden.
>
> But last Tuesday was our gala night. One came down within 6 yards of our window and flung F[136] into my arms. It went through into the garage and destroyed a hundred cars. Only three of the Snowden windows went, but elsewhere desolation and destruction of doors and windows. Another took an adjoining house in St. Georges S[q]uare and covered us with dust; another missed the front of the Square by a yard and blew in a few more windows; another just accross [sic] the road in front wiped out all the remaining windows in front; another landed in the west door of the garage and smashed the windows in the west, but not as high as 903, and killed the ambulance driver; a last pitched into Grenville and burst harmlessly.
>
> The power station[137] and our fortress still stand amid surrounding ruins, but with windows hanging anyhow.
>
> All services still working; and 'nothing could stop that

> astonishing infantry'![138]
> Jos[139] spent one night on the floor here . . . a fairly quiet night; but tonight is as bad as ever. Monday and Tuesday . . . incessant pounding and I cannot hear a single gun.
>
> F has two flats to clean now besides cooking all my meals, but has got a daring woman to come in to help, one of the few left in the neighborhood [sic].
>
> All I want to do is to get back at them with interest. They kill about 200 a night only, but their destruction is offensive . . . Westminster Hall looks like Fountains Abbey . . .
> Your loving father
> J.C.W.[140]

For Costain, wartime management of the Square was hampered by disruption of the property market, rising costs, staff shortages, and the introduction of rent control. Domestic house-building virtually ceased, and the company's activities were redirected to war work. At the AGM for 1940, held in the Chichester Room in June 1941, the directors revealed that the company was working entirely for government departments, and stated that there was no prospect of an ordinary dividend. Similar statements were issued in 1942 and 1943.[141] The workforce not on active war service were engaged in vital, and often secret, work, building Mulberry Harbours, coastal defences, aerodromes, reinforced aircraft hangars, and ordnance factories. Later on, the company co-ordinated supplies for the American Air Force and provided equipment for the Normandy landings.[142] For the company's existing commitments, staff shortages and inflation provided further headaches, and this was particularly evident with a building as complex as Dolphin Square. With the outbreak of war, rent control was hastily reintroduced at levels not seen since the early 1920s. The Rent and Mortgage Interest Restrictions Act of 1939 abolished decontrol by vacant possession and extended control to over ten million houses with rateable values of less than £100 in London, £90 in Scotland, and £75 elsewhere. Essentially this made rent control as extensive as it had been under the Act of 1920.[143] When Dolphin Square was built all but 150 of its smaller flats lay outside control thanks to the decontrol measures introduced in

1923, 1933 and 1938,[144] but the 1939 Act had the effect of freezing most rents at the 1939 level. Very few of Costain's flats were valued at above the £100 mark, and these were the 44 'best' flats on the upper floors.[145] However, equally challenging for Costain was the general difficulty of finding tenants, especially after the bombing of 1940–1. As we have seen, rentals were difficult to sustain at their pre-war levels, even though inflation was beginning to erode their real value. From the middle of 1941, a substantial portion of Dolphin Square became empty, with tenants electing not to seek a renewal of their agreements. At the same time, there were new tenants, especially those who like MPs and key civil servants were required to be in Westminster whatever the state of the war. Most disruptive of all was the fact that four of the Square's houses were transferred to the Government in 1942. Much of Frobisher House was closed due to war damage.[146] Although one might be tempted to assume that maintenance was neglected, the recollections of those living in the Square during the war indicate that Costain was relatively quick to effect repairs, particularly when addressing the damage caused by bombing.[147] But by 1945, with the company having spent six years of its productive time in war work, deficiencies began to surface. Dolphin Square was clearly a more subdued place than it had been in the sparkling days of 1938–9.

POST-WAR AUSTERITY AND AFTER

Tenants returning to or moving into Dolphin Square after the war felt an overwhelming desire to 'get back to normal', and to some extent this occurred. The bank and the shops had remained under the same ownership during the war, and these reopened their doors in peacetime conditions. The 135 bus had disappeared with the war, in May 1940, but the 134 took over the extension to Chichester Street, with 10–15 minute intervals, and evening services were reinstated in 1946.[148] Shortages of men and materials hindered the work of restoration, but in September 1947 the main restaurant and swimming pool reopened. A bar was added in the east balcony in 1949.[149] Squash matches resumed, and *The Times* began to report them in January 1948.[150] And yet post-war Britain was a very different place. After six years of bitter fighting and privation, the newly-elected Labour Government of 1945 expressed egalitarian aspirations, and there was talk of a 'New

Jerusalem'. But this was difficult to attain given the economic difficulties in which the country was placed. Britain was saddled with debt, its international status was being challenged, many of its industries were run-down or skewed towards military production, and there was a substantial housing shortage. Recovery was painfully slow, and new measures such as bread rationing (1946–8) and the control of potatoes (1947–8) underlined the severity of the immediate post-war years.[151] Rationing and other restrictions, which affected both producers and consumers, remained in place into the 1950s. The period from 1945 to 1951 is rightly described as the 'Age of Austerity'.[152] In London, some of the post-war pressures were magnified, notably in relation to housing and industrial disruption.

Nevertheless, Dolphin Square remained an attractive place to either live, or to rest one's head while working in central London. There was no shortage of 'celebrities' in the post-war period. We lack a complete listing of tenants before the early 1960s, but the electoral registers and rate books reveal some famous names. First of all, there were more politicians, who continued to be attracted by Dolphin Square's proximity to the Houses of Parliament. One of the most distinguished was Sir Hartley Shawcross, the barrister and politician, who moved into 201 Beatty House with Joan, his second wife, in 1950. Shawcross was Attorney-General in the Labour administrations of 1945–51, and chief British prosecutor at the Nuremberg war crimes tribunal. He also prosecuted the traitor William Joyce, 'Lord Haw-Haw', who also had a link to Dolphin Square, having been acquainted with, and underestimated by, Maxwell Knight, who allowed him to slip through the net and flee to Germany.[153] Lord and Lady Silkin lived in 314 Rodney House and then in 904 Collingwood House in the mid 1950s. Lewis Silkin was Labour's Minister of Town and Country Planning after 1945, and was responsible for key pieces of legislation on new towns, planning, and access to the countryside.[154] Geoffrey (later Sir Geoffrey) de Freitas, another Labour MP in the Square, occupied 906 Hood House from 1950 to 1961. He was British High Commissioner in Ghana, 1961–3, and in Kenya, 1963–4, and later President of the Council of Europe Assembly.[155] We have already mentioned two Conservatives, Brigadier Smyth and Cdr King-Hall (see p.81). Brigadier Sir John ('Jackie') Smyth, VC, MC, PC, served with distinction in both world wars, and in the Second War commanded troops in Dunkirk and Burma. He held a junior ministerial post in the 1951–5 administration and was Lawn Tennis correspondent for both the *Sunday Times* and the *News of the World*. Cdr Stephen King-Hall, the son of an admiral, founded the Hansard Society in 1944.[156] Also worth mentioning are: Sir Eric Errington, MP, who returned to the Square having been out of the Commons between 1945 and 1954;[157] Cdr Charles Donaldson, Conservative MP for Roxburgh and Selkirk, 1951–64;[158] and George Pargiter, Labour MP for Southall, 1950–66, who was one of the founding members of the Dolphin Square Tenants' Association (see p.120).[159]

Captain Leonard Plugge, MP for Chatham from 1935 to 1945, was a minor politician, but was certainly a colourful character. He receives over a page in Morris's history of Dolphin Square. Plugge lived in a bedsit, No. 701 Beatty House, from 1950 to 1971. He also rented 902 Hood House, from 1963, and his wife Gertrude briefly occupied 702 Beatty House from 1965. A man of many talents – Morris describes him as a 'politician, inventor, painter, sculptor and balletomane' – he was an enthusiastic pioneer of radio, fitted the first car radio in 1926, and claimed to have invented the car telephone. He also established the International Broadcasting Co., a commercial rival to BBC radio, in the 1930s. Plugge's flat, said Morris,

> had to be seen to be believed. In the bathroom all the taps were gilt dolphins; the lavatory pan was concealed in a green velvet throne. Over the bath on extending arms were three telephones each with a different number; at each end of the bath there was a television set. In the bed sitting room there was a richly curtained four poster bed, which he claimed had been Marie Antoinette's, again with three telephones at the head and with a television set at the foot. In the centre of the ceiling there was an Italianate painting of unclothed maidens of junoesque proportions; from the edges of the painting came silk drapes giving the effect of an Arabian tent . . . It is said that Lenny entertained young ladies in the flat – according to the porters very young ladies, who looked as though they might be the grand-daughters

> of the venerable old gentleman in black jacket, wing collar and sponge bag trousers.

His later life was clouded by the death of two of his children, a fire in the flat (said to have been caused by a candle used for illumination when the electricity had been cut off), and an enforced exile to Hollywood when the creditors closed in.[160]

More prosaically, the Square was also home to a number of senior public servants. One of the most pioneering was Dame Katherine Watt, a leading nurse and civil servant. When the war began she was seconded to the Ministry of Health, helping to set up the emergency hospital service. She became the first nurse to be appointed to a permanent post within the civil service when taking up the post of Chief Nursing Officer in 1941. Here she was actively involved in planning for the National Health Service, acting as an adviser from 1948 to 1950. She first rented a furnished flat, 204 Beatty House, and then moved to 708 Grenville House.[161] Sir Donald Fergusson, who lived in 608 Frobisher House from 1945, and later in 411 Rodney House, had been Permanent Secretary at the Ministry of Agriculture, 1936–45, where he directed the food production campaign. As Permanent-Secretary of the newly-constituted Ministry of Fuel and Power, 1945–52, he presided over the nationalisation of coal, electricity and gas. After his retirement he became a director of Costain, from 1957 to 1962.[162] Air Vice-Marshal Sir Conrad Collier was the tenant of 901 Collingwood House from 1947 to 1962. He had a distinguished record with the RAF in both world wars and was subsequently Director-General of Technical Services in the Ministry of Civil Aviation.[163] General Sir Robert Mansergh, of 901 Nelson House, was Deputy Commander-in-Chief of Allied Forces Northern Europe, 1951–3, then Commander-in-Chief, 1953–6. He had been awarded the Military Cross in 1932 while serving in Iraq.[164] Also deserving a mention are: Major Lyndall Urwick, management consultant, founder of Urwick Orr & Partners, and author, with Edward Brech, of the path breaking *The Making of Scientific Management* (1945–8);[165] Dr G.A.H. Elton, food scientist and subsequently Chief Scientific Adviser (Food) to the Ministry of Agriculture, Fisheries and Food;[166] and Phineas Quass, QC, one of the founders of the Institute for the Scientific Treatment of Delinquency (now the Centre for Crime and Justice Studies).[167]

Literature, the arts and the media were also represented. The novelist Angus Wilson knew Dolphin Square well, since his friends, the art historian Francis Wormald, and his wife Honoria, had moved into 506 Beatty House during the war when their flat in Bloomsbury was bombed. In 1948, with Honoria's help, he took a lease on 07 Frobisher House, a one-room flat. His biographer, Margaret Drabble, noted that the lease was dated 24 December 1948 and the rent was £112 a year. Here, she said, Angus, who regarded the Square as 'the height of chic', obtained 'peace, privacy and independence'[168] [Illustration 20 (iii)]. Other writers were early residents, including C.P. Snow and Harry Hoff. Snow was not only a novelist - best known for his *Strangers and Brothers* sequence of novels - but was also a successful civil servant and government minister.[169] Hoff, his former student and friend, wrote under the name William Cooper, and was the author of the comic novels *Scenes From Provincial Life* (1950) and *Scenes from Married Life* (1961). He rented 104 Grenville House with his wife Joyce.[170] Later on, in 1952, Angus Wilson and his partner Tony Garrett also moved into a flat in Grenville House, where the rent was £142 a year. This was given up in August 1959, since Wilson was spending more time in Suffolk. But his time in Pimlico was a fertile period in which he wrote *Hemlock and After* (1952), *Anglo-Saxon Attitudes* (1956), and *The Middle Age of Mrs Eliot* (1958).[171] Harold (later Sir Harold) Hobson, the distinguished drama critic, lived with his wife Elizabeth in 901 Grenville House from 1949, and later in 905/6 Nelson. He was long-serving contributor to both the *Christian Science Monitor* (1931–74) and the *Sunday Times* (1947–76), championing emerging playwrights such as Pinter, Osborne and Beckett. In his autobiography he listed as one of his pleasures 'playing bridge with friends in Dolphin Square'. After his wife died, he married Nancy Penhale in 1981. She was a pre-war tenant of Drake House, and a post-war resident of Howard House; they lived in Nelson House until 1986.[172] Then there was Quentin Crewe, the writer and journalist, notably with the *Evening Standard* and *Queen*, who lived briefly in 806 Hawkins House.[173] The racing driver Donald Campbell was also a resident, of 805 Duncan House. Like his father, Sir Malcolm Campbell, he attacked the world's speed records on land and water, but died in a crash on Coniston Water in 1967. Morris, in his history of the Square, reports that Campbell was superstitious about the number of his flat, and asked for it to be changed to No. 811. His request was granted, but he did not stay there long.[174] Less well-known was William Trotter of the BBC. Nonetheless, he attracted the attention of the *Daily Mirror* in June 1949 when he held a large Spanish party which spilled over into the Spanish garden [Illustration 27].[175]

Proximity to the West End also drew actors and entertainers to the Square. Among them was Jimmy Nervo, the acrobat and comedian, who achieved fame – first with Nervo and Knox and then as a member of The Crazy Gang (1931–62). He lived in 902 Raleigh House from 1949, and in 1953 he and his wife Minna, a dancer, moved to 509 Hood House.[176] They were later joined in Dolphin Square by Bud Flanagan and his wife Ann, who lived in 503 Raleigh House from 1957. Flanagan, a member of the Crazy Gang, was one of Britain's leading comedian-singers, famous for his double act with Chesney Allen.[177] Another major entertainer was the musician and comedian, Vic Oliver, who, after the failure of his marriage to the actress Sarah Churchill, married Dolphin Square resident Natalie Conder, in 1946. They lived in 807 Howard House and later in 103 Nelson House.[178] The comedians Arthur Askey and Tommy Trinder, and the character actor, Thorley Walters, all lived in the Square in the 1950s.[179] Roy Plomley, the radio broadcaster who devised the long-running Desert Island Discs, was also a resident, living in 507 Hawkins House with his wife, the actress Diana Wong from 1947. He presented Desert Island Discs from 1942 until shortly before his death in 1985. In fact, Vic Oliver was his first castaway.[180] Nat Temple, the clarinettist, bandleader and broadcaster, and his wife Freda occupied 409 Hawkins House in 1948, and moved to 02 Drake House in 1950. The flat was subsequently acquired by Jack Hylton Ltd. in 1958. Temple enjoyed a career stretching over 70 years, and was surely the last of the great showmen bandleaders and broadcasters.[181] Much of Susan Hampshire's childhood, which was clouded by dyslexia, was spent in Dolphin Square. The actress, famous as 'Fleur' in the BBC's *The Forsyte Saga*, lived in 903 Raleigh House with her mother, Jane Hampshire, and her sisters, Jane and Ann, from 1946.[182] Of course there were others, some of them obscured by the use of non-stage names. For example, in the electoral register for 1951 we find the following persons listed in 807 Howard House: 'De Greefe, Dorothy I.; Hill, Alan'. It requires some detective work to discover that they are Chili Bouchier, star of the silent screen in the 1920s and an actress until 1990, and Bluey Hill, an Australian film director. Chili had moved into a furnished flat in Dolphin Square, having left her second husband Edward, known as Peter, de Greef. She quickly discovered that an old flame, Bluey Hill, was a neighbour. As she put it, in characteristically florid fashion, in one of her autobiographies, 'almost the first person I encountered at the bus stop was a fellow-tenant, my old Aussie sunshine-face – Bluey!' They soon moved into a single flat, in his name, and were enduring residents of Dolphin Square.[183]

If the war provided the beginning of serious difficulties for Costain as a property manager, Britain's austerity period certainly continued them. The extension of rent control into peacetime made it much more difficult for the company to return a profit on Dolphin Square while costs were rising, but revenues were more or less fixed. Until 1957 the rents of controlled properties were frozen at their 1939 level but prices were 74 per cent higher in July 1945 and 97 per cent higher by 1951.[184] On top of this, furnished properties were also subject to control from 1946. An Act in that year provided a system of protection modelled on Scottish precedent, and involving rent tribunals charged with determining reasonable rents. At least two Dolphin Square flats were the subject of hearings at the new tribunals in 1947.[185] The Chairman and Managing Director of the parent company, Richard R. Costain, made frequent reference to the problem of rent control at successive annual general meetings.[186] In April 1947, reporting on the year 1946, he pointed out that the Rent Restriction Act precluded the raising of rents to meet increased costs. In May 1949, commenting on a slight fall in gross profits for 1948, he attributed the primary cause of this to 'the reduction in profits of your subsidiary Dolphin Square Ltd', which were 'wholly inadequate in relation to the value of the property'. The problems could only be resolved, he maintained, when 'Parliament agrees to give landlords a fair deal'.[187] He reported in similar terms two years later, when reviewing the results for 1950. The operation of the Rent Acts, he said, constituted 'an increasing burden on property owners'.[188] Further complaints followed. At the company's AGM in July 1954 the Chairman, now Sir Richard Costain, had to field a question about the future of the Square, and was quick to emphasise that no negotiations had taken place to sell it. The company, he said, 'would be very reluctant to have to do so, if they could continue to receive a fair return on their investment'. Unfortunately, in the immediate past the profits had been 'little more than sufficient to meet the sinking fund'.[189] There was some amelioration for landlords from the Housing Repairs and Rents Act of 1954, which allowed them to make a 'repairs increase' when properties were in good order. However, Costain maintained that this made only a marginal difference to the economics of housing management.[190] The breakthrough came at last in 1957 when the Rent Act in that year decontrolled all houses with a rateable value above £40 in London and Scotland and £30 elsewhere. No new tenancies were to be controlled unless they were granted to a tenant who was a controlled tenant of the same premises.[191] In Sir Richard's report to the AGM in June 1957 he expressed the view that the new Act would enable the company to secure a 'fair economic return' on its properties.[192]

Given this statement of intent, it came as something of a shock when the company announced, in November 1958, that it had agreed to sell Dolphin Square to the property developer and hotelier, Maxwell Joseph.[193] The reasons for the change of policy are set out in the next chapter, but it is clear that Costain's withdrawal represented a major change of direction for Dolphin Square and its tenants.

NOTES

1 Costain, *Development*, 1, n.d. [1937].

2 One five-room flat - 903 Grenville - was offered at £465 p.a.

3 Dolphin Square register of leases, 1937, DST. 902 Frobisher and 01 Collingwood were discounted by £25, representing a reduction in rental of 12.5% and 16.66% respectively.

4 Two-room flats were offered at £113 p.a. in October 1937 and February 1938, but at £120 p.a. in May and September 1938. See advertisements in *The Dolphin*.

5 *Financial Times*, 31 March 1939, p.5. The rate books suggest that Duncan in particular was not fully let: WCC Rate Book No.5, ½-year ending 30 September 1939, WCA.

6 David George Brownlow Cecil, The Lord Burghley, 6th Marquess of Exeter (1905–81), MP for Peterborough, 1931–43, Governor of Bermuda, 1943–5, and a director of the London & North Eastern Railway and the National Provincial Bank. Michael Stenton and Stephen Lees (eds.), *Who's Who of British Members of Parliament*, III (Brighton, 1979); Norris McWhirter, 'David George Brownlow Cecil', *OxDNB*.

7 Lord Frederick Cambridge (1907–40), son of Prince Adolphus, the Duke of Teck, subs. 1st Marquess of Cambridge; killed in action, May 1940.

8 Mark Everard Pepys, 6th Earl of Cottenham (1903–43): driver for Alvis, Sunbeam and Talbot, author of *Motoring Without Fears* (1928) and *Steering-Wheel Papers* (1932), adviser to the Metropolitan Police Motor Driving School, 1937. *Times*, 21 July 1943, p.7; thePeerage.com; David Gilbert, file note on 'The Earl of Cottenham', Brooklands Museum, Weybridge. On his MI5 activities see Joan Miller, *One Girl's War: Personal Exploits in MI5's Most Secret Station* (Dingle, Co. Kerry, 1986), p.13.

9 Cdr Charles Maurice Elton Gifford, Lord Gifford (1899–1961) was Chairman and MD of Theatre Tickets and Messengers Ltd. and Ashton & Mitchell. *The Times*, 17 April 1961, p.15; thePeerage.com.

10 William Francis Hare, 5th Earl of Listowel, PC, GCMG (1906–97), Labour Chief Whip, 1941–4, Postmaster-General, 1945–7, Secretary of State for India and Burma, 1947, Minister for the Colonies, 1948–50, Governor-General of Ghana, 1951–60. George Ireland, 'William Francis Hare', *OxDNB*.

11 Percival Lee Dewhurst, Lord Perry of Stock Harvard (1878–1956), worked for Ford Motor Co. (England), 1911–19, was Chairman of Ford Motor Co. (UK), 1928–48, and author of *Island of Enchantment* (1926) and *International Balance of Trade* (1932). Richard Davenport-Hines, 'Percival Lee Dewhurst Perry', *OxDNB*.

12 June Hannam, 'Ethel Snowden', *OxDNB*. Only Lord Burghley and Lord Gifford are listed in Appendix 1. The Earl of Halsbury replaced Walker in 602 Nelson in July 1937, while the others moved into the North Block and are listed in the St. George's Westminster electoral register for October 1938 and/or 1939, WCA.

13 Beatrice, Lady Clarke-Jervoise (wife of Sir Harry Cumming Clarke-Jervoise), Sir Stanley Cochrane (1877–1949), Hon. George Cunliffe, Hon. V. Edith Harris, Josephine and Ruth Higham, both former wives of the advertising agent Sir Charles Frederick Higham, Baroness R. Hornstein, Sir Charles Louis, Ethel Lady Mackenzie; Mary, Lady Marston, Dorothy Beatrice Rothschild, and Hon. Bernard Elliot Yorke.

14 Lt Col. Allen Bathurst, The Lord Apsley, was MP for Southampton (1923–9) and Bristol Central (1931–42); Violet Bathurst, The Lady Apsley, was MP for Bristol Central (1943–5). *Who's Who of British Members of Parliament*, III; G.E. Maguire, 'Violet Emily Mildred Bathurst', *OxDNB*.

15 MP for South Salford (1910–23). He was Minister of Labour, 1922–4. *Who's Who of British Members of Parliament*, III.

16 Sir Eric Errington (1900–73), Conservative MP for Bootle 1935–45, Aldershot, 1954–70. *Who's Who of British Members of Parliament,* IV.

17 MP for Cardiff South (1923–4, 1929–31), Kingswinford (1935–50), Rowley Regis & Tipton (1950–66), then was created Baron Rowley. He was Financial Secretary, War Office, 1943–5, Secretary of State for Air, 1947–51. *Who's Who of British Members of Parliament,* IV.

18 MP for Watford (1918–43), then created Baron Hemingford. He was the Deputy Speaker, 1931–42. *Who's Who of British Members of Parliament,* III.

19 Former Liberal; MP for Newcastle-under-Lyme (1906–42), then was created Baron Wedgwood. *Who's Who of British Members of Parliament,* III.

20 Greenwood (1880–1954) was MP for Nelson and Colne (1922–31), and Wakefield (1932–54). He was Minister of Health, 1929–31, Labour's Deputy Leader, 1935–45, Minister without Portfolio, 1940–2, Lord Privy Seal, 1945–7, Paymaster General 1946–7. R.C. Whiting, 'Arthur Greenwood', *OxDNB*; *Who's Who of British Members of Parliament,* IV; St. George's Westminster electoral register for October 1939.

21 Stefan Lorant (1901–97), born in Budapest, film-maker and photojournalist, who had fled from Germany's Nazi regime, did not have British citizenship and emigrated to the US in 1940. He lived in 804 Frobisher (Appendix 1). See Michael Hallett, 'Stefan Lorant [István Reich]', *OxDNB*; *Independent,* 17 November 1997, p.16, *Guardian,* 17 November 1997, p.15. Morris, *Dolphin Square,* p.107, states that Felix H. Man, *Picture Post* photographer, also lived in Dolphin Square.

22 John Stewart, 'Edith Clara Summerskill', *OxDNB*.

23 Frances Lady Ryder CBE (1888–1965) was the daughter of the 5th Earl of Harrowby.

24 *The Dolphin,* 19 (December 1938), pp.12–13, WCA 2518/21.

25 Clementine Mabell Freeman-Mitford (1915–2005), married Sir Alfred Beit in 1939.

26 Lease register, supplemented by information in the St. George's Westminster electoral registers for October 1938 and 1939, WCA.

27 Morris, *Dolphin Square,* p.108, and see Appendix 1. Murphy was succeeded by Dr Manuel Ferris in 1956.

28 Lease register, supplemented by information in the St. George's Westminster electoral register, October 1937, WCA.

29 Una, Lady Troubridge, *The Life and Death of Radclyffe Hall* (1961), p.190; Richard Ormrod, *Una Troubridge: The Friend of Radclyffe Hall* (1984), p.269, 272; Michael Baker, *Our Three Selves: The Life of Radclyffe Hall* (1985), pp.341–9 and 'Marguerite Antonia Radclyffe-Hall', *OxDNB*. Lady Troubridge moved to Lincoln's Inn early in 1944, but for some reason remained on the electoral register for Hood House in 1945 and 1946.

30 WCC Rate Book No.5, ½-year ending 30 September 1943, WCA. Morrison's biographers reject the idea of an affair: Bernard Donoughue and George W. Jones, *Herbert Morrison: Portrait of a Politician* (1973), p.392.

31 *South Wales Post,* 19 October 1940, *Manchester Guardian,* 18 November 1940, Ellen Wilkinson's press cuttings book, Labour History Archive, People's Museum, Manchester, LP/WI/5. Labour Party correspondence indicates that Wilkinson moved to 607 Hood in 1946: Morgan Phillips (General Secretary, Labour Party)-Wilkinson, 27 February 1946, Labour History Archive LP/GS/NEC/39.

32 *Evening News,* 6 February 1947, *The Times,* 11 February 1947, in ibid. and see Betty D. Vernon, *Ellen Wilkinson 1891–1947* (1982), p.233; Beverly Parker Stobaugh, *Women and Parliament 1918–1970* (Hicksville, NY, 1978), p.30; Brian Harrison, 'Ellen Cicely Wilkinson', *OxDNB*. She was also the author of *Clash* (1929) and *The Division Bell Mystery* (1932).

33 Ida Cook (1904–86), Louise Cook (1901–91). See Ida Cook, *We Followed Our Stars* (1950), republished as *Safe Passage: The remarkable true story of British sisters who rescued Jews from the Nazis* (Richmond, 1976 and 2008).

34 Cook, *We Followed Our Stars*, pp.120–1.

35 Ibid. p.133.

36 Puzzlingly, Mary Kewley is listed in the electoral register for 1938 and 1939, Beatrice Derrick and Cecilia and Nesta Guthrie in 1945, and Grace Baxter and Frances Ryder in 1948. St. George's Westminster electoral registers, 1938–48, Cities of London and Westminster electoral registers, 1951–5, WCA. The rate books indicate that Ida took the flat back from Ms Kewley in March 1940, though others were often in residence thereafter: WCC Rate Book No.5, ½-year ending 31 March 1940, WCA.

37 Rebecca A. Pope and Susan J. Leonardi, 'Ida Cook', *OxDNB*; Louise Carpenter, 'Ida and Louise', *Granta*, 98 (Summer 2007), 49–83; Susan Rosenbluth, *Jewish Voice & Opinion*, December 2008; dd.librarything.com

38 *The Times*, 7 March 1938, p.23. The 1937 lease register shows Mrs P. Linney as the tenant of 905 Frobisher House.

39 *The Times*, 19 October 1938, p.7.

40 In Holden Estates Ltd. and Walter Travis (debenture holders) v. the General Mortgage Society (Great Britain).

41 *The Times*, 3 March 1938, p.4, 27 May 1938, p.13, 20 November 1943, p.6; John Tribe, 'Peerage and MP ledger: the 2nd Earl of Halsbury', 26 April 2010, http://www.jordansinsolvencylaw.co.uk/articles/peerage-and-mp-ledger-the-2nd-earl-of-halsbury-barrister-recorder-of-carmarthen-and-bankrupt.

42 *The Times*, 7 December 1938, p.6. Margaret Lockwood (1916–90) starred in films such as *The Lady Vanishes* and *The Wicked Lady*.

43 *The Times*, 11 March 1937, p.11.

44 *The Times*, 30 June 1939, p.12, 6 September 1939, p.7, 12 September 1939, p.4. There were also short letters from Douglas Goldring, of 03 Frobisher, on Croom's Hill Greenwich, and Howard Wilkins, of 502 Beatty, on the selection of a seaplane base: *The Times*, 18 January 1939, p.8, 13 March 1939, p.10.

45 *Economist*, 24 August 1946, p.294, 26 July 1947, p.148, 13 November 1948, p.790. Both Smyth and King-Hall also wrote to *The Times*, e.g. 25 November 1946, p.5, 12 February 1947, p.5, 22 March 1947, p.7, and 17 November 1949, p.5.

46 *The Times*, 16 April 1937, p.17.

47 *The Times*, 12 March 1938, p.15, 6 April 1938, p.17, 16 October 1938, p.5.

48 Herbert, *Dolphin Square*.

49 Costain, *Dolphin Square*, 1936, p.7.

50 *Dorset Daily Echo*, 5 October 1936, *Banffshire Advertiser*, 8 and 15 October 1936, *Gloucester Citizen* and *Grimsby Evening Telegraph*, both 26 November 1936, *Daily Telegraph*, 27 November 1936, *Sunday Times*, 29 November 1936, from Costain, Dolphin Square Cuttings Book, 1936, DST.

51 Costain, *Dolphin Square*, 1936, p. In the South Block rentals brochure, 'half a minute' became 'two minutes': Costain, Rentals and Accommodation, 1936.

52 Costain, *Dolphin Square*, 1936, p.4.

53 *The Dolphin*, 12 (May 1938), cover and pp.1–2; London Transport Bus Map, 11 June 1939, reprint. The 24, introduced in 1912, is one of the oldest unchanged bus routes in London. The 135 was supplementary to the 134, which ran from Potters Bar to Victoria from 1934.

54 Costain, Rentals and Accommodation, 1936.

55 Faber, *Oscar Faber*, pp.49–50; *The Dolphin*, 5 (October 1937), p.3.

56 Maple & Co., invoice and receipt, 11 and 18 May 1937, DST.

57 *The Dolphin*, 5 (October 1937), p.1.

58 *The Dolphin*, 5 (October 1937), pp.6–7.

59 *The Dolphin*, 9 (February 1938), pp.12–13. The electoral register for October 1939 lists Eric Lane at 06 Collingwood, and Neville Lavington at 205 Raleigh.

60 John Stroud, *The Imperial Airways Fleet* (Stroud, 2005), pp.125–9, Robert Bluffield, Imperial Airways: The Birth of the British Airline Industry 1914–1940 (Hersham, 2009), pp.86, 178–82, Arthur W.J.G. Ord-Hume, *Imperial Airways: From Early Days to BOAC* (Catrine, 2010), pp.98. The 'piggy-back' concept was of course deployed in the Americans' space shuttle programme.

61 *The Dolphin*, 10 (March 1938), pp.12–13, 16.

62 *The Dolphin* 12 (May 1938), pp.12–13.

63 Berger was also the author of *Famous Faces* (1950), *Aesop's Foibles* (1951) and *A la Carte* (1951). *The Dolphin*, 4 (September 1937), pp.6, 216, WCA 2518/19; Mark Bryant and Simon Heneage, *Dictionary of British Cartoonists and Caricaturists 1730–1980* (Aldershot, 1994), p.20.

64 *The Dolphin*, 16 (September 1938), pp.8–9, 16.

65 *The Dolphin*, 19 (December 1938), pp.12–13, 16, WCA 2518/21.

66 *The Dolphin*, 3 (July 1937), pp.10–12, 16, WCA 2518/18.

67 *The Dolphin*, 5 (October 1937), pp.14–16.

68 *The Dolphin*, 10 (March 1938), pp.4–5.

69 *The Dolphin*, 9 (February 1938), pp.12–13.

70 *The Dolphin*, 12 (May 1938), pp.3, 14–15.

71 *Dolphin Square for your especial convenience*, brochure, n.d. [1937].

72 *The Dolphin*, 9 (February 1938), pp.1, 10 (March 1938), p.3.

73 *The Dolphin*, 5 (October 1937), p.16.

74 Prices taken from *Dolphin Square for your especial convenience* [1937], and *Dolphin Square for your especial convenience*, handbook, n.d. [1938], WCA 2518/4 and 5; Dolphin Square, Note on Shoe Cleaning, n.d., Squash Brochure, May 1937, Garage Service, n.d. [1937], Dolphin Laundry service, n.d., Restaurant Dinner Menus, 23 January 1937, WCA 2518/7–12.

75 Non-residents were charged 3s. for lunch and 4s. 6d. for dinner.

76 Professional lessons cost 4s. (6s. for guests).

77 John Burnett, *A History of the Cost of Living* (Harmondsworth, 1969), pp.298–301.

78 *The Times*, 9 September 1937, p.1, 14 September 1937, p.1; *The Dolphin*, 5 (October 1937), p.2.

79 Isdell-Carpenter (708 Frobisher), Haines (501 Grenville), Goulston (510 Rodney), Walker (706 Frobisher), Renwick (302 Frobisher), Aris (902 Raleigh), Bankes (106 Collingwood) and Burton (409 Nelson); *The Times*, 28 February 1938, p.1–10 August 1939, p.1.

80 *The Dolphin*, 5 (October 1937), p.16.

81 *The Times*, 13 May 1939, p.17.

82 *The Times*, 22 May 1939, p.15; St. George's Westminster electoral register, October 1939, WCA. *The Times* recorded 11 other engagements and marriages before the war.

83 *The Times*, 22 December 1938, p.1. Elsa Wall was the first tenant (Appendix 1), and the electoral registers for 1937–9 list Elsa and Moira Wall.

84 *The Times*, 28 August 1939, p.7; 22 October 1938, p.9.

85 *The Dolphin*, 1 (May 1937), pp.4–5; Costain, *Reflections*, pp.49–50; Morris, *Dolphin Square*, p.29.

86 Morris, *Dolphin Square*, p.61. The 1962 sale document also identifies Mrs H. Sampson as a former employee: Goddard & Smith et al., Sale documents for Dolphin Square, 1962, DST.

87 Information from General Manager's Report, November 1964, p.12, DST.

88 *The Dolphin*, 1 (May 1937)-19 (December 1938), *passim*.

89 *Melody Maker*, 18 December 1937, pp.1, 3.

90 The staffing complement was 194 in 1964: General Manager's Report, November 1964, p.11, DST.

91 *The Dolphin*, 9 (February 1938), p.5.

92 This was something of an exaggeration. In most houses, the maximum no. of flats per floor was either 11 or 12. Only in Rodney House, floors 2–6, were there 27 flats.

93 *The Dolphin*, 12 (May 1938), p.6.

94 Rose was killed on 11th September. *The Times*, 13 September 1939, p.1, 9 October 1939, p.4.

95 Michael Gammidge (905 Beatty), John Cronhelm, David Braham (904 Collingwood), James Masters: *The Times*, 6 June 1940, p.9–9 January 1941, p.1.

96 *The Times*, 22 November 1939, p.16.

97 *The Times*, 24 October 1939, p.1, 26 January 1940, p.16. £6 6s. was being charged for two-room flats in 1936–7.

98 *The Times*, 27 October 1939, p.5. The depot was visited by the Mayor, Mayoress and Corporation of Westminster on 26 October.

99 Clerk, LCC-Secretary, Dolphin Square Ltd., 10 December 1940, LMA GLC/AR/BR/07/2787.

100 *The Times*, 22 August 1940, p.7, 29 August 1940, p.7.

101 *The Times*, 23 April 1940, p.1, 3 May 1940, p.1, 10 June 1940, p.9. Roy Bird, MP for Skipton from 1924, died in 1933.

102 Jan Prebble, *Wartime in Dolphin Square* (2010), p.7.

103 Westminster Civil Defence records, permanent record book of bombing incidents, WCA CD3/441. The initial report – CD3/441 – indicated '34 approx' casualties; the figure of 58 comes from the situation reports, 1940–5, report at 06.00 hrs, 23 September 1940, WCA CD17.

104 *Westminster & Pimlico News*, 27 September 1940, p.3; *Evening News*, 23 September 1940, p.1, confirmed in Lionel McColvin (Westminster City Librarian), *The War in Westminster: Report of the City Council's Civil Defence and Related Services* (10 July 1945), WCA CD215. Prebble quotes the views of Sir Albert Costain and Harry Bailey, the Square's foreman plumber, that the casualties occurred because the local authority had insisted that its shelter be reinforced: *Wartime in Dolphin Square*, p.7.

105 Westminster Civil Defence records, incident form, 5 November 1940, WCA CD1/897, permanent record book, WCA CD3/897, situation reports, 1940–5, WCA CD17; *Westminster & Pimlico News*, 8 November 1940, p.3. It seems that 80 flats were blown out. See also Miller, *One Girl's War*, p.56.

106 Westminster Civil Defence records, permanent record book, WCA CD3/1258, 1263, situation reports, 1940–5, WCA CD17; Prebble, *Wartime in Dolphin Square*, p.13. Later, the no. of deaths was reported to be 148, with 564 injured: *War in Westminster*, WCA CD215.

107 Westminster Civil Defence records, permanent record book, WCA CD3/1440.

108 Cf. Prebble, *Wartime in Dolphin Square*, pp.6, 14, and her *Square Tales: A short history of Dolphin Square*, n.d. p.7.

109 Westminster Civil Defence records, Analysis of bombs, casualties, alerts, 1940–4, WCA CD20, and *War in Westminster*, WCA CD215.

110 *The Times*, 4 October 1946, p.6.

111 Some of Knight's biographical details are rather uncertain, and not all sources agree. See Anthony Masters, *The Man Who Was M: The Life of Maxwell Knight* (Oxford, 1984); Miller, *One Girl's War*; Eric Homberger, 'Charles Henry Maxwell Knight', *OxDNB*; Christopher Andrew, *Secret Service* (1985), pp.334–5, 368–75 and his *The Defence of the Realm: The Authorized History of MI5* (2009), pp.123–32, 221, 902n; Gill Bennett, *Churchill's Man of Mystery: Desmond Morton and the World of Intelligence* (Abingdon, 2007), pp.72–3, 128–33, 338; Gordon Thomas, *Secret Wars: One Hundred Years of British Intelligence Inside MI5 and MI6* (New York, 2009), pp.83–4.

112 Miller, *One Girl's War*, pp.45–6. Recent work casts doubt on Miller's testimony, and in particular her assertions about Knight's homosexuality and the death of his first wife: Bryan Clough, *State Secrets: The Kent-Wolkoff Affair* (Hove, 2005), pp.7, 26, 33–4.

113 Lois's brother, Anthony Drake Coplestone, is listed in the Westminster Rate Books and St. George's Westminster electoral registers for 1938–9, WCA. Masters states erroneously that the flat was *308* Hood, while Andrew is wrong to suggest that the flat was held in *Miss* Coplestone's name: Masters, *Man Who Was M*, p.78; Andrew, *Secret Service*, p.368.

114 Miller, *One Girl's War*, pp.48–9, 56–7; Masters, *Man Who Was M*, p.79. Miller claimed to be Knight's mistress, though she admitted that their relationship was not consummated.

115 Miller, *One Girl's War*, p.56; Prebble, *Wartime in Dolphin Square*, p.24. Masters suggests that Dolphin Square was a convenient base for Knight because it was close to the 'highly suspect' Anglo-German Information Service in Parliament St.: *Man Who Was M*, p.69.

116 Masters, *Man Who Was M*, p.65.

117 WCC Rate Book No.5, 1939–44, and in particular ½-year ending 30 September 1943, and St. George's Westminster electoral register for October 1939, WCA.

118 Maxwell Knight, 'Report on the Work of M.S. (Agents) During the War 1939–1945', 4 April 1945, pp.7–8, 30, 42–8, TNA KV4/227; Andrew, *Defence of the Realm*, pp.179–80, 221, 224–6; Richard Griffiths, *Patriotism Perverted: Captain Ramsay, The Right Club and British Anti-Semitism 1939–40* (1998), pp.142, 254, 258ff; Clough, *State Secrets*.

119 WCC Rate Book No.5, ½-year ending 31 March 1940, WCA; *The Times*, 24 May 1940, p.6; Prebble, p.26. It has been suggested that the Kent-Wolkoff affair was an MI5 'sting', used by hardliners within the Secret Service to press for the wider internment of fascists and others: Ann Rogers, *Secrecy and Power in the British State* (1997), pp.40–2; Clough, *State Secrets*, pp.127, 256. Sir Oswald Mosley and his wife retained their Dolphin Square flats until March 1951: WCC Rate Book No.5, year ending 31 March 1951, WCA.

120 His crime novels were *Crime Cargo* (1934) and *Gunmen's Holiday* (1935).

121 Knight gave up 02/03 Keyes in 1947 and 315/16 Rodney in 1950. He also rented 502/3 Howard briefly in 1945–6. WCC Rate Book No.5, years ending 31 March 1946, 1948, 1951 and 1964, WCA.

122 Committee on Foreign (Allied) Resistance, Memo. to War Cabinet on 'Organisation of the Free French Movement', 11 March 1941, TNA FO371/28457; Sir Edward Spears, *Two Men who Saved France* (1966), p.140.

123 Cf. Aidan Crawley, *de Gaulle* (1969), p.145; Charles Williams, *The Last Great Frenchman: A Life of General de Gaulle* (1993), pp.135, 171, 206. An exception is Serge Vaculik, *Air Commando* (1954), p.133.

124 WCC Rate Book No.5, ½-year ending 30 September 1942, WCA.

125 See reference to 'Free French Forces 05 Grenville 29/1/41–31/3/41': WCC Rate Book No.5, ½-year ending 31 March 1943, WCA.

126 Vaculik, *Air Commando*, p.133. My thanks to Adrian Wray for this reference.

127 Morris, *Dolphin Square*, p.48; Prebble, *Wartime in Dolphin Square*, p.20.

128 WCC Rate Book No.5, ½-years ending 30 September 1942, 31 March and 30 September 1943, WCA.

129 *The Times*, 23 July 1942, p.7, 17 September 1942, p.2, 8 October 1942, p.2, 5 February 1945, p.7; *British Imperial Calendar and Civil Service List*, 1945.

130 St. George's Westminster electoral registers for October 1939 and August 1946, WCA. Both Mrs Brecknell and Mrs Gallop were Dolphin Square residents until the 1990s. Gallop's post-July 1940 account was published in the Tenants Association Newsletter in 1987, and is reproduced in Morris, *Dolphin Square*, pp.49–53. She also wrote letters to *The Times*: see 27 May 1943, p.5, 2 October 1946, p.5.

131 Morris, *Dolphin Square*, p.49; Prebble, *Wartime in Dolphin Square*, p.19; *The Times*, 29 April 1988, p.16; Sir Edward Lewis, *No CIC* (1956), pp.82–5; Louis Barfe, *Where Have All the Good Times Gone? The rise and fall of the record industry* (2004), p.148; Jerry Proc, 'Decca Navigator history', 2008, jproc.ca/hyperbolic/decca; Terry Gourvish, 'The Giants of the British Music Industry: Chandlerian or not?', mss.

132 Costain Group, *Bulletin*, 1965, 19; Morris, *Dolphin Square*, p.47; Prebble, *Wartime in Dolphin Square*, p.20. Col. [later Brigadier] Bonn was a director of Richard Costain from 1933 to 1960.

133 Marjorie Gallop, 'Dolphin Square in the Blitz', in Morris, *Dolphin Square*, p.52, and Prebble, *Wartime in Dolphin Square*, p.21.

134 In fact, seven were killed.

135 This fatality is not evident from the civil defence records.

136 Wedgwood's maid.

137 Battersea.

138 Dolphin Square staff.

139 His son, Josiah.

140 'Copy of a letter from Father. 19.10.40 during the Blitz . . .', Second World War correspondence of J.C. Wedgwood, Imperial War Museum archives, PP/MCR/104.

141 Costain, *R & A, 1940–2*, Guildhall Library.

142 Costain Group, *Bulletin*, 1965, 19; *Financial Times*, 26 April 1945, p.4.

143 Richard A. Sabatino, 'Rent Control Policy in Great Britain', *Land Economics*, 30:1 (1954), 61–2; Paul N. Balchin, *Housing Policy: An Introduction* (2nd edn, 1985), pp.112–113. Rent control had been an enduring policy of governments since the First World War. The first Act was the Increase of Rent and Mortgage Interest (War Restrictions) Act of 1915, which applied to dwellings with rateable values of up to £35 in London, £30 in Scotland and £26 elsewhere. Control was extended in peacetime by an Act of 1920, which increased the rateable value limits to £105 in London, £90 in Scotland and £78 elsewhere.

144 The 1938 Act had decontrolled all houses with rateable values above £35 in London. In Dolphin Square there were 151 flats in 1939 with RVs below £35. Average RVs were £48.57 in Grenville, £50.94 in Grenville, and £68.53 in Drake: WCC Rate Book No.5, ½-year ending 30 September 1939, WCA.

145 Ibid. The 22 double flats were also valued above £100.

146 See WCC Rate Book No.5, ½-years ending 30 September 1942 and 31 March 1943, WCA.

147 Cf. Stella Brecknell, quoted in Morris, *Dolphin Square*, p.48.

148 London Transport bus map no.2, 1947.

149 L. Burdet (Catering Director, Dolphin Square Ltd.)-Clerk, LCC, 13 August 1947, Clerk, LCC-Secretary, Dolphin Square Ltd., 3 October 1947 and 15 July 1949, LMA GLC/AR/BR/07/2787.

150 *The Times*, 19 January 1948, p.6, 6 March 1948, p.6.

151 Ina Zweiniger-Bargielowska, *Austerity in Britain: Rationing, Controls, and Consumption, 1939–1955* (Oxford, 2000), p.24.

152 Michael Sissons and Philip French (eds.), *The Age of Austerity 1945–51* (1963), and see also David Kynaston, *Austerity Britain 1945–51* (2007).

153 Sir Hartley Shawcross (1902-2003) was Labour MP for St. Helens, 1945-58, briefly President of the Board of Trade (1951), and Chairman of the Bar Council, 1954-7. He became Baron Shawcross in 1959 and was a director of several companies, including Ford, Rank Hovis McDougall and Thames Television. Michael Beloff, 'Hartley William Shawcross', *OxDNB*; Hartley Shawcross, *Life Sentence: The Memoirs of Lord Shawcross* (1995), p.78ff.; Masters, *Man Who Was M*, pp.108–9.

154 Lewis Silkin (1899-1972) was Labour MP for Peckham, 1936-50, Minister of Town and Country Planning, 1945-50, where he introduced the New Towns Act, 1946, the Town and Country Planning Act, 1947, and the National Parks and Access to the Countryside Act, 1949. He was ennobled in 1950. Richard Weight, 'Lewis Silkin', *OxDNB*. The Silkins rented 314 Rodney from 1953 and moved to 904 Collingwood in 1957.

155 Sir Geoffrey de Freitas (1913-82) was Labour MP for Nottingham Central, 1945-50, Lincoln, 1950-61, and Kettering, 1964-79, President, Council of Europe, 1966-9. *Who's Who of British Members of Parliament*, IV; Geoffrey and Helen de Freitas, *The Slighter Side of a long public life* (1985).

156 Brig. Smyth (1893-1983) was awarded the VC in 1915 and commanded the 17th Division in Burma (not without controversy). He was MP for Norwood, 1950-66 and received a knighthood in 1955. He was Parliamentary Secretary at the Ministry of Pensions, 1951-5, and lawn tennis correspondent for the *Sunday Times*, 1946-51, and *News of the World*, 1956-7, and first chairman of the Victoria Cross Association, 1956. He moved to 809 Beatty, then 807/8 Nelson. Cdr King-Hall (1893-1966) was MP for Ormskirk, 1939-45 and founder and hon. director of the Hansard Society. He became Baron King-Hall in 1966. *Who's Who of British Members of Parliament*, III and IV.

157 Sir Eric lived in 306 Nelson while MP for Bootle, 1935-45, then occupied 711 Howard while MP for Aldershot, 1954-70.

158 Cdr Charles Donaldson (1903-64) was Conservative MP for Roxburgh & Selkirk, 1951-5, Roxburgh, Selkirk & Peebles, 1955-64. *Who's Who of British Members of Parliament*, IV. He rented 107 Duncan in 1957, and moved to 502 Duncan in 1961.

159 George Pargiter (1897-1982) was MP for Spelthorne, 1945-50, Southall, 1950-66, then Baron Pargiter. *Who's Who of British Members of Parliament*, IV. He rented 01 Grenville in 1957 and moved to 305/6 Howard in 1958.

160 Leonard Plugge (1889-1981). Morris, *Dolphin Square*, pp.110-11; Michael Petheram, 'Leonard Frank Plugge', *OxDNB*.

161 Katherine Christie Watt (1886-1963) was Matron-in-chief, Air Ministry, 1930-8, and Chief Nursing Officer, Ministry of Health, 1941-8. E.J.C Scott, 'Dame Katherine Christie Watt', *OxDNB*. Watt rented 204 Beatty from 1950, then moved to 617 Rodney in 1955 and 708 Grenville in 1957.

162 Sir Donald Fergusson (1891-1963) was also a director of the Prudential after retirement. Costain, *R & A 1957, 1961*; *The Times*, 22 May 1953, p.13, 6 March 1963, p.12. Fergusson rented 608 Frobisher from 1946, then moved to 411 Rodney in 1951 and 409 Keyes in 1959.

163 Sir Alfred Conrad Collier (1895–1986), was Air Attaché in Moscow, 1934–7, Air Vice-Marshal and Deputy Air Officer Commanding-in-Chief Transport Command, 1943–6. At the Ministry of Civil Aviation he was Director-General of Technical Services, 1946–7, and Controller of Technical and Operational Services, 1947–8. www.rafweb.org/Biographies/Collier_AC.html.

164 General Sir Eric Carden Robert Mansergh, GCB KBE MC (1900–70) had been Commander, British Forces Hong Kong, 1949–51; his last position was Commander-in-Chief British Land Forces, 1956–9. www.generals.dk/general/Mansergh/Sir_Eric_Carden_Robert/GreatBritain.html.

165 Lyndall Urwick (1891–1983), 905 Collingwood, 1943–61. Richard Davenport-Hines, 'Lyndall Fownes Urwick', *OxDNB*; Edward Brech, Andrew Thomson and John F. Wilson, *Lyndall Urwick: Management Pioneer* (New York, 2010).

166 Dr G.A.H. Elton, 101 Howard, 1953–7. *New Scientist*, 29 November 1956, 28 May 1959.

167 Phineas Quass, OBE, QC (died 1961), 902 Drake, 1948–59. Emanuel Miller, 'Mr Phineas Quass', *British Journal of Criminology*, 2:2 (1961), 109–10.

168 Angus Wilson (1913–91), Kt 1980. Margaret Drabble, *Angus Wilson: A Biography* (1995), pp.113, 117–18, 143–4; Malcolm Bradbury, 'Sir Angus Frank Johnstone Wilson', *OxDNB*. Drabble states that the Wormalds moved to Dolphin Square in 1941, but the first mention of them in the rate books is in 1943. They moved to 906 Frobisher in 1949.

169 C.P. Snow (1905–80), Kt. 1957, Baron Snow (1964), PhD. 1929, Christ's College Cambridge, 1930–45, Ministry of Labour, 1940–4, Civil Service Commissioner, 1945–60, PS to Minister of Technology, 1964–6. Stanley Weintraub, 'Charles Percy Snow', *OxDNB*. His flat has not been identified.

170 Harry Hoff (1910–2002), novelist and civil servant, consultant to UK Atomic Energy Authority, 1958–72. D.J. Taylor, 'Harry Summerfield Hoff', *OxDNB*. Hoff rented 104 Grenville, 1952–8.

171 Ibid. pp.194–5, 256. Wilson's flat has not been identified, but was probably 404 Grenville, a furnished flat.

172 Hobson (1904–92). Michael Billington, 'Sir Harold Hobson', *OxDNB*; Harold Hobson, *Indirect Journey: An Autobiography* (1978), p.264; Morris, *Dolphin Square*, p.106. Penhale lived in 501 Drake, 1937–9 (Appendix 1), and from 1947 to 1981 in 705 Howard.

173 Quentin Crewe (1926–98). *Independent*, 16 November 1998. Crewe rented 806 Hawkins, 1958–60.

174 Donald Campbell (1921–67). H.G. Pitt, 'Donald Malcolm Campbell', *OxDNB*; Morris, *Dolphin Square*, p.111. On the renumbering see WCC Rate Book No.5, years ending 31 March 1958–60, WCA. Campbell rented the flat from 1956 to 1959.

175 *Daily Mirror*, 20 June 1949, p.7, cutting in DST. Trotter and his wife Vicenta lived first in 403 Duncan, then in 711 Keyes.

176 Jimmy Nervo (1897–1975) was the son of a circus owner and made his first solo appearance at the age of 12. His double act with Teddy Knox began in 1919. David Goldie, 'Jimmy Nervo', *OxDNB*; Maureen Owen, *The Crazy Gang: A Personal Reminiscence* (1986). Minna Nervo lived in the Square until 1991: Morris, *Dolphin Square*, p.106.

177 Bud Flanagan (1896–1968). Sid Colin and David Goldie, 'Bud Flanagan [Chaim Reuben Weintrop]', *OxDNB*. Flanagan rented 421 Rodney, 1955–7 before moving to 503 Raleigh.

178 Victor Oliver (von Samek) (1898–1964). Vic Oliver, *Mr Showbusiness* (1954). Oliver was married to Winston Churchill's daughter Sarah, 1936–45. She was married to Anthony Beauchamp, 1949–57, and lived in the Square in the early 1960s (see below, p.271). Natalie Conder rented 807 Howard, 1943–51. The tenancy of 103 Nelson is something of a puzzle. Vic Oliver is recorded as the tenant from 1957, but prior to that it was rented by 'Mrs P.L. Oliver'.

179 Arthur Askey, 08 Howard, 1957–65; Tommy Trinder, 602 Beatty, 1954–7; Thorley Walters (1913–91), 523 Rodney, 1943–7, 808 Keyes, 1947–91, appeared in numerous films, including *Two-Way Stretch* and *Carlton-Browne of the FO*, and in Sherlock Holmes and St. Trinian's films.

180 Roy Plomley (1914–85) rented 507 Hawkins until 1958. Richard Baker, 'Francis Roy Plomley', *OxDNB*.

181 Nat Temple (1913–2008), played with the Harry Roy Orchestra, 1931–40, then formed his own band, the Club Royal Orchestra, in 1947. Michael Freedland, *The Guardian*, 5 June 2008, p.35; *The Times*, 13 June 2008, p.70.

182 Susan Hampshire, *Susan's Story: An Autobiographical account of my struggle with words* (1981). Mrs Hampshire lived in 903 Raleigh until 1965.

183 Dorothy Irene Bouchier, aka Chili Bouchier (1909–99), was successful in both silent films (e.g. *Shooting Stars, Moulin Rouge*) and sound films (e.g. *Carnival, Gypsy*). She also enjoyed a long stage and TV career. See Chili Bouchier, *For Dogs and Angels: A true story of a love that survived the transition of death* (1967), pp.33, 45, and also *Shooting Star: The Last of the Silent Film Stars* (1996), pp.186, 192; WCC Rate Book No.5, year ending 31 March 1951, WCA; personal effects, Bouchier papers, Women's Library, London, 7/CHB/1/1/1.

184 W.K. Hancock and M.M. Gowing, *British War Economy* (1949), p.166; Balchin, *Housing Policy*, p.113.

185 Rent of Furnished Houses Control (Scotland) Act, 1943, Furnished House (Rent Control) Act, 1946. At the Westminster Tribunal two sublet flats – one in Keyes and one in Collingwood – had their rents reduced by 36%: *The Times*, 1 March 1947, p.2.

186 Richard R. Costain succeeded Richard A. Costain as chairman in 1945. He was also Chairman of Dolphin Square Ltd. R.A. Costain resigned as a director after the company was required to produce consolidated accounts in response to the recommendations of the Cohen Committee on Company Law Amendment of 1945.

187 Chairman's statements, 22 April 1947 and 14 April 1949, Costain, *R & A 1946 and 1948*, Guildhall Library; *Financial Times*, 2 May 1947, p.2, and *The Times*, 1 June 1949, p.9.

188 Chairman's statement, 1951, Costain, *R &A, 1950*, Guildhall Library; *The Times*, 20 July 1951, p.10.

189 Reported in *The Times*, 24 July 1954, p.11.

190 Chairman's statement, n.d., Costain, R & *A, 1955*, Guildhall Library.

191 Rent Act 1957, 5 & 6 Eliz.II c.25, 6 June 1957, s.11 (1).

192 Chairman's statement, n.d., Costain, R & A, *1956*, Guildhall Library.

193 Sir Richard Costain, letter to shareholders, 14 November 1958, copy in London Stock Exchange company reports, Guildhall Library.

CHAPTER 4

CHANGING TIMES, 1958–64

EXIT COSTAINS

The announcement, in November 1958, of the sale of Dolphin Square to Maxwell Joseph surprised many people, since it came shortly after the Government had at last abandoned rent control, the factor most complained of by Costain and other commercial landlords. Only a few months before the transaction, Sir Richard Costain had indicated to shareholders that his company welcomed the opportunities offered by the new Rent Act of 1957, which by decontrolling London properties with a rateable value of over £40 had had the effect of removing all but 137 of Dolphin Square's flats from control.[1] Why, then, did they sell? The full story is obscured, first by the lack of corporate archives for this period, and second by the fact that the accounts for Costain's subsidiary, Dolphin Square Ltd., include not only Dolphin Square, but also 1,096 houses in Dagenham and Elm Park, east London that were managed by another Costain subsidiary, Rylandes Estates Ltd.[2] In his report to shareholders in April 1947, Richard Costain had expressed some doubt as to whether the Rent Control Acts actually applied to Dolphin Square,[3] but while Dolphin Square Ltd. was able in March 1958 to charge guest room prices which were more than double those of 1937,[4] it was unable to secure comparable rent increases for unfurnished flats over the same period. This is not to say that controlled properties had experienced no increase in rents after 1939. In 1949 Costain explained that their problems would have been far worse 'had not the vast majority of the tenants of Dolphin Square agreed to a voluntary increase in their rents' (despite rent control).[5] The fullest statement of Costain's intentions for Dolphin Square in the wake of rent decontrol was made at the AGM in June 1958. The chairman noted that, following the 1957 Rent Act,

> At Dolphin Square we have offered seven-year leases which the great majority of tenants have accepted at rents which are on average only 45 per cent in excess of the restricted rents based on pre-war values. Expressed in different terms, it can be said that the average net rents so offered are equivalent to 2.3 times the gross value for rating assessment purposes. The rents offered to tenants are below current market value. I would mention that we have always had a large measure of co-operation from our tenants at Dolphin Square who, during the period of restriction, voluntarily agreed to increase rentals above the statutory maximum, since they appreciated the fact that a substantial proportion of the rent income was absorbed in services such as heating, porterage, etc., which had increased in cost several times over the pre-war level. The increased rent will enable maintenance work to be carried out which has had to be deferred, and as a result it is not expected that the net revenue will increase in 1958. It is hoped that by 1959 the arrears of maintenance will have been overhauled and that the Group will receive a reasonable return from its investment.[6]

A sample of rentals for Grenville House and Raleigh House in 1936–7 and 1957 gives an indication of what was happening (Table 4.1). The data indicate that Sir Richard's statement underestimated the increase in rents obtained by the seven-year leases of 1957. The return from 'statutory' flats, generally one-room flats with a rateable value of £40 or less which were still subject to rent control, was increased by an average of 45 per cent in Grenville and 66 per cent in Raleigh. For the non-statutory flats, those with two or more rooms, the greater variety in rents makes an average a less reliable measure. However, the seven-year tenancies, which included a rent review after five years, had the effect of raising rents by just over 80 per cent in comparison with 1936–7. On top of this, the rents were now exclusive of rates. Nevertheless, the main point to emphasise here is that these increases were clearly insufficient to match inflation. Since there had been a threefold increase in prices over the same period, the new rents represented a *reduction* in real terms of 44–51 per cent for the statutory flats and just under 40 per cent for most of the others (Table 4.1).

Table 4.1 Rentals for flats in Grenville House and Raleigh House, 1936–7 and 1957

Flat type	*No. of rooms*	*Average rent in 1936–7 (£)*	*Average rent agreed in 1957 (£)*	*Increase %*	*Change in real terms*
13 Grenville statutory	1	89.61	130.07	45	-51%
8 Raleigh statutory	1	94.37	156.49	66	-44%
12 Grenville	2	148.33	269.33	82	-39%
8 Raleigh	2	148.13	270.63	83	-39%
5 Grenville	3	163.00	296.80	82	-39%
2 Raleigh	3	220.00	369.00	68	-44%
1 Grenville	7	455.00	600.00	32	-56%

Source: Dolphin Square Ltd. register of leases, southern section, 1936–7, and Goddard & Smith, Valuation for the Directors, Lintang Investments Ltd., 28 February 1959, DST.

The fact that Costain elected not to raise rents higher still suggests that rent control was by no means the only problem to affect the management of Dolphin Square. Although, in general, demand for housing greatly exceeded supply, particularly in central London, the growing popularity of owner-occupation was beginning to have an influence on the upper end of the rented market. When Dolphin Square was built, 65 per cent of households were renting their property from a private landlord; by 1956 the proportion had fallen to 36 per cent. At the same time owner-occupation rose from 25 to 34 per cent, and here, owners were financed by building societies, supported by tax relief and encouraged by the prospects of capital gain.[7] It is true that for many tenants, a Dolphin Square flat was a second home, but for others it was their sole residence, and longer leaseholds elsewhere in London offered the prospect of more security. On top of this, private landlords faced higher management costs, additional legislative constraints, and tax disincentives (for example, no offset could be claimed for depreciation). As early as April 1947 Richard Costain had told shareholders that the day-to-day operating costs of Dolphin Square had increased by more than £25,000 a year since 1939.[8] And the problem only became worse over the course of the next decade. Some of the financial pressures were eased when Dolphin Square Ltd., which had been founded with a modest share capital of £2,000,[9] converted itself into a public company in March 1946 and raised a substantial amount - nearly £1.5 million - in debentures. This enabled existing mortgages and money owed to Richard Costain Ltd. to be repaid, and placed borrowings on a more satisfactory and transparent basis.[10] However, the accounts available from 1948 indicate that very modest profits were made, at best only 2.6 per cent of the capital invested. Results were improving, with profits in 1955-7 double those of 1949-51, but the overall position was scarcely encouraging (Table 4.2).

Table 4.2 Dolphin Square Ltd. net profits and return on capital, 1948-57

Period	*Net profits after tax, annual average [£]*	*Return on capital (share capital + debentures[a]) %*	*Return on capital (share capital + debentures[b]) %*
1943–4	16,471	–	–
1948	2,503	0.15	0.2
1949–50	15,743	0.9	1.3
1952–4	19,915	1.2	1.6
1955–7	32,320	1.9	2.6

Source: Dolphin Square Ltd., Report and Accounts, 1959–61, DST; The Exchange Telegraph Co., data card on 'Dolphin Square Ltd.', 1962, DST; Dolphin Square Ltd., prospectus, in *Financial Times*, 25 March 1946, p.6.

a based on £2,000 share capital and £1,469,000 in debentures issued in 1946
b based on £2,000 share capital and £1,038,859 in debentures outstanding at end 1958

Was this, then, merely a matter of selling off an underperforming investment? It is difficult to argue that the Costain Group was under pressure to do so. Prudently run, and embarking on a policy of diversification, it was able to weather most of the post-war storms. Indeed, comfortable returns were made for shareholders. After difficulties in the early war years, dividends resumed in 1943, when four per cent was paid, and they were quickly doubled to eight per cent in 1944. Thereafter the company was able to pay a conservative ten per cent a year to 1956, representing a yield of around four-seven per cent. It also paid capital bonuses of three per cent in 1954-6, and was able to put sizeable amounts into reserve.[11] It is true that there were some question marks about the Group. A large bank debt was built up with Lloyds Bank, amounting to over £1 million by 1951, although this was partially resolved by the issue of £515,000 in 5.5 per cent preference shares in 1955.[12] Furthermore, there was always the danger of over-reaching oneself. The company's expansion overseas was not always profitable, for example in Canada and East Africa, and the joint venture it entered into with John Brown from 1948 carried a notable risk element. A pipeline contract with Iraqi partners resulted in a significant loss, inducing Costain to sell its share in the joint venture in 1957. At home, a substantial investment in opencast mining proved unprofitable.[13] There was also some press speculation about a possible takeover bid in 1958. But the threat was countered when, after experiencing the best results in the company's history in 1957, the directors raised the dividend to 17.5 per cent and made a one-for-one bonus share issue. This did not indicate a company in any difficulty.[14] If the annual reports are anything to go by, then Costain's interest in Dolphin Square seems to have diminished as the Group diversified and extended its activities abroad, with its work in Nigeria, Rhodesia and Kuwait receiving particular attention. At home, the success of its concrete subsidiary, and the attractions of contracts for commercial property, tipped the scales against the private housing market, although this was not neglected entirely.[15] What Costain was facing was merely the beginnings of a general trend for large commercial landlords in London to withdraw from the market and sell off their freeholds to insurance companies or friendly societies, while the latter sold long leaseholds to owner-occupiers.[16] Finally, a psychological blow to Dolphin Square was delivered in 1955, when the company, having moved into new headquarters at 111 Westminster Bridge Road, decided to hold its meetings there and not in Rodney House, where it had met since 1939. In short, Dolphin Square did not fit into what was considered to be the Group's 'core activities'. As Sir Richard made clear in his letter to shareholders, their Pimlico investment was 'very much larger than they would normally contemplate, and involves full time management'. The sale would release important funds for further investment and support overseas contracting, which by 1958 made up about 60 per cent of the Group's activities.[17] In June 1959, he explained to the AGM that 'with an increasingly competitive market in rented accommodation [Dolphin Square] would be more valuable to someone specialising in this business than to us'.[18]

ENTER MAXWELL JOSEPH

Who went on to buy the property? Maxwell Joseph, born Max Joseph in the Whitechapel Road in 1910, was the rising star of hotel management and property development [Illustration 28 (i)]. Like his contemporary, Charles Clore, his business model, much copied since, was to acquire underperforming assets, lick them into shape and either manage them or sell them on at a profit. After the war he built up a small chain of hotels, and in 1957 his London hotels were incorporated as Grand Hotels (Mayfair) Ltd. In the same year he bought the Mount Royal Hotel at Marble Arch for over £1 million. In 1962, these assets were combined to form Grand Metropolitan Hotels Ltd., a business which diversified into brewing, restaurants and dance halls and became one of the largest enterprises in the British leisure sector and indeed the economy.[19] Joseph was a quietly-spoken, courteous man, slim and short in stature. His rather gentle demeanour belied an entrepreneur's drive and a facility for risk taking.[20] A good delegator, he worked on intuition and personal judgement. As he later recalled, 'that's worth more than any calculation that can be made in any scientific way'. David Palmer, management editor of the *Financial Times* in the early 1970s, thought that another consistent element in Joseph's approach was that 'he always does what the professionals say he should not do'.[21]

In the 1950s Joseph was also dealing in rented property, and the abandonment of rent control offered him further opportunities. At the time of the Dolphin Square purchase he had been bidding for the St. James' Court Estate, and was involved in negotiations to buy the 25-acre Hyde Park North Estate, between Lancaster Gate and Paddington Station, which had once belonged to the Church Commissioners.[22] The price paid to Costain was not disclosed, but since the sellers announced that they would make a capital profit of about £1 million, *The Times* estimated it to be between £2.25 and £2.5 million. Subsequently, Neville Faulks, reporting for the Board of Trade (see below), said that it was £2,375,000.[23] In buying Dolphin Square Joseph had made it clear that he was acting on behalf of one of his investment companies, and the vehicle involved was soon revealed to be Lintang Investments. This property company, with an office in Alva Street, Edinburgh, had been created from the shell of a Scottish-registered Malaysian rubber company, Bukit Lintang Rubber Estates, established in 1907. The estate had been sold in 1956, and the change of name came in May 1958.[24] The newly-constituted company was very much a London-based concern dominated by Joseph. He was the managing director, and although the chairman was a City figure - Sir Harold Gillett, a chartered accountant, holder of the Military Cross and Lord Mayor of London in 1958–9 - the other directors - a solicitor, Leonard Tobin, and another accountant, Frank Gaston - were essentially Joseph's nominees.[25]

In March 1959 Joseph sold Dolphin Square Ltd. to Lintang Investments in return for 3.5 million 5s. shares in the company. The purchasers also took on a debt of £100,000 owed to him by Dolphin Square Ltd. Lintang had acquired the Hyde Park North Estate in the month before Joseph had bought Dolphin Square, and these two important properties formed the lynchpin of a capital placing and application to list on the stock exchange on 6 March. After a number of changes to the capital structure, the £2 million in ordinary capital was consolidated into eight million 5s. shares. Then the issued shares - 6.3 million with a nominal value of £1,575,000 - were placed by the company's brokers, Solomon & Co., at 11s. 6d. [57.5p] a share. The listing was followed by a mini 'bubble' in the shares, eclipsing the contemporaneous offer of shares in the *News of the World*.[26] On the first day of trading, 12 March, over a million shares changed hands and the share price quickly doubled to 23s. 6d. [£1.17], prompting a stock exchange embargo on property placings, and an expression of scepticism about Lintang's prospects from *The Times*.[27] One thing is clear. Maxwell Joseph made a tidy paper profit on his Dolphin Square transactions. At 11s. 6d. a share his holding was worth £2 million; at 23s. 6d. it was worth double that.[28]

Prior to the stock exchange listing Lintang Investments had engaged the surveyors, Goddard & Smith, to conduct a valuation of Dolphin Square, which was completed at the end of February 1959.[29] Goddard & Smith reported that the property was producing an estimated income of £394,622 gross, but the operating costs were, they considered, 'on a most extravagant scale', with one staff member for every five flats. The specific examples given were that of 20 telephone operators, the employment of a 'highly paid Engineer with 10 assistants in a block of flats where the central heating and constant hot water is supplied from an external source', and 'unjustifiably expensive' accounting services. Unfortunately for Lintang, any savings effected would, according to the existing tenancy agreements, have to be passed onto tenants for five years, although after that these would accrue to the landlords. The majority of the unfurnished flats had been let at below their market value, and once costs had been reduced, the surveyors anticipated a net income of £241,000 per annum. The capital value 'in the open market' was therefore put at £3.1 million, implying a return of 7.8 per cent.[30] Now a wholly-owned subsidiary of Lintang Investments, Dolphin Square Ltd. had limited opportunities for immediate change, with seven-year leases in force. However, the new owner lost no time in seeking to make his mark in Pimlico. The first change was introduced by Joseph's junior colleague, Stanley Grinstead, who went on to succeed him as chairman and chief executive of Grand Metropolitan in 1982.[31] On 31 March 1959 he announced that the rents on unfurnished flats would rise to take account of the higher maintenance costs incurred by the previous owners in 1958. Costs had risen by 49 per cent in that year in an effort to tackle maintenance arrears.[32] On 6 March Surplices Ltd., a Joseph subsidiary, had signed a 21-year lease on the garage, restaurant, bars and sports facilities. The facilities were let at a rent of £13,500 a year exclusive of rates, with seven-year reviews. Joseph retained a 50 per cent stake in the company. The two main businesses were then sublet to operating companies. A Dolphin Square catering company was incorporated, on 25 March, with Maxwell Joseph and Ian Hart as directors. Most of the capital of 100 shares was held by Surplices Ltd.[33] Tenants must have been rather anxious about these developments and the prospects of higher rents. However, worse was to come and within three months the assets were sold on again, in what were to be even more controversial circumstances. For the second time in 25 years, the Dolphin Square site was bought by someone who was unable to complete the transaction.

THE JASPER-GRUNWALD-MURRAY AFFAIR

Maxwell Joseph was not the only developer-speculator operating in the British economy during the property boom of 1955–64.[34] There were three men whose complex corporate dealings eventually brought them into a disastrous relationship with Lintang Investments: Herbert Murray, Secretary and Managing Director of the State Building Society; Friedrich Grunwald, a relatively young man of 34 who had escaped Nazi persecution to pursue a successful career as a solicitor and whose firm, Harewood & Co., were solicitors to the State Building Society; and Harry Jasper, another German refugee who had established a merchant bank in London in 1946. Jasper & Co. was acting for Murray and Grunwald.[35] Joseph and the Jasper/Grunwald consortium had already crossed swords in a search for corporate control: in the spring of 1959 they had both made a bid for the Palmerston Investment Trust, and were subsequently competing to acquire the Piccadilly Hotel, owned by R.E. Jones Ltd., which Lintang seemed likely to win.[36]

What happened next was exceedingly complex, involving a plethora of financial transactions, many of them disputed. This is not the place to record all the ramifications of the 'Jasper affair', much of which can be found in a critical report by Board of Trade inspector Neville Faulks, QC of December 1959, a report for the Registrar of Building Societies on the State Building Society in 1960, in Harry Jasper's voluminous bankruptcy proceedings from 1961 and in the Mansion House and Old Bailey court reports.[37] Here we must focus on the events which affected Dolphin Square as a Lintang subsidiary. In July 1959 Jasper & Co. made an offer to acquire the directors' controlling stake in Lintang Investments - 51 per cent of the issued capital - for 23s. a share in cash. Most of these shares were held by Joseph who accepted the offer on behalf of the Lintang Board, with the condition that the other shareholders were offered 24s. Jasper then made a formal offer for the rest of the capital on these terms.[38] However, it soon transpired that Jasper was representing third parties, and that these parties were Murray and Grunwald. Faulks, the Board of Trade inspector, later described Murray, aged 68, as 'elderly, unscrupulous and rich', while Grunwald, more than thirty years his junior, was 'young, unscrupulous and poor'.[39] Since 1956 the two men had embarked on a speculative merry-go-round of acquisitions, using the resources of the State Building Society. They concealed their transactions by creating around 500 limited companies, many of them 'shell' companies formed from enterprises which had ceased trading.[40] To begin with, the scheme worked well, since property prices were rising, the acquisitions were relatively small, and Murray had a good eye for a bargain. However, in order to expand their empire, Murray and Grunwald were sucked into a vicious circle of overpaying for assets, and offering building society investors unsustainable interest rates. Lintang, the 14th takeover in the series, proved to be an acquisition too far.

The circumstances were as follows. Grunwald and Joseph had had earlier dealings in May–June 1959, when after Joseph had triumphed over Grunwald in bidding for two companies – the Palmerston Investment Trust and Honywood Hotels – he sold them on to Grunwald at a profit. The two men then agreed to collaborate in the acquisition of R.E. Jones, which was allowed to pass into Lintang's hands.[41] Then in July, Jasper, acting for Grunwald and Murray, announced his bid for Lintang. The price was much too high, and Jasper suggested that Grunwald's determination to acquire Lintang was motivated by annoyance at having been bested in the earlier deals,[42] though Grunwald himself claimed that Murray and a property investor, Sigismund Berger, were the prime movers, with Berger particularly keen to acquire Dolphin Square.[43] Joseph had originally asked for 28s. a share, but eventually settled for 23s. and 24s. Even so, this valued the assets at over double their recent valuation, and required at least £8 million to complete, including £3m for the acquisition of R.E. Jones. Joseph was paid £3.5m for his Lintang shares, and Murray and Grunwald fraudulently applied £3.255m borrowed from the State Building Society for this transaction.[44] However, the high-riding solicitor, who had expected further support from Murray, Jasper, Sigismund and Gerson Berger, the Co-operative Permanent Building Society and the banks,[45] could not find enough money to complete the purchase, and in early September Joseph and Tobin agreed to lend Grunwald a total of £1.5m in order to rescue the deal. The loans may well have had a fraudulent tinge to them, although both Joseph and Jasper were subsequently found to be free of blame. Grunwald put up a total of 3.36 million shares in Lintang as collateral, together with 500,000 shares in Reliable Properties, a Jasper-Grunwald vehicle created for the Bergers.[46]

In September 1959, the speculators' financial difficulties turned into a major scandal. Grunwald lacked about £250,000 to complete the purchase of Lintang, but the immediate cause of his downfall was yet another Jasper and Grunwald operation, this time a brewery takeover. What made Grunwald seek to add to his commitments by buying the Ely Brewery in Cardiff is not known. It was a sound business, and perhaps he overestimated its capacity to act as a cash cow.[47] Whatever the reasons, this was the transaction, rather than that of Lintang, that forced the dealings of Murray and Grunwald into the open and brought the house of cards down. On 6 August Jasper & Co. had made a bid of £1.8 million for the brewery and its subsidiary, the Cardiff Malting Co. Eventually, 70 per cent of the shareholders accepted the offer, which required Grunwald to find £1.25m. In mid September it emerged that he could not do so. By this time, Murray was on holiday in the south of France, and Grunwald panicked and fled to Israel, though he was soon persuaded to return to England to face the music. Dealings in Jasper Group companies were then suspended.[48] The vendors of Ely, and in particular its ex-chairman and managing director, Lazarus Nidditch, regained control and ousted Jasper and Grunwald from the boards of Ely and Cardiff Malting.[49] On 25 September a Board of Trade enquiry was mounted and dealings in Lintang and Dolphin Square Ltd. were suspended. Those in Dolphin Square resumed on 7 October; two days later, Grunwald was arrested and charged with fraudulent conversion. There was then a run on the State Building Society, which was forced to close its doors, a situation familiar to readers who remember Northern Rock's problems in 2007–8. After the completion of the Board of Trade enquiry, Murray and Jasper were arrested in early January 1960, and in the following month there was a preliminary hearing at the City of London Magistrates Court. The case was then committed to the Old Bailey in June, and in July, after a 28-day trial, Jasper was acquitted, but Grunwald and Murray were each sentenced to five years' imprisonment.[50] This example of the excesses of speculative activity gave the City a predictable jolt. Faulks had been particularly critical of the way in which the banks had condoned breaches of Section 54 of the Companies Act 1948, which sought to prevent companies from financing purchases of, or subscription for, their own shares, and had found it 'incredible' that the State Building Society had handed over £3.25 million to its solicitor 'with no written report on title to the properties and no applications in writing for the advances'. Unsurprisingly, the 'Jasper affair' was followed by significant changes in the company law on takeovers, and in the building society rules concerning disclosure.[51] But while the episode was quickly forgotten by the public, for Dolphin Square residents it ushered in a prolonged period of anxiety.

IN LIMBO, 1959–62

Had Grunwald managed to pull off his adventurous gambles and evade detection for his frauds, then the future for Dolphin Square tenants would have been bleak. He had told Jasper that his intention in buying Lintang was to sell the Dolphin Square flats for £5,000 each, which would realise £6.25 million. This somewhat simplistic business model, revealed by the press, ignored the existing leasehold arrangements and took no account of running costs. However, it anticipated the selling of longer leaseholds to owner-occupiers, and certainly indicated the intention of the new owners to squeeze the assets.[52] Of course, all this was academic. Grunwald was in prison in the summer of 1960, and the main effect of the Murray-Grunwald fraud case on Dolphin Square was to emasculate Lintang Investments, the owners of Dolphin Square Ltd. While the latter was able to trade, dealings in the parent company remained suspended. Furthermore, there was a clear division between the directors of the company and those holding the shares. Maxwell Joseph and his associates were left with 3.5 million shares, 56 per cent of the equity, but Joseph could not exercise ownership rights since most of this holding had been given to him as collateral for a purchase made with money from the State Building Society, which was seeking redress. In March 1960, the Society, reorganised under Lord Reith as Chairman, took action to freeze transactions in 3.2 million shares.[53] In fact, Joseph was devastated by the fraud and anxious to redeem his reputation. Consequently, he had personally bought 179,000 shares from smaller shareholders who had not been paid by Grunwald.[54]

Strenuous efforts were made to devise a rescue package for Lintang Investments, along with the other major companies in the Jasper Group, and board changes were made to assist in this regard. Once Jasper and Grunwald had bid for Lintang in July 1959, the existing board resigned to be replaced by Jasper (Chairman), Grunwald, Wolf Brueckmann, Jasper's partner, and Sigismund and Gerson Berger.[55]

However, after the revelation of the fraud, Grunwald resigned as a director in September 1960. He was quickly followed by Jasper. The bad publicity given to his bank's activities by the inspector's report and the trial effectively spelt the end for him and his partner, and it was not long before both were facing bankruptcy proceedings.[56] Subsequently, other directors were added to the Board: Norman Barrington Cork, of chartered accountants W.H. Cork, Gully & Co., whom Jasper had asked to examine the accounts of the Jasper companies; Major-General Howard Goodfellow; Major George Webb, of the Alliance Property Co.; and Eric Rhodes, a director of several Jasper companies. Then, Joseph, having made it known that he did not wish to continue his involvement in Lintang, changed his mind when rival property companies began sniffing at the door. He challenged the right of existing directors to sit, and took legal action to have Major Webb removed. Supported by Gerson Berger and the State Building Society, he successfully blocked Webb's appointment, and in December 1960 Webb, Cork and Goodfellow resigned from the Board.[57] A major complication in this wrangling was the fact that the company's shareholders' register had not been made up since February 1959. The fraud proceedings had revealed that Lintang shares had been bought not only with money from Jasper Group companies but from Lintang's own cash resources, and ownership of much of the capital was affected by litigation brought to resolve the issue. It was difficult to make progress while these uncertainties persisted.

All this delayed a solution to the 'Lintang puzzle'. Several schemes were advanced from October 1959. First, John Dalgleish, Chairman and Managing Director of Camp Bird, a former mining finance company turned diversified industrial group, was invited by Jasper shareholders to draw up a solution to the Group's problem, including that of Lintang. His idea was that a consortium of business interests would take over the companies.[58] However, this was more easily said than done, especially with normal business operations effectively suspended, and ownership of the shares in dispute. Then, in January 1961, it was reported that Charles Forte had come up with a plan to repay the State Building Society and acquire a controlling stake in Lintang and R.E. Jones, but it is not clear how serious this was, and in any case, no more was heard of it. Another scheme was mounted by Continental Bankers, but this also came to nothing.[59] In the autumn of 1961, Isaac Wolfson was identified as the architect of a further initiative, and it was suggested that he was prepared to oil the wheels with cash. Once again the proposal was unsuccessful.[60] It was not until December 1961, while Harry Jasper was facing bankruptcy proceedings, that the Lintang board was reconstituted. A completely new board was established, representing the interests of Joseph and the State Building Society. The directors, three of whom were chartered accountants, had more respectable credentials than their predecessors. The new chairman was Donald House, former President of the Institute of Chartered Accountants and chairman of R.E. Jones, and the other directors were Joseph; Grinstead; Sir Dingwall Bateson, director of the State Building Society and chairman of a number of reconstituted Jasper Group companies; James H. Robertson, former General Manager of Abbey National and a director of the State Building Society; and Barnett Saffron, a solicitor.[61] Dolphin Square's Board, which was reconstituted on 7 February 1962, was the same. When House resigned his directorships, owing to an appointment to the Restrictive Practices Court, Bateson took his place as Chairman of both companies. A partner in the law firm Walters & Hart, Chairman of the Racecourse Betting Control Board, and a director of the Phoenix Assurance Co., he had been awarded the Military Cross in the First World War.[62] In the place of House, Hugh T. Nicholson, another chartered accountant from the City, was appointed a director in April 1962.[63] Lintang then began the process of selling off its main assets: Dolphin Square and the Hyde Park North Estate. Now at last an end to the impasse seemed to be in sight and the future management of Dolphin Square could be addressed.

Thus, the period from 1959 to 1962 was an uncomfortable one. Observers fully expected the owners to seek to drive up rents. At the same time, some Dolphin Square tenants had also attracted adverse publicity, with the eviction in October 1961 of Sarah Beauchamp née Churchill, Vic Oliver's former wife, for unreasonable behaviour, and the arrest of John Vassall on charges of spying in September 1962 (see below, p.272). But as Lintang's board changed, and changed again, and as a number of rescue plans were advanced, then abandoned, it was difficult to see a firm strategy being applied. The Square was effectively in limbo until a solution was found to Lintang's problems.[64]

THE RESIDENTS RESPOND, 1959–62

This is not to say that nothing was done in Dolphin Square in 1959–62. Rents and charges were certainly raised after 1958. By 1961, guest room charges had doubled since 1958 and were now five times higher than the 1937 charges.[65] This was a visible demonstration of the policies favoured by Dolphin Square Ltd. and its newly-installed general manager, Gerald Woolf Rhodes, who was appointed in July 1959.[66] Rents were also raised in 1959, as we have seen, to take account of higher maintenance costs. According to the *Financial Times*, this meant increases of between £3 and £6.50 a month.[67] With residents' concerns increasing, a Dolphin Square Tenants' Association [DSTA] was formed in May 1959, with broad support from tenants. An initial meeting, held on 20 April to discuss 'ways and means of protecting the interests of Dolphin Square Tenants', was attended by Alderman A.N.H. [Noel] Baines of Westminster City Council who lived in Howard House, two barristers, an engineer, an accountant, and three senior military men.[68] A provisional committee was then elected, comprising: Cdr Reginald Hoare, of Raleigh House (Chairman); Harry Mitchell, Keyes House (Deputy Chairman); Henry A. Smith, an accountant, Collingwood House (Hon. Treasurer), and Diana E. Wynn Jones, a journalist, Nelson House (Hon. Secretary).[69] Feelings were certainly running high at this stage, fuelled by the sharp increase in rents to cover higher maintenance costs (see above, pp.123–6). The tenants had no difficulty in attracting the attention of the press, which was indicative of the scale and location of the Square, but also reflected the influence of many of its residents. In April, the *Daily Express* carried a piece entitled 'The bitter battle of Dolphin Square', in which it was claimed that an unsigned telegram had been handed into Sir Harold Gillett, Chairman of Lintang Investments, at the Mansion House, calling on him to resign unless he put a stop to the 'arbitrary increase in rentals by unethical if legal means'.[70] Alderman George Pargiter, MP for Southall, from Howard House, attended a second meeting on 27 April, and a meeting of tenants was arranged in Caxton Hall on 4 May. There was strong support for the idea, and it was unanimously resolved that an Association should be formed with an annual subscription of £1.[71] It was reported that the membership quickly reached 500, and with the future of Lintang Investments uncertain following, first, its purchase by Jasper on behalf of Grunwald, and then the subsequent revelation of the Grunwald-Murray frauds, the Association's executive committee was encouraged to consider more direct action. A sub-committee consisting of Pargiter, Baines, Smith and Wynn Jones was formed to investigate the possibility of forming a Housing Association to buy the flats and manage them on a non-profit making basis. In November 1959, the subcommittee made an informal approach to Westminster City Council and it met with representatives of the housing and finance committees, Alderman C.P. Russell and councillors Sir Charles Norton and Mrs Margaret Ball Wilson, for a preliminary discussion on whether the Council would loan the tenants the purchase money on the security of the property. The Town Clerk, Alan Dawtry [Illustration 28 (ii)], attended the meeting and asked the subcommittee for further information. Having been living in the Square since 1956, he was placed in a difficult position and was at some pains to distance himself from the DSTA.[72] In January 1960, the Council told the tenants that it viewed their aims sympathetically, although concerns were raised about the price they envisaged paying. The Association had obtained a valuation of £1.75 million 'from a reputable surveyor', and it was intending to spend no more than £2.5 million gross. However, this was well short of Goddard & Smith's valuation of £3.1 million in 1959. The Council advised the DSTA to approach Lintang and ascertain what price it would want for the property.[73]

The DSTA, emboldened by a lively annual meeting in March 1960, at which the landlords were roundly condemned, now pressed for more direct action.[74] Shortly afterwards, it made efforts to meet with the Lintang directors, and was successful in making contact with Norman Cork. He was told that the tenants were seriously considering the possibility of buying the Square themselves, through the medium of a housing association incorporated under the Industrial and Provident Societies Acts.[75] At this time the Lintang board was naturally cautious, with the future of the company so uncertain. For its part, the DSTA was frustrated by the lack of engagement with the company, and it raised the temperature with some of its pronouncements, especially those orchestrated by Wynn Jones, who campaigned vigorously for the cause, liaising with other tenants' associations, and appealing to both the Housing Minister, Henry Brooke, and the Prime Minister, Harold

Macmillan, for help.[76] Some of the stories emerged after the DSTA's executive committee circulated a memorandum to the Minister of Housing & Local Government on the effects of the 1957 Rent Act in September 1960. Mrs Wynn Jones was quoted extensively in the *Star*, which pointed out that one-room flats costing £85 p.a. were being decontrolled and let for £350. She was reported to be concerned by the likely situation when leases expired in 1962. 'Dolphin Square is not full of wealthy tenants as is generally supposed', she said. 'We are practically all processional [sic: should be professional] people.'[77] The publicity had some effect in that it induced Sigismund Berger, a director of Dolphin Square Ltd., and Gerald Rhodes, the general manager, to reduce the much higher rentals they were proposing for a renewal of expiring three-year leases.[78] This confrontational climate gave way to a more conciliatory approach once the boards of both Lintang and Dolphin Square Ltd. were reconstituted in 1962. Pargiter, in particular, advocated a more diplomatic engagement with the landlords. Chairman of the Association after the resignation of Cdr Hoare, he held informal talks with Maxwell Joseph in an attempt to establish something of a rapprochement between the parties.[79] With half of the 600 seven-year leases reaching their five-year break point in 1962, Lintang exerted pressure for an increase in rentals. Representatives of the DSTA met with the company and offered to use their influence to obtain the agreement of tenants to an increase if Lintang agreed to look sympathetically at the Association's plan to acquire the property via a housing association. The company promised to do so, and in May 1962 the parties accepted that a 20 per cent increase, to apply from August in the sixth and seventh years of seven-year tenancies, was fair.[80] At this stage the landlords were applying an 18-point rent scale for new three-year tenancies, ranging from £390 a year for one-room flats, £450–570 for two rooms, £550–625 for three rooms, £695–770 for four rooms, and £850–1,050 for the larger flats.[81]

By this time it was evident that Lintang was keen to sell Dolphin Square, and on 14 August the *Financial Times* revealed that tenders would soon be invited for the property and referred to the suggestion that the sale would produce 'something like' £4.5 million. The newspaper expressed some doubts about the proposed method of disposal. While a sale by tender would probably realise the best price, buyers might well be deterred by the fact that the transaction could not be effected via an exchange of shares, and so would require payment in cash.[82] Nevertheless, a sale document was drawn up and distributed at the end of November. It invited tenders for the leasehold interest, which had about 71 years to run (99 years from 24 June 1935), with a deadline of 8 February 1963. It also offered purchasers the alternative of bidding for the issued capital of Dolphin Square Ltd.[83] Thus, by the end of 1962 there was the prospect of yet another owner, the fourth in four years.

How had rents changed in the period 1957–62? With three-year and seven-year tenancies expiring at different periods, and a fluctuating turnover rate, it is hard to be precise about the movement of rents. In his history of the Square, Morris notes that Lintang acted to raise rents for incoming tenants, and gives examples of rentals affected by the policy. For a one-room flat priced at £100 p.a. in 1937, tenants could expect to pay £165 from 1957, and £350 after 1959; for two-room flats costing £135 p.a. in 1937, the new charges were £240 and £555. The post-1959 rentals were thus 250 and 311 per cent higher than in 1937. In addition, rates were now the responsibility of the tenant.[84] A perusal of the existing rentals at the time of the tender document in November 1962 reveals a more confused picture, and for tenants of similar-sized flats, there was a considerable disparity in what they were paying. In part, this reflected the position and amenity of individual flats, with the landlords now working with two to three separate categories for each size of flat (18 in all), but it also depended upon the date at which a tenancy agreement was struck. Thus, South Block tenants who were paying £100 p.a. in 1937 were now being charged anything from £156 (as a controlled rent) to £390, and those paying £135 p.a. in 1937 were being charged ten different rents, ranging from £200 to £470.[85] Dolphin Square had a strong core of existing tenants and for many of them rentals did not rise as sharply as those for newcomers. Thus, one-room flats priced at £85 p.a. in 1937 were in 1962 costing £155 if rent controlled, and if decontrolled, anything from £185 to £390. Two neighbouring three-room flats in Collingwood House, which had cost £165 p.a. to rent in 1937, were in 1962 costing £310 and £600 respectively. The most expensive flats were now costing between £625 and £950, though 11 of these were 'double' flats. Not only were tenants experiencing a wide variety of charges,[86] but the new landlords, for all their posturing, were unable to raise rents to their pre-war levels in real terms. The South Block rentals charged to incomers in 1936–7 (Appendix 1) totalled £67,386, including rates; the same flats were being charged £161,816 excluding rates in 1962 (before rent increases applied in late 1962), an increase of 140 per cent. However, since prices in general more than trebled between 1937 and 1962, in real terms the landlords were getting 29 per cent less, though this was mitigated to some extent by passing responsibility for rates onto the tenants.[87]

Even if there was something in the argument that in Dolphin Square tenants had prospered relative to the landlords since 1939, it was becoming clear by 1962 that the 1957 Rent Act had patently failed to increase the supply of rented accommodation and that in London, where the problem was particularly acute, the actions of less scrupulous landlords were beginning to concern those in the rented sector. In particular, by 1962–3 the attention of the media was being focused on the way in which tenants protected by controlled rents were 'persuaded' to vacate their flats so that much higher rents could be charged, a practice that became associated with the name of Perec (Peter) Rachman. Rachman had died in November 1962, but in the following year his name surfaced during the Profumo scandal. In the trial of the osteopath Stephen Ward, Rachman was revealed to have had a sexual relationship with the 'good-time girls' Christine Keeler and Mandy Rice-Davies, who were later said to have been subtenants in the Square.[88] Rachmanism may have been an extreme example of poor landlord-tenant relations,[89] but the course of action being proposed by the Tenants' Association, which promised to defend 'Dolphinites' from the risk of excessive landlord zeal, was extremely welcome to existing tenants. When, at last, the recent profit record of Dolphin Square Ltd. was revealed in 1962, the results vindicated tenants' concerns. Earlier, we noted that net profits had averaged only £32,000 per annum in 1955–7 (Table 4.2, above); after a post-tax loss of £7,400 in 1958, net profits rose sharply to £69,300 in 1959, £91,500 in 1960, and £98,500 in 1961.[90]

ENTER WESTMINSTER CITY COUNCIL, 1962–3

Westminster City Council, in the early 1960s, was still relatively small. It was not until April 1965 that the borough was merged with that of Paddington and St. Marylebone to create a much larger authority with city status. The issue of Dolphin Square's future therefore arose during the last three years of the old borough council.[91] However, there was certainly continuity in the political composition of the council, which remained a Conservative stronghold. This was important in shaping its attitude to housing in general, and to rented housing in particular, since from 1961 the Conservative administration of Harold Macmillan was heavily criticised for the way in which it had tackled rent control and the housing shortage.[92] The available housing stock was certainly a matter of concern for the inner London boroughs, and when the DSTA approached the Council, raising the spectre of a loss of rented accommodation in the borough, it was no surprise that councillors and officials gave the lobbyists a sympathetic hearing. There was a possibility that Dolphin Square would change fundamentally as a result of a simple sale by tender. Much bandied about was the rumour that Pan American Airways, which had an air terminal in Victoria and also owned a rapidly expanding subsidiary, InterContinental Hotels, were interested in acquiring the Square and using it as accommodation for passengers and crew in transit.[93] Another rumour surrounded the possibility that the Square might be linked in the same way with the BOAC's Terminal in Victoria. The Conservative government was certainly interested in the concept of housing associations at this time. Although their contribution to the housing stock was insignificant, they seemed to offer an alternative approach to the problems caused by the decline in the private rented sector and were the focus of government attention in the early 1960s, in much the same way as the current [2013] Coalition Government is interested in the 'Big Society'.[94] The Council certainly possessed the necessary powers to 'promote and assist' an incipient housing association, under Sections 119–21 of the 1957 Housing Act. Subject to ministerial approval, it could make grants or loans to an association, subscribe for share or loan capital, or guarantee money borrowed by the association.[95]

Council representatives held meetings with the DSTA in October and November 1962. On 15 October the tenants met councillors from the Housing and Finance committees, including their respective chairmen: C.A. (Tony) Prendergast, 31-year-old Chairman of the Housing Committee and recently elected councillor representing Belgravia (1959) [Illustration 28 (iii)]; and Douglas Overall, Chairman of the

Finance Committee, and a chartered surveyor, Fellow of the Institute of Actuaries and partner in the leading firm of auctioneers and surveyors, Hillier Parker May & Rowden. Pargiter, for the Association, repeated its request for the Council's help in forming a housing association and in obtaining a 100 per cent loan to enable it to acquire the leasehold interest of Dolphin Square. He emphasised that their intention was to enable the tenants 'to continue to reside there with some better degree of security and at reasonable rents'. Clearly, the current value of the property was a critical issue. The Association had asked J.H. Bailey, of the auctioneers and valuers John D. Wood & Co. to provide a new valuation, and he had offered them 'spot' valuations of £3.25 and £3.6 million, though at the meeting he stated that the valuation might have to be increased to about £4m. Sir Dingwall Bateson, Chairman of Dolphin Square Ltd., had suggested a figure of £4.5m.[96] After a second meeting on 30 November the councillors expressed sympathy for the tenants' position, but required a more detailed valuation, together with a fuller estimate of the acquisition costs, including maintenance and amortisation, and a more considered estimate of future rental income. They asked the DSTA to base its calculations on fairly stiff terms, viz. a 30-year loan of 90 per cent of the acquisition costs. Dawtry, the Town Clerk, had already been directed to write to the Association to request the necessary information, and specifically to obtain evidence of its ability to service a loan, and the proportion of the existing tenants likely to be able and willing to pay rentals adequate to finance such a scheme. He gave the DSTA a strong steer in his letter of 1 November 1962, noting that while the Council would not press it to charge the highest possible rents, 'some regard must be had to the character of the accommodation and the amenities the premises generally offer'. The Council also took the view that the furnished flats should as soon as possible revert to unfurnished accommodation, and that while it understood that some tenants held 21-year leases, shorter leases, backed by a housing association, ought to offer adequate tenurial protection.[97]

The DSTA replied to the Town Clerk on 24 November, enclosing a report with detailed financial schedules prepared by Bailey of John D. Wood & Co. The tenants intended to charge rents to cover costs on a non-profit-making basis, and while they were unable to give an undertaking on dispensing with the furnished flats, which they said was a matter for the housing association when formed, they were fully in agreement with the policy. They also pointed out that only commercial tenants, mostly Richard Costain Ltd. and its subsidiary companies, had leases longer than seven years. Bailey's detailed report offered a revised valuation of approximately £4.1 million, based on a gross annual income of £501,000, expenditure of £160,000 and net income of £341,000 (Table 4.3). However, Bailey made the assumption that the potential gross income was £525,000 p.a. (based on rentals of £350 p.a. for one-room flats, rising to £500 for three-room flats, £700 for five rooms and £900 for seven rooms), and this was close to the estimate offered in the official tender document published by Goddard & Smith et al. a week later. This showed a gross income of £529,000, costs of £183,000 and a net income of £346,000. However, the expectations of higher rentals from early reversions were expected to produce an additional £100,000 a year by December 1964 (Table 4.3). Using this information, the DSTA considered that £4m would be needed to buy the Square, plus £200,000 in costs. It therefore proposed to borrow £3.6m from the Council, with £600,000 raised from shares taken by members of the housing association.[98]

Table 4.3 Income and expenditure estimates for Dolphin Square, November 1962 (£)

Item	*Bailey valuation for DSTA*	*Marcus Leaver/ Goddard & Smith valuation*
Income:		
Rentals unfurnished flats	338,819	374,727
Rentals furnished flats	113,749	113,749
Rentals offices + basement storerooms	6,399	6,425
Guest rooms	11,637	11,637
Amenities – garage, restaurant etc	13,500	13,500
Shops	3,304	3,304
Miscellaneous	14,024	6,021
Total actual + estimated	501,432	529,363*
Costs:		
Rent	20,250	20,250

Wages	65,815	57,101
Central heating/hot water	25,925	25,890
Housekeeping	15,811	17,663
Electricity/gas	10,385	10,385
Administration	–	10,856
Telephone operators	8,712	8,712
Other costs net of maintenance/service income	13,159	32,373
Total costs	160,057	183,230
Net income	341,375	346,133
Extra rental income from reversions by December 1964	–	100,000

Source: J.H. Bailey, valuation, 21 November 1962, Goddard & Smith et al., Sale documents for Dolphin Square, 1962, DST.

Key: * includes income from rent increases, November 1962.

With only a matter of weeks remaining before the end of the tendering period, both the local authority and the tenants were required to act swiftly. Fortunately, the parties were willing to do this. At the meeting on 30 November it was accepted that the tenants would not be able to complete all the necessary procedures to mount a bid themselves and that Westminster City Council would have to do so on their behalf. Most councillors accepted Prendergast's arguments that action was necessary to safeguard Dolphin Square's middle income group flats, which were a 'vitally important' resource in central London, and that the loss of accommodation for 3,000 people 'by a change of use of the building into something like a Hotel' should be avoided.[99] However, it was difficult for the Council to take part in a tendering process, and following a joint meeting of the Housing and Finance committees on 4 December, Prendergast met Maxwell Joseph informally, opening the way for Dawtry to begin negotiations with the owners to buy the property directly.[100] He also conferred with officials from the Ministry of Housing and Local Government. They advised that the Minister, then Sir Keith Joseph, would be prepared to give his consent to the Council borrowing money for the transaction, providing that the term did not exceed 60 years, and 'on the understanding that, if the Council purchased Dolphin Square, the premises would be managed so as to ensure that the income from the property would, over the whole period of the subsisting lease taking one year with another, balance the expenditure'.[101] Dawtry then met Maxwell Joseph, who agreed to sell Dolphin Square provided their respective valuers agreed a price. Herring Son & Daw acted for the Council, Goddard & Smith for Lintang, and a sale price of £4,500,000 was quickly reached.[102] In the meantime the tenants lost no time in establishing a housing association. A letter circulated to tenants on 10 December invited them to support such a step, and favourable replies were apparently received from over 600 of them. Then, at a meeting in Church House on 17 December the tenants gave the negotiating committee what was described as 'virtually unanimous' approval to proceed.[103]

At a special meeting on 10 January 1963 the Council considered the following recommendations from both the Housing Committee and the Finance Committee: 1) that the Council should buy the lease on Dolphin Square for £4,500,000 [plus £90,090 for land registry fees and stamp duty], and the fixtures and fittings for £33,154; 2) that the Council should approve, in principle, the transfer of the premises to a housing association operating on a non-profit making basis and sponsored by the Council, subject to the constitution and rules of the association being in a form acceptable to it; and 3) that the Council should undertake that all possible steps be taken to ensure that the Square would be managed so that its income would balance expenditure over the whole period of the lease, taking one year with another. Two Labour councillors - Dr T.J.H. Bishop and A.C. Miles - moved that the second recommendation be reconsidered, but this was defeated. The Council then formally agreed to buy the property for £4.5m, with completion expected at the end of March. Application was to be made to the Minister to borrow £4,590,090 on mortgage for the purpose. These decisions were announced publicly on the same day.[104] Six days later, on 16 January, the Dolphin Square Housing Association Limited was registered with the National Federation of Housing Societies by eight of the tenants: Pargiter, Baines, Smith and Wynn Jones, who had acted as the negotiating sub-committee on behalf of the Tenants' Association, and Henry Bliss, Major-General Arthur Williams, Margaret Harper-Nelson, and Colin Marsh, elected members of the executive committee.[105] With the help of Spencer le Marchant, a councillor and partner in the stockbroking firm of L. Messel & Co.,[106] the Council obtained a 60-year mortgage at a fixed interest rate of 6.125 per cent. The Minister, giving his consent, attached the following conditions: there should be no charge on the general rates, and the management of the flats was to be such that income would balance expenditure.[107] It now remained for the Council, having obtained the lease, to sublet it to the Housing Association. However, the tenants had annoyed the Council by forming their housing association without consultation,[108] and the transfer of the property was to prove a much more contentious matter.

COMMITTEE AND TRUST, 1963–4

Having established a housing association, the tenants began serious negotiations with the council to take over the management of Dolphin Square. A sublease arrangement was envisaged. In the meantime, the Council had to make provision for the continuing management of its newly-acquired asset. At the end of January 1963 it therefore set up a special ad hoc committee, which was given the task of managing the Square on an interim basis and negotiating for a transfer of the property to a non-profit-making housing association. The Mayor of Westminster, Paul (Tony) Negretti,[109] and deputy mayor, Jack Dribbell, were appointed *ex officio* as were the chairmen of the housing and finance committees, Prendergast and Overall (the latter soon replaced by Spencer le Marchant). There were two Labour councillors: Ashley Bramall, a barrister, and former MP for Bexley;[110] and John (Jack) Curran, who, as we have seen (Chapter 2), had been employed as a painter in the building of Dolphin Square. He was Site Relations Officer to the exhibition industry and a former trade union official. The remaining members of the committee were: Sir Charles Norton, MC, solicitor and senior partner in Norton, Rose, Botterell & Roche, and Past President of the Law Society; A.L. (Tony) Burton, director of Henderson-Kenton, a furnishing firm; and Geoffrey Gay, partner in estate agents Knight Frank & Rutley. The Committee first met on 5 February with Dribbell as chairman, and Burton as vice-chairman. Dribbell, a councillor since 1946, was in the paper merchants and haulage contracting business. The members immediately decided to limit new lettings to three-year tenancies, and to continue with the 18-point rent scale for new tenants drawn up by Dolphin Square Ltd., viz. £390 per annum for one-room flats, rising to £1,050 for the best seven-room flats. Priority would be given to existing tenants, followed by: those needing to live in or near Westminster because of the nature of their business or profession, e.g. MPs, and people working in the catering and entertainment industries; those displaced by building developments in Westminster; those employed or living in Westminster. No immediate action was to be taken to raise rents or to obtain possession of the flats which would become decontrolled as a result of the purchase by the Council. And no steps would be taken to alter the existing arrangements for letting furnished flats in Rodney House.[111]

However, Westminster councillors and officials soon began to have second thoughts about handing over Dolphin Square to the tenant-sponsored Housing Association. It is clear that the DSTA had not thought through a number of aspects of the process of transfer, including the management of the commercial activities in the Square. The very fact of purchase by the Council was to prove fatal to their aspirations to manage the property themselves. Meetings between representatives of the Housing Association (who were also members of DSTA's executive committee) and Westminster's Dolphin Square (Special) Committee were held in February 1963 and differences of opinion quickly surfaced. One of the areas of disagreement was the contention by Wynn Jones and others that the Council had bought the property 'on behalf of the Housing Association', and after the transfer the Association expected to be in 'full managerial control' of Dolphin Square. The councillors and officers challenged this view, pointing out that Dolphin Square had been bought by the Council on its own account, with the intention of transferring it to a housing association on acceptable terms. The Council should therefore be represented on the Housing Association's management committee. There was also a disagreement about the period of assignment. The Association assumed that this would match the period of the lease, i.e. 71 years, but the Council took the view that it should be for the period of the mortgage, i.e. 60 years.[112] However, the disagreement that brought matters to a head concerned the position of general manager. As we have seen, Gerald Rhodes had been the General Manager under Lintang's ownership, and it was a condition of the sale that the existing management staff should be transferred to the Council's service. Many tenants and

Westminster's representatives came to the conclusion that Rhodes was a competent manager who was doing a good job. Unfortunately, it was evident at an early stage that there was 'considerable friction' between Wynn Jones and Rhodes.[113] The Housing Association suggested that the general manager should also serve as secretary of the Association after the transfer. The Council agreed and it was decided that the new combined post should be publicly advertised and filled. But while the Housing Association expected that it would be an equal partner in the recruitment, the Council took the view that the decision was ultimately its own to make, though it invited three members of the Association to join its three representatives in the interviewing process.[114] After the interviews on 18 March, the Council's representatives proposed that Rhodes should be appointed, but the Housing Association preferred another candidate, and negotiations reached something of an impasse.[115] Eventually Rhodes was duly appointed by the Dolphin Square (Special) Committee, and the Council asked the Association to give it categorical assurances that it would accept the appointment, and that in due course Rhodes would become its Secretary. When the Association failed to concur, the Committee broke off negotiations in May and began to prepare the ground for the transfer of Dolphin Square to an entirely new housing association to be promoted by the Council.[116] This course of action was approved by the Council on 27 June 1963. The basic structure of the new housing association was agreed by the Council's General Purposes Committee in July, and endorsed by the Council in August.[117]

The DSTA and its fledgling Dolphin Square Housing Association continued to lobby hard for their continued involvement in the transfer process, and lost no opportunity to attack the Council.[118] One of the further disagreements they highlighted was the Council's insistence that it be allowed to nominate tenants for vacant flats. As Pargiter explained to the DSTA's annual meeting in June, 'we are not prepared to become merely the servants of the W.C.C., nominally owning the property, but at the same time doing the bidding of the Council as it might be at any time.'[119] On 3 July Pargiter circulated a letter to residents, outlining the progress of negotiations, which Dribbell regarded as so seriously misrepresenting the actions and intentions of the Council that he sought to put the record straight in a circular letter of his own on 1 August.[120] On 22 July, Pargiter wrote to the tenants setting out the Housing Association's vision for the future. In a long memorandum prepared by Henry Smith, the Association explained that it had drawn up a scheme following advice received from its accountants. In particular, it set out the anticipated contributions it expected of tenants under the headings of capital and rent. As members of the Association tenants would subscribe approximately £180,000 in capital, or £2.67 per £1 of rateable value (in 1962). Thus, tenants of the lowest rated one-room flats, rated at £32, would contribute £85; those with two-room flats at £52 would contribute £139, and those with three-room flats at £64 would put up £171. Pargiter explained that a financial stake was 'essential in order to foster the co-operative ownership spirit essential for the [Association's] successful operation'. Future rents were calculated on various assumptions: 1) that tenants would receive personal tax relief under the Finance Act of 1963 on a pro rata share of the mortgage interest; 2) that no relief would be granted; and 3) that all the furnished flats in Rodney House would be converted into unfurnished flats. The Association calculated that tenants would pay a minimum of £235 a year for the one-room flats, £382 for the two-room flats, and £470 for the three-room flats, with rateable values as above. With personal tax relief, these rentals would fall to £183, £297 and £366 respectively. Although these rents were much lower than those being charged by the Council on an interim basis, many tenants reading the memorandum would have regarded the scheme with some anxiety. The tenants paying £155 a year as a controlled rent were facing an increase of over 50 per cent, if tax relief did not apply, together with a capital contribution equivalent to over half a year's rent. Those with larger flats were paying a variety of rents, and for those rated at £64 the range was a wide one, from £310 to £570 a year. Setting a rental of £470 a year (before tax relief) would mean that while some tenants would gain by the proposed arrangement, many would have to pay more. And all tenants, irrespective of the remaining period of their leases, would be required to pay the capital contribution.[121]

Westminster's councillors, while certainly not unanimous on how to treat rents in the future,[122] were busy wrestling with the same issues for their own putative housing association. The taxation question was a complex one, and it was by no means certain that relief would apply to

Dolphin Square. Certainly, no progress could be made on the issue unless the Square's commercial assets were separated from its purely residential assets. Both sides were agreed that tenants would have to join the Housing Association and make a capital contribution, and there should be no subletting (the practice had virtually stopped in Lintang's time) and no corporate lets.[123] However, the proposed treatment of the formerly rent-controlled tenants, now numbering about 110, was a further bone of contention. Councillors were minded to continue a measure of protection, but the leaders of the Housing Association, and Wynn Jones in particular, appeared to be adopting a particularly venomous attitude towards these tenants. Relations scarcely improved when lawyers became involved in August. Hamlins, Grammer & Hamlin, acting for both the DSTA and the Housing Association, wrote to Dawtry to protest at Dribbell's circular letter to tenants of 1 August, pointing out that only the combining of the posts of general manager and housing association secretary stood in the way of the Council handing over the property to their clients as originally proposed. But by this time, the shrill behaviour of the DSTA executive had given councillors no confidence in its future operation.[124] Further evidence of the DSTA's behaviour emerged at its meeting held at Caxton Hall on 4 November. Rhodes, who had resigned as general manager in September,[125] informed Dribbell that in the course of a lively debate Pargiter had said that the Council was 'as black and distorted as any previous Landlord at Dolphin Square'. It was evident that Pargiter had lost control of his executive committee, which was clearly being dominated by the redoubtable Wynn Jones.[126] In any case, Pargiter had already given up his tenancy of 305 and 306 Howard House, and did not stand for re-election in 1964. He was succeeded as Chairman by Alderman Baines.[127] Pargiter's departure from the Square certainly weakened the standing of the DSTA and its housing association. Furthermore, their authority to speak for the tenants was revealed to be somewhat weaker than they had claimed. At the Caxton Hall meeting, for example, a membership of 700 was claimed, with 600 having paid their subscriptions, but the meeting was attended by only 150 tenants.[128]

On 23 October 1963 Dribbell wrote to the tenants outlining the Council's terms for the transfer of Dolphin Square to an alternative housing association. The letter stated unequivocally that 'The City

Council will make no profit from the transaction'. The organisation and policy of the new housing association were in many ways similar to that put up by the tenants' committee. For example, there was to be a management committee of 12, three of them nominated by the Council, and the intention was to convert Rodney House into unfurnished accommodation. However, some concessionary changes were offered. The Council had decided not to reserve for itself the right to nominate tenants to vacant flats, and there was no reference to this in the letter, which reiterated its earlier approach to the selection of tenants. Subletting would be allowed, with the permission of the management committee, and the contribution of loan capital by each tenant might be waived in cases of hardship. On future rents, Dribbell criticised the figures quoted in Pargiter's letter in July, pointing out that they were minima and based on several 'incorrect' assumptions: that the formerly controlled flats would be let at the full rent; that there would be no loss of income from empty flats; that the housing association would be entitled to tax concessions under the 1963 Finance Act; and that the tenants would be able to deduct a considerable proportion of his or her rent for tax purposes. The tax concessions were illusory, said Dribbell, because they required there to be a 'complete identity' between the membership of the Housing Association and the people living in the flats. This was not likely to occur for some time and, in any case, there were shops, a restaurant, garage and other facilities let on 21-year leases; their existence would preclude any tax relief under the Act.[129] Estimating that, with Rodney House converted, an annual rental income of about £492,000 would be required, the Council stated that rents would range from £335 to £905, 14 per cent lower than the existing charges. In order to proceed with the transfer to a housing association, the support of tenants was clearly required, and the Council intended to hold a referendum to gauge this. It informed tenants that unless at least 70 per cent of those eligible to take part voted in favour it would not go ahead with the scheme.[130]

The DSTA's Caxton Hall meeting on 4 November was convened to discuss the Council's proposal. The proceedings indicate that the Association had not given up the battle for Dolphin Square, and was endeavouring to spike the Council's efforts to resolve the issue. The following resolution was passed: 'This meeting . . . is not prepared to accept the terms and conditions stipulated by the Westminster City Council in their document dated 23rd October and calls upon the Council to re-open negotiations with the Executive Committee of the Tenants' Association with a view to the flats being transferred to the Dolphin Square Housing Association Limited, which enjoys our complete confidence'.[131] The resolution was then sent to all tenants, inviting them to send their copy to the Council as an alternative reply to the referendum. The intervention proved effective, and the Council's referendum produced disappointing results. Of the 955 tenants eligible to vote, only 107 had done so by the closing date, 11 November. There were 87 acceptances (9 per cent), and 20 rejections. However, 218 tenants sent in signed copies of the DSTA's resolution.[132] At its meeting on 12 December the Council therefore abandoned the housing association option, and asked the Dolphin Square (Special) Committee to come up with an alternative. Thus, nearly a year after the decision to purchase, the future management of the Square was still uncertain.

Dribbell's Committee considered its options in December 1963 and January-February 1964. Having managed the property, including Rodney House and two of the shops, for nearly a year it was convinced that direct management by the Council was undesirable, since the commercial aspects of the Square were 'difficult to reconcile with local authority management' and should be run by a separate executive.[133] Management by a housing association was clearly preferable, but, given the results of the referendum, the body should not be owned and run by the tenants. The committee raised the possibility of creating a Housing Management Commission (under Section 115 of the 1957 Housing Act), but the Ministry of Housing advised that a Housing Association would be able to exercise much more extensive powers of management. Asked to think again, the Committee, supported by the General Purposes Committee, eventually proposed a housing association promoted and controlled by the Council, using powers under Section 119 of the 1957 Housing Act. This would establish a body similar to the Westminster Housing Trust (see p.165). Seven councillors would be required to apply to the Registrar of Friendly Societies to incorporate the Association under the Industrial and Provident Societies Act of 1893 and form the initial management committee, in the same way as Pargiter, Wynn Jones et al. had done with their Association, but with broader powers. The constitution would be largely similar to that of the earlier scheme, but would of course be amended to take account of the fact that tenants would neither be members nor have control. The General Purposes Committee proposed that a Housing Association to be known as the 'Dolphin Square Trust Limited' be sponsored, and that the eight members of Dribbell's Special Committee be its first members. Future trustees would be nominated by the Council, which endorsed these recommendations at its meeting in March.[134]

The proposals for Dolphin Square had not been unanimous. Some of Dribbell's committee members expressed anxiety about the creation of the Trust. Ashley Bramall, for example, thought it the 'worst of both worlds'. As the Council's creature it would not be responsible to anyone and would be removed from democratic control. Jack Curran referred to the dangers of a 'self-perpetuating oligarchy'. Nevertheless, they both agreed to serve as members of the Trust. Presumably they were reassured by Sir Charles Norton's argument that there were safeguards that would take the Trust out of the political arena.[135] Meanwhile, the Special Committee continued its interim management of the property in 1964. Rhodes was succeeded as General Manager by Lt Col. Bryan Garrard, former Assistant Director of Supplies and Transport at the War Office, with effect from 1 February, with John Dobson serving as interim general manager until then.[136] Before the members of the Dolphin Square Trust first met, the Committee took some important decisions which would inform the new body's early operations. First, taking the advice of council officials, it decided that the proposal to 'defurnish' Rodney House would be abandoned. The retention of the profitable furnished flat and hotel business would make it possible to keep the rents of the unfurnished flats lower by about £20–50 a year.[137] Second, the matter of rents required immediate attention, with 330 seven-year leases due to expire by August 1964, and 60 tenants with expired three-year agreements on hold pending a decision. The Committee therefore drew up a new form of five-year tenancy agreement, with rents set at £320–870, viz. 18 per cent less than the Lintang tariff (£390–1,050), and slightly lower (by £15–35) than the tariff put to tenants in Dribbell's circular letter in October 1963.[138] By July new leases had been offered to 341 tenants whose three- and seven-year leases had expired. At the same time, it was decided to treat the formerly controlled tenants as if rent control were still in place, and to consider cases of hardship on their merits, since the Committee was aware that there were a number of elderly retired women living on small fixed incomes who would not qualify for a council house if they were forced to leave the Square.[139]

The first meeting of the Dolphin Square Trust was held on 27 April 1964. Dribbell was appointed its Chairman, and Garrard was appointed Secretary. The selection of seven councillors from the eight committee members did not arise because Geoffrey Gay was forced to resign as a trustee, since his articles of partnership with Knight, Frank & Rutley precluded him from serving.[140] Rules were drawn up, and the Trust was formally registered on 10 June 1964. The consent to the granting of a sublease was given in a letter from the Ministry of Housing and Local Government on 3 November.[141] Three weeks later the Trust's Committee of Management met to consider the terms. On the last day of 1964 an agreement was duly signed by both parties. The Council, in granting the Trust an underlease of Dolphin Square for the remaining term of the Council's lease - c.71 years - less a few days, did so on the clear understanding that the transaction would produce no costs. The premium, which was advanced to the Trust, was £4,609,837, or about £75m in today's prices. It was to be repaid on the same terms, and at the same rate (interest at 6.125%), as that defined by the Council's mortgage. The Trust also undertook to pay the Council an annual rental of £20,250, which matched the sum to be paid by the Council to the freeholder, the United Kingdom Temperance and General Provident Institution. The conditions attached to the lease were similar to those previously agreed by the Special Committee, i.e. there would be no further corporate lettings, and unfurnished flats would be let with the following receiving priority: i) existing tenants; ii) those displaced by building developments in Westminster; iii) those needing to live in or near central London by virtue of their business, profession or employment, e.g. 'Members of Parliament or persons engaged in the catering trade or in the entertainment business or who are employed in Central London and because of infirmity require to live near the place of employment'; iv) those employed or in occupations in Westminster; and concurrently with the previous criteria, applicants who had lived in Westminster continuously for at least five of the previous ten years.

The Trust was also required to ensure the continued protection of controlled tenants, and to accept the rent structure and leasing policy previously established by the Council, 'and any variation thereof which may from time to time be approved by the Council'.[142]

The DSTA continued to express its opposition to the new arrangements. In January 1964, it conducted its own poll of tenant opinion. Specifically, it asked tenants whether they still favoured a transfer to the original housing association. The results were something of a blow to the Council: 375 in favour, 39 per cent of the tenants eligible to vote; 73 against; and six abstentions.[143] Wynn Jones and her colleagues maintained their campaign of opposition, delaying the process of ministerial endorsement of the Council's underlease by appealing directly to the Housing Minister, Sir Keith Joseph, at the end of March. Joseph met a delegation from the DSTA, but told them that he was unable to help, pointing out that it was not for the Minister to intervene in such disputes.[144] Conciliatory gestures were made by the Council when it agreed to meet the greater part of the consulting costs of the DSTA and its housing association, and responded to its complaints about the disproportionate increase in rentals for one-room flats, which affected some of the executive committee members.[145] It was not until the autumn of 1965 that the air was finally cleared (see Chapter 5, p.200). But at last the status and management of Dolphin Square, uncertain since its sale by Costain, had been resolved. While some nervousness remained among the tenants about the new landlords, represented by a group of Westminster councillors who had certainly not anticipated the outcome when appointed to the Special Committee in February 1963, the terms of the Trust provided safeguards which promised to give the tenants a benevolent management charged with maintaining the property to a high standard and keeping rents as low as possible. On the whole, the mood was optimistic when the Trust took over the Square on 1 January 1965.

NOTES

1 Chairman's statement [to AGM, 5 June 1958], Costain, *R & A, 1957*, Guildhall Library. Data from Goddard, corrected to include three 3-year tenancies at a controlled rent. The number of controlled tenancies had fallen to 118 by 1962: Goddard & Smith et al., Sale documents for Dolphin Square, 1962, DST.

2 Rudimentary accounts are available from 1948, when the accounts of Richard Costain Ltd. and its subsidiaries were consolidated. The Exchange Telegraph Co., data card on 'Dolphin Square Ltd.', 1962, DST.

3 Chairman's statement, 22 April 1947, Costain, *R & A, 1946*, Guildhall Library.

4 17s. 6d. for a single room, 30s. for a double room, 133% and 140% higher than the charges in 1937. Dolphin Square Ltd., guest room charges, February 1958, DST.

5 Chairman's statement, 1949, Costain, *R & A, 1948*, and see also *1950*, Guildhall Library; *The Times*, 1 June 1949, p.9.

6 Chairman's statement, n.d., Costain, *R & A, 1957*, and see also *1956*, Guildhall Library.

7 Fred Berry, *Housing: The great British failure* (1974), pp.112–14; W.D. Rubinstein, *Wealth and Inequality in Britain* (1986), p.87.

8 Chairman's statement, 22 April 1947, Costain, *R & A,1946*, Guildhall Library.

9 The share capital was kept low by a Treasury ban on bonus share issues – i.e. capitalisation of reserves: *Financial Times*, 25 March 1946, p.3.

10 The issue was £1,469,000 in 3¾% First Mortgage Debenture Stock. On 31 March 1945 Dolphin Square Ltd.'s mortgage loans amounted to £985,546, while £499,791 was owed to Richard Costain Ltd. Prospectus, in *Financial Times*, 25 March 1946, pp.3, 6; Costain, *R & A 1946*; *Economist*, 3 May 1947. p.693.

11 Costain, *R & A, 1943–56*, Guildhall Library.

12 With the outstanding redeemable 6% preference shares converted into 5.5% shares, this made a total of £550,000. Costain, EGM, 27 January 1955, Guildhall Library. Lloyds Bank records show Costain's bank debt rising from £531,000 in 1947 to £1.4m in 1951 and 1954, and nearly £2m in 1956–7: Lloyds Bank Board Minutes, 21 November 1947–1 November 1957, Lloyds Banking Group Archives, London, HO/D/Boa/Min/55–61.

13 Costain, *R & A 1956–8*.

14 Ibid. *1957*; *The Times*, 27 March 1958, p.16, 17 April 1958, p.23.

15 Costain attempted to establish a new town at Allhallows, in Kent in 1956, but the project was lost on appeal. *The Times*, 1 June 1956, p.6, 14 February 1957, p.4. Sir Richard Costain was also Chairman of Harlow Development Corporation, 1950–66.

16 Balchin, *Housing Policy*, pp.109–10.

17 Sir Richard Costain, letter to shareholders, 14 November 1958, Guildhall Library.

18 Chairman's statement n.d., Costain, *R & A, 1958*, Guildhall Library.

19 On Sir Maxwell Joseph (1910–82) and Grand Met see the biographies by Christine Shaw, *Dictionary of Business Biography*, III (1985), pp.543–53, and by Richard Davenport-Hines, *OxDNB*.

20 Cf. Edward L. Erdman, *People and Property* (1982).

21 David Palmer, *Financial Times*, 17 August 1971, p.13. Palmer was later chief executive of the FT.

22 *The Times*, 7 September 1957, p.12, 18 December 1958, p.10.

23 Sir Richard Costain, letter to shareholders, 14 November 1958, Guildhall Library; *The Times*, 15 November 1958, p.8 [and cf. lower price of c. £2m, derived from Lintang Investments placing advertisement, 6 March 1959, in *The Times*, 9 March 1959, p.14]; Board of Trade, *Investigation into the Affairs of H. Jasper & Company Limited. Report by Mr. Neville Faulks Q.C.* (1 December 1959), published in June 1961.

24 *Financial Times*, 12 January 1959, p.5; Lintang Investment Ltd. prospectus, in *Financial Times*, 9 March 1959, p.9.

25 Tobin had been a director of the company which had sold the Hyde Park Estate to Lintang.

26 *The Times*, 9 March 1959, p.15; C. Bernard Hill (903 Drake), Memo. on 'Dolphin Square Limited and Lintang Investments Limited', 30 September 1959, in Hill-Morgan Phillips (General Secretary, Labour Party), 7 October 1959, Labour History Archive LP/GS/HOUS/54.

27 Lintang Investment Ltd. placing advertisement, 6 March 1959, in *Financial Times*, 9 March 1959, p.9; *The Times*, 12 March 1959, p.18; 13 March 1959, p.19, 11 April 1959, p.11; *Economist*, 30 May 1959, p.866. The shares settled down at 17–18s. a share in April, but had risen to 22s 6d. by early June: *The Times*, 3 June 1959, p.21.

28 Joseph took some profits, since he also had a holding of Lintang shares acquired for under 2s. a share.

29 At the same time Goddard & Smith, who were managing the 680 properties of the Hyde Park Estate for Lintang, valued that estate at £1.2m.

30 Goddard & Smith, Valuation, 1959, DST.

31 Sir Stanley Grinstead (1924-2003) was Chairman and Chief Executive of Grand Met, 1982–6.

32 *Financial Times*, 2 April 1959, p.2, 23 April 1959, p.12. See also Hill, Memo., 30 September 1959, p.9, Labour History Archive LP/GS/HOUS/54.

33 Surplices Ltd. held 98 of the 100 shares in Dolphin Square Caterers. Lintang Investment Ltd. placing advertisement, 6 March 1959; Dolphin Square Caterers Ltd. Board Minutes, 26 March 1959, DST. At the same time, the garage and petrol station were let to Dolphin Square (Garage) Ltd., operated by the Charles Rickards Group.

34 See Scott, *Property Masters*, p.132ff.

35 George Bull and Anthony Vice, *Bid For Power* (3rd edn, 1961), pp.268–9.

36 *The Times*, 18 March 1959 p.15, *Financial Times*, 9 July 1959, p.1.

37 See Faulks, *Report* (1961), and *Report by the Chief Registrar of Friendly Societies for the Year 1960: Part 5. Building Societies. Appendix III. Reports of the Inspector appointed by the Registrar of Building Societies to examine into and report on the Affairs of the State Building Society*, 29 January [interim] and 7 October [final] 1960. The inspector was William Lawson of Binder, Hamlyn & Co. A good summary of the affair is provided by Bull and Vice, *Bid for Power*, pp.268–79.

38 *Financial Times*, 9 July 1959, p.1, 21 July 1959, p.8, 9 February 1960, p.9. The directors held 3,165,871 shares, including Joseph's stake of 3,063,872 [48.6%].

39 Faulks, *Report*, 1961, p.4.

40 Re Harry Oscar Jasper (No.252 of 1960). Official Receiver's further report, 19 June 1962, p.5, TNA BT226/5929. The first was a Swaziland cotton business called Cotton Plantations which was turned into C.O.P. Investments.

41 *Financial Times*, 21 July 1959, p.8, 26 September 1959, p.9.

42 This was suggested by Jasper. See Harry O. Jasper, affidavit, 5 October 1959, p.12, TNA BT226/5931.

43 'Notes of an interview with Friederich [sic] Grunwald at Wormwood Scrubs Prison on Tuesday 21st March, 1961', TNA BT226/5931. Sigismund and Gerson Berger were wealthy property owners who were involved in a number of deals with Jasper and Grunwald. See Shirley Green, *Who Owns London?* (1986), pp.86-7.

44 *Interim report on State Building Society*, 29 January 1960, p.15. It is not clear why Joseph was willing to sell. Bernard Hill, of 903 Drake, who complained to the Labour Party about 'purely speculative operations', thought that plans for development opposite Dolphin Square - a heliport on the South Bank, and a secondary school in Chichester/Lupus streets, may have influenced Joseph. Hill, Memo., 30 September 1959, p.9, Labour History Archive LP/GS/HOUS/54.

45 Several banks were involved in the Lintang and subsequent transactions, including Lloyds, Martins, Williams Deacon's, and Barclays. In 1959 Lloyds had granted overdraft facilities to Lintang and Tildet, another Maxwell Joseph company, amounting to £1.85m. Security on the Lintang account was provided by 1,992 Dolphin Square Ltd. Shares: Lloyds Bank Board Minutes and Papers, 21 August 1959, Lloyds Banking Group Archives HO/D/Boa/Min/62 and HO/D/Boa/Age/29.

46 Joseph and Grunwald, indenture, 4 September 1959, Jasper bankruptcy proceedings, TNA BT226/5929; Faulks, *Report*, pp.8-9, 16; *Financial Times*, 9 February 1960, p.9, 22 March 1960, p.7; *Economist*, 30 July 1960, p.495; Bull and Vice, *Bid for Power*, pp.270-6.

47 Cf. its 1958 results, reported in *Financial Times*, 5 February 1959, p.6.

48 *Economist*, 19 September 1959, p.951, 26 September 1959, pp.1041-2.

49 *Financial Times*, 21 September 1959, p.1, 26 September 1959, p.9; T.R. Gourvish and R.G. Wilson, *The British Brewing Industry 1830–1980* (Cambridge, 1994), p.464; Bull and Vice, *Bid for Power*, p.275.

50 *The Times*, 10 October 1959, p.1, 11 January 1960, p.12, 23 July 1960, p.4.

51 Faulks, *Report*, pp.17-18; *The Times*, 20 June 1961, p.8; Bull and Vice, *Bid for Power*, p.277; *Companies Act 1948*, 11 & 12 Geo.VI c.38; I; *Building Societies Act 1960*, 8 & 9 Eliz.II c.64 and see also E.J. Cleary, *The Building Society Movement* (1965), p.262ff.

52 Jasper, affidavit, 5 October 1959, pp.13-14, TNA BT226/5931; *Financial Times*, 16 February 1960, p.7; *Economist*, 9 July 1960, p.188; Bull and Vice, *Bid for Power*, p.274.

53 *Financial Times*, 1 April 1960, p.7, 25 July 1960, p.1. 3.36m shares of a total of 3.54m shares in the possession of Joseph and his associates had been pledged as collateral.

54 Peat Marwick & Mitchell and Stephenson Harwood & Tatham (Joseph's solicitors), for Maxwell Joseph, letter to Lintang shareholders, 20 October 1959, London Stock Exchange company reports, Guildhall Library; Stephenson Harwood & Tatham-Lintang Investments Ltd. Shareholders, 20 October 1959, Assistant Secretary, Insurance and Companies Dept., Board of Trade, 1 June 1960, TNA BT58/755; *Financial Times*, 17 May 1960, p.12.

55 *The Times*, 31 July 1959, p.11; H.O. Jasper (Chairman, Lintang Investments)-Lintang shareholders, 28 August 1959, London Stock Exchange company reports, Guildhall Library.

56 Brueckmann committed suicide on 26 March 1961 before his case could be heard: Public examination notes on Wolf Brueckman, n.d., TNA BT226/5929.

57 *Financial Times*, 10 November 1960, p.11, 12 November 1960, p.7, 23 November 1960, p.12, 3 December 1960, p.1.

58 *Financial Times*, 4 December 1959, p.11, 1 January 1960, p.10; *Economist*, 12 December 1959, p.1101.

59 *Financial Times*, 7 January 1961, p.7, *Daily Telegraph*, 6 January 1961, p.2; H.O. Jasper bankruptcy proceedings, TNA B9/1579.

60 *Financial Times*, 18 November 1961, p.1; *Economist*, 2 December 1961, pp.952–3 and 24 March 1962, p.1151; *The Times*, 27 February 1962, p.16.

61 Report of Directors, 5 October 1962, Lintang Investments, *R & A 1961*, Guildhall Library; *The Times*, 29 November 1961, p.20, 22 December 1961, p.12.

62 Dolphin Square Ltd., *R & A, 1959–61*, p.3, DST; *Times*, 30 April 1962, p.17. Sir Dingwall Latham Bateson (1898–1967) was killed in a shooting accident. *Times*, 31 December 1960, p.3, 31 January 1967, p.12.

63 Lintang Investments, *R & A 1961*, Guildhall Library; Exchange Telegraph Co., data card, 1962, DST. Bateson, Robertson and Nicholson had been co-opted onto the State Building Society board at the invitation of the Chief Registrar of Friendly Societies. *The Times*, 1 April 1960, p.7.

64 It was not until 1964 that the affairs of Lintang, the State Building Society, and other parties were finally resolved: Bateson-Lintang shareholders, 27 August 1964, London Stock Exchange company reports, Guildhall Library; *Economist*, 29 August 1964, p.348. The EGM to wind up Lintang was held on 2 October 1964.

65 Guest room prices per night in August 1961: single 35s., double 63s., cf. 7/6 and 12/6 in 1937. Dolphin Square Ltd., Charges for Rodney House furnished flats and guest rooms, August 1961, DST.

66 Gerald Woolf Rhodes, affidavit, n.d., Treasury Solicitor's papers on W.J.C. Vassall: Tribunal of Inquiry, TNA TS58/639.

67 *Financial Times*, 15 March 1960, p.9.

68 The barristers were J.V. Naisby, 02 Keyes, and W.V. Sinclair, 07 Howard; the engineer was H. Blackman, 308 Hawkins; the accountant was H. Smith, 502 Collingwood; and the military men were Lt Col. L. Edwards, 303 Keyes, Cdr R.M.R. Hoare, RN [retd], 701 Raleigh, and Major-Gen. Arthur Williams, 901 Hood.

69 Interview with Sir Alan Dawtry, 11 February 2011. Wynn Jones is not to be confused with the writer of fantasy fiction, Diana Wynne Jones (1934–2011).

70 *Daily Express*, 21 April 1959, cutting in DST.

71 R.M.R. Hoare, Notices to Dolphin Square tenants on 'Proposed Tenants' Association', April 1959, 28 April, 1 and 9 May 1959, deposited by G. Wadlow, 805 Drake, DST.

72 Dawtry rented a furnished flat for £5 a week in 1956, and obtained a lease on 802 Nelson in 1957. Interview with Sir Alan Dawtry, 11 February 2011.

73 Alan G. Dawtry (Town Clerk, WCC), Report to the Housing and Finance Committees, 19 February 1960, and DSTA, 'Tenants' Association – Summary of Negotiations', 1959–63, in Pargiter (Chairman, DSTA), Letter to All Residents, 3 July 1963, DST.

74 *The Times*, 2 March 1960, p.6.

75 *The Times*, 8 March 1960, p.7; *Financial Times*, 8 March 1960, p.9, 15 March 1960, p.9.

76 *Westminster and Pimlico News*, 12 August 1960, p.1; *Daily Express*, 20 September 1960, p.9, cuttings in Dolphin Square Trust file on 'Formation Trust', DST.

77 DSTA, Notice No.16, enclosing Memorandum on 'Some Effects of the 1957 Rent Act', September 1960, and *Star*, 13 September 1960, p.4, cutting in ibid.

78 G.W. Rhodes (General Manager, Dolphin Square Ltd.), letters to Ministry of Housing & Local Government, G.A. Pargiter, and S. Berger, 16 September 1960, ibid.

79 Cdr Hoare vacated his flat, 701 Raleigh, in August 1961.

80 *The Times*, 30 April 1962, p.8, 22 May 1962, p.6; Morris, *Dolphin Square*, p.71. The *Observer* reported that there were 587 such leases: 20 January 1963, p.4.

81 The scale was reported in WCC Minutes, 14 March 1963, WCA.

82 Cf. the discussion in *Financial Times*, 14 August 1962, p.1, 6.

83 Goddard & Smith et al., Sale documents for Dolphin Square, 1962, DST; *Guardian*, 28 November 1962, p.17. The document was leaked to the *Financial Times*, 22 November 1962, p.9.

84 Morris, *Dolphin Square*, p.70. Here the two-room rental after 1959 quoted by Morris should have been £430 [+218%], not £555. See DSTA, Notice No. 16, September 1960, Dolphin Square Trust file on 'Formation Trust', DST.

85 Goddard & Smith et al., Sale documents for Dolphin Square, 1962, DST, and Appendix 1. No one in a flat originally priced at £135 p.a. was paying £555 in 1962. This tariff was being applied to flats with an original rental of £165+.

86 Something complained of by Gerald Rhodes, the General Manager. See G.W. Rhodes-S. Berger, 16 September 1960, Dolphin Square Ltd. file on 'Formation Trust', DST.

87 Appendix 1, and Goddard & Smith et al., Sale documents for Dolphin Square, 1962, DST. Prices rose by 236%, 1937–62 [combining Board of Trade wholesale prices to 1948 and the GDP deflator at market prices from 1948]. The 1962 rate, at 17/6 in £1, amounted to £28 p.a. for controlled flats paying £155, and £92–139 p.a. for dearer flats. For our sample in the South Block, the rates bill amounted to £23,103.5, reducing the real loss to landlords to 18 per cent.

88 See Nicholas Timmins, *The Five Giants: a Biography of the Welfare State* (1995), pp.188–92, Peter Malpass, *Housing and the Welfare State: The Development of Housing Policy in Britain* (Basingstoke, 2005), pp.88–9, and Alan G.V. Simmonds, 'Raising Rachman: The Origins of the Rent Act, 1957', *The Historical Journal*, 45:4 (2002), 863. Rachman's name first appeared in *The Times* on 1 July 1963, p.6. See also Shirley Green, *Rachman* (1979), pp.146–50, 158–61, 209. On Keeler, Rice-Davies and Dolphin Square see Morris, *Dolphin Square*, p.107, and www.dolphinsquare.co.uk/village-living/famous residents/.

89 For a more measured assessment of Rachman's own activities see *Report of the Committee on Housing in Greater London (Chairman: Sir Milner Holland, CBE, QC)*, March 1965, Appendix II, and Green, *Rachman*, pp.218–24.

90 Dolphin Square Ltd., *R & A 1959–61*, DST. Net profits after tax for 1962 have not been found, but pre-tax profits were £238,500, cf. £216,700 in 1961: Dolphin Square Ltd., draft accounts for 1962, 8 March 1963, DST.

91 The change was made by the London Government Act 1963, 1963 c.33, Schedule 1. The Greater London Council was also established and given a primarily strategic role.

92 Cf. Timmins, *Five Giants*, pp.188–92.

93 Interviews with Sir Alan Dawtry, 11 February 2011, and Jack Dribbell, 12 May 2011.

94 See Peter Malpass, *Housing Associations and Housing Policy: A Historical Perspective* (Basingstoke, 2000), pp.133–7, and his 'The Uneven Development of 'Social Rented Housing: Explaining the Historically Marginal Position of Housing Associations in Britain', *Housing Studies*, 16:2 (2001), 225–42.

95 *Housing Act 1957*, 1957 c.56, S.119–21.

96 Notes of a 'Conference between the Chairmen and Vice-Chairmen of the Finance and Housing Committees and representatives of the Dolphin Square tenants, Monday, 15th October 1962', DST.

97 Dawtry, letter, 1 November 1962, cit. in Dawtry, 'Report of the Town Clerk to the Joint Meeting of the Finance and Housing Committees – 4 December 1962: Dolphin Square – Proposed Formation by Tenants of Housing Association – Application for Loan from Council on Security of Premises', 3 December 1962, DST.

98 DSTA, Memorandum to WCC, 24 November 1962, Appendix A of Dawtry, Report, 3 December 1962, DST.

99 Tony Prendergast (Chairman, Housing Committee, WCC)-Group Capt. G.H. Pirie (Councillor and leader of WCC), 5 December 1962, DST. Sir Arthur Howard was the

fiercest opponent of purchasing the Square. A former MP for St. George's Westminster (1945–50), he was Treasurer of St. Thomas's Hospital, 1943–64. *Who's Who of British Members of Parliament*, IV.

100 Ibid. Prendergast made the point that direct action was necessary because while the Council was precluded from buying shares under the Housing Acts the vendors had introduced the option of a purchase of Dolphin Square Ltd. shares.

101 WCC Minutes, 10 January 1963, WCA.

102 Draft Resolutions of the Finance and Housing Committees, 4 December 1962, DST; Interview with Sir Alan Dawtry, 11 February 2011.

103 DSTA, 'Tenants' Association – Summary of Negotiations', 1959–63, DST.

104 WCC Minutes, 10 January 1963, WCA; *Financial Times*, 11 January 1963, p.1.

105 DSTA, 'Tenants' Association – Summary of Negotiations', 1959–63, DST. Bliss, 05 Hawkins; Harper-Nelson, 205 Hood; Marsh, 704 Nelson, Williams, 901 Hood.

106 Sir Spencer le Marchant (1931–86), Westminster councillor (1956–71), Conservative MP for Derbyshire High Peak (1970–83), Chief Secretary to the Treasury, 1972–4, Minister for Energy, 1974. *Who's Who of British Members of Parliament*, IV. Margaret Thatcher begins her memoirs with the observation that Le Marchant was 'famous for his intake of champagne': *The Downing Street Years* (1993), p.3.

107 Reports of WCC Housing Committee, 2 January 1963, and Finance Committee, 22 January 1963, WCA. Morris, *Dolphin Square*, p.72, incorrectly states that the interest rate was 6.75%.

108 Cf. Tony Prendergast-Group Capt. G.H. Pirie (Councillor and leader of the Council), Confidential Note on 'Dolphin Square', 31 December 1962: 'I was horrified to learn that the Association was to be registered this week with a set of rules quite unacceptable to the Council.'

109 Chairman of Negretti & Zambra, scientific instrument manufacturers. *Directory of Directors*.

110 Bramall was MP for Bexley, 1946–50, when he was defeated by Edward Heath. He was Chairman of ILEA, 1965–7, and Leader, 1970–81. He received a knighthood in 1975. His younger brother Edwin, later Lord Bramall, was Chief of the Defence Staff, 1982–5.

111 WCC Minutes, 31 January and 14 March 1963, WCA; Dolphin Square (Special) Committee Minutes, 5–6 February and 21 March 1963, DST; Interview with Jack Dribbell, 12 May 2011.

112 Later on, the Council changed its mind, and favoured an assignment for the 71-year period of the lease less a few days.

113 Cf. Leslie Howard (Secretary & Agent, Westminster Conservative Association)-Councillor Anne Marsh, 5 February 1963, Marsh-Councillor Tony Prendergast (Chairman, Westminster Housing Committee), 6 February 1963, Jack Dribbell (Chairman, Dolphin Square (Special) Committee)-Prendergast, 11 February 1963, DST. The animosity between Wynn Jones and Rhodes probably stemmed from the fact that she, along with fellow DSTA executive members Mitchell and Smith, had been forced to move from Rodney House (nos. 304, 320, and 421) in order for the flats to be converted into furnished properties. See WCC Rate Book No.5 for years ending 31 March 1955–9, WCA. Rhodes also felt strongly that Rodney House should not be 'defurnished' as the DSTA wanted. See Dawtry and E. Ockenden, City Treasurer, WCC, Report to Dolphin Square (Special) Committee, 30 December 1963, DST.

114 Report of the Dolphin Square (Special) Committee, 5, 6 and 22 February 1963, WCC Minutes, 14 March 1963, WCA.

115 Unsurprisingly, the reports of the two sides on these events do not concur: cf. Pargiter, Letter to Residents, 3 July 1963, and Dribbell-Dolphin Square Residents, 1 August 1963, DST. The DSTA was also unhappy that Rhodes was not resident in Dolphin Square.

116 Dawtry-Wynn Jones, 8 May 1963 and reply, 11 May 1963, Dolphin Square (Special) Committee Minutes, 21 March and 17 May 1963, DST; WCC Minutes, 27 June 1963, WCA.

117 WCC Minutes, 27 June and 1 August 1963, WCA.

118 See press coverage in 1963, e.g. *Daily Telegraph*, 11 and 12 June, 10 August and 14 November, press cuttings in WCA.

119 Pargiter, Letter to Residents, 3 July 1963, DST.

120 Ibid. and Dribbell-Dolphin Square Residents, 1 August 1963, DST.

121 Pargiter-Dolphin Square Residents, 22 July 1963, DST. The capital contribution was to be returned when a tenant left the Square.

122 Some councillors favoured charging market rents to all, e.g. Peter Laszlo of Marconi and English Electric: Peter Laszlo-Prendergast, 7 February 1963, Laszlo-Dribbell, 25 February 1963, DST.

123 Dolphin Square (Special) Committee Minutes, 11 July 1963, Dawtry, Report to Dolphin Square (Special) Committee, 6 September 1963, DST. Councillors envisaged a capital contribution of £1, plus a subscription of loan capital.

124 Hamlins, Grammer & Hamlin-Dawtry, 12 August 1963, DST. Pargiter also challenged the statements in Dribbell's letter to residents of 1 August: Pargiter-Dolphin Square residents, 17 August 1963, copy in Dolphin Square (Special) Committee papers, 12 September 1963, DST.

125 His resignation took effect on 30 November 1963. Dolphin Square (Special) Committee Minutes, 12 September and 21 November 1963, DST.

126 Rhodes-Dribbell, 5 November 1963, enclosing 'Notes on a Meeting of the Dolphin Square Tenants' Association held on the 4th November 1963', Dribbell papers, 2001, DST.

127 Wynn Jones-Dawtry, 16 January 1964, DST. Pargiter accepted a financial inducement to quit. See Dolphin Square (Special) Committee Minutes, 5 February 1963, DST. His tenancy ended on 28 February 1963: WCC Rate Book No.5 for year ending 31 March 1963, WCA.

128 Rhodes-Dribbell, 5 November 1963, Dribbell papers, 2001, DST.

129 The separation of Dolphin Square into residential and commercial entities was regarded as 'completely impracticable'.

130 Dribbell-Dolphin Square residents, 22 October 1963, DST.

131 Reproduced in WCC Minutes, 12 December 1963, WCA.

132 Ibid. and Dribbell-Dolphin Square residents, 12 November 1963, Dolphin Square (Special) Committee Minutes, 21 November 1963, DST. The Council subsequently revealed the number of responses received by 28 November, viz. 95 acceptances (10%), 20 rejections, and 256 copies of the DSTA resolution.

133 'Suggested speech for use by Chairman of the General Purposes Committee', February 1964, Dribbell papers, DST; Dolphin Square (Special) Committee, presentment, 7 February 1964, DST.

134 Report of General Purposes Committee, 5 March 1964, WCC Minutes, 19 March 1964, WCA.

135 See annotations on Dawtry, Report to Dolphin Square (Special) Committee, 4 February 1964, DST; *Westminster & Pimlico News*, 3 April 1964, p.6; Interview with Jack Dribbell, 20 May 2011.

136 Dolphin Square (Special) Committee Minutes, 21 November 1963, and Rhodes-J.A. Dobson, 22 November 1963, DST; *The Times*, 23 October 1963, p.6.

137 Dawtry and Ockenden, Report, 30 December 1963, Dolphin Square (Special) Committee Minutes, 2 January 1964, DST.

138 Dawtry, Report on 'Future of Rodney House', 30 December 1963, Dolphin Square (Special) Committee Minutes, 2 January and 7 February 1964, DST; Morris, *Dolphin Square*, pp.76, 121. The original intention to charge rents of £315–£850 was modified when the Committee accepted the advice of the City Treasurer to abandon the proposal to charge rents with two separate components: i) to service the council loan; and ii) to cover repairs, renewals and management costs. Ockenden, Report to Dolphin Square (Special) Committee, 4 February 1964, DST. Rents of £320–870 are about £5,200–14,100 in today's prices.

139 Garrard, Report on 'Cases of Hardship in Dolphin Square', 16 July 1964, Joint meeting of Dolphin Square (Special) Committee and representatives of the WCC Housing Committee, 20 July 1964, DST; Interview with Jack Dribbell, 20 May 2011.

140 Dolphin Square Trust Minutes, 27 April 1964, DST.

141 J.R. Niven (Ministry of Housing & Local Government)-Dawtry, 3 November 1964. Niven, reporting the Minister's consent in principle, promised that a separate letter would be sent to the Council setting out matters of detail, but this does not appear to have been sent. It is possible that a change of government led to the omission, with Sir Keith Joseph having been succeeded by Richard Crossman as Minister on 18 October.

142 Dolphin Square Trust Committee of Management Minutes, 23 November 1964, DST; Report of WCC General Purposes Committee, 26 November 1964, WCC Minutes, 10 December 1964, WCA; WCC and DST, underlease, 31 December 1964, DST; 'Agreement between the Mayor Aldermen and Councillors of the City of Westminster and Dolphin Square Trust Ltd.', 31 December 1964, DST.

143 Dawtry, Report to Dolphin Square (Special) Committee, 4 February 1964, DST. Those eligible to vote (952) are listed in Appendix 2.

144 *Daily Telegraph*, 6 May 1964, p.17; *Westminster and Pimlico News*, 8 May 1964, p.5.

145 WCC Minutes, 19 March and 10 December 1964, WCA; Garrard, Report on 'Rents of One Room Flats', 22 April 1964, Dribbell papers, DST. The Council agreed to pay £5,920 of the DSTA/DSHA's costs.

CHAPTER 5

THE DOLPHIN SQUARE TRUST, 1965–93

THE TRUSTEES, 1965–93

Seven Westminster councillors met as the first Dolphin Square Trust Committee of Management in November 1964. However, the Trust's rules stipulated a committee of between seven and 16 members, and in March 1965 five further Council nominations were received and accepted: Geoffrey Ball, FRICS, a quantity surveyor; Peter Dew, former Chairman of Westminster Chamber of Commerce; William Hayhurst, FIMTA, FCA, former Council Treasurer and a director of Sterling Estates; James Macnabb, FCA, a chartered accountant and housing expert (he was, inter alia, Chairman of the National Federation of Housing Societies); and Valerie Shafto, joint managing director of Enjoy Britain and the World Ltd. Macnabb was a particularly useful recruit. He was a member of the Westminster Housing Trust, a past president of the Institute of Housing, and a member of the Ministry of Housing's Central Housing Advisory Committee. He was also an administrator of the Peabody Trust (Table 5.1).[1] What was this group like? Housing associations are often criticised for being 'self perpetuating oligarchies' of middle-class people, and the Dolphin Square Trust was no exception.[2] However, it could not be said that the Trust lacked expertise. The members were drawn from business and the professions. Two were Labour councillors, Curran and Bramall, but in general the trustees reflected Westminster's conservative leanings. No fewer than eight Mayors (from 1965 Lord Mayors) came from the Trust's ranks.[3] Initially, there were only two tenant-trustees, Ball and Shafto, but the number was increased to three in 1968 when Spencer le Marchant, one of the founding members, took a lease on 508 and 509 Frobisher House, and to four when Prendergast's wife Simone leased 804 and 805 Hood House in 1969.[4] None of them had been active in the Dolphin Square Tenants' Association.

Table 5.1 Dolphin Square Trust members, March 1965

Trustee	*Office*	*Background*	*Term of office*
J.L.C. [Jack] Dribbell	Chairman	WCC Councillor; Business	1964–7
A.L. [Tony] Burton	Vice–Chairman	WCC Councillor; Business	1964–7
Geoffrey W. Ball, FRICS		Tenant 209/10 Duncan; Surveyor	1965–76
[Sir] Ernest Ashley Bramall		WCC and GLC Councillor; Barrister; Chairman/Leader, ILEA 1965–7, 1970–81	1964–8
J.J. [Jack] Curran		WCC Councillor; Trade Unionist	1964–83
Peter Dew, OBE		Business (Chairman Westminster Chamber of Commerce, 1963–5)	1965–71
William Hayhurst, CBE, FIMTA, FSAA		WCC Treasurer, 1945–62	1965–75
Sir Charles Norton, MBE, MC		WCC Councillor; Solicitor	1964–74
Spencer Le Marchant		WCC Councillor; Broker; Tenant 508/9 Frobisher 1968–72	1964–72
James Macnabb, FCA		Accountant; Chairman, National Federation of Housing Societies	1965–72
C.A. [Tony] Prendergast		WCC Councillor; Business (Lloyds)	1964–98
Valerie Shafto		Tenant 106 Keyes; Business	1965–75

Source: DST.

Inevitably, there was a turnover in membership as time passed, but only 25 trustees were required in the three decades from 1964 to 1993, and there were only two chairmen, Jack Dribbell (1964–7), and Tony Prendergast (1967–93) [Illustration 28 (iv)]. The office of vice-chairman changed hands more frequently. Tony Burton resigned on succeeding Sir Charles Norton as Lord Mayor in 1966, and left the Trust in the following year; he was succeeded by Prendergast (1966–7), who, in turn, was succeeded by Peter Dew (1967–71). Dew was followed by Roger Dawe, FCIS (1971–86), a chartered surveyor, councillor and director of Bovis. Later a Lord Mayor, he was one of the two members recruited in 1967–8 to replace Bramall and Burton.[5] The other newcomer was Wilfred Bowdell, FIMTA, the serving Westminster City Treasurer. There was a major change in the Trust's membership in 1971-2, when four trustees - Dribbell, Dew, Le Marchant and Macnabb - resigned at a time when the City Council came to the view that trustees who were either councillors or tenants should resign their position on ceasing to be either.[6] Initially, they were replaced by only three new trustees: Gordon Pirie, former Mayor and Leader of the Council, 1961-9, who served briefly as Vice-chairman of the Trust in 1975-7; Alan (from 1974 Sir Alan) Dawtry, the former town clerk and chief executive of Westminster until 1977 who was in many ways the architect of the Council's purchase of the Square, succeeded Dawe as vice-chairman in 1986; and Joan Quennell, MP for Petersfield since 1960, who had recently been PPS to Ernest Marples at the Ministry of Transport (1962-4), and, like Dawtry, was a Dolphin Square tenant. The number of trustees briefly increased to 12 again in 1974, with the appointment of John Bamford, CIPFA, FRVA, another Westminster Council Treasurer.[7] However, in the same year Sir Charles Norton died and four more trustees resigned in 1975-6: Hayhurst, Quennell, Shafto and Ball. They were succeeded by three Dolphin Square tenants: Jan Reid (from 1994 Jan Prebble), a *Daily Mail* columnist, subsequently Press and Public Relations Officer of Capital Radio, and active member of the DSTA, 1973-87;[8] Barry Pinson, QC and specialist in taxation law; and Maurice Stonefrost, CIPFA, a leading practitioner of local government finance, Comptroller of Financial Services at the GLC, 1964-73, and its last Director-General (1984-5).[9] Membership now fell to ten, and stayed at this level thereafter. Bamford, the City Treasurer, was replaced by his successor, David Hopkins, in 1979, and when Jack Curran stepped down after nearly 20 years as a trustee in 1983, David Weeks, a marketing specialist and Westminster councillor, 1974-98, joined the Committee. He served as Shirley Porter's deputy from 1983 and succeeded her as leader, 1991-3. He was heavily involved in Porter's gerrymandering activity under the banner 'Building Stable Communities' (see below, p.236).[10] In 1986, Bowdell and Dawe, who had also served for 20 years, were followed by Rodney Brooke and Alan Bradley. Brooke, Westminster's chief executive, 1984-9, had his period in that office cut short by his opposition to Porter.[11] Bradley, a leading actuary and Westminster councillor from 1978, took a particular interest in planning and the environment and served as Lord Mayor in 1995-6.[12]

While the Trust began as a body of Conservative councillors and senior local government officers, who provided nearly two-thirds of the total, more than half the trustees were residents, and their representation increased over time. By 1977, tenants made up half of the membership, and since the last seven trustees to be appointed in the period 1975–86 were all resident in the Square, from 1986 the proportion rose to 80 per cent (see Table 5.2).[13] Thus, from the 1980s the Trust began to reflect the views of those who had a direct and personal interest in Dolphin Square, rather than merely a watching brief on behalf of the City Council.

Table 5.2 Dolphin Square Trust members, 1972–93

Trustee	*Office*	*Background*	*Term of office*
C.A. [Tony] Prendergast, CBE	Chairman, 1967–93	WCC Councillor; Business (Lloyds); Tenant 804/5 Hood 1969–75	1964–98
Roger M. Dawe, FCIS	Vice-Chairman, 1971–5, 1976–86	WCC Councillor; Business (Co. Sec & Dr, Bovis until 1983)	1968–86
J.J. [Jack] Curran		WCC Councillor; Trade Unionist	1964–83
Sir Charles Norton, MBE, MC		WCC Councillor; Solicitor	1964–74
Geoffrey W. Ball, FRICS		Surveyor (senior partner, C.E. Ball & Partners); Tenant 209/10 Duncan	1965–76
Peter Dew, OBE		Business (Chairman Westminster Chamber of Commerce, 1963–5)	1965–71
William Hayhurst, CBE, FIMTA (CIPFA), FSAA		WCC Treasurer, 1945–62; director, Sterling Estates	1965–75
Valerie Shafto		Business (Jnt MD, Enjoy Britain and the World); Tenant 106 Keyes	1965–75
Wilfred Bowdell, CBE, FIMTA (CIPFA)		WCC Treasurer, 1962–74	1967–86
[Sir] Alan G. Dawtry, CBE	Vice-Chairman, 1986–99	WCC Town Clerk/Chief Executive, 1956–77; chairman Sperry Rand Ltd, 1977–86; Tenant 806 Collingwood/901 Grenville	1971–2002
[Sir] Gordon H.M. Pirie, CVO, CBE, DL	Vice-Chairman, 1975–6	WCC Councillor; RAF; Tenant 103 Beatty, 1978–82	1971–98

Joan M. Quennell, MBE, MP		MP for Petersfield, 1960–74; director, Winchester & Alton Railway; Tenant 106 Grenville	1972–5
John W. Bamford, CIPFA, FRVA		WCC Treasurer, 1974–8	1974–8
Jan K. Reid [from 1994 Prebble]		Journalist (*Daily Mail*), later P&PRO, Capital Radio until 1987); Tenant 904, 902 Howard	1975–2011
Barry Pinson, QC		Lawyer; Tenant 804/5 Hood	1976–2011
Maurice F. Stonefrost, CBE, DL, CIPFA		Dr-Gen. GLC, 1984–5; Tenant 807 Howard, 611 Hood	1975–2001
David J. Hopkins, CIPFA, FRVA, AMBIM		WCC Treasurer, 1979–90; Tenant 403 Hawkins	1979–2000
David P. Weeks, MCIM		WCC Councillor; Business (Marketing: E. Gomme, Y.J. Lovell); Tenant, 408 Frobisher	1983–98
[Sir] Rodney G. Brooke, CBE, DL		WCC Chief Executive, 1984–9; Solicitor; Tenant 706 Grenville	1986–2011
Alan Bradley, FIA		WCC Councillor; Actuary (Partner, Clark & Peacock); Tenant 710 Collingwood	1986–2004

Source: DST; Morris, ***Dolphin Square***, p.118; supplementary information.

THE SENIOR MANAGERS AND STAFF, 1965–93

In 1964–5 the staff of just under 200 people was led, as before, by a general manager, then Bryan Garrard, who also acted as secretary to the Trust. The number of employees remained relatively stable for over 30 years. In 1964, there were 194 full-time posts; in 1993, the number was 193.[14] Garrard presided over ten senior functional managers, covering accounting, building superintendence, lettings, the hotel, housekeeping, porterage, telephones, printing, and the news and hardware shops (Table 5.3). These were a mixed bag of activities varying in size and importance, and with some departmental heads paid less than more junior staff in the larger departments.

Table 5.3 Dolphin Square senior managers, 1964–5

Office	*Manager*	*Term of office*
General Manager	Bryan C. Garrard, FCIS	1964–74
Chief Accountant	J.S. Austin, CA	1964–74
Building Superintendent	John. A. Dobson, MIPHE, MJIE	1936–70
Letting Office Manager	Eve Parsons	1954–72
Head Receptionist (Rodney House Manager)	Judy Morgan	1963–87
Head Housekeeper	Ms N.L. Payne	1961–6
Head Porter	H.W. Phillips	1961–72
Telephone Exchange Supervisor	Nena G. Howe	19#–76
Printing Manager	J.G. Flynn	1963–7
Newsshop Manager	J. Hillcoat	1960–7
Hardware Shop Manager	George K. Lindsay	1963–#
Other senior staff:		
Chief Engineer	William Groves	1956–80
Accountant	A.E. Mapledoram	1962–70
Maintenance Manager	D.C. Roshier	1960–6
Secretary	Ms C.B. Harris	1965–81

Source: DST.

Note: Dates are in some cases approximate [information is incomplete]

In terms of staff numbers the major departments were maintenance and engineering (51), porters and cleaners (48), housekeeping (42), and telephony (18).[15] Over the next 30 years, finding suitable managers for the principal posts was not without its problems, since the Trust was required to balance income and expenditure at a time of inflation, which averaged 8.2 per cent a year, 1964–93, and was sometimes rapid, as in 1974–7, 1978–81, and 1989–90.[16] A not-for-profit enterprise could only be cautious in handling salaries and wages, and it was sometimes difficult to recruit able people at the remuneration being offered given the competition in central London's labour market. Filling the key posts of general manager and chief accountant proved to be particularly challenging for the trustees, and in the 30 years to 1993 there were five general managers, three of which were asked to resign,[17] and eight chief accountants, excluding interim managers (Table 5.4). The post of general manager called for a wide range of skills – organisational, financial and personal, in an operation which combined property management, landlord and tenant relations, and commercial activities, including a hotel. Ex-military men were generally favoured. Bryan Garrard, a Fellow of the Chartered Institute of Secretaries and Administrators, was general manager from 1964 to 1974. He had experience of military administration at a relatively high level, having been Assistant Director of Supplies at the War Office. At Dolphin Square he quickly got to grips with the problems surrounding the property, tackling the backlog of maintenance, and streamlining the rather cumbersome administration.[18] Garrard was succeeded by his deputy, Kenneth Morris, who also had a military background – he had been a staff quartermaster in the Royal Army Service Corps, later the Royal Corps of Transport – and was particularly popular with staff and tenants during his period of office (1974–83)[19] [Illustration 31]. His successor, Commodore John (Ian) Wood, general manager, 1983–5, was a Fellow of the British Institute of Management, and had been awarded a CBE for services to the RAF, where he was a director of personnel services.[20] While the policy of appointing military men was not always a success, as the departures of Garrard and Wood indicated,[21] it was the only civilian to be appointed who was the subject of a very public resignation. The career of John Cumming, general manager from 1986 to 1991, had begun in higher education, but he certainly had experience of property management, although not with an enterprise as large as Dolphin Square. Alongside his teaching of management at Croydon College from 1971, he took an active interest in estate management, and the latter became a full-time occupation in 1983. Prior to his appointment as general manager at Dolphin Square he was Chairman and Estate Manager of Chinfort Ltd., a company that helped residents in large mansion blocks to buy their freeholds and manage the properties. In 1985, the company was managing ten blocks in Battersea, Sloane Square and Fulham.[22] After five years at Dolphin Square, he complained strongly about his dismissal to the tenants, appealed to an industrial tribunal and took his story to the press.[23] He had certainly clashed with members of the DSTA. In March 1987, its newsletter recorded dissatisfaction with his response to general maintenance problems. And in the following October four key members of the Association – Deirdre Marshall, chairman, Peter James, vice-chairman, Jan Reid, secretary, and Ralph

Gurnett – resigned en bloc. In a letter to members they referred to the 'considerable frustration' they had experienced when trying to raise tenancy issues with the general manager.[24] Fortunately, Cumming's successor, Tony Crawford, CBE, proved to be an entirely satisfactory appointee. He also made an immediate positive impression with the tenants by improving communication levels via his 'Round-Up' letters.[25] Previously a brigadier and Director of the Intelligence Corps, he was general manager until 1997 (Table 5.4).

Table 5.4 Dolphin Square major departmental heads, 1965–93

General Manager and Secretary:	Bryan C. Garrard, FCIS Ken F. Morris John P. (Ian) Wood, CBE, FBIM John L. Cumming, MIPM A.K. (Tony) Crawford, CBE	1964–74 1974–83 1983–5 1986–91 1991–7
Assistant to General Manager/ Deputy General Manager:	Ken F. Morris David Collins, MIMBM	1968–74 1991–7
Secretary to General Manager/ PA to General Manager:	C.B. (Betty) Harris Phyllis Gordon Catie M. Bland Sally A. Watson	1964–81 1981–9 1989–91 1991–2011
Chief Accountant:	J.S. Austin, FCA A.R. Dale, AMBIM Bernard A.G. Cloke F. Rioch, FCA H.T.B. Legg, FCA, FCCA J.E. Webb, ACMA, MBIM R.J. (Bob) Morley, FCA Gordon E.F. Jacques, ACMA	1964–74 1974 1974–7 1978–83 1983–4 1984–5 1985–7 1988–97
Accountant:	A.E. Mapledoram P. Symons	1962–70 1971–#
Building Superintendent/ Head of Maintenance:	John A. Dobson, MIPHE, MJIE Joseph Judd David Collins, MIMBM	1936–73† 1973–6 1977–97
Chief Engineer:	William Groves Doug Durand	1956–80 1980–8
Maintenance Manager/ Assistant Head of Maintenance:	D.C. Roshier Joseph Judd P.W. (Paddy) Moore G. Hare David 'Bob' Morley	1960–6 1967–73 1973–85 1985–8 1988–#
Letting Office Manager/ Flats Manager:	Eve Parsons M. Perkins (Mrs) Win King Peter B. Bicknell	1954–72 1973–81 1981–4 1984–93

Rodney House Manager*:	Win King Janetta .M. Devon, AIPM John R. Firrell, MHCIMA	1985–8 1989–91 1991–6
Head Housekeeper:	Ms N.L. Payne Enid K. Pedraza George Paget	1961–6 1966–79 1981–91
Head Receptionist:	Judy Morgan	1963–87
Head Porter/ House Superintendent:	H.W. Phillips Charles 'Andy' Anderson A. 'Buster' Brown George Burton	1961–72 1972–4 1974–85 1985–2008

Source: DST.
Note: Dates and descriptions are in some cases approximate [information is incomplete]

Key:
† Employed on a consultancy basis, 1970–3
* Also known as Commercial House Manager, Hotel Operations Manager

The post of chief accountant also gave the trustees some headaches, since turnover was particularly high (Table 5.4). After J.S. Austin retired in 1974, three accountants were tried before some stability was restored, and there were further recruitment difficulties in 1983-5, coinciding with Wood's period as general manager. The Trust's surviving records provide relatively little information on this problem, though Garrard noted in 1974 that recruitment and retention in accounts had been troublesome, and that consultants had been engaged in 1973 to review the department.[26] It is well known that smaller charities face tough competition for able accountants as they can command much higher salaries elsewhere. At Dolphin Square the problem was compounded by an extremely high turnover rate in 1973-4. In four posts there had been no fewer than 24 different individuals in 15 months, and the post of cashier changed hands 14 times in nine months. The machine room lacked continuity, and this threatened the integrity of the accounting process. As Garrard observed, this 'places an intolerable strain on senior members of the staff who are forever sorting out errors made by others instead of getting on with their own jobs'. It certainly did not make the post of chief accountant a particularly attractive one.[27]

In his ten years as general manager, Garrard made efforts to streamline the organisation of Dolphin Square. When he arrived in November 1964, he thought that the number of departments should be reduced to three, i.e. Operations, under the letting office manager; Building, under the building superintendent; and Administration, under the chief accountant.[28] However, a year later he suggested that there should be four main departments, namely Building, Accounts, Unfurnished flats, and Rodney House (including the sports centre). Under the existing arrangements, the management of both the unfurnished and furnished flats was shared between the letting office manager (letting of both unfurnished and furnished flats), the head receptionist (letting of guest rooms), and the head housekeeper (servicing of Rodney House and guest rooms). Garrard argued that this was unsatisfactory, since the Rodney House operation had grown out of all proportion to the number of staff responsible for it.[29] However, reforming zeal seems to have diminished with Garrard's departure, and his immediate successors were content to work within a modified version of the existing framework. When Morris retired in 1983 the organisational chart supplied to applicants for his job was still rather imprecise. While four senior managers were identified - general manager, building superintendent, chief accountant and letting officer - reporting lines were far from clear. It seems that while there was clarity in the maintenance department, the management of the flats was as divided as it had been when Garrard complained about it in 1965. The letting officer remained responsible for both unfurnished and furnished flats, and the head housekeeper and head receptionist reported to her. However, the house superintendent continued as a separate function, embracing the porterage, security and cleaning of the common areas (excluding Rodney House). And in common with the telephone supervisor, printer, sports centre manager, and sauna manageress (a sauna had opened in 1970), the house superintendent seems to have reported directly to the general manager.[30]

It was not until September 1985 that Garrard's suggested reform was implemented. The growing importance of Rodney House was reflected in the appointment of a Rodney House manager to manage the letting office manageress, head housekeeper, and head receptionist. There were now four senior managers below the general manager: building superintendent, David Collins, responsible for the planning and supervision of installation, maintenance and repair work; flats manager, Peter Bicknell, responsible for the letting of and day-to-day management of the unfurnished flats; Rodney House manager, Win King, responsible for the letting of and day-to-day management of the furnished flats; and chief accountant, Bob Morley, responsible for the maintenance of the Trust accounts, rent records, staff records, and wages and salaries. The administration of Dolphin Square was now more balanced, with similar numbers of staff in each of the main departments. Printing was placed under the building superintendent, telephones under the flats manager.[31] In 1988, further changes were made to the organisation of the Square during John Cumming's time as general manager. Recognising that the maintenance of the building was becoming a major priority, the Maintenance department was reorganised in March. Its head, David Collins, was now to be known as 'head of maintenance' instead of 'building superintendent'; the responsibilities of the newly-appointed assistant head of maintenance, David ('Bob') Martin, were clarified; and the post of chief engineer disappeared with the retirement of Doug Durand.[32] In November, it was decided to reduce the number of main departments from four to three. The Flats and Rodney House departments were merged into a single department under the flats manager, Peter Bicknell, who was to be supported by an assistant. The detailed administration of tenancies was combined with oversight of the Rodney House functions, and the change was justified given the managerial pressures that had been created by the requirements of the 1988 Housing Act and the marketing drive for a revamped Rodney House (see below, pp.188-9).[33] However, the appropriateness of this change was immediately challenged by trustees, and in March 1989 they considered a further report by Cumming, which in some ways represented a return to the position *ex ante*. In addition to the appointment of an assistant flats manager, a further appointment was proposed, that of front of house or commercial manager, who would manage Rodney House, together with its new conference centre, the sports centre and new health club. The trustees endorsed the plan, and Janetta M. Devon, AIPM, was appointed commercial house manager. Jerry Murphy took up the post of assistant flats manager.[34] The final organisational change in the period took place after Cumming's departure. David Collins, who had acted as general manager from April 1991 until Crawford's arrival in September, became deputy general manager in addition to head of maintenance.[35]

*

Otherwise, recruiting and retaining staff were continuing concerns, and some fine judgments were required at the annual reviews of wages and salaries, usually held in the spring of each year. The involvement of the Transport and General Workers Union (TGWU) made the negotiations more difficult.[36] Trustees recognised that the smooth running of Dolphin Square depended, to a considerable extent, upon the loyalty and long service of key personnel, notably: John Dobson, building superintendent for 34 years; William Groves, chief engineer for 24 years and a Costain employee since 1940; Eve Parsons, a Costain employee since 1928 and letting office manager for 18 years; and Harry Bailey, who contributed 50 years' service as a plumber before retiring as foreman plumber in 1988. Replacing these key figures often led to problems. For example, Dobson's successor, Joseph Judd, found it difficult to cope with the demands of the job as the plumbing renewal programme intensified. Having been chief electrician under Dobson, he became maintenance manager in 1966 and building superintendent in 1974, but was asked to step down in 1977.[37] Suitable junior employees were also difficult to find, and Garrard made frequent references to the 'human resources' challenges he faced in his decade as general manager. Thus, in 1970 he highlighted the six activities with a particularly high turnover rate: accounts (already mentioned), telephone exchange, news-shop, porters, housekeeping, and maintenance and engineering. Turnover amounted to 38 per cent of the number employed in the years 1967–9, with particularly high rates in porterage (78 per cent), accounts (67 per cent) and telephones (61 per cent). Garrard noted that without the 79 'stalwarts', those with five years' service or more, 'the situation would be chaotic'.[38] Two years later he reminded trustees that while staff morale had greatly improved, in comparison with the situation in 1963, goodwill was threatened by pay awards elsewhere. Turnover remained high in areas where Dolphin Square was uncompetitive: machine operators in the accounts department (turnover rate: 80 per cent in six months), receptionists (75 per cent), and the sports centre (100 per cent).[39] A substantial pay award was agreed for the Square's maintenance and engineering staff, and although this was affected by the Heath Government's pay and price freeze of 1972–3, when it was finally implemented it highlighted anomalies in the Square's pay structure which created further problems elsewhere. Garrard continued to press for urgent action to raise wages and salaries in 1974, following a period of further pay restraint, and as the rate of inflation began to increase.[40]

Some changes to the management structure were reactive, a necessary response to new issues. Thus, Morris's appointment first as assistant to Garrard in 1968 and then as deputy general manager from 1971–4, was prompted by the initiative of the DSTA in asking the Trust to explore the proposal that tenants should have the right to buy their flats under a co-ownership scheme. The additional work that arose in connection with the idea – first raised in 1967 and ultimately abandoned in 1970 after opposition from the Ministry of Housing – led to the appointment of Morris, who later on enjoyed success as a general manager.[41] He too found labour relations to be his most enduring challenge. In his 1980 report he revealed difficulties in filling vacant posts for maids, porters, and night attendants, and had to cope with particularly high turnover rates. In 1979–80, 15 day porters had left in a team of nine, and there had been a turnover of 20 night attendants for eight jobs.[42] Two years later he identified several occupations where pay was lagging behind that of comparable posts in London: housekeepers, receptionists, telephone operators, and masseuses.[43] In Morris's final annual report, drafted for the trustees in 1983, when the wage bill exceeded £1 million for the first time, he noted that recruitment continued to be difficult in London and reiterated Garrard's point that only the exceptional loyalty of key staff enabled Dolphin Square to function. For example, there were four maintenance foremen with a total of 142 years' service, and eight maids, each with over 20 years' service.[44] At times, urgent corrective action was required when Dolphin Square wage rates fell below those of comparable employers, as, for example, in 1986–8, when increases amounting to 30 per cent above inflation were made in order to restore parity.[45]

FINANCIAL PERFORMANCE, 1965–93

The overriding requirement of Dolphin Square Trust Ltd. was to balance its books, viz. to equate income and expenditure. This did not preclude deficits in particular years, but in common with charities reporting to the Charity Commissioners, the Trust had to ensure that its money was spent on the purposes for which it had been established, and it was expected to avoid building up large reserves. No set of company accounts is presented in exactly the same way over a 30-year period, of course, and over the years the Trust altered the way in which it treated particular items in its published accounts. These included taxation, depreciation, provision for renewals and dilapidations, transfers into and out of reserves, and investment income. The principal changes came in 1983, when the Trust was required to change its reporting format in response to the Registered Housing Associations (Accounting Requirements) Order of 1982, and in 1992, after the Trust had de-registered as a housing association (see notes to Appendix 3). By adjusting the annual accounts on a consistent basis we discover that, in overall terms, the Trust did indeed balance the books with income exceeding expenditure before tax by £3.01 million (£5.44 million in constant 1993 prices), or under four per cent of total turnover (Table 5.5). Over the period 1965–93 £1.6 million or two per cent of turnover was left after tax, and of this, £0.75 million was set aside in 1965–82 to meet repairs and dilapidations (Table 5.5 and Appendix 3).[46] Some elements were clearly beyond the trustees' control, notably changes in taxation, including value added tax and selective employment tax, and particular problems were caused by liability for VAT in 1982–3.

Table 5.5 Income and expenditure, margins before tax, net income and accumulated surplus/deficit, 1965–93

*Period (years to 30 September)**	*Income [£m., rounded]*	*Expenditure before tax [£m., rounded]*	*Margin before tax [£m.]*	*Net income after tax – consistent basis [£'000]*	*Reported accumulated surplus/(deficit) at end period [£'000]*
1965–70	4.25	4.25	0.00	4.0	(82.0)
1971–5	5.54	5.56	(0.02)	(37.6)	(38.8)
1976–80	9.66	8.67	0.99	573.5	1.98
1981–5	15.71	14.81	0.90	285.7	48.5
1986–90	23.81	23.07	0.74	258.3	50.1
1991–3	18.61	18.21	0.40	509.2	1,904.3
Total 1965–93	*77.58*	*74.57*	*3.01*	*1,593.1*	

Constant 1993 prices					
1965–70	36.13	36.31	(0.18)		
1971–5	30.98	30.92	0.06		
197–80	26.24	23.48	2.76		
1981–5	25.87	24.36	1.51		
1986–90	30.51	29.63	0.88		
1991–3	18.90	18.49	0.51		
Total 1965–93	*168.63*	*163.19*	*5.44*		

Source: Appendix 3.

* 1st nine months in 1965

However, the essential task was to maintain the fabric of the Square and keep the property in as attractive a condition as possible. In the early years this meant tackling maintenance issues which had been postponed during the Lintang years. As Appendix 3 indicates, expenditure exceeded income in 1966-8, and the reported accumulated deficit, after tax and provisions, was nearly £169,000 on 30 September 1968. Deficits were also reported in 1973-5, when once again there was an accumulated deficit. This was reported as £69,000 on 30 September 1974, and the deficit would have risen to £106,000 in the following year had not £75,000 been transferred from reserves. Deficits were also experienced in 1988 and 1992, and in the latter case the blow was softened by the return of £1.43 million in reserves to the profit and loss account (Appendix 3, cols. 6 and 7). But in general, a margin of income over expenditure was maintained. Margins before tax were particularly high in the period 1976-85 (Table 5.5, col.4). The surplus after tax, but before special provisions, amounted in total to £221,000 in 1969-72, £513,000 in 1976-9, and £305,000 in 1980-3. The annual surplus was particularly high in 1976-7, 1990-1, and in 1992-3, following rent increases (see below), when a surplus of £0.54 million was recorded (Appendix 3, col.5). It may be unwise to draw too many conclusions from the data expressed in constant prices, but it does seem that in periods of high inflation both income and expenditure lagged behind the price level, as, for example, in 1976-85. It may be that higher margins were recorded in this decade because expenditure, especially on wages and salaries, failed to keep pace with the rate of inflation.

MANAGING THE CORE BUSINESS: UNFURNISHED FLATS

The income from the 1,047 unfurnished flats at Dolphin Square[47] produced 50 per cent of the Trust's income over the period 1965–93, and it scarcely needs to be said that fixing rents was a critical element in the trustees' work. However, the importance of this income stream changed over time. In the accounts for 1965, the rents from unfurnished flats provided no less than 68 per cent of the Trust's total income. As the Rodney House hotel was developed and marketed, and external factors such as government legislation began to affect the freedom to charge, this proportion fell gradually but steadily, until 1982 when it was only 37 per cent. Unusually high annual increases in rental income in 1983 (17 per cent) and 1984 (16 per cent), explained in the main by higher service charges (see below), heralded a reversal of this process. In 1992 and 1993, the annual income from flats increased significantly, by 23 and 31 per cent respectively, and this source of income was almost as important as it had been in the early 1970s, providing 53 per cent of the Trust's income (see Appendix 4).[48] We have seen that in earlier years in Dolphin Square's history, rents failed to keep pace with inflation. After 1965, a similar trend may be observed. Rental income in 1993 was in real terms very similar to that in 1965–70, but this apparent 'steady state' is misleading, since it was essentially caused by belated increases in the early 1990s. From 1970 the real value of rental income fell steadily, until by 1982 the income was under half its real value in 1970. Only with the increase in 1993 were rents restored to their real value in 1965–70 (Appendix 4).

Our account of the developing rent policy must take account of these general trends, while recognising that the Trust's actions were more complex than a simple annual adjustment to rentals. In the first place, an 18-point scale was inherited from the previous owners, reflecting the variety of flats, with their one to seven rooms, and differences in location and amenity. This was increased to 20 points in 1965. The business of executing tenancy agreements became even more complicated with time. From 1974, 33 categories were in use, when the Trust and the rent officer began to distinguish between unmodernised flats and those which, having been improved under the duct renewal and modernisation programme (see below, pp.190–1), commanded a higher rent. By 1992, the Trust was working with a 36-point scale. Distinctions were then made between new tenants, who were to be charged market rents, and existing tenants seeking to renew three- or five-year leases, who were offered a measure of discount via a Byzantine system of graduated incremental increases. Also inherited from the immediate past was a commitment to offer a group of previously protected tenants, 79 in number in 1968, a measure of protection from the ravages of the market.[49] A further complication was the requirement to respond to the changing charitable framework in which the Trust was expected to operate, together with compliance with the emerging national legislation on rents, and notably the 'fair rent' scheme introduced by the Heath Government's Housing Finance Act of 1972 (see below, p.182).

In the early years of the Trust, action was clearly taken to adjust rents in line with inflation, market conditions and rising costs, and, in particular, to address the generosity of the rent scale introduced by Westminster's special committee in 1963–4 (above, pp.154–5). In July 1965, the Committee of Management therefore introduced increases via a 20-point scale, intended to apply to both new tenants, and existing ones when their agreements became due for renewal. In future, only three-year tenancies would be made. The scale, from £325 to £1,200 a year (Appendix 5), charged tenants of larger flats proportionately more. Thus, one-room tenants faced an increase of only 6.5-9.5 per cent, while the rents of two-room flats were to rise by 15–26.5 per cent, and three-room flats by 21–24 per cent. The rent of the largest flats, with seven rooms, was raised from £870 to £1,200 a year, an increase of 38 per cent.[50] A revised rent scale was introduced for new tenants in 1966, in response to rising costs, and, in particular, the imposition of selective employment tax.[51] The new scale was 7.5 per cent above the 1965 scale. Established tenants seeking renewals were offered renewals on the 1965 scale.[52] In 1968-9 there was a further increase of 8–9 per cent (6–6.5 per cent for one-room flats). Tenants renewing their agreements were offered renewals on the 1966 scale, but some of the older tenants, who had narrowly missed earlier renewals and were still on the 1964 scale, were offered a staggered rent which brought them up to the appropriate scale in the last year of their three-year tenancy.[53] The next change came in 1971, when increases of 9–11 per cent were made (see

Appendix 5). Some of the trustees expressed concern at the creation of different classes of tenant, each paying significantly different levels of rent, but after considerable discussion it was agreed that established tenants be offered renewals on the lower 1968–9 scale, while the formerly controlled tenants were treated more generously still and given five years to bring their rents up to the 1968–9 scale.[54] The policies followed in 1965–71 were driven by the need to balance income and expenditure, but the overall approach was liberal, with new tenants being charged rents around 15–20 per cent below market rents, and old tenants receiving additional discounts.[55]

Legislative changes introduced by alternating Labour and Conservative administrations then affected the rent-setting process. In 1965, Wilson's Labour Government reintroduced rent control with its Rent Act. This complex and wide-ranging measure created an independent rent officer service in England and Wales, which was first introduced in Westminster. It applied to dwellings with a rateable value of up to £400 in London, and £200 elsewhere. Rent officers, responding to applications by either the landlord, or tenant, or both, were to establish 'fair' rents, basing their decisions on the rents of comparable properties in the area and making the assumption, somewhat puzzlingly in the case of central London, that the supply of rented housing was more or less equal to demand. A fair rent could be registered on the application of one or both of the interested parties, and any objections would be referred to a Rent Assessment Committee. Although the Act was found not to apply to housing associations or trusts, or, for that matter, local authorities and housing co-operatives, the 1965 Act certainly influenced the climate in which the Dolphin Square Trust elected to treat its tenants, whether new, long-established, or formerly protected.[56] And since, like earlier legislation, it tended to produce rents below the market level, it did nothing to prevent the decline of the private rented sector.[57] In 1972, Heath's Conservative administration passed the Housing Finance Act, the purpose of which was to require public sector authorities to charge economic rents. This measure was more directly relevant to Dolphin Square, since, inter alia, it extended the 'fair rent' principle to all dwellings, including those of housing associations and trusts. Applying to London properties with a rateable value of up to £400, it affected most of Dolphin Square, viz. all the one- to three-room flats, and the majority of the four-room flats. From 1 January 1973, the rents of unfurnished flats could not be higher than those established by the rent officer and operative for three years before revision.[58] Whatever the merits of this short-lived measure – it was much debated in the Commons and received considerable criticism at the time for failing to address the decline in unfurnished tenancies – its fair rent system was retained in subsequent legislation. Although Dolphin Square rent levels were usually set below the fair rents eventually established for its properties, the trustees and managers lost some flexibility in the setting of rents, and were presented with an intrusive and protracted bureaucratic layer. The process was often frustrating, since it was difficult for the rent officer to find Westminster properties which were comparable with flats in Dolphin Square, and especially its two-room flats.[59] On top of this, the Conservatives' hopes of introducing more economic rents were dashed by an economic crisis, and the counter-inflation measures adopted by the Heath Government froze national rents at their existing level from November 1972 to April 1973.[60] Then Wilson's Labour Government introduced a rent freeze from March 1974 to March 1975.[61] However, although the freezes were irksome for the Dolphin Square management,[62] they did give the general manager time to begin the process of establishing a fair rent framework in the Square. On the other hand, the second freeze, which utilised powers contained in the previous administration's Counter-Inflation Act of 1973, also extended control to properties with a rateable value of up to £600 in London (on revaluation, £1,500). The rest of Dolphin Square was thus included within rent control, in common with most of London's luxury flats.[63]

Labour, in power from 1974 to 1979, modified the policy of rent control, abolishing the earlier provisions affecting council house tenants. Its Housing, Rents and Subsidies Act of 1975 ended the 1974–5 freeze on rent increases and provided for limited and phased increases.[64] For landlords such as Dolphin Square, the schedules of fair rents were used to set rentals for new tenants, but existing tenants continued to be treated more favourably since the restrictions established by the 1972 Act, which limited annual increases to £0.75 a week or £39 per annum for those with over a year's residence, continued to apply.[65] Furthermore, the 1977 Rent Act, while providing for higher fair rents, also retained the £39 limit.[66] The trustees decided in 1973 to give existing tenants renewals at the fair rent less five per cent,[67] but the statutory limit meant that the increases the Trust obtained were lower than those incremental increases which it had applied, before rent control, in 1968–71. Thus, by the end of the decade most tenants were paying rents well below the fair rent calculation, which itself was also falling behind both prices and the market.[68] It became increasingly evident to trustees that the yield from rents was failing to keep pace with inflation, and since examples of fair rents were published in the Trust's annual reports from 1979–80 to 1987–8, the disparity was equally evident to tenants and the DSTA. At the same time, the establishment of a fair rent system did not make the execution of tenancy agreements more straightforward. The trustees received regular reports from the general manager on the tenancies he had agreed. For example, the agenda for the management committee meeting on 6 November 1979 reveals that over a four-month period 132 new tenancies had been signed, using 17 different tariffs, including the fair rent scales for 1975, 1976, 1978 and 1979.[69]

More flexibility in tenure and greater increases in rents were permitted under the Thatcher Government's Housing Act of 1980, which represented a shift to a more market-based approach to housing provision, and encouraged council house tenants to buy their homes. The Act also introduced the re-registration (i.e. recalculation) of fair rents every two years, instead of every three, and provided for the rents charged to existing tenants to be increased to the registered rent in two annual steps from the date of registration by the rent officer.[70] Although there was now legislative encouragement to raise rents to the fair rent level, the Dolphin Square management continued its rather cautious approach to rent-setting. Nevertheless, with maintenance costs rising, rents were necessarily increased. In July 1980, the Management Committee agreed that while it would continue to charge the full registered fair rent to new tenants, existing tenants, on obtaining new tenancies, would have their rents increased by annual increments of £60 for a one-room flat, £84 for two rooms, £108 for three rooms, rising to £205 for a seven-room flat. Over 500 tenants had signed the new agreements by November 1982.[71] The Trust also began to take a tougher line with those tenants who were in breach of their tenancy agreements, viz. absentees who were subletting, or those who were behaving antisocially. The ability to raise rents substantially above the existing level was a useful weapon in the armoury.[72] The new policy produced higher rental income than under the 1972 Act, but the Committee of Management had set annual increases which were well below those necessary to bring all its tenants up to the fair rent level. For example, the fair rent for a bedsit (type 1B) rose steadily from £480 in 1973 to £1,068 in 1982, and a three-room flat (type 3A) from £840 to £1,992 (Appendix 5), rates which did not keep pace with inflation.[73] However, the charges to existing tenants were much lower. For example, in 1981, Ken Morris informed trustees that a tenant of ten years' standing was able to rent a 1B flat for only £597, just over half of the 1982 fair rent, and a 3A flat was being let at £930, under half of the fair rent. In the first case, the three annual increments would add only £180, instead of the £470 permitted under the 1980 Act; in the second, the increments would total £324, instead of the £1,062 permitted. In the following year, he pointed out that a 3A flat with a fair rent of £1,992 had just been re-let to an existing tenant for three years at an annual rent of £1,038, rising to £1,146 and £1,254. The fact that many rents were below the fair rent level was revealed to both the rent officer and the London Rent Assessment Panel when they adjudicated on a dispute with a tenant in the same year. The Trust had proposed to raise the rent on a double-flat in Drake House from £1,785 to the fair rent level of £2,900. After the tenant appealed against the rent officer's decision, which supported the Trust, the Rent Assessment Panel decided that the fair rent should be £4,500.[74]

Morris continued to press for the rents paid by existing tenants to be brought closer to the fair rent level, but he was largely unsuccessful.[75] The policy of charging discounted annual increments continued unchanged until 1992, widening the gap between the rents of new and established tenants. The only adjustment that was made for existing tenants was prompted by a rise in the service element in the rent. Higher heating costs resulted from the closure in 1983 of Battersea power station, which had provided excess heat to the Pimlico Heating Undertaking, suppliers to Dolphin Square and Churchill Gardens. The Trust also decided to pay Thames Water's sewerage and environmental charges, instead of leaving the responsibility to individual tenants.[76] In 1983, the first of the three annual increments established in 1980 was raised to take account of these higher costs. The increase in rent over three years was of the order of 50 per cent.[77] Higher rents were also charged to new tenants of flats which had been repaired and modernised as part of a long-term renewal programme.[78] But while it could be shown (as the Trust did in its annual reports) that fair rents, used as a proxy for market rents, continued to rise steadily, and certainly kept pace with inflation over the longer term,[79] most tenants were established residents enjoying a measure of discount. This is also evident from the waiting list, and the number of new tenancies. Thus, with over 1,000 unfurnished flats potentially available, the turnover rate was generally below ten per cent, and in some years was very low indeed, with only 29 new tenants in 1984/5, and 18 in 1989/90, producing turnover rates of 2.8 and 1.7 per cent respectively. Only in the early 1990s did the number of new tenants exceed 100, with a turnover rate of 14.3 per cent in 1991/2 and 12.7 per cent in 1992/3.[80] At the same time, there was a sizeable waiting list for flats. In January 1977, there were 583 on the list, and although the number fell to 273 in 1980, it had risen to over 500 in January 1983 when the list was closed.[81] The majority of tenants were paying incremental increases, it is true, but their rents remained substantially below the fair rent, let alone the market rent. The cross-subsidisation afforded by the commercial activities in Dolphin Square, especially Rodney House, and the charitable purposes of the Trust, made this possible.

The late 1980s and early 1990s heralded a change of policy, encouraged partly by further legislation, and partly by a sharp decline in Rodney House income in 1990/1 and 1991/2 (Appendix 4) and a substantial post-tax loss of £0.3 million in 1991/2 (Appendix 3). The Housing Act of 1988 aimed to revive the dwindling private rented sector by abandoning rent control and introducing new forms of tenancy. It also sought to encourage housing associations to expand by attracting private finance. Henceforth they were expected to shed their quasi-public role and behave more like independent, private sector institutions. The Act gave the Trust greater freedom to vary rents, by allowing it to charge market rents instead of fair rents to newcomers from January 1989.[82] Anticipating the legislation, the Trust appointed the surveyors Daniel Smith to draw up a schedule of market rents, and following the exercise a trustee sub-committee recommended the introduction of bands of market rents for each type of flat, ranging in 1988 from £2,800–4,100 for bedsits to £12,000–13,500 for seven-room flats (see Appendix 5). The bands were between 23 and 54 per cent above the calculated fair rents in that year. The subcommittee also developed a more sophisticated approach in dealing with tenants who were forced to move flats while theirs were being modernised, and for absentee tenants enjoying the benefits of a low rent. These measures were endorsed by the Committee of Management in March 1988.[83] In 1989, the rent bands were increased by eight per cent, and in each of the years 1990 and 1991 the Committee of Management approved a 15 per cent increase in rents for one- and two-room flats, and a ten per cent for three-room flats.[84] In 1992, with the financial deficit a pressing matter, the trustees agreed to raise rents still further. First, full rents for new tenants were increased by ten per cent. Then the incremental rent increases applied to renewals of tenancy since 1980 were raised by 50 per cent for renewals in 1992–4. Tenants would then pay further ten per cent increases in the second and third years of their agreements.[85] There were also increases in 1993: five per cent for new tenancies, ten per cent for one-room flats. Deregistration as a housing association, effected in 1992 (see below), meant that the Trust was no longer bound by the fair rents structure, but the trustees gave an undertaking to pre-1989 tenants that their rents would not exceed the fair rent calculation.[86] At the same time, the rents for newcomers had risen substantially, by between 39 and 80 per cent in the period 1988–93 (see Appendix 5).

Was the rental policy sound? With the benefit of hindsight, and given the public criticism of its rental policy in the 1990s (see below, p.235–7), the Trust might have pursued a more determined policy to bring rentals in line with fair rents, which, in any case, were substantially below the market rents. However, given the existing mix of commercial and non-commercial activities in the Square, this would have produced substantial annual surpluses for the Trust, something that would have been frowned upon by the Housing Corporation and the Charity Commissioners. Furthermore, the sums involved were not small. In 1991, the degree of subsidy, i.e. the difference between the market rents that could have been charged and the actual rent received, was put at £3.5 million, at a time when the unfurnished flats were yielding £2.5 million. The 1992 figure was higher because all tenants could now be theoretically charged market rents. The subsidy was now £4.6 million, compared with an income of just over £3 million.[87] Dolphin Square was thus a novel, even unique, example of co-operative, quasi-public housing activity for the middle class. It may have been vulnerable to criticism, but no one could argue that it did not benefit its tenants, and the benefits increased the longer they remained in the Square and observed the conditions of their leases.

THE RODNEY HOUSE 'HOTEL'

The furnished flat business in Rodney House grew in importance over time, producing a strong income stream for the Trust. In the early years the 150 furnished flats, together with the 30 guest rooms in Keyes and Hood, produced about a quarter of total income, but this proportion increased steadily, thanks to buoyant demand, and the management's ability to price the facilities freely. Income rose steadily from £170,000 in 1965/6 to £1.1 million in 1978/9 and £3 million in 1989/90 (a rise of 136 per cent in real terms).[88] Consequently, Rodney House's share of total income increased from 25 per cent in 1965/6 to 51 per cent by 1978/9, and the proportion was 53 per cent in 1989/90 (Appendix 4). In the quarter-century of growth, occupancy rates were high, often in the 70–80 per cent range,[89] and charges for its 150 apartments were competitive with London hotels. Tariffs were raised each year. Thus, the charge for a night in a single room went up from £3.50 in 1965 to £22 in 1979 and £88 in 1991, representing a rise in real terms of 180 per cent, 1965–91.[90] The price per week of a larger flat, with a lounge and twin bedroom, rose from £26.75 in 1965 to £170 in 1979 and £774 in 1991, an increase in real terms of 222 per cent (see Appendix 6). Guest rooms, for hire by the tenants, were less important, but they produced a steady if modest contribution to Rodney House income, of around six per cent (see Appendix 4).

As we have already observed, Rodney House experienced something of a crisis in 1991–3. For some time, the business had been reliant on the North American market, supported by a marketing activity initiated by Garrard in the 1960s. In the early 1990s demand fell away, the product of terrorist activity in London, and compounded by the onset of the Gulf War. More general factors were also at work, notably the prolonged recession of 1989–93. Managers were also aware that, as with all hotel operations, there was a tendency for standards to decline gradually, and certainly in Rodney House some aspects required modernisation at this time. It was accepted by 1991 that the regular increases in prices had probably reached a ceiling.[91] In the financial year 1990/1 occupancy rates fell sharply, and income fell by a third compared with 1989/90. Charges were frozen in 1991/2, but the increase in income in 1991/2 and 1992/3 was relatively modest.[92] Nevertheless, by 1993 there were signs of improvement, the product of a concerted marketing campaign introduced by specialist managers, and accompanied by a room modernisation programme and improved facilities. Over the long run, of course, the setback did not undermine the benefit which the hotel operation had provided to the Trust's overall financial and rental strategies.

THE COSTS OF PROVIDING FOR DOLPHIN SQUARE

The Trust's expenditure was straightforward at first sight. In 1965/6 the principal components were: loan interest (41 per cent); wages and salaries (including maintenance labour) 20 per cent; and repairs and maintenance (excluding maintenance labour) 19 per cent (Appendix 7). Over time, loan interest declined in importance while the other items became more prominent. Thus, by 1979/80 wages and salaries made up nearly 40 per cent of total costs, while maintenance costs accounted for 29 per cent. Loan interest was now only 12 per cent of the total, and it fell to five per cent in 1988/9. Accounting changes in the early 1980s and early 1990s prevent an exact comparison over the entire period. From 1983, for example, maintenance labour was not distinguished in the accounts. However, we can say that maintenance costs, and wages and salaries remained the largest cost components. On a consistent basis, spending on maintenance and repairs (excluding labour costs) exceeded 30 per cent of total expenditure in 1984/5–1989/90, as the Trust addressed the pressing problem of duct and plumbing renewal (see below).

Clearly, one of the immediate challenges for the Trust was to address the backlog of maintenance and renewals, which had been allowed to build up by Costain and Lintang, and which was exposed in Garrard's initial report in November 1964. The general manager made particular reference to the condition of the exterior brickwork, woodwork and joinery, subsidence, the internal plumbing system, the roofs of the sports centre/restaurant and garage, and the passenger lifts.[93] From 1965 to 1993 the Trust spent a not inconsiderable £19 million on maintaining the fabric and services of Dolphin Square (Appendix 7). If maintenance labour were added, the total would be something like £26 million. In addition to routine tasks such as repainting, re-carpeting, and refurbishment of the common areas, etc., large sums were required for more exceptional items, such as replacement of the plumbing and lifts, asbestos removal, and replacement of the labour-intensive manual telephone system. Spending was inevitably lumpy, and was particularly high in 1966/7 (lift replacement), and in 1972/3–3/4, 1979/80 and 1983/4–89/90 (plumbing), but there was a tendency for costs to rise as the building aged, and major parts of the infrastructure required renewal or replacement. In the 1960s, attention was focused on the replacement of all 26 lifts by the Otis Elevator Co. and A. Bell & Son. The project was financed by a special 25-year loan of £211,000 from Westminster City Council, with interest fixed at 7 per cent.[94] In the same period the swimming pool and sports centre were renovated, and a special repairs equalisation account was established (in 1968/9) to help smooth out future spending.[95] In the 1970s, the eight calorifiers (water heaters) were replaced (in 1970–2), and the ageing telephone system was replaced by a smaller manual system in 1976, followed by the progressive withdrawal of the original house telephones. Then in 1986 a new, automated system was installed. The project was managed by Morris, and the equipment was purchased from British Telecom for £345,600.[96] But by far the biggest project, in both the 1970s and the 1980s, was what became known as the duct replacement and modernisation programme.[97] In 1971, Dobson, the former building superintendent, reported that the internal plumbing and drainage system, with its 89 ducts, needed to be completely replaced. This was a major task, requiring unrestricted access to the flats. However, the project also enabled the management to take the opportunity to modernise the bathrooms and kitchens and to do essential rewiring work, as well as building a house-linking corridor at ground level. The first stage of the project, undertaken from January

1973 to February 1976 by A. Bell & Son and Cliden Construction, resulted in the renovation of over 150 flats at a cost of £589,000.[98] The work was temporarily halted for financial reasons, since it was funded entirely from revenue, but it resumed in April 1978, with Cliden, Bell & Son (to 1980) and the London Electricity Board as the contractors. By September 1980 the bill for the works exceeded £1 million, and by September 1984, 336 flats had been treated (about a third of the stock of unfurnished flats) with a total spend of over £2 million.[99] This second stage was further complicated by the need to engage specialists to remove asbestos in the main ducts under strict control following the asbestos regulations of 1983 and 1987.[100] By September 1993, a total of 658 flats had been renewed (about two-thirds of the total) at a cost of at least £5.5 million.[101] It is a tribute to the soundness of the trustees' financial approach that this major work was accomplished without further borrowing.

THE SQUARE'S AMENITIES

The Trust, in its annual report, made little reference to the Square's amenities, other than to record, from 1977–8, that they included a hot water supply, heating, communal gardens, an indoor swimming pool, squash courts, a tennis court, sauna, shopping arcade, underground garage and petrol station, restaurant, guest rooms and a communal television aerial.[102] This comparative reticence may be explained by the fact that the principal services were managed at arm's length. Garrard, on becoming general manager, was critical of the fact that both the garage and the restaurant had been sublet to commercial companies. He found this to be 'a source of many difficulties. Quite naturally, both are run with the profit motive as the prime consideration, and this results in neither being operated primarily for the benefit of tenants in Dolphin Square'.[103] As we have seen, Surplices Ltd., a Maxwell Joseph subsidiary, had taken a 21-year lease on the facilities in 1959, paying £13,500 a year. The garage and petrol station were sublet to Charles Rickard Group, while the restaurant was sublet to Dolphin Square Caterers Ltd. [DSCL], in which Surplices had a controlling interest. When the Trust was established, the inadequacy of these arrangements quickly became evident. A dispute over the liability for urgent roof repairs produced the finding that the Trust was in fact liable, leading Garrard to complain that the underleases had been hastily drawn up and were unsatisfactory, with the rights and obligations of the respective parties ill-defined.[104] The standing of the DSCL directors was also a matter for debate. In April 1964, the company's 100 shares were transferred to Louis and Phyllis Gossman, who became, respectively, chairman and secretary of the company. Maxwell Joseph and his associates then stood down. However, it does appear that Joseph retained some interest in the business, since in 1960 the catering company had assigned its lease to Surplices, and taken a sublease at a rental of £5,000 a year.[105] But the restaurant had been losing money, and after negotiations with the Gossmans the Trust decided to buy the company and run it as a subsidiary. This it did in August 1965, paying £4,000 and taking on liabilities of up to £7,500. The aim was to align the operation of the restaurant and sports centre more closely with the requirements of Rodney House.[106] After periods of closure both facilities were reopened. The restaurant and cocktail bar were completely redecorated, reopening in November 1965 after an operating agreement had been made with Alan Da Costa, an experienced restaurateur and the Chairman of Empire (Catering) Co.[107]

The first directors of DSCL under its new owners were two trustees (Dribbell [chairman] and Dew), and the general manager (Garrard). This form of directorate persisted until the company was wound up.[108] The subsidiary's income grew steadily, rising from £23,000 in 1966/7 to £374,000 in 1991/2, an increase in real terms of 89 per cent.[109] But costs more than matched this growth, rising in the same years from £22,000 to £407,000 (Appendix 8). In general, income and expenditure were in alignment, and modest profits were obtained between 1965 and 1980 (see Table 5.6). Under the terms of the underlease with Surplices, now held by the Trust, the subsidiary was required to pay its parent rent of £5,000 a year,[110] and it also declared dividends totalling £50,000 in the period 1972–8 (Appendix 8). Thereafter, losses were as likely as profits, and in the period 1980/1–5/6 post-tax profits were negative to the tune of £8,000 or £1,300 per annum. It was in the period 1986/7–91/2 that more serious financial problems emerged, with the subsidiary's post-tax losses amounting to £329,000 or nearly £55,000 per annum (see Table 5.6).

Table 5.6 Dolphin Square Caterers Ltd., income, expenditure and post-tax losses, 1965–1992 (£, annual averages)

Period	*Income*	*Expenditure*	*Profit/(loss) after tax*	*Dividends paid to DST*
1965/6–67/8*	24,889	24,709	569†	–
1968/9–73/4	61,690	53,001	7,085	3,333
1974/5–79/80	129,433	120,954	5,203	5,000
1980/1–85/6	199,198	200,183	(1,339)	–
1986/7–91/2	290,049	344,911	(54,863)	–

Source: Appendix 8.

Key:
* 3.5 years
† includes return of over-provision for rates, 1964–7

At this stage, the Trust decided to take over responsibility for the business and to leave the company dormant (effective from October 1992 [the company was eventually dissolved in January 2004]).[111] If the restaurant's problems provided the impetus for the acquisition of the company, its contribution to total income was rather modest, in comparison with that of the other facilities (Appendix 8). Strong real income growth was exhibited by the squash courts, the refurbished swimming pool, and the sauna (from 1970), this last boosted by sunbed income from 1985/6 (Appendix 8). Restaurant income was more modest, and its contribution to income, in 1965/6 as high as 48 per cent and close to 30 per cent in the late 1960s, fell to 13 per cent in 1972/3 and was under two per cent by the late 1980s, until a new agreement was made in 1989 (see below). In contrast, the squash courts and sauna each contributed about a third of total income, and the swimming pool just under a quarter (Appendix 8).

The restaurant faced the problem of making a profit while remaining open to provide breakfast, lunch and dinner for Rodney House guests as well as tenants and visitors. The challenge for DSCL was to find restaurateurs able to provide the required services at a quality that would attract custom sufficient to ensure a satisfactory profit over the length of their contracts. Empire Catering, which provided a full restaurant and bar service from November 1965 (Illustration 30), obtained a

21-year concession with a commitment to pay DSCL ten per cent of gross turnover (excluding tobacco sales), while having use of the premises free of rent, rates and electricity.[112] After initial teething problems,[113] the arrangement appears to have worked well for some years. However, in the late 1970s difficulties were apparent, and the commitment to provide three meals a day, seven days a week was becoming more onerous. Support for the restaurant from the tenants was sporadic at best, and Rodney House guests were often attracted to the flats by the opportunity they afforded for self-catering. In March 1979, Morris informed the trustees that the restaurant was now 'unsatisfactory' and plans were made to place Empire Catering on an annual contract. However, a year later it emerged that the company, by this time a subsidiary of United Biscuits, wanted to quit. The news heralded a tricky period with the venture.[114] The restaurant franchise attracted expressions of interest from the emerging Italian chain, Pizza Express, and two established London-based restaurants, Mon Plaisir and Villa dei Cesari. The trustees eventually chose Alain L'Hermitte, owner of Mon Plaisir since 1972, and Janet Baker (who would go on to be one of its directors 1991–8); they began operating as licensees in February 1981. Their agreement provided for a payment to DSCL of £15,000 in the first year, followed by 7.5 per cent of gross receipts (up to £250,000).[115] The change produced an investment of £90,000 by the incomers, improved meals and spending on publicity, but it was not long before L'Hermitte and Baker reported that they were in financial difficulties. Although business had improved in comparison with that of Empire Catering, the revenue was only half of their required breakeven point. With liabilities in excess of £150,000 the licensees reported in October 1982 that they might be forced to cease trading. The Trust agreed to supply them with a loan of £25,000, and to improve the terms of their agreement, viz. a reduction in the payment to DSCL to £5,000 a year, credit for guest room breakfasts and consent to Sunday evening closing.[116] The situation did not improve, however, and by 1984 the business had been put on the market. The outstanding loan amounted to £20,000 when the business, together with its liabilities, was sold in late 1985 to Shaun Wilson, general manager of London Capital Hotel, and Nicholas Crawley, proprietor of two hotels in the Prestige Group in 1985. They obtained a 15-year franchise, on much the same terms as L'Hermitte and Baker, and began trading in the Square as Crawley Wilson

Restaurants in January 1986. The restaurant was renamed 'Brasserie'.[117] Yet Wilson Crawley had no more success than had L'Hermitte and Baker, and in 1987 they too were experiencing difficulties in meeting the terms of their agreement. The trustees once again agreed to give the licensees financial assistance, by waiving the initial annual payment due and providing an interest-free loan of £50,000.[118] Although the standards provided seem to have been high, Crawley Wilson continued to trade at a loss. In January 1988, the trustees agreed to waive a further annual payment, and a year later Crawley Wilson revealed that it had put the restaurant on the market.[119]

There were greater expectations of the Parasol Corporation, a subsidiary of Allied Breweries, who took on the business – Brasserie and Lighthouse Bar[120] – in July 1989, paying the previous licensees £495,000. The new operators negotiated a 25-year concession, but in other essentials the agreement was the same as that entered into with Crawley Wilson.[121] However, to the trustees' exasperation they too wanted to quit after a relatively short time, though the prolonged recession of the 1980s and the withholding of investment support by the parent company were additional elements in the decision. As early as November 1989 they extracted concessions in relation to trading hours. Relations between Cumming, the General Manager, and Parasol managers became strained, and in July 1990 John Lee, MD of Parasol, reported that he could not sustain weekly losses of £2,000 and expressed a desire to withdraw the provision of breakfasts and to close on Sundays.[122] A new management team at Parasol made optimistic noises at the beginning of 1991,[123] but it soon became apparent that they too wanted to sell. In 1992 Crawford, who had replaced Cumming as general manager, reported that while no serious applicants had emerged for the concession, four companies were interested in taking on the restaurant on a management agreement basis: Sutcliffe (P & O), the Roux Brothers, Justin de Blank and Gardner Merchant (Trust House Forte). The last emerged as the favoured bidder, and in October 1992, on the recommendation of an ad hoc subcommittee comprising Prendergast, Dawtry and Reid, the Trust decided to buy back the concession from Allied Breweries and manage the business itself. An initial budget of £100,000 was approved, and Gardner Merchant was engaged. The firm negotiated a management buyout from Forte shortly afterwards. The restaurant was renamed the 'Dolphin Square Restaurant', and the Trust agreed to invest an estimated sum of £141,000 for refurbishment, but in fact, £149,000 was spent in total.[124] Once again the residents and guests were promised something better,[125] but Gardner Merchant reported losses in 1993, and the move heralded the beginning of an expensive commitment for the Trust.[126] The subsidiary company, DSCL, which owed its parent £551,000 and had accumulated losses of some £325,000 by 30 September 1992, became dormant on that date, and the restaurant became a direct responsibility of the Trust for the first time.[127]

Turning to motoring aspects, in 1965 the garage and petrol station were the responsibility of Dolphin Square Garage Ltd., a subsidiary of Charles Rickards Ltd., who since 1960 had been paying a rent of £8,500 per annum for premises which were badly in need of modernisation.[128] In the early days of the Trust, there was some dissatisfaction about the garage, which was being operated largely for commercial reasons (including an arrangement with security firm Securicor), rather than as a facility for the benefit of residents. Parking was also becoming a serious problem. During the Trust's negotiations with Surplices and Charles Rickards about the roof repairs, Rickards offered to surrender its lease in return for a management agreement on improved terms (for the Trust). However, no agreement was reached. In January 1967, the Trust approached Maxwell Joseph in an attempt to gain control of the garage; he replied that his companies would be prepared to surrender the lease for £35,000.[129] In the end, Joseph accepted £27,500 and Westminster City Council was asked whether it would be interested in acquiring the garage. In July, proposals from the Council and from National Car Parks [NCP], which had also offered consultancy advice to the Trust on how to address the issue of parking and roads management, were considered. The latter was chosen as the favoured bidder and in October the Trust entered into what was to prove a long, if not always harmonious, arrangement with the company.[130]

NCP took over responsibility for the garage, service and petrol stations and the parking bays on the interior, private roads. The company also agreed to undertake a major programme of renovation at a cost of £55,000. In return it acquired a lease for an initial term of 14 years. It paid premiums of £27,500 to Charles Rickards and £7,500 to the Trust, and contracted to pay an annual rent of £10,000 for the garage, petrol station, workshops and roadways parking, plus five per cent of the gross parking receipts over £20,000 a year, and 40 per cent on receipts over £40,000 a year.[131] Free parking on roadways was stopped, and paid bays were created at a cost of 30s. [£1.50] a week. Parking following renovation was to cost £2 a week for small cars, rising to £3 15s. [£3.75] for large cars (over 16 feet). A ten per cent discount was offered to residents entering into parking contracts of 12 weeks.[132] As with Empire Catering and the restaurant, the initial operation of the garage worked to the mutual benefit of all parties, and the tenants benefited from an agreement that restricted increases in parking charges to the change in the Retail Prices Index (RPI). Furthermore, the facilities were improved, and although the business was barely profitable, concerns expressed by the Trust, together with the continuation of price control via the Price Commission, deterred NCP from passing on the full RPI increase in 1970, 1974 and 1976.[133] By 1977, however, the relationship had become less satisfactory. While some tenants had little alternative but to use the garage, there was an element of price elasticity in total demand, and NCP was anxious to make up lost ground. Although price control was given further impetus by the Labour Government's strengthening of the Price Commission's powers in that year,[134] NCP was able to raise charges by 15–20 per cent in November 1977, and by a further ten per cent in 1978.[135] The Trust gained additional revenue – which rose from £600 in 1967/8 to nearly £11,000 in 1977/8 – but by this time it faced a similar situation to that of the restaurant. NCP was unable to make a profit while satisfying the levels of service demanded by the Trust. On the other hand, tenants were dissatisfied with the way the garage was being run. For some time the practice had been to let casual users park in bays reserved for tenants if they were not in use, but this required the employment of attendants to sort out any problems this might cause when tenants returned with their cars. However, faced with operating losses, NCP cut its labour force, making unresolved disputes over parking spaces more common. There was also an increased level of theft and vandalism. The situation was such that the tenants took independent action through the DSTA to alleviate some of the problems by erecting signs to enable season ticket holders to park in the same space.[136] At the same time parking charges rose sharply. For example, the cost of garaging a car of 14–16 feet for 12 weeks (exclusive of VAT), which had risen from £32.40 in 1967 to £58.80 in 1978, was raised by 33 and 40 per cent respectively in 1979 and 1980. This took the cost to £101, although it was £40 short of the sum that NCP could have charged had the full RPI increase been applied. With the lease set to expire in September 1981, a prolonged period of negotiation followed. Agreement could not be reached, however, and in February 1982 Healey & Baker, a leading firm of international real estate surveyors, were engaged to assess the rental value and act for the Trust.[137]

Eventually an agreement was reached, on more advantageous terms for the Trust. A new lease was signed in October 1984. Applying for 20 years from 25 March 1983, NCP agreed to pay the Trust a rental of £32,500 a year for the first five years, with reviews every five years. The parking tariff for residents' 12-week season tickets was specified exclusive of VAT, at £88.20 for small cars, rising to £129 for vehicles of 14–16 feet and £180 for those over 16 feet.[138] A separate agreement gave NCP management of the roadways parking at a rental of £3,500 a year. Parking charges were also specified.[139] However, this was not the end of a fraught relationship, and very soon new problems emerged. In 1985, NCP informed Ian Wood, then general manager, that the car sales, service workshops and petrol station facilities were to be discontinued. The obligation to provide these apparently unprofitable services had become permissive under the terms of the 1984 lease, and after being run for a short time by W.P. Allen & Co. on NCP's behalf, they ceased in 1986.[140] NCP did promise to reinstate them via another third party, raising eyebrows when they asked a potential operator, J.C. Abbot & Co., for rent of £22,000 a year.[141] This deal fell through, but in February 1988 NCP sublet part of the garage to a car hire firm, Town & Country Cars (TCC), a subsidiary of Henlys. TCC undertook to reopen the petrol station and servicing shops, and the sublessees were allocated 20 parking bays for their hire business. The rental was the same as that asked of Abbott's. However, before the ink on the lease had dried TCC was acquired by another company, Guy Salmon, and the new owners concentrated their attention on car hire, cordoning off 53 car parking spaces in the process.[142] This action, which limited parking for tenants and Rodney House customers, was regarded by the Trust as a breach of the lease, and legal proceedings were instituted in 1989.[143] Something of an impasse was created, and two years later there remained four outstanding areas of dispute with NCP: the rent (due for review in 1988); the parking spaces occupied by the car hire firm, now Alamo; the extent of dilapidations, which had resulted in the Trust serving a Section 146 notice on NCP for breach of its agreement in March 1989;[144] and unauthorised parking on the petrol station area and ramps. In 1991–3 efforts were made to reach an accommodation with NCP, and considerable work was put into drafting a management agreement to replace the existing lease.[145] Eventually, after the Trust obtained £137,900 in back rent and interest following the judgment of an independent expert, there was an anxiety on both sides to settle. At a meeting of trustees in November 1993 it emerged that NCP had undertaken to quit at the end of March 1994, though the issue of repairs and dilapidations remained unresolved. The Trust agreed to manage the facility itself, employing Opus Security to operate the garage on its behalf, initially on a trial basis. At last there was a resolution of what had been a rather unsatisfactory relationship.[146]

The services provided by the arcade of shops in Rodney House rarely appeared to concern the trustees, though this does not mean that there were not issues relating to letting, maintenance and so on. While Lloyds Bank closed its sub-branch in 1980, eventually providing an ATM machine on Chichester Street, in general the shopping services were maintained, although as with the restaurant, the facilities were reported to be poorly supported by the tenants. A return drawn up in April 1989 reveals that there were nine shops: a bakery and coffee shop, chemist, dry cleaner, greengrocer, grocer, butcher, hairdresser, newsagent, and off-licence. The properties were primarily let on seven-year leases and the annual rent amounted to about £31,000. By 1991, the rent had increased to £38,000.[147] In 1991, the trustees undertook a review, given the introduction of a unified business rate in Westminster, which had the effect of raising the rate burden.[148] The decision was taken to involve the DSTA in reviewing the needs of tenants and exploring the appropriate retailing policies to be followed. Notwithstanding some doubts about the future viability of retailing in the arcade, the shops were an undoubted asset both to tenants and to hotel guests, giving Dolphin Square the feel of a self-contained community. Trustees in general felt they should be supported.[149]

TENANT RELATIONS AND THE STATUS OF THE TRUST

In 1965 the Trust's relations with the DSTA were fraught, the product, as we have seen, of the circumstances in which the Trust had been created. Dribbell and Garrard in particular took steps to repair the damage, but the DSTA's officers, Baines, Bliss and Wynn Jones, continued to offer a strident opposition to the Trust's decisions. Their principal grievance was the raising of rents in July 1965 (noted above, p.181). Following a somewhat acrimonious meeting on 28 July, the DSTA mounted a campaign of opposition, which included sending several solicitors' letters. The letter sent on 13 September asserted that the Trust's failure to convene a special meeting to discuss the tenants' requests was 'a callous disregard of the anxieties which they are suffering', and advised tenants who had not renewed their leases and faced legal action to apply to the court for the suspension of a possession order pending the completion of negotiations.[150] This unsatisfactory state of affairs was finally resolved at an informal meeting of the Trust and the DSTA in September. After going over the ground, Dribbell told the tenants that the Trust 'was entitled to know where it stands'. He considered the hostile wording of circulars and letters to be 'tantamount to the Tenants' Association declaring war on the Trust'. He emphasised the point that the Trust was now the landlord and its actions could not be vetoed by the DSTA. The tenants were invited to withdraw to consider their position. On their return, Baines, the chairman, apologised for the solicitor's letters and offered a rapprochement.[151] A few days later Baines and Wynn Jones (secretary) resigned from the Association, being succeeded by Dr Alan Fisk and Nancy Penhale. A series of meetings were held in which the new tenancies for residents whose seven-year leases had expired were treated sympathetically via a formula of staggered increases.[152] Lower proportional increases in the rents of the one-room flats also helped to diffuse some of the tenants' anxieties, and Garrard's subsequent dealings with the tenants were more circumspect, with cases of hardship reviewed by the Committee whenever they arose.[153] A tradition of what Fisk called 'open eyed friendliness' was evident in Morris's time, and was only disturbed by Wood's difficulties, and then the breakdown in relations with Cumming in the late 1980s. Tenants' concerns were generally dealt with promptly, and with the 'right to buy' issue in 1967–8 the Trust went out of its way to examine the options before they were ruled out. The same degree of communication was evident in the way the Trust briefed tenants about the important changes to its status, notably its registration with the Housing Corporation in 1976 and its deregistration in 1992, and to its relationship with the freeholder, the United Kingdom Provident Institution. We now turn to these events.

It was in January 1975 that the Trust applied to the Housing Corporation for registration as a housing association under the Housing Act of 1974. Three factors made this an attractive course of action. First, it was assumed that the move would make the Trust eligible for grants from Housing Corporation funds, an important consideration given anxiety about future maintenance costs. Second, it would place Dolphin Square residents outside the protection of the Rent Acts, facilitating the easier termination of problematic tenancies. Finally, it promised to give the Trust an exemption from corporation tax under section 93 of the 1965 Finance Act.[154] The Housing Corporation was reluctant to register the Trust, on the grounds that its commercial activities appeared to be inconsistent with section 13 (3) of the Act.[155] There followed a prolonged period of negotiation, and the engagement of counsel by both sides before registration was finally obtained in December 1976. In fact, approval was conceded reluctantly, and only after the Trust had given the Corporation an undertaking that it would not seek grants from public funds (except possible loans from the local authority).[156]

The Trust's position as a housing association was re-examined by trustees in the wake of the Housing Act of 1980, which created the status of 'secure tenant' and gave housing association tenants the right to buy their homes as well as the right to exchange properties.[157] The 'right to buy' had engaged the attention of trustees much earlier. In 1967, Alan Fisk, chairman of the DSTA, approached the Trust suggesting that the tenants should be given the right to buy their own homes through a co-ownership housing association to be formed by the tenants. Encouraged by the Trust, Council officials approached the Ministry of Housing and Local Government to seek approval for such a move. Work on a scheme proceeded and draft documents were lodged with the Ministry in November 1968. But after a year's prevarication the Ministry rejected the proposal.[158] The issue resurfaced in 1984, when the Housing and Building Control Act strengthened the 'right to buy' and the right to exchange provisions of the Housing Act of 1980, which had introduced more security and rights for tenants, and required improved consultation arrangements with them.[159] The Trust was convinced that it enjoyed exemption from the right to buy sections of the 1980 and 1984 Acts, since it was a housing association which had received no grants, and was operating with a relatively short lease: with only 50 years to run in 1984, and a restrictive covenant prohibiting it from granting underleases beyond 2024.[160] Nevertheless, the Act encouraged the Trust to review its existing status with the help of its solicitors, Woodroffes. The general manager, Wood, introduced a serious discussion of the Trust's status in March 1985. He pointed out that the three reasons for seeking registration in 1975–6 were now largely redundant. In reluctantly agreeing to registration, the Housing Corporation had indicated that the Trust should not seek grants from public funds.[161] Furthermore, the 1980 Housing Act had protected housing association tenants by creating the status of 'secure tenant', who could only be deprived of his/her tenancy by a court order for possession. The right to take in lodgers, and to sublet (with the landlord's permission) had also been included. Finally, the Trust had never pursued exemption from corporation tax, on the advice of its auditors. Exemption could only be obtained on the earnings from the Trust's housing activities, but these were difficult to separate from its other activities. In addition, relief was discretionary and could be withdrawn. Informal soundings taken with the Department of the Environment in 1984 were unpromising. Wood suggested that registration now seemed to confer few advantages, and there was a danger that the 'right to buy' might be extended to bodies such as Dolphin Square. Counsel's opinion was that it might be advantageous for the Trust to deregister, and thus be regulated as a private sector body, but at this stage the Trustees decided not to act, taking the view that deregistration offered no positive assurance that it would be better protected from future legislation affecting the 'right to buy'.[162] Later, the climate changed and the Trust again sought to deregister. Among the new factors taken into consideration were the changes introduced by the Housing Act of 1988, which indicated that deregistration would remove Dolphin Square's

1. Thamesbank, Pimlico, prior to development: the New Ranelagh Cottages

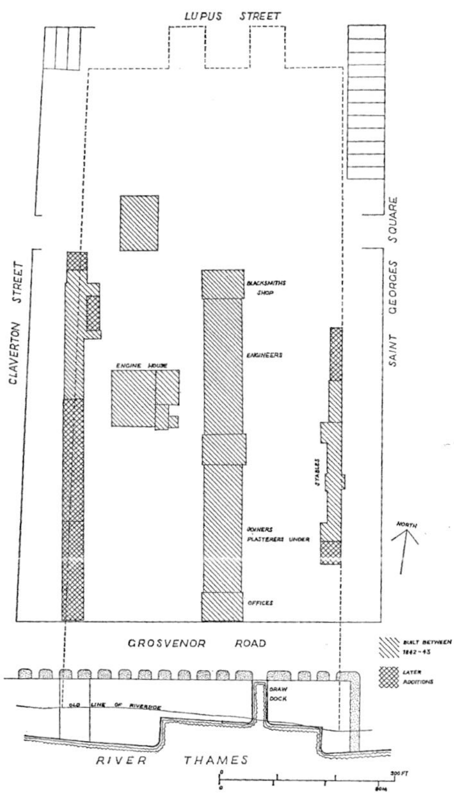

2. Plan of Thomas Cubitt's works, Pimlico, 1842–56

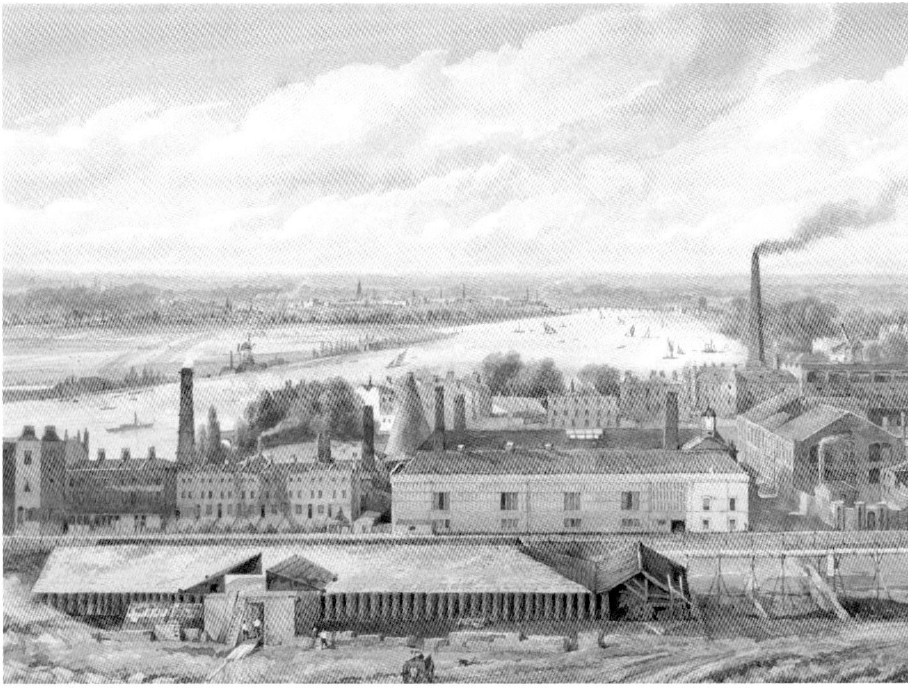

3. Cubitt's works, c.1842, looking west

4. Central Hall of the Royal Army Clothing Depot, c.1877

GROSVENOR/WCA

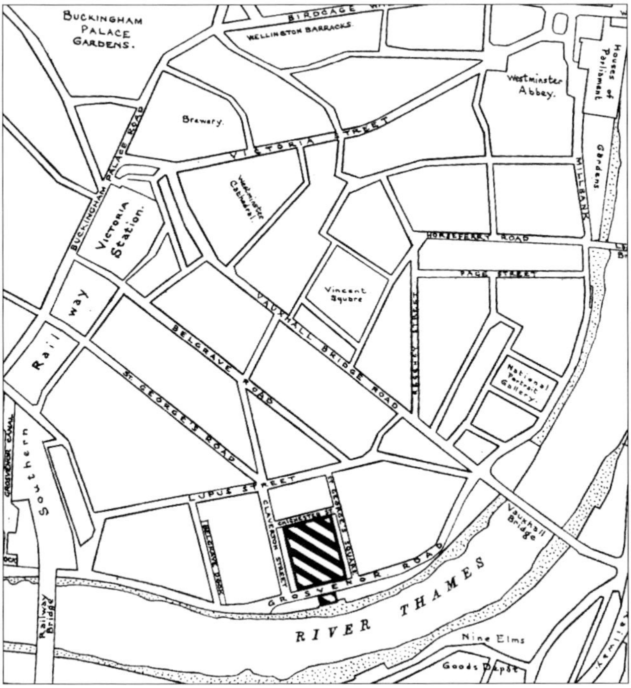

5. Royal Army Clothing Depot sale particulars, 1933: key plan

GROSVENOR/WCA

6. Royal Army Clothing Depot sale particulars, 1933: aerial view

7. Founders: 7 (i) Fred F. French; 7 (ii) Sir Richard Costain; 7 (iii) Sir Albert Costain, MP; 7 (iv) Oscar Faber, bust on Bank of England building (*New York Times*, 31 August 1936; Costain Group, *Bulletin*, June 1965; Bank of England)

TERRY GOURVISH

8. Tudor City New York, 2012: Tudor Tower

TERRY GOURVISH

9. Knickerbocker Village, New York, 2012: East River frontage

FRED F. FRENCH COLLECTION, NYPL

FRED F. FRENCH COLLECTION, NYPL

10 and 11. Original conceptions for 'Tudor City London', 1934: 10. Bird's Eye view with central 23-storey block; 11. With central 10-storey block

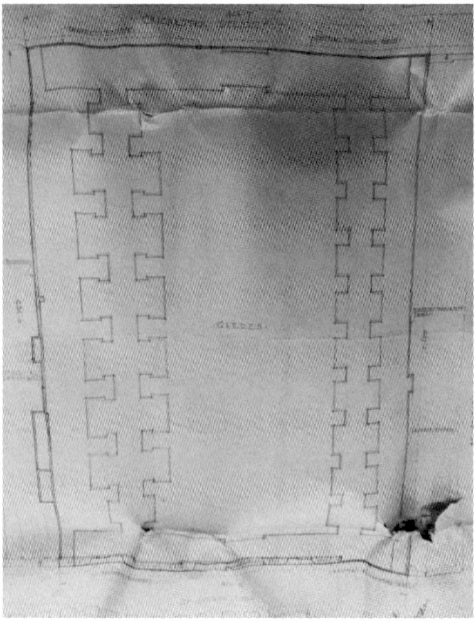

LMA

12. Frederick F. French & Co. Ltd., site plan for 'Ormonde Court/Square', in preliminary plans submitted to LCC, 5 November 1934

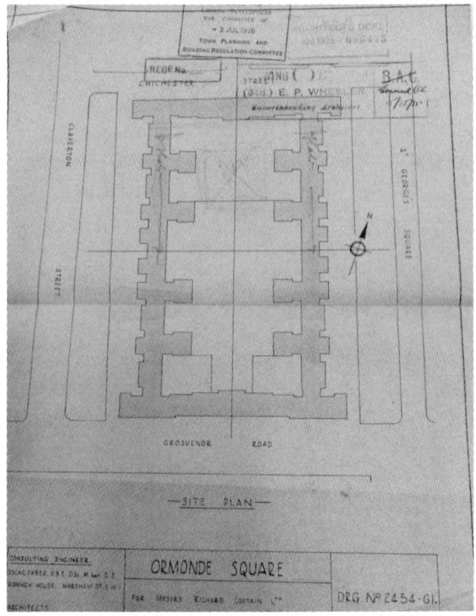

LMA

13. Gordon Jeeves, site plan for 'Ormonde Court/Square', July 1935

DST

14. Construction of Dolphin Square: Work in progress on the South Block, December 1935

DST

15. Completion of the South Block, November 1936: exterior on Grosvenor Road

DST/SYDNEY NEWBERY

16. Petrol station, 1938

DST

17. The rose garden, fountain and pool, 1937, from the cover of *The Dolphin*

DST

18. Opening of Children's Centre, November 1936: Lady Diana Cooper presented with flowers by Ann Costain

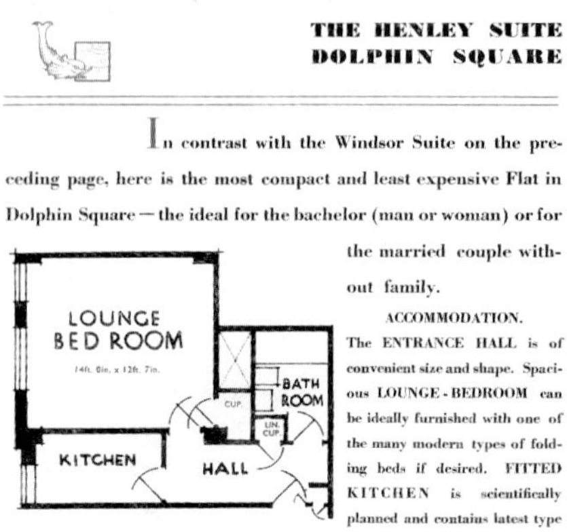

THE HENLEY SUITE
DOLPHIN SQUARE

In contrast with the Windsor Suite on the preceding page, here is the most compact and least expensive Flat in Dolphin Square — the ideal for the bachelor (man or woman) or for the married couple without family.

ACCOMMODATION.

The ENTRANCE HALL is of convenient size and shape. Spacious LOUNGE-BEDROOM can be ideally furnished with one of the many modern types of folding beds if desired. FITTED KITCHEN is scientifically planned and contains latest type

DST

19 (i) Flat designs – The Henley Suite

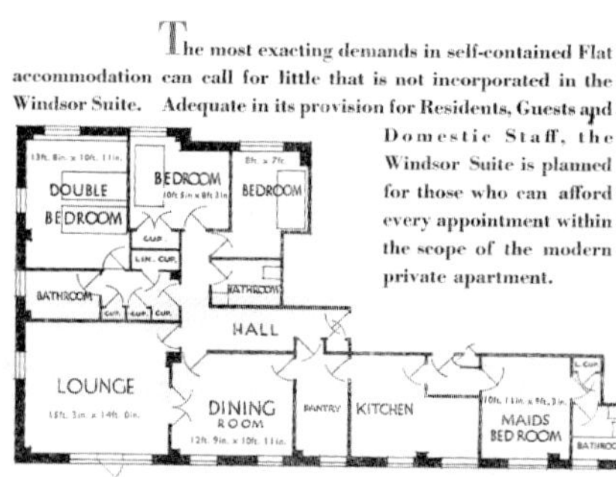

The most exacting demands in self-contained Flat accommodation can call for little that is not incorporated in the Windsor Suite. Adequate in its provision for Residents, Guests and Domestic Staff, the Windsor Suite is planned for those who can afford every appointment within the scope of the modern private apartment.

DST

19 (ii) Flat designs – The Windsor Suite

HARLEQUIN

NORMAN DUNN COLLECTION

GETTY IMAGES

DST/RICHARD ROWAN

Residents 1: 20 (i) Ida Cook with Maria Callas, 1964; 20 (ii) Ellen Wilkinson MP, on the Jarrow March, October 1936; 20 (iii) Angus Wilson, 1963; 20 (iv) Robert Mayo's composite plane, 1938

M.H. BATEMAN DESIGNS

21. The Dolphin Square restaurant, according to H.M. Bateman

DST

DST/EDWARD SMETTEM

22. Thames-side views from Dolphin Square: 22 (i) Balcony view as portrayed in the Dolphin Square brochure, 1936; 22 (ii) Actual view, including the Nine Elms warehouse, 1937

DST/SYDNEY NEWBERY

23. Interior of a flat, July 1938

DST

THE DOLPHIN, SEPTEMBER 1938 7

AT THE DOLPHIN EXCHANGE

. . . *Sir, you left your tennis racket at the Restaurant. . . . Sorry, your number is engaged. . . . Flat 705 are on holiday. . . . You have a piano at the goods depôt, Madam. . . . May I take a message, Sir? . . . Sorry, your number is engaged. . . . Baby won't leave the Children's Centre, Madam. . . . Sorry. Thank ou, Sir.*

24. The telephone service: Oscar Berger's cartoon in *The Dolphin*

DST

DST

DST

25. The staff in 1939: 25 (i) Nurses (the matron, Evelyn Pantin, is seated in the centre); 25 (ii) Restaurant staff; 25 (iii) Porters and page boys

WCA

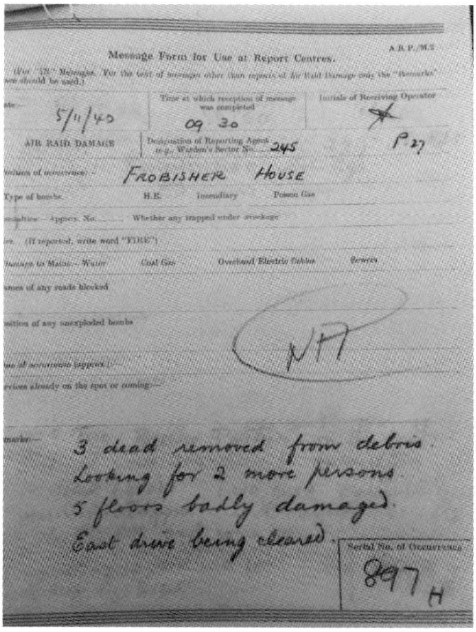

A.R.P./M.2

Message Form for Use at Report Centres.

(For "IN" Messages. For the text of messages other than reports of Air Raid Damage only the "Remarks" ...ace should be used.)

...ate:— 5/11/40 | Time at which reception of message was completed 09 30 | Initials of Receiving Operator

AIR RAID DAMAGE | Designation of Reporting Agent (e.g., Warden's Sector No. 245 | P.27

...osition of occurrence:— FROBISHER HOUSE

Type of bombs. H.E. Incendiary Poison Gas

...sualties—Approx. No. ...... Whether any trapped under wreckage

...ire. (If reported, write word "FIRE")

Damage to Mains:—Water Coal Gas Overhead Electric Cables Sewers

...ames of any roads blocked

...osition of any unexploded bombs

...me of occurrence (approx.):—

...rvices already on the spot or coming:—

...marks:— 3 dead removed from debris.
Looking for 2 more persons.
5 floors badly damaged.
East drive being cleared.

Serial No. of Occurrence 897 H

26. Bombing of Frobisher House, 5 November 1940: 26 (i) civil defence message form; 26 (ii) photograph of damage

DAILY MIRROR

27. William Trotter's Spanish party, 1949

NATIONAL PORTRAIT GALLERY
DST/REX COLEMAN
DST
DST; DST/JOHN BIGNELL

28. Protagonists: 28 (i) Maxwell Joseph; 28 (ii) (Sir) Alan Dawtry; 28 (iii) Tony Prendergast; 28 (iv) Jack Dribbell

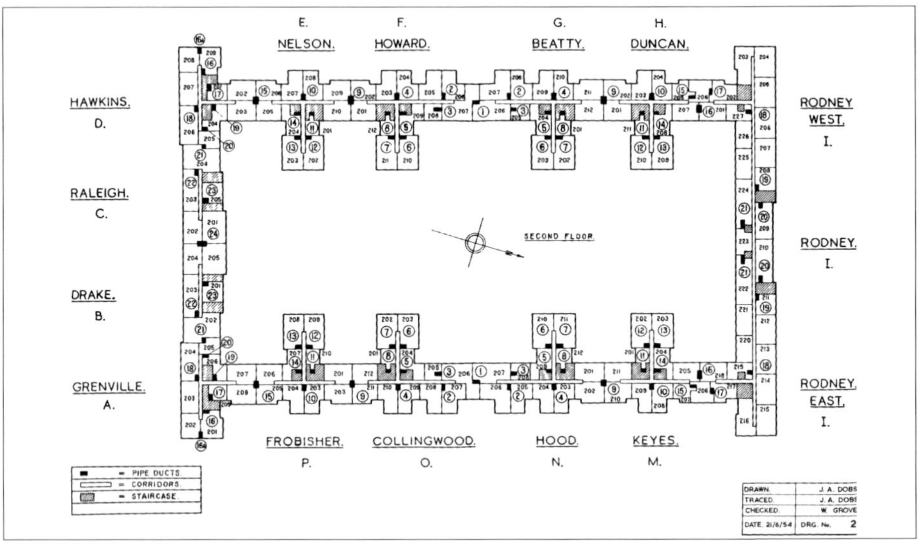

DST

29. Plan of the Square, 1954: second floor

DST

30. Empire Catering menu, 1965

THE NEWS

31. General managers: Bryan Garrard (1964–74) and Kenneth Morris (1974–83, 1985–6), in 1970

MAIL ON SUNDAY

32. Dolphin Square staff, 1987

33. Dolphin Square Trust Committee of Management and senior managers, March 1999 (DST). Standing, left to right: Clare Stewart (Hotel Manager), Adrian Wray (Secretary and General Manager), Rodney Brooke, Geoffrey Lander, Bruce Clitherow, John Holmes (Facilities Manager), Bernard Bindman (Chief Accountant), Sally Watson (PA to General Manager); seated, left to right, Barry Pinson, Sir Alan Dawtry, Maurice Stonefrost (Chairman), Alan Bradley (Vice Chairman), Jan Prebble. Absent: David Hopkins, Jane Salt (Flats Manager).

GETTY IMAGES

34. Residents 2: 34 (i) John Vassall, 1972; 34 (ii) Sid James and Barbara Windsor, 1973; 34 (iii) David (later Lord) Steel, 1980; 34 (iv) William and Ffion Hague, 2001

MIRRORPIX/RANDOLPH CAUCHIE

MIRRORPIX

PRESS ASSOCIATION IMAGES/PA ARCHIVE/PETER JORDAN

MIRRORPIX/STAN JAANUS

35. The brothel in Duncan House, 1971

TERRY GOURVISH

36. The Bud Flanagan bench

tenancies from rent control, and the fear that the Corporation would seek to interfere in the Trust's rental policy. The latter arose after tensions emerged between Wood's successor as general manager, John Cumming, and the DSTA, from 1987. Eventually, tenants' complaints provoked the DSTA into approaching the Housing Corporation, which stirred up a hornet's nest. Corporation officials then began to take a closer interest in the Square and its operations. In May 1990, the Corporation's regional monitoring manager wrote to Cumming to point out that the Trust had never been monitored, and to inform him that it would be included in his monitoring programme for that year.[163] And after a visit of inspection conducted in the autumn, the Corporation came to the conclusion that the Trust was not operating adequately as a housing association. Its registrar, James Tickell suggested that in order for Dolphin Square to comply with its requirements, attention would need to be given to the following issues: access to housing; committee and association accountability; race equality and equal opportunities; management control; and finance. There would need to be 'fundamental changes to the nature of the Trust, its client base, and the day to day operation of the Square'. In short, the Corporation's view was that Dolphin Square should play its part in tackling the need for social housing in the borough and that the flats, including those in Rodney House, should be made available to those unable to find accommodation in the private sector or on the Council's waiting list. The ethnic imbalance of the Square, whether tenants, staff or trustees, was also a matter for criticism.[164] The counsel engaged to advise the Trust considered it unlikely that the Corporation would interfere in rental policy, and he also doubted whether deregistration, which he felt offered limited advantages, could be achieved.[165] Notwithstanding his advice, the Trust pressed ahead with an application to de-register. After receiving a positive vote of support from the tenants (683 for, 8 against), the Trust applied to deregister in January 1992, and the change was effected in March.[166]

In the course of the deliberations about registration, the question was raised as to whether the Trust's lessee status should also be reconsidered. In fact, the Trust had made an approach to the freeholder, the mutual life insurance society, the United Kingdom Provident Institution (UKPI), in 1980, indicating that it was willing to buy the freehold. UKPI responded by making it clear that it was unwilling to discuss such a sale.[167] Then in 1985 the freeholder took the initiative, stating that it wished to buy back the lease in order to sell the flats to the tenants. However, the Trust replied that the proposal was contrary to the terms of the sublease with the City Council, and was rejected.[168]

The freeholder persisted, however. Its chairman and managing director, S.G. Brooksbank, then had discussions with Dame Shirley Porter, leader of Westminster City Council since 1983, and asked for a meeting with the Council to 'restructure the lease'. A meeting attended by Prendergast, Dawe, Morris and Cumming for the Trust, G.E. Touchard, Westminster's Director of Property Services, Brooksbank, and Tim Simons of Savills, UKPI's estate agents, took place on 10 December 1985. Brooksbank pointed out that since the existing lease had only 49 years to run, the lessees should sell the lease back to UKPI, who would then offer the flats for sale on 99-year leases to the existing tenants. He contended that most tenants would wish to buy, and the move would be consonant with Government policy on the 'right to buy'. Prendergast restated the Trust's implacable opposition to the idea. No fewer than six reasons were given: the Trust had been set up to provide rented accommodation for people working in Westminster; its long-term policy was to provide reasonable rents no higher than the designated fair rent; given the shortage of such accommodation in Westminster, the Trust had every intention to continue to provide it; there was no evidence that the tenants wished, or were able, to buy flats on long leases; the Trust was busy with its long-term duct renewal programme, which required short tenancies in order to obtain vacant possession and had 20 years still to run; and this programme was dependent on the continuation of the substantial income from Rodney House. UKPI's response was to challenge the Trust's view of tenant opinion and to suggest that a poll of the tenants be conducted. The Committee of Management considered the position in January 1986. By selling the underlease the Trust would make a short-term financial gain, which it did not want. The financial advantages for UKPI would be much greater, of course, but the process of sale and resale, and the likely future sale of the freeholds on individual houses in the Square, would produce complex legal and residential problems. It was agreed that no further action would be taken unless UKPI made an approach to the tenants.[169] In fact, UKPI kept up the pressure. In February, Brooksbank informed Prendergast that UKPI would conduct a poll of the tenants. The Trust responded by writing to the tenants informing them that the option was ruled out under the rules of the Trust, and that the trustees had firmly rejected the approach. The DSTA, then led by Deirdre Marshall (chairman) and Jan Reid (secretary), also wrote to the tenants expressing its support for the Trust's stance.[170] It later emerged that UKPI was in financial difficulties and within weeks it had to be rescued by the Friends' Provident Life Office via an operational merger. Its sluggish property portfolio may have been one factor, but the main reasons for its collapse were poor investment decisions, coupled with the high cost of obtaining new business.[171] Friends' Provident then took a closer interest in Dolphin Square, in particular when it updated its property portfolio. It was also the case that its chairman from 1988, Lord (Patrick) Jenkin, who had joined the board in 1986, knew the Square well, since he was a tenant.[172] The company undertook a broad survey of the property in 1992, and asked to be kept informed of any developments. As Crawford rightly observed, 'it seems inevitable that, as the end of the lease comes nearer, they will become even more interested.'[173]

In many ways, the early 1990s mirrored the mid 1960s in terms of uncertainty for the future of Dolphin Square. In between, changes of housing legislation frequently required the trustees to be on their toes. Nevertheless, the Committee of Management had steered the property on a sound course for nearly 30 years, and while the tenants had their gripes, they could not deny that principles of sound financial and administrative management had been applied to the letting of flats and the maintenance of the property. By 1993, it was becoming evident that adhering to those principles in the face of a more intrusive interest from the freeholder would create considerable problems, not least in attracting the attention of Westminster City Council, which since 1965 had left the Trust to its own devices. These are the subject of the following chapter.

NOTES

1 DST Committee of Management Minutes, 27 November 1964 and 11 March 1965, DST. Macnabb (1901–90) won a gold medal in rowing at the 1924 Olympic Games and was Treasurer of the Amateur Rowing Association for 20 years: *The Times*, 10 April 1990, p.14.

2 Cf. Malpass, *Housing Associations and Housing Policy*, pp.5, 132.

3 Mayors: Pirie, 1959–60; Dribbell, 1961–2; Lord Mayors: Norton, 1965–6; Burton, 1966–7; Prendergast, 1968–9; Pirie, 1974–5; Dawe, 1975–6; and Bradley, 1995–6.

4 Annual Return of Land and Housing Society Committee of Management, 1969 and 1970, DST; WCC Rate Book for years ending 31 March 1969 and 1970, WCA. Le Marchant and Prendergast rented their flats until 1972 and 1975 respectively.

5 Dawe, who served as Lord Mayor, 1975–6, stepped down as vice-chairman in 1975–7. Pirie took his place. DST Committee of Management Minutes, 19 March 1975, 28 March 1977, DST.

6 DST Committee of Management Minutes, 18 March 1971, DST.

7 There were in fact 13 trustees from the time of Bowdell's appointment on 8 February 1967 until Burton's resignation on 11 August 1967. The number fell to 11 in 1972–4.

8 Reid was Hon. Secretary of DSTA, 1974–7 and 1981–7, newsletter editor, 1973–81 and 1985–7, and social secretary, 1977–81. DSTA newsletters, 1973–87, passim, DST.

9 Tony Travers, *Guardian*, 5 November 2008, p.39, *The Times*, 7 November 2008, p.85, George Jones, *Independent*, 26 November 2008, p.42. Stonefrost was secretary of IMTA (subsequently CIPFA), 1964–73.

10 There is an unflattering portrait of Weeks in Andrew Hosken, *Nothing Like A Dame: The Scandals of Shirley Porter* (2006), p.77, and see also Paul Dimoldenberg, *The Westminster Whistleblowers: Shirley Porter, homes for votes and twenty years of scandal in Britain's rottenest borough* (2006).

11 Hosken, *Nothing Like A Dame*, pp.251, 257–9. Brooke had been Chief Executive of West Yorkshire CC, 1981–4. He was hon. secretary of the London Boroughs Association (1984–90), secretary of the Metropolitan Authorities (1990–7), and Deputy Lieutenant of Greater London (1989–). His publications include *Managing the Enabling Authority* (Harlow, 1989) and *The Environmental Role of Local Government* (Luton, 1990).

12 See www.westminster.gov.uk/councillors.

13 Of the 25 trustees 1964–93, ten were WCC councillors and six were WCC officers; 14 tenants were trustees, though three of these became residents after their appointment.

14 Garrard, Initial Report, 11 November 1964, p.11, DST, *R & A 1992/3*, DST. There were some minor fluctuations in staffing between 1964 and 1993. Reported numbers of full-time staff were 200 (1978), 183 (1979), 185 (1980), 202 (1982), 199 (1983), 197 (1984), 210 (1990), and 197 (1992).

15 Garrard, Initial Report, 11 November 1964, p.11, DST. An organisational chart of 1982 revealed similar figures, viz. maintenance and engineering 51; porters and cleaners 48; housekeeping 50; and telephone 15: Organisational chart, in papers for DST Committee of Management, 13 July 1982, DST.

16 RPI all-items index, in ONS, *Economic Trends Annual Supplement 2006*.

17 Garrard claimed to be the 9th general manager since 1936, but did not list them: ibid.

18 Cf. DST Committee of Management Minutes, 28 September 1965, DST; Morris, *Dolphin Square*, pp.80, 92. Garrard's salary was £4,000 a year. DST Committee of Management Minutes, 17 May 1965, 21 January 1969, DST.

19 *Supplement to the London Gazette*, 25 June 1957, 21 May 1963, 16 April 1968. On Morris see Jan Prebble, 'An Anecdotal Tribute to Ken Morris', *A Hotchpotch of Tales from Dolphin Square* (January 2006), p.18.

20 DST Committee of Management Minutes, 21 September 1982, DST.

21 See Garrard-Prendergast, 10 September 1974 and reply, 22 September 1974, DST Committee of Management Minutes, 25 September 1974, 16 July 1985, DST.

22 DST Committee of Management Minutes, 19 November 1985, DST.

23 DST Committee of Management Minutes, 16 September 1985, 27 March and 9 April 1991, Prendergast-John Cumming, 9 April 1991, DST; Cumming-Dolphin Square tenants, April 1992, DST; Mira Bar-Hillel and John Passmore, 'The secret society of Dolphin Square', *Evening Standard*, 12 May 1992, pp.21–2. David Collins, the Head of Maintenance, became acting general manager until Crawford's appointment w.e.f. 30 September 1991.

24 DSTA newsletter March 1987; Deirdre Marshall (Chairman, DSTA) et al., letter to DSTA members, 5 October 1987, DST. The tenancy issues included the future impact of the duct renewal programme.

25 Tony Crawford-Dolphin Square Tenants, 9 December 1991, et seq., DST.

26 The management consultants were Turquand, Youngs & Layton-Bennett. When Gordon Jacques was appointed Chief Accountant in 1988 the auditors Ernst & Whinney advised on the appropriate salary level: Cumming, report, DST Committee of Management Minutes, 26 January 1988, DST.

27 Garrard, report on 'Staff Problems', 16 July 1974, DST.

28 Garrard, Initial Report, 11 November 1964, DST.

29 Garrard, report, 4 November 1965, DST Committee of Management Minutes, 12 November 1965, DST.

30 Organisational chart, 13 July 1982, DST.

31 Organisational chart, 11 November 1985, in papers for DST Committee of Management, 19 November 1985, DST. Staff numbers were building supt. 42; flats manager 59; Rodney House manager 65; chief accountant six. The sports centre and sauna managers do not appear in the chart.

32 Cumming, report on 'Re-organisation of the Maintenance Department', 18 March 1988, DST Committee of Management Minutes, 29 March 1988, DST.

33 Cumming, report on 'Senior Management Reorginization [sic]', DST Committee of Management Minutes, 23 November 1988, DST.

34 Cumming, report on 'Proposals on the development of the Flats Department and the appointment of a Commercial Manager', 14 March 1989, DST Committee of Management Minutes, 21 March and 25 July 1989, 27 January 1992, DST; DST, *R & A 1988/9*, pp.3, 6. John Firrell succeeded Janetta Devon in 1991, and in the following year the post was renamed hotel operations manager: DST Committee of Management Minutes, 27 January 1992, DST.

35 DST Committee of Management Minutes, 19 November 1991.

36 DST Committee of Management Minutes, *passim*.

37 Morris, report, 10 January 1977, DST Committee of Management Minutes, 20 January 1977, DST.

38 Garrard, Note, 20 January 1970, DST Committee of Management Minutes, 20 January 1970, DST.

39 Garrard, report on 'Staff Matters', 13 November 1972, DST.

40 Garrard, report on 'Staff Problems', 16 July 1974, DST Committee of Management Minutes, 25 July 1974, DST.

41 DST Committee of Management Minutes, 24 January and 21 March 1968, 20 January 1970, DST. The DST had endeavoured to take advantage of Section 43 of the Finance Act, 1963. Morris later acted as interim general manager from July 1985 until Cumming's appointment in January 1986.

42 Morris, report, 6 March 1980, DST Committee of Management Minutes, 18 March 1980.

43 Morris, report, 16 March 1982, DST Committee of Management Minutes, 16 March 1982.

44 DST, *R & A 1982/3*, p.6.

45 Cumming, report, DST Committee of Management Minutes, 21 March 1989, DST.

46 It was a condition of the lease with WCC that the DST should establish a 'dilapidations fund' of £150,000 over the period of the lease: WCC and DST, underlease, 31 December 1964, s.3. Before 1983 such transfers, together with transfers to/from a repairs equalisation fund, were shown after net income had been determined. Thereafter, they were included in the main accounts. See Appendix 3.

47 This was the stated figure in 1979–93. Earlier the number had been slightly higher, viz. 1,072 at the time of the sale in 1963, 1,063 in 1970, and 1,050 in 1977. DST, *R & A, passim.*

48 These trends can also be seen in the annual rate of increase of unfurnished flat income: 8.3% p.a., 1965–93, but 5.4%, 1965–82, and 19.6%, 1990–3. Calculated from DST, *R & A 1965–92/3.*

49 Garrard, report, 12 March 1968, DST Committee of Management Minutes, 21 March 1968, DST. The number of formerly protected tenants had fallen to 58 by November 1972: Garrard, report, 9 November 1972, DST.

50 Garrard-Dolphin Square tenants, 29 July 1965, and annex to Garrard, report, 4 November 1968, DST Committee of Management Minutes, 3 August 1965 and 11 November 1968, DST.

51 Finance Act 1966, 1966 c.18 s.44.

52 DST Committee of Management Minutes, 8 November 1966, DST.

53 Thus, for those on the 1964 scale: the 1965 scale in year 1, the median of the 1965 and 1966 scales in year 2, and the 1966 scale in year 3. This represented a change of policy, since the Committee had opposed 'graduated rents' in 1966. DST Committee of Management Minutes, 8 November 1966, 11 November 1968, DST; DST, *R & A 1967/8*, p.5.

54 Garrard, reports, 8 July and 10 September 1971 and 9 November 1972, DST Committee of Management Minutes, 13 July and 21 September 1971 and 16 November 1972, DST. The policy was explained to the DSTA on 11 October 1971.

55 Cf. Garrard, reports, 2 November 1966 and 8 July 1971, DST.

56 Ashley Bramall, a trustee and expert on housing law, raised the issue as to whether the 1965 Act applied to Dolphin Square: DST Committee of Management Minutes, 8 March 1966, DST. He was the author of *The Rent Act 1965* (1965).

57 Paul N. Balchin, *Housing Policy: An Introduction* (2nd edn, 1989), pp.118–19.

58 Garrard, report, 9 November 1972, cit.; Piers Bierne, *Fair Rent and Legal Fiction: Housing Rent Legislation in a Capitalist Society* (1977), p.148ff; Balchin, *Housing Policy*, pp.120, 151; Morris, *Dolphin Square*, p.83.

59 DST Committee of Management Minutes, 16 November 1972, DST.

60 Counter-Inflation (Temporary Provisions) Act, November 1972, 1972 c.74.

61 *The Times*, 9 March 1974, p.1, 7 November 1974, p.1.

62 Cf. Garrard-Christopher Tugendhat MP, 11 March 1974, DST Committee of Management Minutes, 19 March 1974, DST.

63 There was one exception, a flat in Nelson which had been converted from three flats. DST Committee of Management Minutes, 14 March 1973, DST; Balchin, *Housing* Policy, pp.120–2; Counter-Inflation Act, March 1973, 1973 c.9.

64 Housing, Rents and Subsidies Act, February 1975, 1975 c.6; Balchin, *Housing Policy*, p.122.

65 Garrard, report, 5 March 1973, DST; Housing Finance Act 1972, 1972 c.47 s.84 (2), Housing, Rents and Subsidies Act 1975, s.7; DST, *R & A 1979–80*, p.5.

66 Rent Act 1977, 1977 c.42, s. 89 (2); Philip H. Pettit, *Private Sector Tenancies, being a second edition of Landlord and Tenant under the Rent Act 1977* (1981), pp.174–7; Morris, report, 21 October 1977, DST.

67 Where the rateable value was under £600, but the increase not to produce a rent lower than the 1971 scale: DST Committee of Management Minutes, 14 March and 5 July 1973, DST.

68 Morris pointed out that in 1974–8 fair rents had increased by 45%, but the RPI had increased by 64%: report, 22 June 1979, DST.

69 Agenda for DST Committee of Management Meeting, 6 November 1979, DST.

70 Housing Act 1980, 1980 c.51; Balchin, *Housing Policy*, pp.127–31; Peter Malpass, 'Housing policy and the housing system since 1979', and Peter Kemp, 'Rebuilding the private rented sector?', in Peter Malpass and Robin Means (eds.), *Implementing Housing Policy* (Buckingham, 1993), pp.24, 27, 62–3.

71 Morris, report on 'Rents – Unfurnished Flats', 4 November 1981 and 1 November 1982, DST Committee of Management Minutes, 17 November 1981 and 9 November 1982, DST.

72 Morris, report, 4 November 1981, DST.

73 These fair rents increased by 122% and 137%, but the RPI increased by 242%, 1973–82.

74 Morris, reports, 4 November 1981 and 1 November 1982, DST. See also Morris, *Dolphin Square*, pp.83–4.

75 Cf. Morris, report, 1 November 1982, DST. Morris also floated the idea of switching from fixed to periodic term tenancies for new tenants, but the trustees did not agree: Morris, report, 14 March 1983, Wood, report, 1 November 1983, DST Committee of Management Minutes, 22 March, 13 July and 8 November 1983, DST.

76 The water supply itself came from the Square's own artesian wells.

77 Wood, report, 1 November 1983, DST Committee of Management Minutes, 9 November 1982, annex B, DST. Instead of £60 in the first year, tenants paid £144–162 for one room, £198–246 for two rooms, and £258–288 for three rooms. The increase for a three-year tenancy ranged from 45% for a 2C flat to 64% for a 2A+ flat. This appears to have been a 'one-off' increase, since in the early 1990s the original incremental tariff was being quoted (though the seven-room increment was given as £204 instead of £205): cf. Crawford, report [n.d.], DST Committee of Management Minutes, 24 November 1992, DST.

78 DST, *R & A 1980/1*, pp.4, 6, *1983/4*, pp.6–7. Higher rents for modernised flats were first reported in 1973: Agendas for Committee of Management Meeting, 12 July 1973 and 25 July 1974, Garrard, report, 1 November 1973, DST. A relatively generous discount for tenants returning to their flats after modernisation was agreed in 1984: Wood, report, 9 November 1984, DST Committee of management minutes, 20 November 1984, DST.

79 The fair rent for a 1A flat (in constant 1993 prices) was £2,844 in 1973, £3,656 in 1988 and £4,700 in 1993.

80 DST, *R & A, passim.* Data = 1980/1 80; 1981/2 73; 1982/3 65; 1983/4 50; 1984/5 29; 1985/6 45; 1986/7 51; 1987/8 33; 1988/9, 34; 1989/90 18; 1990/1 42; 1991/2 150; 1992/3 133. The low turnover rate was also affected by the policy of retaining empty flats to house tenants affected by the duct renewal programme.

81 DST, *R & A 1975/6–1984/5.* The Trust did not publish waiting list numbers in its annual report after 1984/5.

82 Housing Act, 1988, 1988 c.50; Bill Randolph, 'The re-privatization of housing associations', and Peter Kemp, 'Rebuilding the private rented sector?', in Malpass and Means, *Implementing Housing Policy*, pp.39–40, 67.

83 Cumming, reports, 14 January and 18 March 1988, DST Committee of Management Minutes, 26 January and 29 March 1988, DST. The subcommittee had expected market rents to be higher than Daniel Smith's valuation, and proposed to charge 'full rents', i.e. rents between the market rent and the fair rent. When Smith's tariff proved to be lower than expected, they accepted it as the basis for rent-setting.

84 Cumming, reports, 14 November 1988, and in 1989 and 1990 [n.d.], DST Committee of Management Minutes, 23 November 1988, 23 November 1989, 27 November 1990, DST.

85 Crawford, report [n.d.], DST Committee of Management Minutes, 19 November 1991, DST.

86 Crawford-Geoffrey Lander (Honorary Secretary, DSTA), draft letter, 19 May 1992, and Crawford, report [n.d.], DST Committee of Management Minutes, 24 November 1992, DST.

87 Crawford, report, DST Committee of Management Minutes, 25 November 1993, DST. 1993 data: subsidy £4.74m., rent collected £4m.

88 In constant 1993 prices, Rodney House income rose from £1.55m in 1965/6 to £2.73m in 1978/9 and £3.66m in 1989/90, an increase, 1965/6–1989/90, of c. 3.6% p.a. See Appendix 4.

89 In 1972 an occupancy rate of 81% (apartments and guest rooms) was reported, which compared favourably with the London hotel average of 65%. Occupancy was also high in the mid 1980s, e.g. 73.3% in 1985/6, 79.2% in 1986/7, 78.7% in 1987/8 (apartments only). Garrard, report, 1 November 1972, DST Committee of Management Minutes, 16 November 1972, 23 November 1988.

90 Including a switch to higher quality (premium rates). The standard rate was increased by 138%.

91 GM, report [n.d.], DST Committee of Management Minutes, 5 February 1991, and see also 26 June and 19 November 1991, DST.

92 See Appendix 4 and 6.

93 Garrard, initial report, November 1965, pp.3–5, DST.

94 WCC and DST, further charge (limit: £220,000), 7 November 1966, DST.

95 DST, *R & A 1968/9*, p.6; DST Committee of Management Minutes, 20 January 1970, DST. The shopping arcade was also refurbished, and a major crack in the outside wall of Rodney House was repaired. DST, *R & A 1970/1*, p.5.

96 DST Committee of Management Minutes, 19 November 1985, DST; DST, *R & A 1975/6*, p.6, *1985/6*, p.5; Morris, *Dolphin Square*, pp.59–60.

97 See Morris, *Dolphin Square*, pp.86–9.

98 The annual reports for 1974/5 and 1975/6 stated that 154 flats had been renovated, but Morris later put the figure at 155: DST, *R & A 1970/1*, p.5, *1971/2*, p.5, *1974/5*, p.5, *1975/6*, p.5; Morris, report, 3 November 1980, DST Committee of Management Minutes, 18 November 1980, DST.

99 DST, R & A 1979/80, p.5, 1983/4, p.6.

100 DST Committee of Management Minutes, 28 March 1984, 25 March 1993, 29 March 1994, DST.

101 Collins (Head of Maintenance), report [reprises history], DST Committee of Management Minutes, 27 March 1991, DST; DST, *R & A 1987/8*, p.6, *1992/3*, p.9. Confidence in the Trust's calculations is undermined by an unexplained discrepancy in the annual reporting. Thus, in September 1990, 504 flats were reported to have been renewed at a cost of £5.049m, but in the following year the total was given as 600, at a lower cost of £4.674m. DST, *R & A 1989/90*, p.5, *1990/1*, p.5.

102 DST, *R & A 1977/8*, p.4. A health club was added to list in *1988/9*, p.4, a conference centre in *1991/2*, p.5, and a gymnasium in *1992/3*, p.7.

103 Garrard, initial report, November 1964, p.9, DST.

104 Garrard, report, 4 March 1965, Dribbell and Garrard, report [n.d.], DST Committee of Management Minutes, 19 January, 17 May and 12 July 1965.

105 DSCL Board Minutes, 26 September 1960, 13 and 24 April 1964, DST. Unfortunately, the information revealed by the board minutes is extremely limited. For example, on 13 April 1964 Rupert Mostert was also elected a director, along with the Gossmans, but he was not assigned any shares, and was reported to have resigned on 3 May 1965: Minutes, 3 May 1965, DST.

106 DST Committee of Management Minutes, 17 May, 12 July and 3 August 1965, 25 July 1966, DST; Dribbell-Gossman, 6 May 1965, Dribbell papers.

107 Da Costa had provided catering for special events such as the Royal Windsor Horse Show, Wimbledon Tennis Championships and the Royal Norfolk Show. Advertisement in *Westminster and Pimlico News*, 12 November 1965, p.1; DST, *R & A 1965*.

108 DST Committee of Management Minutes, 3 August 1965, DST. In the period 1965–93 Prendergast succeeded Dribbell as chairman in 1967, Dew was succeeded by Ball (1971–7), then Reid (1977–). Dawtry was co-opted to the board in 1989.

109 Derived from Appendix 8.

110 DSCL Board Minutes, 5 September 1966, DST.

111 DST Committee of Management Minutes, 21 July 1992, 27 November 2003, DST.

112 DSCL Board Minutes, 5 September 1966, DST.

113 Cf. DST Committee of Management Minutes, 25 July 1966, DST.

114 DST Committee of Management Minutes, 14 March 1979, 23 July 1980, DST.

115 The payment was reduced to 5% of gross receipts, if between £250,000 and £500,000. The contractors were also to pay for electricity and gas. DST Committee of Management Minutes, 18 November 1980, Agenda, 31 March 1981, DST.

116 Morris, reports, 12 January, 16 March and 1 November 1982, DST Committee of Management Minutes, 19 January, 23 March and 9 November 1982, DST.

117 Morris, report, 11 November 1985, Cumming, report, 12 March 1986, DST Committee of Management Minutes, 16 July and 19 November 1985, 19 March 1986, DST; DST, *R & A 1986/7*, p.4. The agreement of 6 January 1986 required a payment of £15,000 in the first year, then for the next four years 7.5% on gross receipts up to £250,000, 5% on £250,000–500,000, then 7.5% up to £350,000, and 5% on £350,000–500,000, for the next five years.

118 Cumming, report, 19 July 1987, and correspondence, May-June 1987, DST Committee of Management Minutes, 29 April and 21 July 1987, DST.

119 Cumming, reports, 14 January 1988 and 17 January 1989, DST Committee of Management Minutes, 26 January 1988 and 24 January 1989, DST.

120 The Lighthouse Bar also offered food, and was the forerunner of the cheaper 'brasserie' when Dolphin Square offered both a 'restaurant' and 'brasserie' from 1998.

121 Cumming, report, 18 July 1989, DST Committee of Management Minutes, 25 July 1989, DST.

122 Cumming, report [n.d.], DST Committee of Management Minutes, 23 November 1989, 23 January, 20 March and 24 July 1990, DST.

123 Christopher Faulkner (Operations Director, Parasol)-Cumming, 28 January 1991, DST Committee of Management Minutes, 23 January 1990, DST.

124 Sub-Committee report [n.d.], DST Committee of Management Minutes, 27 January, 21 July and 24 November 1992, 27 January 1993, DST; DST, *R & A 1992/3*, p.8.

125 Cf. Crawford-tenants, 1 and 30 Sept 1992. DST.

126 DST Committee of Management Minutes, 25 March and 22 July 1993, DST.

127 DST Committee of Management Minutes, 25 November 1993, DST; DST, *R& A 1991/2*, p.18.

128 Charles Rickards was in turn a subsidiary of Giltspur Investments, whose chairman was Maxwell Joseph.

129 Dribbell and Garrard, report, n.d. (May 1965); historical summary in Garrard, report [n.d.], DST Committee of Management Minutes, 29 March 1967, DST.

130 Sub-committee report, 5 May 1967, Garrard, reports, 6 July and 22 September 1967, DST Committee of Management Minutes, 9 May, 11 July and 2 October 1967, DST. Garrard received advice from F.S. Mcfadzean, a Dolphin Square tenant who was an MD of Shell International and Chairman of Shell-Mex and BP Ltd., and from P.M.H. James of L.F. Dove Ltd.

131 Garrard, report, 22 September 1967, DST; Morris, *Dolphin Square*, p.64. Indicative of the problems with NCP was the fact that the lease was not signed until September 1984: DST and NCP, underlease, 18 September 1984, DST.

132 Garrard-Dolphin Square tenants, 22 September 1967, DST.

133 DST Committee of Management Minutes, 8 July and 18 November 1969, 25 July 1974, 12 November 1975, DST.

134 Price Commission Act, July 1977, 1977 c.33.

135 Morris, reports, 4 November 1977 and 6 July 1978, DST Committee of Management Minutes, 23 November 1977, 19 July 1978, DST.

136 A trial scheme became permanent with the introduction of blue plastic signs. Reid-Cumming, 4 August 1986, Cumming-Raymond S. Durrant (Director, Estate Management, NCP), 26 February 1991, DST.

137 Morris, reports, 9 March 1979, 14 July 1980 and 14 March 1983, DST Committee of Management Minutes, 14 March 1979, 23 July 1980, 9 November 1982 and 22 March 1983, Oliver Blunt (Chairman, DSTA)-Morris, 16 November 1980; DST Committee of Management Agenda, 19 January 1982, DST; Morris, *Dolphin Square*, p.64.

138 DST and NCP, underlease, 19 October 1984, DST. The principal rental was less than the Trust had wanted: cf. DST Committee of Management Minutes, 9 November 1982, DST.

139 DST and NCP, counterpart agreement, 19 October 1984, DST.

140 Wood-Woodroffes (DST's solicitors), 28 March 1985, DST. The decision to substitute a permissive clause in the 1984 lease was blamed on the previous general manager, Wood: Dawtry-Sir Donald Gosling (Jnt Chairman, NCP), 24 April 1987, DST.

141 Durrant-Dawtry, 12 May 1987, DST.

142 Cumming-G.R. Duncan (Commercial Manager, NCP), 16 March 1988, Michael Davies (Matthews & Son)-Cumming, 10 May 1988, DST.

143 Cumming, 'Notes on the Dolphin Square Trust - National Car Parks Dispute', 22 June 1988, and report [n.d.], DST Committee of Management Minutes, 26 July 1988, Geoffrey Lander (Hon. Secretary, DSTA)-Cumming, 15 July 1988, Richard Day (Charles Russell Williams & James)-Cumming, 30 March 1989, DST.

144 A Section 146 notice under the Law of Property Act 1925 warns a tenant who is in breach of a covenant of the landlord's intention to forfeit the lease.

145 Collins, report [n.d.], Notes of meeting, 16 October 1991, and progress reports, DST Committee of Management Minutes and papers, 26 June and 19 November 1991, 27 January, 24 March and 27 July 1992, 27 January and 22 July 1993, DST.

146 DST Committee of Management Minutes, 25 November 1993, DST.

147 Cumming, Memo. on 'Shops Leases: Schedule of Rents', 26 April 1989, Memo. on 'Review of Arcade Shops', n.d., DST Committee of Management Minutes, 27 March 1991, DST. The greengrocer and dry cleaner had five year leases and the newsagent and off-licence appear to have been held on 'indefinite' leases.

148 The unified business rate was based on rateable value x a multiplier set by the local authority.

149 Cumming, report [n.d.], DST Committee of Management Minutes, 27 March 1991, DST.

150 Garrard, report [n.d.] and accompanying correspondence, including Graham Page & Co. (for DSTA)-Garrard, 13 September 1965, DST Committee of Management Minutes, 28 September 1965, DST.

151 Notes of an informal meeting of DST and DSTA, 17 September 1965, DST; Dribbell, interview, 2011.

152 So in the first year: 1964 scale; second year: midpoint of 1964 and 1965 scales; third year: 1965 scale. DST Committee of Management Minutes, 28 September 1965, DST.

153 Garrard-Dolphin Square tenants, 29 July 1965, and annex to Garrard, report, 4 November 1968, DST Committee of Management Minutes, 3 August 1965 and 11 November 1968, DST.

154 Morris, report, 9 January 1975, DST; Wood, report, 12 March 1985, DST Committee of Management Minutes, 20 March 1985, DST; Charles Russell (solicitors), instructions to counsel Re Dolphin Square Trust Ltd., 19 July 1990, DST.

155 Housing Corporation-Secretary, DST, 19 February 1975, V.D. Hibbs (Registrar, Housing Corporation)-Morris, 16 February 1976, Morris, report, 15 March 1976, DST Committee of Management Minutes, 24 March 1976, DST.

156 Notes of meeting of Housing Corporation and DST, 3 November 1976; Morris, report, 4 November 1976, Committee of Management Minutes, 9 November 1976, DST.

157 Housing Act 1980, c.51; Balchin, *Housing Policy*, pp.165-8.

158 Garrard, reports, 4 November 1968 and 15 January 1970, Garrard, draft letter to Dr Alan Fisk (Chairman, DSTA), 15 January 1970, DST Committee of Management Minutes, 11 November 1968 and 20 January 1970, DST.

159 Morris, report, 16 March 1982, DST Committee of Management Minutes, 23 March 1982, DST.

160 Wood, report, 12 March 1985, DST Committee of Management Minutes, 20 November 1985, DST.

161 Morris-V.D. Hibbs (Registrar, Housing Corporation), 18 September 1976, Morris, report, 4 November 1976, DST Committee of Management Minutes, 9 November 1976, DST.

162 Report, 12 March 1985, DST Committee of Management Minutes, 20 March 1985, Charles Russell, instructions to counsel, 19 July 1990, DST.

163 Bill Hennessy (Regional Monitoring Manager, London & Home Counties (North West), Housing Corporation)-J. Gumming (sic), 17 May 1990, DST.

164 James Tickell (Registrar, Housing Corporation)-Prendergast, 19 November 1990, DST Committee of Management Minutes, 27 November 1990, DST. The visit of inspection was conducted by Mrs Vowles and Ms James.

165 Jonathan Gaunt, QC, opinion, 18 September 1990, DST Committee of Management Minutes, 25 September 1990, DST.

166 Prendergast, letter to tenants, 15 July 1991, Crawford-Judith Warner (Chairman, WCC Housing Committee), 29 October 1991, DST Special General Meeting Minutes, 27 January 1992; Housing Corporation, consent, 3 February 1992; E.M. Davison (Housing Corporation)-Crawford, 9 and 26 March 1992, DST.

167 DST Committee of Management Minutes, 18 November 1980, DST.

168 DST Committee of Management Minutes, 16 July and 19 November 1985, DST.

169 Cumming, report, 20 January 1986, DST Committee of Management Minutes, 30 January 1986, DST.

170 S.G. Brooksbank (Chairman and MD, UKPI)-Prendergast, 24 February 1986, Cumming-Dolphin Square tenants, 3 March 1986, DSTA, notice to tenants, n.d., annexes to Cumming, report, 12 March 1986, DST Committee of Management Minutes, 19 March 1986, DST.

171 *Financial Times*, 8 April 1986, p.1, 9 April 1986, pp.1, 8, 8 May 1986, p.8; Morris, *Dolphin Square*, p.92.

172 *Financial Times*, 8 July 1986, p.28; *Who's Who*. Jenkin was chairman of Friends' Provident, 1988–98.

173 Crawford, report on 'General Matters' [n.d.], DST Committee of Management Minutes, 24 November 1992, DST.

CHAPTER 6

CHANGING TIMES, 1993–2006

THE TRUSTEES AND MANAGERS, 1993–2010

The year 1993 saw changes in the composition of the committee of trustees and also heralded a period of change for the Trust. First, Tony Prendergast stepped down as chairman after a period of 26 years at the helm. There was certainly no loss of expertise or experience, however. His vice-chairman, Sir Alan Dawtry, continued in office until 1999, and his successor as chairman was Maurice Stonefrost, who had been a trustee since 1975, and was a leading expert in local authority affairs, having been Director-General of the GLC before its demise in 1986. He then became chief executive of the British Railways Board Pension Fund, 1986-91 (Table 6.1). The ten-strong committee was dominated by tenants of the Square. Eight of the ten trustees gave Dolphin Square addresses in 1993, and the two 'outsiders', Prendergast, who lived in Warwick Square, SW1, and Pirie, with an address in Dorset, had both been tenants in the past. Furthermore, this domination became even greater. The replacements for Prendergast, Pirie and Weeks, who resigned in 1998, were two tenants: Bruce Clitherow, a chartered surveyor and head of property management at the Teesland Group, who had lived in the Square since 1976; and Geoffrey Lander, a property expert and partner in the leading commercial property law firm, Nabarro Nathanson.

Table 6.1 Dolphin Square Trust members, 1993–2011

Trustee	*Office*	*Background*	*Term of office*
C.A. [Tony] Prendergast, CBE	Chairman, 1967–93	WCC Councillor; Business (Lloyds); Tenant 804/5 Hood 1969–75	1964–98
Maurice F. Stonefrost, CBE, DL, CIPFA, DPA	Chairman, 1993–2001	Dr-Gen. GLC, 1984–5; Tenant 807 Howard, 611 Hood	1975–2001

Sir Rodney G. Brooke, CBE, DL	Chairman, 2002–11	WCC Chief Executive, 1984–9; Solicitor; Tenant 706 Grenville	1986–2011
Sir Alan G. Dawtry, CBE	Vice-Chairman, 1986–99	WCC Town Clerk/Chief Executive, 1956–77; Chairman Sperry Rand Ltd, 1977–86; Tenant 806 Collingwood/901 Grenville	1971–2002
Alan Bradley, FIA	Vice Chairman, 1999–2002	WCC Councillor; Actuary (Partner, Lane, Clark & Peacock); Tenant 710 Collingwood	1986–2002
Sir Gordon H.M. Pirie, CVO, CBE, DL	Vice-Chairman, 1975–6	WCC Councillor; RAF; Tenant 103 Beatty 1978–82	1971–98
Deirdre A. Marshall	Vice-Chairman. 2002–11	Civil Servant; Tenant 503 Raleigh	2001–11
Jan K. Reid [from 1994 Prebble]		Journalist (*Daily Mail*), later P&PRO, Capital Radio until 1987); Tenant 904, 902 Howard	1975–2011
Barry Pinson, QC		Lawyer; Tenant 804/5 Hood	1976–2011
David J. Hopkins, CIPFA, FRVA, AMBIM		WCC Treasurer, 1979–90; Director, CIPFA Loans Bureau, Citibank Investment Management; Tenant 403 Hawkins	1979–2000
David P. Weeks, MCIM		WCC Councillor; Business (Marketing: Dr, Y.J. Lovell); Tenant, 408 Frobisher	1983–98
Bruce C.T. Clitherow, ARICS		Surveyor (Farebrother, Teesland Group); Tenant 201 Hood	1997–2011
Geoffrey I. Lander		Real estate (Nabarro Nathanson); Tenant 806 Collingwood	1999–2011
Richard Pulford		Civil servant/arts manager (Society of London Theatre); Tenant 905 Beatty	2001–11
Rodney Pennington Baker-Bates		Business (Arthur Andersen, Chase Manhattan, Midland Bank, etc.); Tenant 611 Collingwood	2001–11

Source: DST; Morris, ***Dolphin Square***, p.118.

Lander's appointment arose when, in 1998, Friends Provident expressed the intention to realise the value of its freehold in Dolphin Square. Both Clitherow and Lander became members of a leasehold interest subcommittee which was established to monitor negotiations and safeguard the Trust's position (see p.240).[1] Clitherow's appointment in July 1997 had been prompted by Westminster Council's anxiety that the Trust should not be regarded as a local authority influenced company within the meaning of the Local Government and Housing Act of 1989. One of the criteria defining such a company was if 20 per cent of its directors were associated with the Council. With two councillors - David Weeks and Alan Bradley - on the committee of ten, the Trust could be so defined; after Clitherow's appointment, the proportion of trustees with Westminster connections was now regarded as falling below the 20 per cent mark. However, with the eleven-strong committee including two former chief executives (Dawtry and Brooke), a former treasurer (Hopkins), and two former councillors (Prendergast and Pirie), experience of the Westminster 'machine' was much greater than the directorial proportion implied.[2] As we noted earlier, trustees who were no longer members or officers of the Council or tenants were supposed to stand down. The rule applied to Pirie and Prendergast, who nevertheless had retained their positions after ceasing to be either in 1982 and 1990 respectively. This anomaly was rectified when both retired on 1 January 1998. From this point, all the trustees were Dolphin Square tenants. When Weeks stepped down in the following March, having resigned as a councillor following his part in Shirley Porter's Homes for Votes affair, the number of trustees fell to eight. Lander's appointment in April 1999 increased the number to nine, but this fell to eight again when Hopkins died in August 2000. In 2001/2 Stonefrost, Dawtry and Bradley resigned, but there were three new appointments, all of them tenants: Deirdre Marshall, a barrister and retired civil servant; Richard Pulford, a former civil servant and arts manager, who had been Deputy Secretary-General of the Arts Council and General Director of the South Bank Centre;[3] and Rodney Baker-Bates, an accountant turned banker, with a wide experience of both the City and corporate boardrooms.[4] A committee of eight then served from November 2004 until the Trust sold its interest in Dolphin Square in January 2006, continuing in office until the Trust was wound up in 2011 (Table 6.1). At the beginning of 2002 Stonefrost was succeeded as

Chairman by Rodney Brooke, Sir Rodney from 2007, former chief executive of Westminster City Council during part of Shirley Porter's controversial period as leader. In 1999 Dawtry was succeeded as vice-chairman by Alan Bradley, who in turn was succeeded by Deirdre Marshall in 2002.

The senior management team in 1993 was led by Tony Crawford, the general manager, and David Collins, his assistant, but there was a complete change in personnel in 1996–7. First the hotel operations manager, John Firrell resigned, and was succeeded by Clare Stewart. Then the chief accountant and deputy general manager retired. Gordon Jacques was followed by Bernard Bindman,[5] and in Collins's place J. Holmes was appointed to the post of facilities manager. Crawford retired, owing to ill health, in October 1997. His successor was Adrian Wray, a retired brigadier and formerly Chief of Staff to the Commandant-General, Royal Marines.[6] Finally the flats manager, Sandy Crane, was succeeded by Jane Salt. The only continuity was provided by the general manager's personal assistant, who remained Sally Watson (Table 6.2). Nevertheless, with the exception of Holmes, who was replaced by Phil Rickett in 1999, this team remained in post until the end of the Trust's period as lessee of Dolphin Square. And while times had clearly changed, the Square continued to benefit from the contribution made by loyal and long-serving employees, notably George Lincoln, who retired from the garage in 1984 having been on the staff since 1936, and Serge Bernard, the stores manager, who retired in September 1990 after nearly 40 years' service.[7]

Table 6.2 Dolphin Square senior managers, 1993–2006

General Manager and Secretary:	A.K. (Tony) Crawford , CBE Adrian D. Wray	1991–7 1997–2006
Deputy General Manager and Head of Maintenance:	David Collins, MIMBM	1991–7
PA to General Manager:	Sally A. Watson	1991–2006
Chief Accountant:	Gordon E.F. Jacques, ACMA Bernard Bindman, FCA	1988–97 1997–2006
Facilities Manager:	John Holmes, ACIOB Phil J. Rickett, MCIOB	1997–9 1999–2006

Flats Manager:	Peter B. Bicknell Sandy G. Crane (Mrs) Jane E. Salt	1984–93 1993–7 1998–2006
Hotel Operations Manager/ Hotel Manager:	John R. Firrell, MHCIMA Clare Stewart, MHCIMA	1991–6 1996–2006

Source: DST.

Note: In 2006 the officers transferred to Mantilla Ltd. Wray and Bindman continued to act for the Trust on a consultancy basis until 2010.

BUSINESS AS USUAL? INCOME AND COSTS, 1993–2005

With leading local authority executives such as Dawtry, Stonefrost and Brooke on the committee of trustees, not to mention their colleagues, all of whom had professional expertise, it would have been a major surprise if Dolphin Square's affairs had not been managed effectively and efficiently. For the remainder of the Trust's leasehold interest in Dolphin Square, under the chairmanship of first Stonefrost (1993-2001), and then Brooke (from 2002) financial performance continued to be soundly based. Over the period 1993/4-2004/5 income exceeded expenditure by £9.4 million before tax, or £11 million in constant 2005 prices (Table 6.3), about six per cent of total turnover, the margin being a little higher than in the period 1965-93.[8] In 1993/4-2004/5 the total after-tax 'profit' was £3.7 million, and after sums set aside for maintenance and repairs, the total was £1.9 million, in current prices (see Table 6.3 and Appendix 9). The trading activity was much greater than in the previous 12 years, 1981/2-92/3. Both income and expenditure were nearly double that of the earlier period in real terms, and post-tax 'profits' were much higher (see Appendices 3 and 9). As before, annual deficits were made occasionally, notably in three of the last four years of operation, viz. 2001/2, 2003/4 and in 2004/5 [11 months]. In the first of these years Rodney House experienced a four per cent fall in income, there was a large back-dated bill for business rates, and a 15 per cent rise in spending on maintenance; in the last two years, income from the unfurnished flats rose by only a modest amount (1.6 per cent in each year), while Rodney House income fell, by 2.0 and 2.5 per cent respectively.[9]

Table 6.3 **Income and expenditure, margins before tax, net income and accumulated surplus/deficit, 1994–2005**

*Period (years to 30 September)**	*Income [£m.]*	*Expenditure before tax [£m.]*	*Margin before tax [£m.]*	*Net income after tax – consistent basis [£'000]*	*Reported accumulated surplus/deficit at end period [£'000]*
1994–6	28.73	26.83	1.90	1,085.2	2,989.5
1997–9	37.86	34.48	3.38	2,329.4	5,270.0
2000–2	45.91	42.62	3.29	1,151.1	5,138.2
2003–5	50.01	49.21	0.80	(817.7)	4,177.2
Total 1994–2005	***162.51***	***153.14***	***9.37***	***3,748.6***	
Constant 2005 prices					
1994–6	37.06	34.60	2.46		
1997–9	44.85	40.81	4.04		
2000–2	50.85	47.17	3.68		
2003–5	51.47	50.61	0.86		
Total 1994–2005	***184.23***	***173.19***	***11.04***		

Source: Appendix 9.

* 11 months in 2005

The Trust's letting policy continued as before, with flats let to newcomers on 'assured tenancies' ('assured shorthold tenancies' from 1997, after the Housing Act of 1996), at about 80 per cent of Pimlico's market rent levels.[10] Complex as it may have seemed to outsiders and many tenants, the approach to letting and rents was a straightforward matter for the trustees. A statement clarifying the Trust's position was drafted by Alan Dawtry in 1997. The policy was to let flats to persons of working age (generally under 60) without London homes, who were employed full-time in central London. Given these restrictions, the rent obtained, known internally as the 'full rent' or subsequently as the 'restricted rent', was around 20–25 per cent lower than the market rents for the area. Furthermore, the Trust's secure financial position, boosted by its commercial activities, allowed it to increase rents for existing tenants 'at a much more modest rate than is allowed by law'. Thus tenants who remained employed in central London, or who were occupying a flat as their sole or principal home, were offered renewals of their three-year agreements at a discount to the market.[11] From 1993/4 to 2004/5 the income produced by Dolphin Square's 1,047 flats - 1,058 flats from 1996/7[12] - contributed 55 per cent of the Trust's total income, compared with 46 per cent in the period 1965-92/3. There was a tendency for the proportion to rise: the percentage increased from 52 per cent in 1993/4 to 59 per cent in 2004/5. And the real value of the rental income increased until 2002/3 (Appendix 4 and 9).

Did the Trust adopt a more market-oriented approach to rents after 1993? The trustees were anxious to make it clear that their overall policy had not changed. However, the policy of raising full rents each year for new tenants continued, though the approach was not uniform. In several years, across-the-board increases were applied: in 1994, 1999, 2000 and 2002 (5, 6, 5 and 7 per cent respectively). At other times, differential increases were made. In 1998, for example, the tariffs for one-room flats were frozen, and a sliding scale was then applied, the increase for two-room flats being two per cent and for three-rooms four per cent, rising to 6-7 per cent for four- and five-rooms.[13] Sometimes the differentials worked in the opposite direction. Thus, having agreed a six per cent increase to apply from January 1999, in April a further two per cent was added to the rentals for one-three room flats, following advice from local estate agents. And the only increases made in 2004 were for one-room flats (see p.224).[14] From 2000, the Trust engaged the leading estate agents, Knight Frank, to advise them on appropriate rents for new tenants. This was a response to the pressure exerted on letting policy by both Friends Provident and Westminster City Council in connexion with the battle for ownership and control of the Square (see pp.242-4). The increases introduced in 2001 reflected this advice. Knight Frank had concluded that the variations by type of flat were unnecessarily complex, and recommended that a number of flat types warranted the same rental value. This meant that the range of increases in that year was greater than normal: 5-17 per cent for two-room flats, 3.5-17 per cent for three rooms, 26-40 per cent for four rooms, and 17-28 per cent for five rooms. However, the Trust felt that it could not implement Knight Frank's recommendation that the rents for one-room flats be reduced, and these were raised by a uniform three per cent.[15] After these changes, it quickly emerged that at the upper end of the market the response was disappointing, with some of the larger flats becoming more difficult to let.[16] In 2002, when the number of vacant flats was found to be higher than usual, Knight Frank was asked to enhance the Trust's marketing, and the decision was taken to let most of the future properties complete with carpets and white goods. In general, the letting market was felt to be buoyant, and a seven per cent increase was made for 2002. However, the situation changed very quickly and, following advice from Knight Frank, rents were frozen in 2003 and 2004, with the exception of one-room flats, where rents rose by ten per cent in 2004.[17] Knight Frank were more positive in the following year, and rents were raised by three per cent for one to three roomed flats, two per cent for four to five rooms, and one per cent for six to seven rooms.[18] The impact of these several modifications was that over the period 1993–2005 'full' or 'restricted' rents increased by 60–80 per cent for one-room flats, slightly more than those for two-room flats, which increased by 58–71 per cent. Rentals for three rooms rose rather more, by 73–88 per cent. The highest rise was experienced by those renting four rooms, where the increase was 115–116 per cent. Rents of £5,050–20,400 in 1993 had risen to £8,100–40,850 by 2005 (Appendix 5). In real terms, rents for newcomers had been raised by between 16 and 47 per cent.

The liberal treatment of established tenants via the discount or incremental system was certainly modified after 1993. As we have seen, save for a special increase in relation to heating costs (see pp.185–6) this had remained unchanged from 1980 to 1992, when a tenant renewing a three-year agreement was presented with an increase of 50 per cent in the first year, followed by an additional ten per cent in each of the second and third years. The same was done with tenancies renewed in 1993 and 1994, by which time the 50 per cent increase had been applied to all tenancies. Thereafter the increase in increments was fixed at ten per cent a year. Tenants became concerned by this regular increase as the rate of inflation fell. Thus, those renewing in 1995 were presented with increments which were 120 per cent higher than the pre-1992 rates (Table 6.4). By 1997, the incremental burden was 167 per cent higher than it had been for 1991 renewals (Table 6.4), in real terms a hefty increase of 126 per cent.

Table 6.4 Incremental increases in rents for established tenants, 1980/2–2005/7 (£)

Rooms	*1980–2 to 1991–3*	*1992 renewals*	*1995 renewals*	*1997 renewals*	*1999 renewals*	*2001 renewals*	*2005 renewals*
		1992–4	1995–7	1997–9	1999–2001	2001–3	2005–7
1	180	300	400	482	581	701	1026
2	252	418	556	671	810	978	1429
3	324	536	716	867	1048	1267	1854
4	396	656	873	1056	1276	1541	2254
5	468	774	1029	1245	1505	1820	2663
6	540	894	1192	1444	1746	2110	3088
7	615*	1014	1348	1631	1971	2383	3488

Source: DST.

* sometimes given as £612

In July 1997, Geoffrey Lander wrote to the Trust to complain about the continued imposition of an annual ten per cent increase, and there were similar complaints from the DSTA. In response Adrian Wray and Jane Salt prepared a detailed review of the rent regime, and this was considered by the trustees in July 1998. Lander had argued that the policy of increasing the increments in this way was adversely affecting retired tenants on fixed incomes, particularly as the rate of inflation was falling. Instead, he favoured a sliding scale, dependent on the length of time a tenant had been resident in the Square, with those of longer standing paying less. Research indicated that this was not a minor problem. Over 400 tenants had lived in Dolphin Square for more than ten years, 180 of them for over 20 years. Wray and Salt opposed the idea of a sliding scale, but felt that a reduction in incremental increases to five per cent was feasible and could be funded from an additional increase in the rents charged to new tenants. The trustees expressed sympathy for the tenants concerned, but noted that many of them were still enjoying a substantial discount to the market, and the degree of 'subsidy', i.e. the difference between the income obtained from rents and the income that could have been derived from open market rent levels, was put at £4.5 million (or 40 per cent of full rents) in 1997, much the same as it had been in 1992.[19] A subcommittee consisting of Stonefrost, Dawtry and Clitherow was appointed to consider the matter, but with the freeholder, Friends Provident, and Westminster Council showing heightened interest in the future management of the Square, this was not the time to provide tenants with additional support, and the trustees decided to retain the annual increases of ten per cent in 1999, in spite of protests from the DSTA.[20] The same policy applied for the next six years, by which time the increments, set in November 2004 for the period 2005–7, were £1,026 (one room)-£3,488 (seven rooms), over five times higher than they had been before 1992 (Table 6.4). Allowing for inflation, established tenants were now being presented with increases which were nearly four times higher than those before 1992, and 75 per cent more than the three-year increments which had applied in 1997. If these tenants enjoyed a substantial discount to the market, it had certainly been reduced in size by 2005.

Accompanying these changes, a tougher stance was taken with people abusing the discount system by holding on to flats after ceasing to work in London, or by subletting while absent for long periods. Dawtry, in his statement, admitted that the serious drawback of the concessionary rents policy had been to tempt tenants moving out of London to sublet, or to retain their flats as a pied-à-terre. Following the discussion on increments in 1998 the trustees clarified their definition of acceptable tenants. These should be under the age of 60 and be working in or near central London. They were required to reside in the Square for at least four nights a week.[21] Tenants and/or their spouse/partner should not own any residential property in London. Once they had ceased working, such tenants could continue to live in the Square if their flat was their sole or principal residence. The changes formed part of revised tenancy agreements applying from 1999.[22] The trustees also took a firm line with tenants employed by the Ministry of Defence. In 1996, the Ministry informed the general manager that it was changing its method of funding the accommodation required by servicemen. Instead of giving them a tax-free lodging allowance and leaving them to find the accommodation, it intended to use a letting agency, Hambros, to provide the accommodation for them. Hambros would sign rental agreements and pay the rent, thus avoiding a tax liability. Crawford discovered that there were 44 tenants who had first acquired their flats via the allowance system, though only 14 of them were still serving officers. The Ministry wanted Hambros to sign Dolphin Square leases for their servicemen in the future, which the trustees regarded as amounting to corporate lets, which were prohibited under the terms of their lease with the Council. They therefore declined to initiate a special arrangement with Hambros, but agreed to enter into one-off agreements with the agent for existing MOD tenants.[23]

The Trust's Special Case Tenants Subcommittee, established in 1992, dealt with tenants who were in breach of Dolphin Square's restrictive covenants, and in particular those who were absentees. The Committee's remit was subsequently extended to cover those who were behind with their rent.[24] The extent of rent arrears was monitored regularly, and managerial attention was focused on their reduction. Sometimes, as with a few foreign nationals who refused to pay the full rent, the sums outstanding had to be written off.[25] The trustees' deliberations also indicate a particular attention to breaches of covenant. Those found to be transgressing were usually placed on the full rent on the expiry of their existing agreements.[26] At the same time, the plight of older tenants living on dwindling fixed incomes was regarded with some sympathy. There were 100 tenants in receipt of housing benefit in 1997, and their financial difficulties were dealt with on a case-by-case basis, for example, by enabling such tenants to move to a cheaper flat for the same percentage of the established 'fair rent' that they were paying previously.[27] In the period to 2005 there was regular reporting of outstanding debts, which often exceeded £100,000 in total. In 2001/2 two tenants were proceeded against, and others followed. At the same time, sympathetic consideration was given to tenants with personal problems.[28]

When we last looked at the Rodney House business, it was at something of a crossroads after several years of growth. The period from 1993 saw determined efforts to modernise the 'hotel' and its facilities as competition in London intensified, and to respond to the challenge provided by market fluctuations in the leisure market. As we have seen, Dolphin Square's dependence on North American customers was particularly heavy, and income tended to fall during periods of crisis, for example, at the time of the Gulf War and in the wake of the September 2001 attacks on the United States ('9/11'). Profit and loss depended on the state of the economy, and the success or otherwise of marketing activity, including the management of discounted rates. To summarise, hotel income, including guest room and conference centre revenue, contributed 30 per cent of the Trust's income in the period 1993/4–2004/5 (Appendix 4). Turnover rose by 93 per cent (63 per cent in constant prices) from 1993/4 to 1999/2000, when in a single year the increase was 27 per cent, largely due to a substantial improvement in the occupancy rate following refurbishment. Income then fell back in the wake of '9/11' by around nine per cent (12 per cent). A modest recovery in 2002/3 of 11 per cent (eight per cent in real terms), was then sustained (Appendix 4). A major programme of investment was effective in improving standards. By 1995/6 the 152 apartments and 30 guest rooms had been reduced to 151 and 17 units via this process, notably with the introduction of en suite facilities in the guest rooms. From 1997 to 2001 there was five-year programme of renewal which produced an upgrade of the remaining apartments in Rodney House for £4.6 million. The hotel, which now had 148 suites and 17 guest rooms, was awarded a four-star rating by the English Tourism Council in 1999.[29] With improvements to the sports centre, health club, restaurant, and swimming pool, a capital expenditure of £6.4 million was invested in the six years to 2001/2.[30] The rates charged are more difficult to generalise about, due to the reclassification of apartments following refurbishment, and the practice of charging discounted rates, including the offer of 'downgrades' (cheaper guest rooms offered to hotel clients).[31] For example, in 1997/8 the average room rate was £100–110 in the summer and autumn months, but fell to £83-87 in winter.[32] After relatively small pricing changes during the recession of 1989-93, incremental increases were introduced in 1994-8. A more substantial increase in rates was introduced in 1999, but thereafter reduced demand, in the wake of the '9/11' atrocity, together with more intense competition in the London hotel market, affected marketing decisions. As an example, the full quoted cost of a 'premier' single studio remained at £99, 1995-7, but was raised to £130 in 1999. The rate was £140 in 2001, £165 in 2003 and £185 in 2005, by which time it was four times higher in real terms than in 1965 (Appendix 6). However, with discretion to discount, the rate actually achieved was often much lower than this. Indeed, the average rate achieved for all apartments was pretty flat at £98 a night, 1997/8–2004/5 (lower at £92–95 for the three years after '9/11') (Table 6.5). Occupancy rates for the hotel suites and guest rooms were generally good. They recovered well from 47 per cent in 1991/2 to 68 per cent in 1993/4, 74 per cent in 1994/5, and 79 per cent in 1995/6.

Table 6.5 Rodney House average room rates, 1997/8–2004/5

Year	*Average room rate suites, £*	*Average room rate suites and guest rooms, £*
1997/8	97.6	90.2
1998/9	100.4	93.1
1999/2000	99.1	93.6
2000/1	103.1	97.5
2001/2	94.9	90.5
2002/3	93.2	89.9
2003/4	91.8	88.6
2004/5	100.8	97.0
Average rate 1997/8–2004/5	97.6	92.5

Source: Reports to DST Committee of Management, 1998–2005, DST. Rates quoted exclude VAT and breakfast (earlier data include VAT and breakfast).

There was a fall when rooms were taken out of use for refurbishment, and only 66 per cent was achieved in 1998/9, at a time when the swimming pool was also closed. A rate of 86 per cent was achieved in 1999/2000, though it fell back to 82 per cent in both 2000/1 and 2001/2 with the reduction in North American leisure travel which followed '9/11', but it then recovered well and reached an impressive 89–92 per cent over the next three years to 2004/5.[33] Although the market was much tougher, the management of Rodney House became more professional, and the facility continued to make a substantial contribution to the Trust's profit and loss account. However, the precise extent of this was a matter for debate, since estimates of profitability depended on the amount of maintenance work being carried out in a particular year, and on the share of overhead costs allocated to the hotel (it was a moot point whether the operating burden of the restaurant should be charged to Rodney House). A profitability exercise carried out for the Trust by KPMG Peat Marwick in 1994 found that the hotel operation made pre-tax profits of £367,000 in 1992/3, 65 per cent of the total profits in that year.[34] Although the results are not strictly comparable with the KPMG exercise, operating surpluses were comparatively large in 1995/6–2000/1, averaging £612,000 a year (see Appendix 10).[35] However, subsequent trading was not so favourable. In 2001/2, as a result of reduced demand, and the imposition of an exceptional rates demand, the Rodney House apartments and guest rooms made an operating loss of £1.2 million. Although there was a subsequent improvement, losses were made in both 2002/3 and 2003/4 (£162,200 and £360,500 respectively) (Appendix 10). At a time when the future of both the Square and the hotel operation was being actively discussed, the prospects of the supporting plank of Rodney House for the Trust's financial health seemed more uncertain.

In 1993/4 the cost profile of Dolphin Square remained much as it had been since 1965. The principal items of expenditure were staffing costs, repairs and maintenance, heating and lighting, and VAT. Together these items made up 76 per cent of total expenditure.[36] However, by 2004/5 the proportion had fallen to 55 per cent, and the explanation for the change is to be found in increased spending on other items. A new element in the account was the cost of the restaurant, which had returned to direct management in 1992. In fact, the cost burden of the restaurant was considerable, and increased over time, as the accounts reveal, though they were of course partly offset by revenue. These costs rose from under £600,000 in 1993/4–1994/5 to £1.7 million in 1998/9, and remained at about £1.5 million thereafter, approximately nine to ten per cent of total expenditure (Appendix 11). Provision for depreciation was another element of increased cost. This was low in 1993/4 - only £153,000, but accompanying the extensive refurbishment of Rodney House and other assets, the figure rose steadily, to £680,000 in 1997/8, £1.75 million in 1999/2000, and £2.42 million (15 per cent of total costs) in 2001/2. Provision was reduced thereafter, but still amounted to £1.1 million in the eleven months of 2004/5[37] (Appendix 11). Finally, as the struggle for the Dolphin Square leases intensified, spending on legal and professional fees rose sharply. Amounting to £150,000 a year or one per cent of total costs in the 1990s, these costs rose to £370,000 in 2000/1, £680,000 in 2002/3, and in the 11 months of 2004/5 consumed the considerable sum of £2.9 million, or 17 per cent of total expenditure. The costs of defending a Section 146 notice served on Westminster Council and the Trust by Friends Provident in 2002, alleging a breach of the leasehold covenants, and advice taken in connexion with the sale of the Square, were major elements (see below). Together, these three items - the restaurant, depreciation and legal fees - made up 32 per cent of costs in 2004/5 (Appendix 11).

The largest single item of expense, unsurprisingly, was labour, and spending under this head, including national insurance, pension and recruitment costs, accounted for 32 per cent of total costs, 1993/4–2004/5 (derived from Appendices 9 and 11). Staffing levels were maintained at around 200 full-time and 15-20 part-time employees. Numbers of full-time staff crept up from 193 in 1992/3 to 218 in 1999/2000, but there was a limited degree of rationalisation thereafter and at the end of August 2005 there were 166 full-time and 23 part-time staff, a reduction of 12 on the number in 2001/2.[38] Labour relations were generally amicable, but the pressure on low-paid workers in central London complicated the pay-setting process, and in July 2002, the TGWU'S 99 Dolphin Square members - mainly cleaners, chambermaids and maintenance staff - were called out on two one-day strikes after a pay offer was rejected. The union had sought a flat rate London allowance of £1,000 on top of the offered three per cent increase. The striking workers received some support from tenants, and notably from Labour minister Beverley Hughes, and Labour peer Meghnad Desai. In the end, the union accepted an improved offer, and undertook to join management in a job evaluation exercise.[39]

The other major item of expenditure was, as before, maintenance. As Dolphin Square grew older, maintenance and renewal became major concerns. Spending on this issue certainly accelerated. In 1992/3 only £1.29 million had been spent under this head. Thereafter activity intensified, and spending (on both revenue and capital accounts) increased each year until 1998/9, when it reached £5.5 million in 1998/9. After a fall of about 20 per cent in the next two years, expenditure exceeded £5 million again in 2001/2. Only in 2004/5, the last full year of the Trust's management, did spending fall below £4 million (see Appendix 11). Another phase of the duct modernisation programme was carried out, and by 1995 over £6 million had been spent on this since 1973. Attention was then focused on a five-year programme of asbestos removal, 1995-9.[40] Other work included:

re-asphalting the roofs, 1994–8; replacing the old heating system provided by the Council's Pimlico District Heating Undertaking with the Square's own boilers, 1998–2000;[41] repairing the Square's external brickwork; window replacement; corridor refurbishment and lift modernisation; the renovation of apartments in Rodney House; the maintenance of the restaurant and bars, sports centre, gymnasium, health centre and gardens; and an extensive programme of kitchen and bathroom replacement. The expenditure accounts reveal that a total of £32.5 million was spent on maintenance and repairs, 1993/4–2004/5, 21 per cent of total costs (Appendix 11). However, this does not capture the total amount, since a further £13.7 million was spent and charged to capital account. The total spend was therefore an impressive £46.2 million (see note to Appendix 11).

How did Dolphin Square's amenities fare in the recent past? There was now no subsidiary company to preside over these activities, but the trustees seem to have made a concerted effort to preserve the 'character of the Square', by maintaining the garage, restaurant and bars, meeting rooms, sports centre with gymnasium and six squash courts, swimming pool, health club, shopping arcade, gardens, tennis court and croquet lawn.[42] The costs of doing so were an important matter, of course, and required close supervision. It was difficult to calculate operating profits for each of these amenities precisely, owing to cost sharing, but there was also the notion that the amenities should be considered as a necessary support to the hotel business as well as supporting the prime activity, the letting of unfurnished flats. A calculation for 1994/5 sheds light on the situation. It showed that operating profits of £91,000 on the hotel apartments/guest rooms and of £119,000 on the shops/offices provided enough to cover operating losses of £62,000 on the sports centre/health club and £112,000 on the restaurant and bars.[43] In terms of income generated, the most popular of these several amenities were the restaurants and bars, which had a combined turnover of £1.4 million, 1999/2000–2004/5, though these facilities were also the most costly to run (Appendix 10). The sports (swimming pool, gymnasium, squash courts) and health clubs/spa, marketed from 2001 as Zest!, had a turnover of £0.5 million in the second half of the 1990s, rising to £0.7 million in 2003/4–2004/5. But costs more than matched this, and operating losses were indicated, though the deficits were not large, averaging £171,000 per annum in the period 1993/4–2003/4 (Appendix 10). Elsewhere, annual surpluses were made by the shops/offices and garage/parking bays, amounting to £75,000 and £68,000 respectively, 1994/5–2003/4 (Appendix 10).[44]

The restaurant business was in general a commercial disappointment, in spite of all the attempts to transform it via an association first with the television chef Gary Rhodes and his Michelin-starred establishment, 'Rhodes in the Square' (1998–2003); and then with Anton Edelmann and his 'Allium' restaurant (2003–6). As we saw in Chapter 5, the relationship with operators Gardner Merchant was initially disappointing, but the prospects were better after 1994. First of all, in 1995 Gardner Merchant merged with the giant French catering company Sodexho and its three-year contract with the Trust was converted into a continuous contract. Then, in November 1997 the parties agreed to meet refurbishment costs of about £900,000 on a 50-50 basis and to share any operating losses.[45] The strengthened company had already begun an association with Gary Rhodes, which led to the opening of a new restaurant in the City of London - 'City Rhodes' - in January 1997. In Pimlico, the Trust was encouraged to invest substantially in its restaurant at this time, creating an art deco 'fine dining' restaurant, making the association between Rhodes and Dolphin Square very clear by naming it 'Rhodes in the Square', and adding a second, cheaper facility by changing the 'Lighthouse Bar' to the 'Brasserie', and converting the residents' lounge into the 'Clipper Bar'.[46] The quality of the new venture was not in doubt, and although the new restaurant attracted some rather snotty reviews in the media when it opened in June 1998,[47] a Michelin star was gained and retained.[48] However, this ambitious initiative did not stem the tide of regular operating losses, and the Trust was soon raising concerns about labour costs, attempting to have the agreement with Sodexho modified, and discussing rationalisation plans.[49] Losses over the period 1993/4–1997/8 amounted to £689,000 or £138,000 per annum. Subsequent results were no better. When Rhodes in the Square was in operation, losses, excluding Sodexho's share, totalled £1.08 million, or £216,000 a year, 1998/9–2002/3 (Appendix 10). Sodexho replaced Rhodes in the Square with established chef Anton Edelmann's[50] 'Allium' in 2003, but the new restaurant's turnover was half that of its predecessor in 2003/4–2004/5, and the operating losses of the total catering and bar businesses were £209,000 a year. Indeed, losses continued to be experienced until the Square was sold.[51] When we add the burden of the Trust's 'landlord's costs' and its share of refurbishment costs to the operating deficits, the price of maintaining the catering and bar services was very high indeed, something in the order of £4.2 million, or £350,000 a year, 1993/4–2004/5 (Appendix 10). The 'golden age' of catering in Dolphin Square may have been enjoyed by many people, but it was not a commercial success.

In March 1994, the garage was also brought back under direct control, when the vexed relationship with NCP described in Chapter 5 came to an end. With the car hire firm Alamo moving to NCP's car park in Porchester Road at the beginning of January 1995, the Trust was able to enter into a management contract with Opus to run the garage on its behalf: the initial price was £88,400 per annum.[52] The Trust put up about £150,000 for repairs and improvements, 1994–6, and most of the 176 spaces were then made available to tenants. The switch to direct management was immediately reported to be a 'success story', with direct income exceeding direct expenditure by about £36,000 in 1994/5.[53] The operating profit and loss data subsequently collected indicated a healthy average surplus of £75,000 a year, 1995/6–2003/4 (Appendix 10). Charges were raised in line with inflation, but were competitive with charges elsewhere. For example, by 2004 a season ticket for the garage cost between £850 and £1,250 a year, compared with £600–1,240 in 1991.[54] The contracts with Opus for security and the garage seem to have operated successfully, and with parking spaces increasingly at a premium in the borough, the garage was clearly a valuable amenity for tenants.[55]

POLITICAL AND BROADER CONCERNS ABOUT DOLPHIN SQUARE, 1993–2001

The 1990s heralded a difficult time for Dolphin Square. The spotlight fell on Westminster generally, with the exposure of the Shirley Porter 'Homes for Votes' scandal, together with the publicity given to the state of the East Finchley, Hanwell and Mill Hill cemeteries, which Porter had insisted on selling for a peppercorn 15p in 1987.[56] The early part of the decade also marked the beginning of more negative media publicity given to the Square by some Westminster Labour Councillors and journalists eager to point out the perceived privileges enjoyed by its tenants, and the apparent anomalies in housing costs in comparison with the experience of council house tenants in the borough. Paul Dimoldenberg, Labour councillor for Harrow Road, 1982–90, and Queen's Park, from 1997, and leader of Westminster's Labour Group, 1987–90 and from 2004, was a fierce opponent of Conservative policies in the borough. His views on Dolphin Square were made plain in his book *The Westminster Whistleblowers*, published in 2006. Commenting on a number of 'scandals' in 1998 which followed the Porter case, including the attempt to abolish the Church Street ward, a damning report by the ombudsman on housing benefit payments of £750,000 paid to the cockroach-infested Clarendon Court Hotel, and a proposal to pay legal bills totalling £700,000 for Conservative councillors and council officers caught up in the Homes for Votes investigations,[57] he suggested that Dolphin Square was a 'longer running scandal'. Dimoldenberg criticised both Westminster's original decision to purchase the Square and the operations of the Trust. 'From 1964 onwards', he wrote,

> Dawtry and his DST colleagues, who include a posse of former Lord Mayors of Westminster - including Tony Prendergast and Alan Bradley - and City Council chief officers such as David Hopkins and Rodney Brooke (who is the current DST chairman), ran Dolphin Square like a colonial outpost of City Hall. Despite Dolphin Square having the status of a housing association, in its forty-year life the trust did not house a single person from the council housing waiting list. Instead it operated a unique housing policy of subsidising rents from the surplus of running one of the blocks, Rodney House, as a hotel. As a result, long-standing Dolphin Square residents enjoyed the lowest social housing rents in London. For over thirty years, the Council turned a blind eye to this scandal, claiming it could do nothing about it.[58]

This was written after the event of course, but it gives a good indication of the changing climate towards the Square.

Undoubtedly the 'Building Stable Communities' programme of 1986, mounted by Westminster Council under the leadership of Shirley Porter, leader of the council from 1983, and David Weeks, deputy leader, 1983–91, came to affect the attitude to Dolphin Square after the scandal broke. The strategy pursued by Porter was to improve the Conservatives' electoral chances in marginal wards by selling, or preparing for sale, the council housing stock in those wards. Exposed in a BBC Panorama programme in 1989, which used information provided by Dimoldenberg, and subsequently accused of gerrymandering, Porter had stood down as council leader in 1991. Created a Dame of the British Empire for her services to local government, she resigned as a councillor two years later. Weeks, her deputy, succeeded her as leader, but he was ousted by his colleagues in July 1993. With Lady Porter, and officials such as Bill Phillips, her short-lived chief executive, he was subsequently found to have been guilty of 'wilful misconduct' by the district auditor, John Magill, in his provisional report of January 1994. This marked the beginning of a protracted campaign to hold Porter and Weeks to account for their actions, which included public hearings (1994–5), a final auditor's report (1996), and references to the High Court (1997), Court of Appeal (1999) and House of Lords (2001), the ramifications of which persisted until 2005.[59] Weeks's successor as council leader, Simon Milton, and his senior officials were all too anxious to avoid any suggestion of improper intervention in housing management. They were also still smarting from criticism of the actions of their predecessors in placing over a hundred homeless families in two run-down, asbestos-filled tower blocks in 1989.[60] Thus, in the wake of Porter's demise the new guard in Westminster became aware of what they regarded as a somewhat anomalous relationship with Dolphin Square via the lease they held with Friends Provident, and, as we have seen, took steps to establish an arms-length relationship with the Trust. Westminster's more proactive and less supportive response to the housing project it had helped to shape was soon to be encouraged by an interest shown by the freeholder (see p.238ff).

Initially, however, the spotlight fell on Dolphin Square for other reasons. The Trust's decision to deregister as a housing association in 1992 had attracted a critical article in the *Evening Standard* magazine in April. Written by Mark Edwards under the headline 'TENANTS'

LAAGER', it suggested that faced with the choice of protecting their privileged amenities and low rents, or fulfilling their obligations to house the homeless as a housing association, the residents had chosen the former. Much was made of the low rents paid by tenants such as the MP Sir David Steel, one of 60 MPs in residence. The piece, which appeared to have made use of the judgments of the Housing Corporation (above, p.203), made reference to snobbery and discrimination.[61] The publication was scarcely in the forefront of media analysis, of course, but it was followed by an unflattering piece in the main body of the newspaper in May. Written by Mira Bar-Hillel and John Passmore, it used the sacking of the general manager, John Cumming, to pose 'awkward questions about vested interest and patronage'.[62] The spotlight became much brighter some months later with the decision of Cdr Timothy Laurence, who was employed at the Ministry of Defence, and his wife, Anne, the Princess Royal, to rent a flat on the 4th floor of Drake House shortly after their marriage in December 1992. The move attracted an extensive, tabloid-style coverage from just after Christmas until well into 1993.[63] The Trust had engaged the services of Square Mile Communications to provide public relations advice following the critical reporting in April 1992,[64] but the assistance of the firm did not prevent an unflattering 'spin' being put on this and other events. Here we may trace the origins of a more hostile attitude to Dolphin Square and its place in the Westminster housing market. Thus, Valentine Low, writing in the *Evening Standard* in February 1993 about the Princess's decision to live in the Square, used the opportunity to criticise the 'positively incredible' system for fixing rents, with over 40 different types of flat, and the discount system provided for established tenants. Later, the same newspaper attacked the council tax banding for the Square. Under the headline 'Anne's Tax Same As Council Tenants', the piece claimed that while Dolphin Square was 'home for some of the wealthiest and most influential people in Britain . . . they will be paying one of the lowest council taxes'.[65] The *Daily Mail*, which obtained photographs of the flat and pressed a number of tenants for interviews, called the Square a 'privileged ghetto' with rents 'pitched well below market value', while *Private Eye* chose to focus on the requirement that tenants should spend four days a week in residence, casting doubt on the royal couple's ability to meet this requirement. Robert Shrimsley, writing in the *Daily Telegraph*, was a little more whimsical. 'The arrival of the Princess Royal may lift the rather nefarious image of Dolphin Square. The brothels and spies may have disappeared, but quirky goings-on continue to this day.'[66] Several commentators contrasted the earlier luxurious days of the Square with its rundown shabby state. Thus Sebastian Faulks, writing in the *Guardian*, suggested that it had 'moved via the raffish to the edge of seediness', and Nick Foulkes noted that the 'corridors that once smelt of expensive perfume nowadays hold the lingering aroma of boiled cabbage'.[67] Most of this was fairly harmless and ephemeral stuff, of course, but the arrival of Princess Anne provoked an enduring series of somewhat sniping entries in the *The Times*'s diary column, including pieces on the tenants' association and the opening of a croquet lawn in 1993, the contamination of the water supply in 1997, and the observation, also in 1997, that Princess Anne had left after apparently describing the area as 'totally naff'.[68] Further press coverage, by no means all of it positive, accompanied the death of tenant Iain Mills, MP in 1997, the use of Dolphin Square by other MPs, notably William Hague, Mo Mowlam and Hazel Blears, and the arrival of television chef Gary Rhodes at the restaurant.[69] All this kept the flats in the public eye at a time when the freeholder began to take a renewed interest in its property.

THE FREEHOLDER AWAKES, 1997–2003

Given the brighter spotlight falling on the Square it was no surprise when the freeholder began to take a renewed interest in its property. As we have seen, from 1985 UKPI had expressed an intention to buy back the lease, even though it had between 40 and 50 years to run. The pressure had eased temporarily with the financial difficulties which had forced UKPI into an operational merger with Friends Provident, but the latter also cast its eye over the property. With its chairman, Lord Jenkin, a tenant, it had conducted a survey of the property in 1992 as part of a general review of its property portfolio. At first, relations between the Trust, Westminster Council and the freeholder were cordial. For example, when Stonefrost became chairman in 1993, Jenkin wrote him a personal note congratulating him on his appointment.

> You will probably know that, as well as being your tenant [he lived in Howard House], I am also your Head landlord – in the

> guise of the Chairman of Friends Provident! So you can't escape! (You will no doubt be relieved to know that I have no plans to abolish the Trust!).[70]

Jenkin's informal patronage may have discouraged intrusive interest for a while, but regular valuations were conducted in accordance with the Insurance Acts.[71] And more interest was shown from 1997 by Simon Lacey, of Friends Provident Property Services, who admitted to Tony Crawford, then general manager, that he had lived briefly in Drake House as an 'unauthorised sub-tenant'. In an off-the-record meeting he wondered whether the Trust might be interested in purchasing the freehold or making another arrangement.[72] The freeholder became more persistent after Adrian Wray succeeded Crawford as general manager. Wray, reporting to Stonefrost on a lunch meeting with Lacey and Nigel Jupp of George Trollope, Friends Provident's property consultants, in February 1998, noted that the conversation had been 'frank' and he 'gained the impression of people in something of a hurry'. Lacey argued that Dolphin Square's existing leasehold arrangements were 'somewhat anachronistic', and suggested that a large capital investment was required to maintain the assets. Friends Provident would therefore endeavour to realise the true market value of the property (estimated at around £200 million), and give tenants the opportunity to buy their flats. Lacey was keen to involve Westminster City Council in tripartite discussions about the future.[73] Stonefrost's view was that the Trust should not be pushed into change. Its primary responsibility was to manage the existing lease until 2034, and its 'paramount right and obligation' was 'not to forego any value or asset arising from the terms of the Sub-Lease'.[74] This was put to Bill Roots, the Council's chief executive, in September. Roots, however, felt that Friends Provident's desire to realise its asset by selling the freehold provided a 'window of opportunity' for both the Council and the Trust to explore the advantages of a change in Dolphin Square's status. Here was the first intimation that the Council, which in the early 1960s had been adamant that it should not profit from the acquisition of Dolphin Square, was now willing to consider the financial advantages of selling its lease.[75]

A draft document prepared in October by Derek Barnden, the Council's corporate property controller, went further. Pointing out that a substantial amount of 'marriage value' was locked up in the property, he suggested that the creation of some kind of 'restructured management company', which would operate a new set of tenancies, would be beneficial to all parties. He concluded that:

> Westminster paid the equivalent of £50M in today's money to buy the Square in the 1960's. The council created a vehicle to manage the Square according to its stated objectives. This was very successful. However the world has moved on, and there is no longer any need for the Council to be involved. It makes sense to divest ourselves of any further interest in control of the Square. This will bring in a return on our original investment, in either revenue or capital.[76]

Westminster's position was repeated in a semi-official letter from Roots to Stonefrost in November 1998. Westminster was undertaking a cyclical review of all its property assets, he said. Assets should either be fully utilised for operational purposes or generate a market return. 'Assets not fulfilling the above criteria are disposed of'. The approach from the freeholder was being considered in this context. The Council received no benefit from the head lease, since the income received was the same as the rent paid. Stonefrost's response matched his name. He told Roots: 'From the fact that an inquiry was made as to whether I had "hit the ceiling" on reading it, you will guess that I do not regard it as on all fours with our discussion.' He pointed out that the 'marriage value' resided with Dolphin Square's underlease, and not with the Council's lease. It was therefore erroneous to suppose that it was an asset to be shared between Westminster and Friends Provident. In something of a holding operation, the Trust told Westminster that it could not negotiate until it had taken legal advice on its position and powers.[77] Roots had informed the Trust that the officers intended to report on the issue at a meeting of Westminster's Policy and Resources Committee in February, and the Trust was asked to supply it with information on Dolphin Square. The Trust therefore established an ad hoc Leasehold Interest Subcommittee to oversee the negotiations, organise the necessary advice, and report to the Committee of Management. The initial members were Stonefrost, Dawtry, Bradley and Clitherow, together with Geoffrey Lander, who was recruited to provide expert advice in the property field. This body, which Stonefrost thought would be needed for a year or so, was to meet regularly over the next three years.[78]

It quickly emerged that the Dolphin Square Trust could not reasonably stay outside the negotiating arena. After approaching its solicitors, Charles Russell, it was advised by Christopher McCall QC in January 1999 that the trustees had public interest duties, similar to those which charity trustees had, with a primary objective to let housing accommodation in Dolphin Square (Rule 2 of the Trust, as amended in February 1992). The Committee 'owed fiduciary duties consistent with the objects and powers of the trust. These did not permit distributions to tenants or to Members of the Trust or the carrying out of activities with a view to creating profit for the tenants or Members'. The Trust's status as an Industrial & Provident Society created 'a quasi public interest which the Committee members had to pursue'. They were therefore 'required in law to take steps so far as commercially reasonable' to exploit the apparent marriage value in order to 'produce benefit for present and future tenants'. While counsel considered that it was not a proper exercise of the Committee's powers to raise money to buy the freehold itself, it could not stand aside. 'Doing nothing was not an option'.[79] An additional complication was the condition in the sublease that no leases were to be granted for a period expiring after 2024. If the Council held the Trust to this, it would affect its letting activities from c. 2020, much earlier than the expiry date of 2034. Fortunately, legal opinion supported the view that the restriction did not preclude the Trust from continuing to grant periodic tenancies.[80]

For a time, the negotiations appeared to stall. The Trust put much effort into gathering information for Westminster, engaging Cluttons to undertake a valuation, but the reference to the Council's Policy and Resources Committee was deferred, and there was no direct contact with Council officers until June 1999. In fact, in April Friends Provident, who had agreed to deal directly with Westminster, had made an outline offer to Westminster, although it was not revealed to the Trust until September.[81] Eventually communicated to Stonefrost by Lacey in October, it involved a merger of the three parties' interests to form a special purpose company, in which Friends Provident would have a majority stake. A 'minimum payment' of £50 million would be paid to

Westminster for part of its stake over the first three years. The Council would thus 'benefit substantially, reaping the financial rewards of its entrepreneurial 1964 purchase'.[82] The Trust was told that the capital might be used to buy out the concessionary rents of the existing tenants. The new company would apply fair rents. This, apparently, was the '"window of opportunity" in which everyone would win!'.[83] At the same time, some hefty 'sticks' accompanied Friends Provident's financial 'carrot'. Early in 1999, the freeholder had argued that Westminster was in breach of its lease by allowing Dolphin Square to run a hotel and sell alcoholic liquor outside the restaurant. It then made it clear that the underlease, together with the associated agreement between the Council and the Trust, gave Westminster control of letting and rental policy at Dolphin Square, and it expected the Council to intervene in the Trust's affairs by insisting on higher rents. These implied threats were of course passed on to the Trust by Roots and his colleagues. As Stonefrost recalled later: 'The implicit assumption of the Freeholder was that the Trust was a secondary creature of the Council which would be persuaded, manoeuvred or cajoled into giving up its Sub-Lease.'[84] In an exchange of letters in June-July, Roots informed Stonefrost that the Council's legal advice was that it possessed the powers to determine rent structure and policy, and that tenants' rebates were included in its remit. As we have seen, the agreement of 31 December 1964 had stated that 'The Trust shall (i) accept the rent structure and policy previously laid down by the Council for the granting of occupation leases of the unfurnished flats at Dolphin Square and any variation thereof which may from time to time be approved by the Council.' It had been included to ensure that the position of formerly controlled tenants continued to be protected, and that the Trust should begin its work by applying the rental schedules introduced by the Council in 1963–4. It was by no means clear that it was intended to give the Council powers to determine rents thereafter.[85] Roots also pointed out that there was 'no legal basis to the suggestion that either the Trust represents the tenants or that the tenants are the beneficiaries of the Trust'. He therefore asked for a note on the Trust's current position in relation to rent policy and profits.[86] Stonefrost assured Roots that the Trust was ready to negotiate constructively. Wray had met Barnden to discuss the alleged breaches of the lease, and it was pointed out that the use of Rodney House had not changed materially since before the underlease was granted. But on the substantive matter of rents the Chairman adopted a firm stance. The Trust's policy, which had been applied for 35 years on a non-profit-making basis, had 'not been questioned explicitly or implicitly until our most recent exchange'. Its own legal advice was that the disputed clause empowered the Council only to approve variations to the existing policy. The temperature was raised when he added that 'your current interest derives from searching for a possibility of gaining a monetary reward for the Council never intended by or structured in the current Agreement'. [87] Roots replied in kind. He asked for details of the rents charged, suggesting that changes might be required if it were found that rents were lower than those charged to council house tenants on neighbouring estates (e.g. Churchill Gardens and Lillington Gardens). The future of the Square was finally to be discussed more publicly at a meeting of the Policy and Resources Committee on 1 November.[88] By this time, as we have seen, the Trust was made aware of Friends Provident's offer to Westminster; and the Council's committee meeting had the effect of alerting both the media and the tenants to the developing situation. Here the councillors resolved that the officers be authorised to negotiate a restructuring of the parties' interests, 'on the basis that the City Council's view is that the following rental policy should be applied from 1 July 2000', viz. that no rental be less than the average rental of comparable flats in the Council's housing stock; and that all rentals should move to market levels by no later than 1 July 2003.[89] Kevin Maguire, writing in the *Guardian* on 5 November 1999 with the help of leaked documents, referred to 'a new homes scandal', and contrasted the '£62 a week for one of London's best addresses' with the '£90 for a council flat'.[90] Stonefrost later asserted that the Council's motive in taking action on rents was to mobilise tenants to put pressure on the Trust to settle the dispute by surrendering its lease.[91] Tenants certainly became alarmed, and Stonefrost immediately sent them an explanatory letter, and briefed Diana Halliday, Chairman of the DSTA.[92]

Something of an impasse then developed – Stonefrost later referred to 'several years of attrition'. Friends Provident made no financial offer to the Trust, nor was the 'obvious obligation' which the Trust had to tenants formally recognised.[93] Although the Chairman felt that the possibility of the Trust buying the freehold or obtaining a long leasehold was a remote and risky prospect which would do nothing for tenants' interests,[94] this was a course of action which had to be explored. The Trust's newly-stated objective was to 'secure the continued fulfilment of its objects beyond 2034'. It had in mind a sum of £30 million, the book value in the freeholder's accounts, but since the market value of the property without leases was around £260 million, Friends Provident refused to discuss the matter.[95] Westminster expressed its opposition to the corporate solution suggested by Friends Provident, preferring instead to negotiate a cash deal. The pressure on the Trust continued in 2000, with Friends Provident persisting with its threat of legal action on a Section 146 basis regarding the alleged breaches of the lease; and the Council continuing to demand that the Trust introduce market rents for all. And although tripartite meetings were convened in February, April and October 2000,[96] each side stuck to its guns, with the Trust adamant that the Council could not impose rent policy, and insistent that in any outcome existing tenants should be protected.[97] In July 2000, Sir Gordon Pirie and Sir Alan Dawtry, writing as leader and town clerk at the time of the purchase of Dolphin Square by the City Council, issued a statement which reiterated the purpose of the transaction: to protect the tenants, who were in danger of losing their homes, and to preserve a pool of privately rented housing in the borough. Westminster's role was a facilitating one, and 'the idea of at any time using the transaction to make a profit for the council would have been unthinkable and unconscionable'.[98] Council officials (Peter Rogers had succeeded Bill Roots as chief executive) now realised that the trustees were more determined than they had thought. Fearing that they might lose a legal action on the rent issue, since they appeared to be seeking to raise rents in order to obtain more cash from the freeholder, they backed off, and by November 2000 were eager to detach the two issues, though they were not abandoned.[99] Meanwhile, the Trust commissioned valuation work from Knight Frank, and from Bacon & Woodrow, its actuaries.[100] The climate was sometimes unpleasant, accompanied by pressure from the other two parties, and disparaging and often ill-informed comments in the press and elsewhere about the intransigence and 'social anachronism' of the 'oligarchic' Trust. For example, the *Evening Standard* discomfited tenants when it suggested that the Square might be used to house council tenants whose homes were being repaired.[101] As a result, the anxieties of the residents came more and more into play, and the Trust came to the view that its 'starting gate' position in any negotiation should be that the 'reasonable expectations of existing tenants be safeguarded'.[102] The DSTA and the tenants were briefed by Kit Malthouse, Deputy Leader of the Council, a St. George's Ward councillor and member of the Policy and Resources Committee, at a meeting on 16 January 2001. He provided a blunt précis of the negotiations which, he said, had been conducted 'in a very aggressive and unstructured manner'. But now the parties were talking sensibly, and a preliminary offer from Friends Provident was expected in the next few weeks.[103]

A week later, Friends Provident, acting through its subsidiary, Friends Ivory & Sime, sent its proposal to both Westminster and the Trust. Westminster would receive a cash sum of £60 million for its lease; the Trust would obtain rent concessions for tenants which were held to be worth £30 million. While new lettings would be on the basis of market rentals after a year, existing tenants would enjoy improved security of tenure through longer leases, of 4–15 years, dependent on previous occupancy. Their rents would increase to market levels over a 33 year period, by about 3.25 per cent a year. There was also the promise of a five-year moratorium before any flats would be sold.[104] There was not enough in the offer for either party: Westminster felt that £60 million was too low, while the Trust did not feel that it was being adequately compensated for its marriage value, or that there would be adequate relief for existing tenants. On the latter issue, Friends Provident explained that tenants would enjoy a subsidy until 2034, with rents in the first year increased by market levels and thereafter by market increases plus one year's diminution of the present subsidy. But with only £60 million on the table for Westminster, and the Trust reckoning that the current cost of safeguarding rents levels was at least £47 million, while the offer was worth only £10 million, no agreement could be reached.[105] Furthermore, the leaseholders' position had been strengthened by the emergence of another bid. In November 2000, Allied Commercial, a property company headed by Jack Dellal, had offered £125 million for the two leases.[106] The two issues in contention – rent levels, and the alleged breaches of the lease – continued to be used by Friends Provident in an attempt to force a settlement. The likelihood of legal action was very real, and the Trust regarded this as an implied threat to surrender its underlease. In April 2001, Westminster's Policy and Resources Committee passed a further resolution reasserting its right to require Dolphin Square to charge rents at market levels, and setting an implementation date of 1 August. A final decision was deferred until June to enable consultation with the tenants and DSTA to take place.[107] The move provoked a strong and well-organised protest from around 500 tenants and in July, Westminster again deferred a final decision on rents until 1 November 'at the earliest'.[108] On the other hand, the matter of breaches of the lease was less favourable. Six elements had been identified by Herbert Smith, acting for Friends Provident, in 1999. The Trust's legal advice was that most of these were clear breaches, and in particular, the use of Rodney House as a hotel and conference centre, the sale of alcohol to non-residents, the existence of an off-licence, and the letting of offices.[109] With negotiations in effect suspended, the Trust considered an alternative option, that it should revive its proposal to buy Westminster's interest, i.e. the lease and agreement, which would probably cost it at least £30–35 million. In doing so it received some brief encouragement from Westminster officials. At the same time, it also examined the possibility of buying the freehold from Friends Provident. 'Project Status Quo' was launched with the help of Knight Frank to analyse the Square's asset base in order to assess the practicalities of raising around £65–70 million for this purpose.[110]

The matter had now reached a delicate stage. Friends Provident, which had demutualised in July 2001, was anxious to resolve the matter, and sought a meeting with the Trust. Its preference was to take Dolphin Square to a capital sale of long leases; however, it was also prepared to explore alternatives. In September Stonefrost, Bradley and Wray met Lacey and Jupp. The freeholder was anxious to avoid legal action and to settle either by a tripartite deal ('option 1') or with the Trust buying out Westminster ('option 2'), and yet Lacey's response made it plain that the company was unlikely to raise its existing offer by very much.[111] The Trust then worked up a bid for Westminster's lease. The valuers' calculations indicated that £28 million was available, but counsel's opinion was that this was far too high a sum to pay for the lease, and the trustees decided that they might offer Westminster £10 million, plus the sum outstanding on mortgage, £3.8 million, together with up to 50 flats for key workers. A letter was sent to Rogers, the chief executive, on 15 November, outlining the proposal and promising to provide the financial 'parameters' after further consultation.[112] However, the move was interrupted by a further offer from Friends Provident, made on the same day. That this was now more serious was evident by the fact that Lacey was replaced at the negotiating table by Paul Herrington, Managing Director of Friends Ivory & Sime, at a subsequent meeting with the Trust on 29 November. The freeholder's 'package' was apparently worth £130 million; £90.25 million in cash would be shared between the Council and the Trust. Rents would be raised to market levels on the same basis as before, including a five-year moratorium on flat sales, but short-term payments or 'rebates' would be made to existing tenants, amounting to £13,000 each and paid over the first three years. In addition, Friends Provident undertook to allocate 30 per cent of all studio flats becoming vacant over a five-year period to key workers, with annual tenancies at 50 per cent of the market rent.[113]

At this point Stonefrost, who was now in poor health, decided to stand down. His successor, Rodney Brooke, was no less a champion of the Trust's cause, and, ably assisted by the tireless Wray, they continued to negotiate with Westminster and Friends Provident on two fronts. The issues facing the trustees were complex, and the demands they faced from all sides - freeholder, Council and anxious tenants - were growing. There was also the implied threat from Westminster that it might use its powers to approve the appointment of members of the Trust in order to change the composition of the Committee of Management and force through change. In these circumstances, it is unsurprising that there were some differences of view. Some members had a strong preference for continuing to operate the Trust's underlease regardless of the pressures being applied, while others placed too much faith in finding a solution (e.g. purchasing Westminster's lease) which did not involve surrendering its lease. In addition, there was the tricky problem of how much the tenants should be told. However, it became increasingly evident that a preference for the status quo would have to give way to the objective of safeguarding the interests of existing tenants and ensuring that a proper share of the emerging financial benefit was deployed to help those needing to live and work in central London.

There was thus general agreement that while the freeholder's offer deserved serious consideration, the tenants' reasonable expectations regarding rents, security of tenure and quality of life should be safeguarded.[114] When Brooke conveyed this to Friends Provident, Herrington was somewhat exasperated to find further resistance to what he considered to be a fair offer; he took this to be a rejection.[115] In January 2002, the Trust pressed ahead with its own proposal to Westminster, following a revised opinion from counsel. It increased its offer to £15 million (including the mortgage) for its interest, the most it felt it could afford. A meeting with tenants to explain the options was held at the Queen Elizabeth II Conference Centre on 7 February.[116] However, the Council could not accept such a sum when it could do much better by transacting with the freeholder or with other parties,[117] and by this time the Allied Commercial consortium had submitted improved offers including £82 million for the Trust and a windfall payment for tenants of £15,000, subsequently raised to £17,500.[118] Despite its dissatisfaction with the Trust, Friends Provident came up with an improved proposal in April 2002. This promised more for the tenants within the existing £130 million package. The sum to be shared between the Council and the Trust was increased to £65,250,000. On rents, tenants would now be offered a further concession, viz. that increases in market rents would be pegged at two per cent per annum over the term of the first lease. Rent rebates were also increased to take account of length of residency. Tenants were promised the following: a 'retrospective' rebate of £10–15,000, based on twice the annual rent paid; a 'standard' rebate of £10,000; and a 'residency' rebate of £1,000 for each year of occupancy. Each tenant would receive a total of £21,000–85,000 (average: £38,000). This offer was to form the basis of further negotiations with the freeholder in 2002–3.[119]

From April 2002 to November 2003 there was another long period of negotiation. The tenants, who received a number of direct approaches from Friends Provident, were by this time somewhat exhausted by the plethora of information to which they had been subjected, and it was no surprise when a Council-sponsored MORI poll conducted in July 2002 concluded that there was no consensus among them about a solution. Some were undoubtedly tempted by the prospect of longer leases and cash payments, while others favoured the status quo.[120] The Trust had found the April 2002 offer to be unacceptable, since it did not give existing tenants security of tenure at reasonable rents,[121] and with its proposal to buy out Westminster having lapsed, it spent this period refining its own solution. It also explored the Council's suggestion that it might introduce longer leases of up to 31 years for tenants who preferred the status quo. Trustees were firm on their negotiating principles, which involved offering tenants a choice between accepting Friends Provident's terms (Option A) and accepting the Trust's continuing arrangements (Option B). The latter would seek to capture their 'reasonable expectations' by providing security with specified rentals, a binding agreement between the freeholder and the tenants, quiet enjoyment of the Square, and some guarantees about service levels and parking.[122] The Council, led by Simon Milton, seems to have made genuine attempts to resolve the impasse, suggesting some concessions on its favoured rent policy, and taking on board the Trust's desire to give the residents' tenure and rent levels a 'reasonable' level of protection. It therefore agreed that a 'twin-track' approach to Friends Provident's offer might be pursued, with tenants being given the choice of accepting the freeholder's terms or remaining under Trust conditions.[123] It also set out its thoughts on how the sale proceeds might be used to create a ring-fenced fund for key worker and social housing.[124] Sometimes a deal seemed likely, for example, after a more constructive tripartite meeting in October 2002, when ISIS Asset Management (formerly Friends Ivory & Sime) spoke more frankly about drawing up heads of agreement;[125] at other times the prospects were more gloomy, with Friends Provident preferring to approach the tenants directly via the DSTA, promising them additional cash payments in July 2002 (presumably at the expense of the Council and the Trust), and showing little appetite for a deal that embraced the Trust's option.[126] The freeholder also continued to threaten the Trust, raising the issue of business rates and planning consent in respect of Rodney House, and continuing with its Section 146 legal action over the breaches of the lease (notices were served in September and October 2002). There were also wide variations in the valuations placed on the Trust's interest in Dolphin Square, which ranged from £207 million (Trust's advice) to £35 million (Westminster's approach).[127] And the waters were again muddied by the intervention of outside interests, with bids from the real estate company Civic Asset Partnerships in July 2002, a more tentative offer by Crown Dilmun, a subsidiary of the Bahrain International Bank, in October 2002, and approaches in 2003 from, inter alia, a consortium led by Justin Cadbury and from an acquisition group advised by property specialists Friend & Falcke.[128] Eventually, matters came to a head. With litigation on the Section 146 issues imminent, there was yet another tripartite meeting in September 2003, leading to a further offer from Friends Provident. Westminster, acting for both parties, had asked for £142 million plus agreement to the Trust's option ('Option B') being offered to all tenants. It wished to retain £30 million of this. Friends Provident was willing to pay only £105 million, and it expressed opposition to aspects of the protection embodied in the Option B proposal. Consequently, negotiations broke down on 4 November.[129] With the Cadbury consortium putting pressure on the parties for a fair hearing, Westminster and the Trust agreed to 'market their joint interests, setting a time limit for the negotiation of a credible and acceptable offer'.[130] This course of action required a resolution of the Section 146 issue, and on 25 November the Trust, supported by a favourable view of its chances from its solicitors, initiated proceedings to determine the validity of the claims in the High Court.[131]

THE SALE OF DOLPHIN SQUARE, 2004–6

With the Friends Provident deal having broken down irrevocably, Westminster and the Trust put Dolphin Square out to open tender. A marketing pack was assembled, and expressions of interest were invited by 26 March 2004, with final bids to be received by 28 May. A National Opinion Poll survey of tenants' requirements was conducted to help interested parties submit 'best and final bids' by 19 July.[132] From the several expressions of interest, 13 outline bids were submitted, and from these, four had been shortlisted by August: AR&V Investments, a private property investment firm, in association with the William Pears Group and Galliard Homes; Grainger Trust, the UK's largest quoted residential property investor; Nomura, a Japanese Bank with substantial property interests in the UK; and Westbrook Partners, a privately owned American property investment management firm, which owned residential property in New York and Paris.[133] The bids provided tenants with the choice of accepting either Option A (an offer to tenants comprising cash and/or rent rebates in return for either vacant possession, a switch to market rents, or a long lease) or Option B (a lease protecting, as far as possible, their existing tenure and rent expectations). However, even at this late stage the policy of the Trust had not been finalised. At a meeting in August the Committee of Management was surprised at the high sums being offered by those who had been shortlisted, although, as Knight Frank pointed out, the top bids were within five per cent of the valuation of £150–180 million which it had placed on the vendors' interests.[134] Indeed, trustees such as Clitherow and Lander had doubted whether the tendering process would lead to an offer higher than the one already on the table from Friends Provident.[135] It was noted that the freeholder had entered an unsuccessful bid which was about £100 million less than the top bidder. But far from giving the trustees comfort about the opportunities the large sums offered in relation to future social housing and the protection of existing tenants, the bids produced concerns that in order to derive a return on their investment, the successful bidder would not only have to raise rents to market levels and/or sell flats, but also reduce running costs to the detriment of current levels of service in the Square. Furthermore, there were those on the Committee of Management who remained unhappy with the way the shortlisting process had been conducted, and there was more than one reference to a feeling of having been 'bounced' into a decision.[136] Some trustees, notably Lander, Clitherow, and Baker-Bates, argued strongly for the retention of the status quo by offering money for Westminster's head lease and Friends Provident's freehold. As to the bids, Nomura was dropped since its Option B cash sum was lower than those of the other parties, TUPE costs would not be met, and it had not confirmed that it would proceed unconditionally on the Section 146 proceedings.[137]

The critical meeting of the trustees was held on 13 September 2004. First, there was a long discussion with counsel on the duties and liabilities of Committee members. Then Knight Frank gave a presentation on the strengths and weaknesses of the remaining bids, in which Westbrook emerged as the favoured bidder, having offered a base price of £190 million to Westminster and the Trust. The process was, however, interrupted by Clitherow, who argued that a purchaser would try to purchase the freehold, and would probably grant 29-year leases to tenants in order to force the issue, e.g. by extracting 90-year leases from Friends

Provident. This would surely depress the value of the freehold, and provide an opportunity for the Trust to buy it. However, Brooke informed trustees that a letter he had received from Westminster that day confirmed that the Council had not agreed to sell its interest to the Trust. Furthermore, the advisers were far from convinced by Clitherow's line of argument, and they suggested that bidders might withdraw if there were further delays in reaching a decision. Brooke concluded by referring to four options: '1. The status quo; 2. Try to buy FP's interest (with or without WCC); 3. Try to buy WCC's interest alone; 4. Sell to an external bidder.' The advisers withdrew, and 'after a lengthy debate', it was agreed that:

> The Trust's preferred option was to maintain the status quo for tenants by purchasing Westminster's interest for £65M which represented the full value of that interest, together with 100 flats for key worker housing at, say, half open market rent . . . If Westminster continued to refuse the Trust's offer, and bearing in mind the Council's threat to increase rents, then the Trust would reluctantly agree a sale to Westbrook on the terms offered, subject to contract and final approval.[138]

In spite of these resolutions, it was no great surprise when Westminster rejected the Trust's last throw of the dice, and in 2004–5 negotiations began in earnest on finalising a sale to Westbrook. Tenants received a letter from Westbrook on 22 October, and on the 27th they were invited to another meeting at the QEII Centre to discuss this news.[139]

In all the long negotiations over the future of Dolphin Square, a sale to a commercial party was never a favoured course of action as far as the trustees were concerned. The unease about the future management of the Square raised by Lander et al. was very real, whatever the prospects of an alternative policy, and they were undoubtedly fed by concerns from the tenants about the future, not only from the DSTA, led by Diana Halliday, but from a newly-formed action group operating under the banner SOS ('Save Our Square'). Indeed, the tenants continued to present a formidable lobbying group, and there was substance to many of their anxieties. In 2002–3 the DSTA had been disturbed by the revelation that Westminster and the Trust had decided to take Friends

Provident's April 2002 offer as the basis of further negotiation, and not its offer to tenants in July, which promised them £20,000 more in cash.[140] The SOS campaign, led by Celia Scott and Rosemary Henley, was also active, expressing strong opposition to a sale to a commercial concern and putting in its own bid for the Square during the bidding process, which envisaged withdrawing the property from the market and negotiating with Friends Provident for an extension of the existing lease.[141] There were also tenants who were upset that the 'right to buy' was excluded from the agreement with Westbrook.[142] At the end of the second QEII meeting in October 2004, tenants were asked whether they wanted the Council to change its mind about selling the Square; an overwhelming majority expressed support for this motion.[143] At critical moments there was evidence that tenant activists had had the benefit of leaked documents.[144] The protests of the SOS campaigners culminated in an unsuccessful appeal to the Local Government Ombudsman about the Council's behaviour, although the latter was rebuked by the Information Commissioner for failing to provide requested documentation until the sale had been completed.[145] However, all too often the tenant activists combined the intemperate with the inaccurate, and some of their more extreme pronouncements not only irritated the negotiating parties, but provoked further hostile responses from sections of the media.[146] Particularly trenchant comments came from Lucy Barnard, writing for the *Estates Gazette*, Mira Bar-Hillel, the property correspondent of the *Evening Standard*, and Edward Simpkins of the *Sunday Telegraph*. Their main thrust, as before, was that the tenants were a wealthy group enjoying privileges denied to others in Westminster.[147] And tenants often failed to appreciate that the Trust's room for manoeuvre was becoming increasingly constrained. Its lease represented a declining asset, and although counsel's opinion was comforting, within 20 years there would be a technical embargo on entering into new leases. To refuse to sell would make the Section 146 action more difficult to defend, while there was a very real possibility that the Council would impose a rent policy of draconian proportions.

In the autumn of 2004 initial impressions of Westbrook as a future landlord were favourable. The purchaser had been investing in UK commercial property since 1997. The company made it clear that it had no intention of seeking an imminent short-term sale, and wished to maintain the amenities of Dolphin Square, with the exception of the Rodney House hotel. Brooke found their representatives, Mark Donnor and Jeffrey Caplin, to be 'open and frank'. They intended to establish a management company to operate Dolphin Square, based on the existing employees.[148] The period to September 2005 was taken up in turning outline heads of agreement into a final agreement. There was much work to be done, to: amend the rules of the Trust to enable it to sell its interest; refine the Option B lease alternative; set up a new company to protect the interests of the Option B leaseholders; set up a new charitable foundation to receive the Trust's proceeds from the sale, which would be deployed on social housing initiatives; obtain indemnities for trustees from Westminster; deal with taxation issues; and safeguard the interests of the staff.[149] One of the more serious issues concerned Westbrook's revelation that the purchase would be made by a subsidiary, initially Westbrook Acquisitions LLC, and not the parent company, which caused the trustees, led by Lander, to call for assurances in relation to financial guarantees and restrictions on assignment, given the absence of accounts. It subsequently emerged that the landlord was to be a non-resident company with Dolphin Square as its only asset.[150] There was also the outstanding Section 146 action, which now centred on three alleged breaches: the use of Rodney House as a hotel; the installation of telecom masts on the roof of Duncan House; and alterations made to Rodney House without consent. Here, Westbrook made it clear that it was not willing to take on the action, while the Council was unhappy about spending large sums on the defence.[151] Furthermore, the lawyers now advised that the Trust's position on Rodney House was not as strong as they had previously believed, and there was a very real prospect that it would have to make substantial alterations to the property. The action was settled out of court in January 2005. The Trust agreed not to brand or market Rodney House as a hotel after 21 July 2006, and paid the freeholder a substantial sum in compensation plus a contribution to costs.[152]

Final heads of terms were exchanged in April 2005; contracts were exchanged in September, amended in November, and completion took place on 10 January 2006. The final negotiations in the summer of 2005 centred on a number of thorny issues. Westbrook wanted to effect the purchase through three separate companies: a WCC lease buyer; a

Trust lease buyer; and a business buyer. It also sought a price adjustment of £8.98 million to take account of additional maintenance work identified following a building survey. Westbrook was also opposed to some of the Trust's plans for Option B leases, viz. succession rights being extended for a further generation to 378 pre-1992 tenants, in accordance with a promise made in 1991,[153] car parking charges being included in the leases, and the proposed rent review schedule.[154] Eventually, these matters were resolved. On succession, the pre-1992 tenants were to be offered £5,000 to relinquish their extended rights.[155] Westminster's lease was transferred to Tannenberg Ltd., one of Westbrook's Jersey-based companies, the Trust's underlease and associated assets went to Westbrook Dolphin Square Ltd., a Westbrook subsidiary, and the commercial businesses, staff and associated assets went to Mantilla Holdings Ltd., Westbrook's property management company registered in Jersey in 2006. The final deal with Westbrook provided for the following. Westminster received an initial cash sum of £60 million.[156] The Trust received £120.6 million, and a further £8 million, based upon the proportion of the 841 eligible tenants who chose Option A, and the proportion entitled to enhanced succession rights who elected to relinquish those rights.[157] The process was generally amicable, but some trustees continued to express anxieties about Westbrook. Although now reconciled to the prospect of a sale, Lander, Clitherow and Pulford continued to raise objections to aspects of the developing deal for tenants, including the formulation of a rent schedule, Westbrook's decision to organise the purchase via three separate companies, and the absence of what they regarded as adequate 'step-in' rights for the Dolphin Square charity should Westbrook become insolvent or commit a breach of the covenants. Lander subsequently went so far as to announce his resignation from the Committee of Management, although this was subsequently withdrawn.[158]

AFTER WESTBROOK

The eligible tenants, 841 in number, made their choice in November 2005. Option A was chosen by 398 tenants (47 per cent), who each received a cash payment from a £28.5 million fund provided by Westbrook, the amount dependent on whether they were pre-1992 tenants or not. Given the choice of moving to a one-year tenancy at market rent or leaving the Square, most (330) opted for the latter. Option B was taken up by 432 tenants (51 per cent), who moved to new leases at protected rents.[159] Of those with '1991' status, 216 waived their rights to extended succession.[160] For Option B electors a complex procedure was to be followed in setting their rents until 2034. New leases would run until October 2018, with a right, exercisable on payment of a premium (expected to be £1,000), to a new lease until 2034. For the period to 2018 low rents were preserved according to the following formula. A market rent would be determined for each flat by Knight Frank. Then a 'restricted rent' (market rent minus a reduction to take account of Dolphin Square restrictions) would be set at five per cent below this, plus a 'fair rent' at 27.5 per cent below the restricted rent. The calculated rents would then rise by two per cent per annum until 1 October 2018. Tenants' rents would increase by the Trust's customary ten per cent increments until they reached the notional fair rent or restricted rent. Thereafter rents would increase by RPI, subject to a maximum of four per cent per annum.[161] To protect their interests a new company, Dolphin Square 2005 Ltd., was established. The Trust agreed to fund it to the extent of £10.6 million. Of this £5 million was ring-fenced to provide a default fund to protect against breaches of its obligations by the landlord, while the remainder was to enable the company to assist tenants in the event of disputes with the landlord, or to assist tenants to pay the premium due on lease renewals. In addition, an initial sum of £5 million was paid to the Dolphin Square Trust Pension Scheme in order to ensure a fully-funded buyout of benefits accrued in the scheme. The initial directors of Dolphin Square 2005 were all Option B tenants: three were appointed by the Trust – Marshall (chair), Pulford and Prebble; and three were elected by the Option B tenants, viz. Warwick Bergin, Daniel Bexfield and Nicholas Walker.[162]

Westminster and the Trust had agreed that the greater part of the proceeds from the sale should be used to fund a new housing charity, the Dolphin Square Charitable Foundation. The Trust made it an initial gift aid payment of £80 million; a further £10 million was paid in five annual instalments in 2006–10. The Council gave certain indemnities to the Trust in connexion with these transactions, to protect against both non-disposal related and disposal related liabilities.[163] The Foundation was to engage in key worker and affordable housing projects. Its precise objects, membership and governance were determined after further lengthy discussions between the Trust and the Council in 2004–5. In general, the Trust's wishes prevailed. For example, no precise figure was put on the balance of activity between key worker housing and social housing (the Council had argued for a 50-50 distribution). Trustees also expressed the wish that the charity should give priority to help Option B tenants who were unable to afford rents or became homeless after 2034.[164] The Foundation's governors were to comprise representatives of: the Trust; the Council; private sector landlords; employers of key workers in Westminster; and registered social landlords. The initial membership was: Ian Henderson, former Chief Executive of Land Securities, and a consultant to Quintain Estates, chairman; Rodney Brooke; Graham Hindes, Chief Executive of Octavia Housing; Rosemary Westbrook, Westminster's Director of Housing; Anu Vedi, Chief Executive of Genesis Housing; Colin Redman, Director of Trusts, Grosvenor Estate; Rachel Whittaker, member of the Metropolitan Police Authority; and Catherine Longworth, a former Lord Mayor of Westminster and a director of Westminster Primary Care Trust; and Andrew Whitley, director of CityWest Homes.[165]

CONCLUSION

From 1999 to 2006 the Trust had been involved in a complex, shifting, difficult and often unpleasant battle over Dolphin Square. In January 2005, it calculated that £2.6 million had been spent on professional and legal fees in connection with the sale.[166] The final bill was much larger, something in excess of £6 million.[167] Negotiations with the Council and Friends Provident had been tortuous over a number of years, but one can understand why the Trust was unwilling to settle quickly. On the face of it, there was no compelling reason to give up the lease, the status quo was working well, and the protection of long-standing tenants was an important consideration. But once tripartite negotiations had been started, they were not easy to control, and the trustees became increasingly boxed in. Indeed, the outcome might have been foreseen, especially as Friends Provident made it clear that it was unwilling to raise its offer to the levels demanded by the Council and Trust. We may sympathise with the uncertainty and anxiety suffered by those on three-year leases who had expected to roll these over at a discount, or else receive substantial financial inducements to quit. But that was not how it turned out. The Option A deals were scarcely generous given the price of property in central London, and although the Trust had clearly done the best it could to protect those who wished to stay on at something approaching the existing terms and conditions, the character of the Square in the future was set to change. Having been set up in 1964/5 to prevent an uncertain future with a commercial landlord, the Trust sold its interest to a commercial landlord whose future policy could not be predicted. Option B tenants were protected, certainly, but this was a dwindling band of relatively elderly people – 316 in January 2012.

Many tenants continued to regard the Trust as primarily to blame for the change of ownership. This was exemplified by an acrimonious correspondence with tenant activists in 2005. Letters exchanged between Rosemary Henley and Brooke in April–May, and in July–August between Brooke and Lord Russell-Johnston, the redoubtable Liberal/Liberal Democrat and Scottish railways campaigner who had succeeded Halliday as chairman of the DSTA, provide a good indication of the matters in dispute (see Appendix 12). Even at this late stage the DSTA, briefly dominated by members of SOS, challenged the right of the Trust to sell its lease. Rosemary Henley, Russell-Johnston, Andrew Probert and Gillis Burgess contended that the Trust was acting in disregard of its prime duty. The publication of a chronicle of events in its newsletter fanned the flames.[168] The complainants were able to point to changes in the Trust's stated purposes, which appeared to challenge the proposal to use the sale proceeds for wider housing purposes. The primary objective of the Trust, when it was first registered as an Industrial and Provident Society in 1964, was relatively broad: 'to carry on the industry, business or trade of providing housing for letting'. However, following deregistration as a housing association in 1992 the Trust amended its rules, and the 'primary purpose' was made much narrower, 'to carry on the business of letting flats in the building known as Dolphin Square'. Then, when in December 2004 the rules were further amended to allow the Trust to sell its interest, a clause was added changing the objects again, in order to allow the Trust to make provision for 'residential accommodation of all kinds in the Area of Benefit' (Greater London).[169] The changes enabled Henley and Probert to challenge the Trust's decision to sell. Henley writing to Brooke in April 2005, contended that the Trust's duty 'is to the tenants of Dolphin Square, which the Trust was created to protect. It has NO responsibility to housing in Westminster'.[170] Russell-Johnston's subsequent interventions were more personal and vitriolic. They culminated in his claim that the answer to a question raised in 1991 during the Trust's deregistration as a housing association - in which the continuance of the Trust as a non-profit-making housing association was confirmed - undermined the Trust's ability to sell. In a personal letter to Brooke, the feisty Scot questioned the morality of the sale and asserted that the Trust had connived in Westminster's 'policy reversal'.[171]

While some of the tenants' arguments were eloquently put, the reality was that the Trust was not a private concern acting for the benefit of the residents. As Brooke pointed out to Henley, the legal advice was unequivocally clear that throughout its life the Trust was a disinterested body with a public interest duty. It could not merely enrich the existing tenants.[172] Furthermore, the several opinion polls revealed that the tenants were never a united body. Some wanted the right to buy, and had argued for this intermittently since the 1960s; others wished to be compensated financially for the loss of their privileged rents; others wished to retain the discounted rents they enjoyed in the Dolphin Square cocoon. While activists wished to 'Save' the Square, the obvious response was: for whom? For what?

Of course, the Trust had an obligation to meet the reasonable expectations of the existing tenants. In fact, the active tenants were, in the main, people who had made Dolphin Square their homes, many of them continuing to live there after retirement. For them, and the other Option B tenants, at least, the sale produced a greater measure of protection than would have been available had the Trust continued to operate until its lease ran out. Standing apart from events, we may suggest that things would have turned out very differently had Friends Provident handled the negotiations differently. If the freeholder had been prepared to offer a little more, and make a serious effort to meet the concerns of existing tenants, then it might now be enjoying the position of unencumbered owner. It might also have been better for the Trust to have called the Council's hand, and challenged it to change rentals. If it had done so, then there would have been a clear and unequivocal 'villain' of the piece as far as the tenants were concerned. Instead, the Trust, which was attacked on all sides, had tried to balance the conflicting considerations before it, and in doing so, had shifted its ground in order to make a sale possible and retrieve the maximum benefit to both existing tenants and London as a whole. The motives of an unpaid group of tenant-trustees, who were all of course affected by the change of ownership, were unimpeachable. But it is scarcely surprising that some of them felt a profound sense of regret about the events of 1999–2006.

NOTES

1 Stonefrost-Bruce Clitherow, 22 December 1998, DST.

2 At the same time the Trust elected to resign from the National Housing Federation. See Stonefrost-Bill Roots (Chief Executive, WCC), 1 May and 25 June 1997, and paper on 'Westminster City Council and the Status of a Local Authority Influenced Company and the Trust's Status as a Housing Association' [n.d.], DST Committee of Management Minutes, 22 July 1997, DST.

3 Pulford became Chief Executive of the Society of London Theatre. He died in 2011: *The Times*, 26 August 2011, p.68.

4 After service with Arthur Andersen and Chase Manhattan Bank, Baker-Bates joined the Midland Bank in 1984, and was MD of Midland UK Banking, 1989–91 and Director, Group Financial Control, 1991–3. He was a member of the BBC's Board of Management and Executive Committee, 1993–9, and chief executive of Prudential Financial Services, 1998–2001. He holds numerous directorships, and is currently [2012] Chairman of the Stobart Group.

5 Bindman's appointment began on a temporary basis: DST Committee of Management Minutes, 25 March 1997, DST.

6 Wray saw active service in Oman, Northern Ireland, Cyprus and Northern Iraq.

7 DSTA Newsletter, January 1985, p.4; DST Committee of Management Minutes, 22 July 1999, DST.

8 In 1965–92/3 the margin was 4%. Note that the data used here include investment income, and interest paid, to make the calculations comparable with earlier data.

9 DST, *R & A*. The rounded data in Appendices 4 and 7 produce slightly different % changes. The rates bill for 2001/2 was £819,000 cf. £196,000 in 2000/1.

10 Assured tenancies, with more limited security for tenants, were introduced by the 1988 Housing Act. Assured shorthold tenancies were created by the 1996 Housing Act, giving landlords greater freedom to evict tenants, and limiting tenants' rights of appeal to a rent assessment committee.

11 Dawtry, statement of 'The Trust's letting and rents policy', n.d. [1997], DST. A tenant changing flats lost this concession unless he/she moved to a smaller flat.

12 In 1999/2000, the number of flats was briefly 1,059. Additional flats were created by converting the offices on the 9th floor of Duncan House into three flats, and dividing some large flats into two smaller ones. Adrian D. Wray (General Manager, Dolphin Square)-Paul Richards (George Trollope), 26 November 1997, DST.

13 DST Committee of Management Minutes, 20 November 1997, DST. In 1996–8, the increases for 6- and 7-room flats were left to the discretion of the flats manager and general manager. DST Committee of Management Minutes, 19 November 1998, DST.

14 Ibid. 25 November 1999, 25 November 2004.

15 Ibid. 23 November 2000. The increases for 6- and 7-room flats were lower: 12–20% and 0.3–9.0%.

16 DST Committee of Management Minutes, 31 October and 22 November 2001, DST. The estate agents Dauntons were instructed to let the larger flats: ibid. 31 January 2002.

17 Robert Orr-Ewing (Knight Frank)-Wray, 25 October 2002, DST Committee of Management Minutes, 21 November 2002 and 27 November 2003, 25 November 2004, DST. Second-year rents for those obtaining tenancies in 2002 were also frozen.

18 Rebecca Richardson (Knight Frank)-Jane Salt (Flats Manager), 15 November 2004, DST Committee of Management Minutes, 25 November 2004, DST.

19 Lander-Crawford, 17 July 1997 and reply, 22 July 1997, DST Committee of Management Minutes, 20 November 1997; Wray and Salt, paper on 'Review of Dolphin Square Rent Regime' [n.d.], DST Committee of Management Minutes, 23 July 1998, DST.

20 Diana Halliday (Chairman, DSTA)-Stonefrost, 7 October 1999, DST.

21 Previously, compliance with only one of these two criteria was required.

22 Rent Subcommittee report [n.d.], DST Committee of Management Minutes, 19 November 1998, DST. The proposal to replace 'Central London' with 'London' [defined as inside the M25 ring] was dropped: cf. statement on 'Letting Policy', 1999, DST Leasehold Interest Subcommittee papers, December 1999, DST.

23 Commodore D.S. Lewis (Director, Service Personnel Policy 1, MOD)-Crawford, 1 October 1996, Crawford, Report [n.d.], DST Committee of Management Minutes, 21 November 1996, DST. The issue was raised again in 2003, when some difficulty was experienced in letting flats, but the Trust's legal advice was not to pursue the matter given the negotiations with Friends Provident and Westminster Council. Norman Starritt (Charles Russell)-Wray, 7 May 2003, DST Committee of Management Minutes, 24 July 2003, DST.

24 The committee had begun work in 1988 as an ad hoc committee before being formally constituted. In 1996, it was renamed the 'Special Case Tenants and Arrears Subcommittee'. DST Committee of Management Minutes, 21 July 1992, 18 July and 21 November 1996, DST.

25 Cf. the case of a Nigerian chief: DST Committee of Management Minutes, 28 March and 15 November 1996, DST.

26 Dawtry, statement, 1997, DST.

27 DST Committee of Management Minutes, 20 November 1997, DST.

28 Cf. DST Committee of Management Minutes, 22 November 2001, 21 March and 18 July 2002, 25 November 2004 and 20 July 2005, DST.

29 DST, *R & A 1997/8–2000/1*; DST Committee of Management Minutes, 22 July 1999, DST.

30 Clare Stewart (Hotel Manager), report on '4* status of Dolphin Square Hotel' [n.d.], DST Committee of Management Minutes, 25 November 1999, DST.

31 Cf. Leasehold Interest Subcommittee papers, 24 July 2003, DST.

32 Stewart, report on 'Hotel Yield Management' [n.d.], DST Committee of Management Minutes, 23 July 1998, DST.

33 DST Committee of Management Minutes, *passim*, and in particular Crawford and Stewart, report, DST Committee of Management Minutes, 21 November 1996, 23 November 2000, 22 November 2001, 31 January 2002, and 27 November 2003, DST.

34 In this exercise none of the restaurant deficit was charged to Rodney house, and general costs were allocated on the basis of the number of apartments, not the floor area occupied. KPMG Peat Marwick, 'Dolphin Square Trust Limited: Hotel income and expenditure analysis' (4 March 1994), DST Committee of Management Minutes, 29 March 1994, DST.

35 Conference Centre and Business Centre results are excluded.

36 DST, *R & A 1993/4*, p.30.

37 Reduced reporting period following change of financial year.

38 DST, *R & A*. In 2001/2 there was a redefinition of 'full-time' and part-time', which prevents a long-run assessment.

39 DST Committee of Management Minutes, 18 July and 21 November 2002, TGWU news releases, 5 and 19 July 2002, Wray, industrial factsheet, 12 July 2002, DST; *The*

Times, 6 July 2002, p.14, *Independent on Sunday*, 14 July 2002, p.7, *Morning Star*, 17 August 2002, p.7.

40 Crawford-tenants, 24 October 1994, DST Committee of Management Minutes, 26 July and 24 November 1994 and 3 February 1998, DST. The estimated cost was £1.6m.

41 This followed numerous interruptions to the supply of heat in 1995–6: DST Committee of Management Minutes, 28 March 1996, DST. The contract with the Council was terminated in October 1998.

42 See statements in DST, *R & A, 1993/4–2002/3*.The croquet lawn was added in July 1993; the number of squash courts was reduced to five in 1997/8; communal satellite TV was replaced by cable TV in 1995.

43 DST Committee of Management Minutes, 28 March 1996, DST. The conference centre made a surplus of £25,000, the business centre a loss of £9,000, while the garage broke even.

44 Offices were let to Cliden Construction, The Sugar Bureau, Genever & Partners, The Entertainments Agents Association, and the NTL Group, among others.

45 DST Committee of Management Minutes, 26 January and 23 November 1995, 18 July and 24 November 1996, 21 January, 25 March, 22 July and 21 November 1997, DST.

46 Ibid. 3 February and 23 July 1998.

47 For example, *Dine Online*, 3 July 1998, Hugh Fearnley-Whittingstall, *Independent*, 5 July 1998, p.49, *Evening Standard*, 7 July 1998, *Time Out* [n.d.], cuttings in DST Committee of Management Minutes, 23 July 1998, DST. The restaurant also suffered a food poisoning outbreak in 1999: DST Committee of Management Minutes, 28 January 1999, DST.

48 DST Committee of Management Minutes, 27 January 2000, 31 January 2002, DST.

49 Ibid. 22 July 1999, 27 January 2000.

50 Edelmann had spent 21 years at the Savoy.

51 Ibid. 13 February and 24 July 2003.

52 DST Committee of Management Minutes, 25 March and 24 November 1994, 26 January 1995, DST.

53 Ibid. 23 November 1995.

54 Ibid. 24 March and 21 July 2004; NCP-DST, 8 March 1991, DST. The charges included VAT.

55 Ibid. 20 July 2000, 27 March 2003.

56 See Hosken, *Nothing Like A Dame* and Dimoldenberg, *The Westminster Whistleblowers*.

57 Dimoldenberg, *The Westminster Whistleblowers*, pp.101–4.

58 Ibid. pp.104–5.

59 See Dimoldenberg, *The Westminster Whistleblowers*, esp. pp.xxi-ii, 70–1, 84–7, 106–9, 147ff., and Hosken, *Nothing Like A Dame*, esp. pp.310–12, 322–5, 358–64.

60 The decision was taken by Porter a week after the resignation of Brooke, who had opposed the move. Hosken, *Nothing Like A Dame*, pp.236–56.

61 *ES [Evening Standard Magazine]*, April 1992, pp.9–10.

62 *Evening Standard*, 12 May 1992, pp.21–2.

63 Beginning with *Evening Standard*, 29 December 1992, p.8. The flat was 402 Drake.

64 DST Committee of Management Minutes, 24 March and 27 July 1992, DST.

65 *Evening Standard*, 3 February 1993, pp.1, 3, 18 February 1993, pp.17.

66 *Daily Mail* and *Daily Telegraph*, both 4 February 1993, and see also *Daily Mail*, 8 February 1993, pp.14–15, *Private Eye*, 30 December 1994, p.7, cuttings in DST archive.

67 *Guardian*, 6 February 1993, p.25; *Evening Standard*, 3 February 1993, p.3.

68 *The Times*, 4 February 1993, p.3, diary, 15 March 1993, p.14, 6 April 1993, p.18, 7 December 1993, p.18, 7 September 1994, p.154, 13 September 1997, p.22, 13 October 1997, p.20. The origin of the 'totally naff' comment was the *Sun*, which had reported Anne's 'departure' in September 1993, giving 'nosy neighbours, noisy traffic, and the sight of hookers who ply their trade nearby' as reasons: 10 September 1993, p.7. However, Anne did not give up her flat until 1995.

69 For example, *The Times*, 17 January 1997, pp.1, 21, 27 February 1997, p.3, 10 May 1997, p.11, 27 October 1997, p.18; *Daily Mail*, 8 August 1994, p.18; *Observer*, 19 January 1997, p.5, *Guardian*, 27 February 1997, p.3. *The Times* diary also included a piece about former education minister Robin Squire's failure to be appointed as general manager: 22 January 1998, p.18.

70 Lord Jenkin-Maurice Stonefrost, 26 July [1993], DST.

71 Cf. Jane A. Ferrett (Estates Dept., Friends Provident)-Crawford, 17 November 1994, DST. Jenkin was Friends Provident's chairman until 1998.

72 Simon J. Lacey (FP Property Services)-Crawford, 2 June 1997, and DST Leasehold Interest Subcommittee report, 28 January 1999, DST.

73 Wray-Stonefrost, 23 February 1998, DST,

74 Cf. Wray-Peter Rogers (Director, Resources, WCC), 6 October 1998, DST.

75 Wray, Record of a Lunch meeting, 16 September 1998, and DST Rent Subcommittee Minutes, 30 September 1998, DST. Roots had been Chief Executive since 1991.

76 Derek Barnden (Corporate Property Controller, WCC)-Wray, 28 October 1998, enclosing strictly confidential memo. on 'Dolphin Square London, SW1', 27 October 1998, DST.

77 William Roots (Chief Executive AND Director of Finance, WCC)-Stonefrost, 10 November 1998, and reply, 17 December 1998; DST Rent Subcommittee Minutes, 24 November and 17 December 1998, DST.

78 Stonefrost-Clitherow, 22 December 1998, and Report of Leasehold Interest Subcommittee, DST Committee of Management Minutes, 28 January 1999, DST. The Subcommittee's first meeting was on 21 January 1999. It seems to have met until early 2002, when monitoring was left to extraordinary meetings of DST.

79 Richard Crouch (Charles Russell)-Wray, 27 January 1999, enclosing draft 'Note of conference with Counsel, Christopher McCall QC, on 20 January 1999', 27 January 1999, DST. The reason for the provision was unclear, but Dawtry suggested that it might have been inserted to allow time for redevelopment of the property before the end of the lease: DST Leasehold Interest Subcommittee Minutes, 26 May 1999, DST.

80 Charles Russell, Case to Advise, 23 February 1999, and Derek Wood QC, Opinion, 7 April 1999, DST.

81 Revealed at a meeting of Stonefrost, Wray, Lacey (FP) and Jupp (George Trollope), 15 September 1999: Wray, file note, 15 September 1999, DST.

82 Lacey-Stonefrost, 13 October 1999, enclosing Friends Ivory & Sime-WCC, 15 April 1999, DST.

83 Wray, file note, 15 September 1999, DST.

84 Stonefrost-Dawtry, 2 May 2008, enclosing Stonefrost, 'Dolphin Square Trust', March 2008, p.9. My thanks to Sir Alan Dawtry for this reference.

85 Agreement between WCC and DST, 31 December 1964, DST.

86 Roots-Stonefrost, 22 June and 12 July 1999, DST.

87 Stonefrost-Roots, two letters, 15 July 1999, DST. Stonefrost later recalled that neither he nor Dawtry had ever 'experienced the use of fine print in [an] agreement to pursue an

object directly contradictory to the main agreement which Westminster City Council had made itself': Stonefrost, 'Dolphin Square Trust', 2008, pp.13–14.

88 Roots-Stonefrost, 1 October 1999, and reply, 19 October 1999, DST Leasehold Interest Subcommittee Minutes, 19 October 1999, DST.

89 WCC Policy and Resources Committee Minutes, 1 November 1999, extract in Roots-Stonefrost, 2 November 1999, DST Committee of Management papers, 13 December 1999, DST.

90 *Guardian*, 5 November 1999, p.3.

91 Stonefrost, 'Dolphin Square Trust', 2008, p.14.

92 Stonefrost-tenants, 5 November 1999, and DSTA, Dolphin News, November 1999, p.1.

93 Stonefrost, 'Dolphin Square Trust', 2008, pp.10–11.

94 Stonefrost, 'Chairman's financial note', n.d., DST Committee of Management papers, 13 December 1999, DST.

95 Charles Russell-C.T. Wilson (Director of Legal Services, WCC), 9 February 2000, DST Leasehold Subcommittee Minutes, 15 February 2000.

96 On 21 February, 20 April and 4 October 2000. See papers for DST Leasehold Subcommittee meeting, 10 March, 11 July and 10 October 2000, DST.

97 Stonefrost did concede that some Dolphin Square rents fell within the 'Lillington Gardens' test and were too low. See papers for DST Leasehold Subcommittee meeting, 10 October 2000.

98 Pirie and Dawtry, statement, 21 July 2000, DST. Dawtry wrote a similar letter to Rogers on 21 May 2001.

99 On 6 November 2000, WCC's Policy and Resources Committee resolved to defer the issue of rental policy. DST Leasehold Subcommittee Minutes, 10 March and 10 October 2000; DST Committee of Management Minutes, 4 April, 12 October and 23 November 2000; Wilson (WCC)-Charles Russell, 22 September 2000, Wray-Peter Rogers (Chief Executive, WCC), 29 September 2000; Stonefrost, informal note for Deirdre Marshall and Roger Pulford, 12 July 2001, DST Committee of Management Minutes, 19 July 2001, DST.

100 Subsequently Hewitt Bacon & Woodrow.

101 *Evening Standard*, 3 February 2001, p.4, and see also Stonefrost-Marshall and Pulford, 12 July 2001, DST. The 1964 agreement had made rehousing 'those displaced by building developments in Westminster' a priority.

102 Cf. Wray-tenants, 25 October 2000, Stonefrost-tenants, 10 January and 29 June 2001, Stonefrost-Halliday, 12 September 2001, DST.

103 DSTA, Minutes of a meeting held in St. Saviour's Church Hall . . . 16 January 2001', n.d., DST. For a more critical view of the proceedings see Prebble-Wray, 17 January 2000, DST.

104 Friends Ivory & Sime Property Asset Management-WCC and DST, 23 January 2001, and supplementary letter, 16 February 2001, DST. Friends Ivory & Sime was the product of a merger of Ivory & Sime and FP Asset Management in February 1998.

105 Stonefrost-Marshall and Pulford, 12 July 2001, DST.

106 The bid was mentioned in DST Leasehold Interest Subcommittee Minutes, 7 February 2001, DST, and in *Daily Mail*, 23 October 2001, p.39.

107 WCC Policy and Resources Committee Minutes, 30 April 2001, extract copied to tenants in Stonefrost-tenants, 16 May 2001, DST.

108 DST Committee of Management papers, 19 September 2001, DST.

109 Ann McAllister QC, Opinion, 5 June 2001, DST Committee of Management papers, 19

July 2001, DST. The underlease made no reference to a hotel ('the lessee will not use or permit to be used the said demised premises or any part thereof otherwise than as high class residential flats with garages shops a restaurant swimming pool recreation ground tennis and squash courts'). Sale of alcohol was only permitted in the restaurant. Underlease, 31 December 1964, DST.

110 Wray-Stephan Miles-Brown (Knight Frank), 19 June 2001, DST Leasehold Interest Subcommittee Minutes, 11 July and 13 September 2001, DST. Wray told Knight Frank to 'consider every angle to make our assets "sweat"'.

111 Wray, 'Record of a meeting . . . on 25 September 2001', 26 September 2001, DST.

112 Michael Briggs QC and Ann McAllister QC, Opinion, 12 October 2001, Stonefrost-Rogers, 15 November 2001, DST Committee of Management Minutes, 19 September, 31 October and 22 November 2001, DST.

113 Paul Herrington (MD, Friends Ivory & Sime)-Stonefrost, 15 November and 6 December 2001, Wray, 'Record of a meeting with Friends Provident . . . 29 November 2001', 3 December 2001, DST Committee of Management papers, 12 December 2001, Stonefrost-tenants, 20 December 2001, Brooke-tenants, 25 January 2002, DST.

114 Cf. the discussion in DST Committee of Management Minutes, 12 December 2001, DST.

115 Herrington-Brooke, 11 January 2002, DST.

116 DST Committee of Management Minutes, 15 January 2002, Brooke-tenants, 17 and 25 January 2002, DST. The £15m bid included £3.5m for the mortgage. WCC did not feel the mortgage repayment should be included in the calculation, but the provision of 50 key workers flats had an NPV of £5.5m, making the package worth £17.0m excluding the mortgage.

117 Wray, 'Record of a meeting [DST and WCC] . . . 29 January 2002', 30 January 2002, DST.

118 Martyn Chappell (Allied Commercial consortium)-Wray, 18 December 2001 and 5 February 2002, Minutes of Dolphin Square Trust Ltd. meeting with tenants, 7 February 2002, Brooke-tenants, 26 March 2002, DST; *Sunday Telegraph*, 31 March 2002, p.O2, 14 April 2002, p.O2.

119 Herrington-Brooke and Rogers, 9 April 2002, DST.

120 MORI, 'The Future of Dolphin Square', August 2002, DST; DST Committee of Management Minutes, 15 May and 18 July 2002, Brooke-tenants, 26 March and 30 May 2002, Milton-tenants, 1 October 2002, DST. Of 1,068 tenants polled, 619 replied; 43% preferred the Friends Provident proposals, but 48% preferred a continuation of the status quo.

121 It should be noted that Friends Provident's offer did not promise existing tenants security of tenure of the flats they were currently occupying.

122 Brooke-tenants, 23 September 2002, 2 April and 14 May 2003, DST Committee of Management Minutes, 10 July, 18 September and 21 November 2002, 13 February 2003, DST.

123 Simon Milton (Leader, WCC)-tenants, 1 February and 1 October 2002, 10 April 2003, Meeting between Brooke and Milton, 30 October 2002, DST Committee of Management Minutes, 21 November 2002; Brooke, opening remarks to DSTA Committee, 26 March 2003, DST.

124 Barnden, Memo. on 'Potential Ring-fenced Fund for Affordable Housing', April 2003, DST.

125 Wray, 'Minutes of a Tripartite Meeting . . . 15 October 2002', 12 November 2002, DST Committee of Management papers, 21 November 2002, DST. ISIS Asset Management was formed after the merger of Friends Ivory & Sime with the Royal Sun Alliance's funds subsidiary in July 2002.

126 Cf. Milton-tenants, 1 October 2002, Lacey-Milton and Brooke, 7 March 2003, and Barnden-Rogers et al., 29 September 2003, DST.

127 DST Committee of Management Minutes, 15 May 2002, 27 March 2003, DST. The Trust's calculation was based on 31 years @ full market rents, the Council's calculation on an extrapolation of existing rents.

128 Ibid. 10 July and 18 September 2002, 27 March 2003, Brooke-tenants, 10 September 2003, DST. Peter Darvall of Civic Asset Partnerships was a Dolphin Square resident (Howard).

129 Milton and Brooke, joint statement, 5 November 2003, DST Committee of Management papers, 27 November 2003, DST.

130 Martyn Chappell (now representing Cadbury Consortium)-Ken Livingstone (Major of London), 3 October 2003, copied to Milton, 11 November 2003, Milton-tenants, 18 December 2003, DST Committee of Management Minutes, 27 November 2003, Brooke-tenants, 16 December 2003, DST; DST, *R & A 2002/3*, p.4. Chappell's letter referred to an offer of 'over £200m' for the leases, made in March 2003.

131 Christopher Lockhart-Mummery QC and Tim Mould (Charles Russell), Opinion, 4 July 2003; DST Committee of Management papers, 21 January 2004, DST.

132 There were 504 replies, with 49% stating a preference for Option A, 28% for Option B.

133 'Notes of a meeting between shortlist of bidders . . . 28 July 2004', DST Committee of Management Minutes, 31 July 2004; Knight Frank-DST, 6 August 2004, DST. The rejected bids were from Olympian Homes, ISIS Property Asset Management, Cooper Group, First Westminster Estates (Cadbury Consortium), Dorrington, Owengate Securities, Dolphin Square Resident's Consortium, and Dolphin Square Consortium.

134 The size of the bids was complicated by the fact that tenants' choice of A or B would determine the eventual cost of the bid. But the parameters of the Option A and B bids ranged from £190.5–211.5m and £170–191m.

135 Cf. the discussion in DST Committee of Management Minutes, 24 February 2005, DST.

136 On Lander's concerns about having been bounced into a shortlist with key elements of Option A and Option B remaining unresolved, see Lander-Brooke et al., 2 August 2004, DST.

137 Chairman's opening remarks and discussion, DST Committee of Management Minutes, 9 August 2004, DST. Nomura had been added to the original shortlist of three on the recommendation of WCC's legal advisers.

138 Ibid. 13 September 2004, DST.

139 WCC Cabinet minutes, 20 September 2004; Brooke-tenants, 21 and 22 September 2004; Minutes of Dolphin Square Tenants' Meeting, 27 October 2004, DST.

140 Cf. Halliday-Brooke, 23 October 2002 and 8 January 2003, Lacey-Halliday, 7 February 2003, Halliday-tenants, 11 February and 6 May 2003, Halliday-Milton, 15 April 2003 and reply, 28 April 2003, Lacey-Halliday, 3 June 2003, DST.

141 See Dolphin Square Residents Consortium bid, and *Westminster and Pimlico News*, 5 August 2004, p.3; SOS circular, 21 September 2004, DST. There was also embarrassment when SOS asked to see a copy of the minister's letter consenting to the setting up of DST in 1964. The letter could not be found, though as we have seen, his consent was conveyed by a civil servant: DST Committee of Management Minutes, 16 December 2004, DST, and see Chapter 4, above, p.164, note 141.

142 Cf. Minutes of Dolphin Square Tenants' Meeting, 27 October 2004, DST.

143 Ibid.

144 Cf. Ibid. 14 July 2005.

145 Celia Scott (SOS)-Lindsey Homer (Office of the Local Government Ombudsman), 23 June 2005, DST, and *Evening Standard*, 18 September 2006, p.9.

146 Cf. Milton-Brooke, Halliday and Herrington, 30 October 2002, Halliday-Brooke, 8 January 2003 (circulated to tenants), Halliday-tenants, 11 February 2003 and refutation in Brooke-tenants, 20 February 2003, Brooke, remarks to Dolphin Square Tenants Meeting, QEII Centre, 14 February 2004, DST.

147 For example, Lucy Barnard and Mira Bar-Hillel, in *Estates Gazette*, 16 February 2002, p.52, 21 February 2004, p.48; Edward Simpkins, in *Sunday Telegraph*, 17 November 2002, p.O2, 31 August 2003, p.O2. See also Bar-Hillel-DST, 27 January 2002 (email); Valentine Low, *Evening Standard*, 7 February 2002, p.23, Catherine Moye, *Daily Telegraph*, 5 July 2003, p.P9, Tim Walker, *Sunday Telegraph*, 16 May 2004, p.34. The press also exploited strike action by T&GWU members in July 2002. See Wray-tenants, 9 July 2002, DST.

148 DST Committee of Management Minutes, 18 October 2004; Mark Donnor and Jeffrey Caplin, remarks to Dolphin Square Tenants' Meeting, 27 October 2004, DST.

149 DST Committee of Management Minutes, 18 October 2004–10 January 2006, and WCC Cabinet minutes, 21 February 2005, DST.

150 Lander-Wray, 7 December 2004, Donnor-Wray and Rogers, 21 December 2004, DST Committee of Management Minutes, 8 and 23 December 2004, DST. There was a further scare when Rosemary Henley, a Nelson tenant, sent Brooke an item from the *Wall Street Journal* of 10 March 2004 which alleged that Westbrook had walked away from a deal, an allegation that was refuted by Donnor: Henley-Brooke, 17 March 2005, and Donnor-Brooke, 23 March 2005, DST.

151 Total costs were likely to reach £1.5m, of which DST's share would be £400,000. Ibid. 25 November 2004.

152 Ibid. 21 January, 11 November and 1 December 2004, 20 and 26 January 2005; Herbert Smith, Settlement Agreement, 21 January 2005, and WCC Cabinet minutes, 21 February 2005, DST; DST, *R & A 2003/4*, p.4.

153 Tenants were assured in 1991 that the DST'S current policy on succession rights would continue, viz. that they would apply to 'the surviving spouse, or close relative living in the flat for the previous twelve months'. Prendergast-tenants, 15 July 1991, and see also Peter Elliot (Charles Russell)-Wray, 28 June 2005, DST.

154 Donnor-Rogers and Brooke, 11 July 2005, DST Committee of Management Minutes, 14 July 2005, Elliot, note, 19 July 2005, DST.

155 Elliot, note, 19 July 2005, DST.

156 Westbrook Partners, Heads of Terms, 22 April 2005, DST.

157 WCC, DST, Tannenberg, Westbrook Dolphin Square, Mantilla Holdings, Westbrook Acquisitions and Dolphin Square 2005, Agreement for Sale, 9 September 2005, amended by further agreement, 18 November 2005 (consequent on a revised offer and refund for 126 rent-adjusted tenants), DST; DST, *R & A 2004/5*, pp.5–6, *2005/6*, pp.5–6, 12.

158 Lander, statement, 26 January 2005, Lander-Brooke, 6 July 2005 (email), Lander-Wray et al., 25 August 2005 (email), and DST Committee of Management Minutes, 20 and 26 January, 3 February, 3 March, 7 and 28 April and 5 and 26 May 2005, DST.

159 Eleven tenants had died or failed to respond.

160 Forsters-Charles Russell, 9 January 2006; Wray, report, DST Committee of Management Minutes, 26 January 2006, DST.

161 Brooke-tenants, 5 August 2005, DST.

162 Dolphin Square 2005, Register of Directors, 9 August 2005, Extraordinary GM Minutes, 9 March 2006.

163 DST, *R & A 2009/10*, p.3.

164 WCC Cabinet minutes, 21 February 2005, DST Committee of Management Minutes, 3 and 24 February, 3 and 21 March 2005, etc.

165 Ibid. 20 July 2005; Articles of Association of Dolphin Square Charitable Trustee, 19 April 2005, DST; *Local Government Chronicle*, 10 January 2006.

166 DST Committee of Management Minutes, 6 January 2005, DST.

167 From October 1999 to 31 August 2006 legal and professional fees for all purposes amounted to £7.1m, with £2.9m spent in the 11 months to 31 August 2005, and £1.6m in the following year: DST, *R & A 1999/2000–2005/6*.

168 Lord Russell-Johnston (Chairman, DSTA)-Brooke, 16 June and 13 July 2005; DSTA, 'Tenant Times' (July 2005); Brooke-tenants, 21 July, Russell-Johnston-Brooke, 22 July and 20 August, and Russell-Johnston-tenants, 25 July, Brooke-Russell-Johnston, 5 and 26 July 2005, DST. See also Andrew Probert (tenant)-Brooke, 27 July 2004 [sic: 2005], DST.

169 DST, Rule 2, 4 June 1964, Rule 2, 27 February 1992, Rule 2, 16 December 2004, DST.

170 Henley-Brooke, 17 April 2005 and reply, 19 April 2005 (see Appendix 12). See also Probert-Brooke, 19 April 2005, Henley-Brooke, 25 April 2005 and reply, 4 May 2005, DST.

171 Russell-Johnston-Brooke, 29 August 2005, a response to Brooke-Russell-Johnston, 26 August 2005, DST (see Appendix 12). Russell-Johnston, Scott, Henley, Probert and Pami Preller resigned from the DSTA in October 2005.

172 Brooke-Henley, 14 and 19 April 2005, Note of Conference with Counsel, Christopher McCall QC, 20 January 1999, with McCall's annotations, 27 January 1999, DST; Interview with Brooke, 2012.

CHAPTER 7

LIVING IN THE SQUARE, C. 1960–2010

THE RESIDENTS, REAL AND IMAGINED

In the early 1960s Dolphin Square was a vibrant, not to say 'edgy', place to live, as the activities of some of its residents indicated. The actress, Sarah Churchill (daughter of Sir Winston) recalled in her autobiography how she used her earnings from a part in *Peter Pan* to take a flat in Dolphin Square.[1] She was already acquainted with the place, since her first husband, Vic Oliver, had lived there after their divorce in 1945:

> These were indeed lively times for me. It was then that I got to know April Ashley.[2] I had met her for lunch in parties before her operation and she joined us in Dolphin Square after undergoing her sex-change operation in Casablanca - the only place in those days where this emotionally and physically delicate operation was available. We tried to support and protect April against the press and sometimes from her own more exuberant follies.

Sarah's own outrageous behaviour, fuelled by drink, led to her being remanded to Holloway Prison in July 1961 after being found drunk and disorderly in Lupus Street.

As she recalled: 'I was already on probation after a series of mishaps ending in court . . . Dolphin Square was my chosen retreat and I would choose to take my midnight prowls mostly up and down along the river.'[3] In the following September the Dolphin Square management was granted an injunction restraining her from throwing bottles and leaving broken bottles in the common parts of the Square. She left in early October.[4]

The exploits of Mandy Rice-Davies and Christine Keeler also embraced Dolphin Square for a brief period. The two women became notorious in the 1960s following the resignation of John Profumo as Secretary of

State for War and the suicide of Dr Stephen Ward in 1963, in a heady mix of sex, lies, drugs, espionage, violence, race, hypocrisy and class.[5] Profumo was briefly one of the more respectable of Keeler's lovers, but it was her troubled relationship with the Jamaican singer and drug dealer Aloysius 'Lucky' Gordon that reached its final denouement in Pimlico. The circumstances are recalled in each of Keeler's autobiographies.[6] She explains how Rice-Davies invited Keeler to move in with her in Dolphin Square, presumably sometime in early 1962. Mandy had gone there after a row with her boyfriend, Peter Rachman, the notorious London landlord, using money which he had given her to pay for the rental.[7] While Rice-Davies soon went back to Rachman, Keeler, who was pregnant, stayed on at Dolphin Square and had an abortion. Her departure from the Square followed a chance meeting with Gordon. Keeler invited him back to her flat, whereupon he terrified her and a female friend by brandishing an axe. She recalls how he assaulted and raped her, keeping her and a friend prisoner in the flat for two days. Eventually the police were called and Gordon was charged with grievous bodily harm. Keeler contends that she dropped the charges after an appeal from Gordon's brother, but Gordon persisted in stalking her at the Square and she fled.[8] It is difficult to find corroboration of this account, especially since her subsequent testimonies carried with them an element of doubt. After a further incident involving Gordon, this time in 1963, Keeler admitted perjury and was sentenced to nine months' imprisonment.[9] We certainly know that she swam in the pool in Cliveden, home of Lord and Lady Astor, where she first met Profumo;[10] whether she ever swam in Dolphin Square's pool is not documented.

Topping the list of Dolphin Square's notorious 1960s residents was John Vassall, an assistant private secretary at the Admiralty, who lived in some style at 807 Hood House from 1959 until his arrest for spying for the Russians in September 1962. The Vassall and Keeler cases were linked because the media, which had been effectively intimidated during the deliberations of the Vassall Tribunal, exacted its revenge on the establishment when details of the 'Profumo affair' began to surface.[11] Its unlikely accomplice was the Labour MP for Dudley, George Wigg. When rumours about Keeler's simultaneous affairs with Profumo and Yevgeni 'Eugene' Ivanov, a Soviet naval attaché and GRU officer, began to circulate,[12] Wigg raised the matter in the Commons during a debate in which concern was expressed about the imprisonment of two journalists for failing to disclose their sources to the Vassall Tribunal. Clearly intent on pursuing Profumo for a perceived deception over army conditions in Kuwait, he used parliamentary privilege to put the allegations about the Keeler/Profumo affair into the public domain.[13] Here he was supported by Barbara Castle, who referred to Keeler as 'the missing "call girl"'.[14] As for the Vassall case, it placed Dolphin Square at centre stage in much the same way as Maxwell Knight had done during the Kent-Wolkoff trial and the internment of Oswald Mosley in 1940. In particular, it indicated how an expensive way of life, inappropriate for a relatively junior civil servant on a modest income, could be enjoyed without attracting attention for some time. Whether Vassall could or should have been detected earlier is a matter for debate. Much of the subsequent criticism of the authorities was being wise after the event, though at least one of his former employers felt that he 'had always seemed to have very much more money than he would expect the normal Admiralty clerk to have'.[15] On the other hand, it was difficult to suspect an urbane and relatively sophisticated man with a love of 'classical music, model railways and theatre going'.[16]

John Vassall moved into Dolphin Square in February 1959. He had originally wanted a studio flat, but there was a long waiting list, and he was willing to consider something larger. He was subsequently offered, and accepted, a seven-year lease on a two-room flat on the 8th floor of Hood House overlooking the gardens. The rent, with maintenance and service charges but exclusive of rates, was £358 a year. As Gerald Rhodes, general manager, and Eve Parsons, the lettings manager, revealed in their evidence to Lord Radcliffe's Tribunal of Inquiry, Dolphin Square customarily obtained references for prospective tenants from an applicant's bank, solicitor, previous landlord, and a personal referee. Employers were only approached in exceptional circumstances, and the Admiralty was not contacted. Three satisfactory references were obtained for Vassall, from his bank, solicitors, and doctor. No landlord was written to because he was living with his parents.[17] It is evident that Vassall was living well beyond his visible means. His net annual salary was £673 in 1959 and £700 in 1961, but his minimum outgoings were at least twice that while he was living in Dolphin Square – £1,750 in 1959 and £1,250 in 1961.[18] He spent 18 months in furnishing and decorating his flat, which he clearly loved.[19] Further indulgences included clothes – comprising three dozen expensive suits – and foreign holidays. Vassall had been recruited by the KGB in 1956 and it was some time before he was caught. Although there had been suspicions for some time that someone recruited in Moscow was spying for the Russians, it was not until August 1962 that Vassall emerged as the principal suspect.[20] His flat was searched on 12 September and cameras and copies of documents were discovered. He was found guilty of espionage and sentenced to 18 years' imprisonment. The release from his agreement at Dolphin Square was obtained with effect from 1 December 1962.[21] Much was made of his homosexuality at a time when this was still regarded as a scandalous vice. However, as David Leitch put it, 'Vassall was accused at his trial of 'selling his country for lust and greed'. But his real downfall was a pernicious and now largely extinct English vice: that wistful Pooterish aspiration to being a gentleman, or at least being mistaken for one.'[22]

A rather unsavoury by-product of the Vassall case was the allegation, erroneous as it turned out, that the spy had had an inappropriate relationship with his former boss, Tam Galbraith, Conservative MP for Glasgow Hillhead, and Civil Lord of the Admiralty, 1957–9, which may have worked against his discovery. It emerged in the course of the inquiry that Galbraith and his wife had once visited Vassall's flat in Dolphin Square, although in his statements Galbraith was anxious to both play down the significance of the visit, and refute any suggestion that he could have been aware that his employee was living beyond his means. However, there was a family connexion. Galbraith's father, Commander T.D. Galbraith, MP for Glasgow Pollok, 1940–55 and subsequently Lord Strathclyde, had been a tenant since the war, first in Frobisher House, then in Nelson House.[23] As his son explained to the Minister of Defence in 1962, 'I had no idea what the cost of a flat in Dolphin Square was. My father who has lived there ever since the Blitz has always said it is cheap and rather slummy, but perhaps these are relative terms.'[24]

This was not an end to Dolphin Square's connections with allegations of spying. In 1968, Niall MacDermot resigned from Wilson's Labour Government 'for personal reasons' – he had been Financial Secretary at the Treasury from 1964 to 1967, and was at the time Minister of State in the Ministry of Housing and Local Government. MacDermot left politics altogether two years later, went to live in Geneva, and served as Secretary-General of the International Commission of Jurists from 1970 to 1990. The reasons for the departure of this extremely able politician were something of a mystery at the time. However, twenty years later he told the *Observer* that he had become disillusioned when his political trustworthiness was challenged and, in particular, when his Russian-born second wife, Ludmila Benvenuto, was interrogated by MI5. In the course of a long article it emerged that the couple were living in the Square, in Beatty House, when the week-long interrogations were conducted. Certainly, MacDermot had been engaged in intelligence work during the war, and MI5 appears to have felt that there were reasons for doubting his reliability. But some of his colleagues in the Labour Party tell a different tale, and in 1996 his obituarist, Tam Dalyell, suggested that there was something of a scandal in 1966 when MacDermot divorced his first wife, Violet Maxwell, and married his Russian-Italian lover.[25] The defection of KGB archivist Vasili Mitrokhin in 1992 led to the allegation that another Dolphin Square tenant, Raymond Fletcher, had once passed nuclear secrets to Moscow. Fletcher, Labour MP for Ilkeston from 1964 to 1983, was briefly PPS to Roy Mason, Minister for Defence Equipment, in 1967. In 1974, he took up the tenancy of 304 Frobisher House.[26] Mitrokhin's notes indicate that Fletcher (codename: PETER) was recruited in 1962 before he entered the Commons, when as a journalist he was an outspoken critic of Britain's nuclear deterrent. He subsequently acted for the Czechs as well as the Russians. However, the evidence suggests that Fletcher had ceased contact with the East before he moved into the Square.[27] Finally, in 1983 the *Observer* revealed that an MI6 mole had infiltrated the Soviet trade delegation, when a team of double-glazers were hired. It was pointed out that the mole had met his 'minders' in a rented room in Dolphin Square.[28]

From the start, Dolphin Square attracted literary representations, either by residents or by others familiar with the place. One of the first was a novel written by the actress and playwright Joan Morgan. In *Citizen of Westminster* (1940), she apparently based many of her characters on people she had met in Dolphin Square while living in 305 Collingwood House. Her depiction of 'Borlase House', and the characters Roger Borlase, Adrian van Rijn, Pamela Thurlmere and Gay Mansfield may have been reminiscent of the Square and its tenants, but the association was at best oblique.[29] However, the best-known depiction is in A.N. Wilson's first novel, *The Sweets of Pimlico*, published in 1977, which contains several scenes set in a thinly-disguised 'Fish Square'. We are quickly introduced to 'Baron Dietrich Gormann', known as Theo Gormann, of 98 Kempenfelt House, Fish Square, a charismatic German gentleman. When the heroine Evelyn Tradescant first visits Gormann in the Square,

> She half imagined a rococo *schloss*, set back from pools where dolphins gambolled with mermaids and sea-horses . . . [But] It had the air of having been modern in the late thirties. Now, it seemed simply big; something between a colossal office-block and a hospital. It was not a square at all; it was a cube. The whole of a block, from street-corner to street-corner, was taken up with this solid complex of buildings. There were a number of different entrances, all barred by automatic traffic barriers . . . At the front, and in the very centre, a neon sign advertised the presence of a restaurant and sports club. Other entrances bore the names of famous admirals; there was a Drake, a Rodney, an Anson, an Effingham, and so on . . . Inside, it was rather like an hotel . . . Carpeted corridors, all blue and decorated with fish, led off in every direction to doors with numbers on them. There were no windows in the corridors, so that, however high one rose in the building, it felt subterranean. It was the perfect setting for a life of total anonymity . . . Perhaps the whole Nazi leadership, rather than dead or in South America, were discreetly pottering about the carpeted recesses of Fish Square, paying their rent and giving offence to no one.[30]

Dolphin Square's reputation for anonymity was recently confirmed by Margaret Drabble, in her biography of another resident, Angus Wilson. She wrote: 'It was and is inhabited by a wide range of characters – diplomats, politicians, conmen, artists, spies, call girls, minor royals, and many others with a good reason to wish for trouble-free, well-run anonymity.'[31] Wilson managed to contrive Dolphinesque references to both Christine Keeler and Mantilla in his Pimlico novel: '"I remember a charming little woman called Christine . . . We called her the Blessed Virgin Keeler . . . [She] used to arrive on a Sunday morning, clutching a mantilla and off they went to High Mass at Westminster Cathedral." '[32] Wilson also included an anecdote about Dolphin Square in his biography of John Betjeman, Poet Laureate from 1972 to 1984. Betjeman's 'old mentor', the Revd A.F. 'Freddy' Hood, lived in Dolphin Square, in Rodney House. He had been priest of St. Mary Aldermary, 1954–61 and then a canon of St. Paul's, until 1970. In 1975, he was reported to be close to death, and Betjeman decided to pay him a call. He was asked to stay for lunch, and went down to the restaurant with Canon John Lucas, vicar of St. Thomas's, Oxford. 'As they entered the modernistic restaurant, the Poet Laureate said, "Oh dear, is this what Purgatory is going to be like?" '[33]

Novelists have made more recent references to Dolphin Square. In *Hung Parliament*, a thriller written in the early 1990s by Conservative MP Julian Critchley, the central character was placed in Dolphin Square. Emma Kerr, MP for 'Corve Dale' and the Conservative Party's 'piece of crumpet', 'lived during the week on the river at Dolphin Square in a small flat paid for by her Parliamentary London Allowance'.[34] There are several references to the flat being used to entertain MPs with whom she was having an affair:

> Emma's tiny flat in Dolphin Square was proximate, warm and soundproofed. It was as well that the walls were thick, for Emma was a noisy lover, much given to loud laughter, shouts of ecstasy and cries of encouragement . . . However, the flat was not ideal for their purposes. Dolphin Square, with its swimming pool and pool-side restaurant, was a weekday 'home' for at least twelve[35] other MPs, three of whom, including Peter Worthington Evans, lived in Beatty block.[36]

And the risqué character of the Square continues to be portrayed. In *The Blue Book*, A.L. Kennedy described it as 'the nest of scrimping aristos, MPs and spies and shaggers, singles and nutters and incognitos'.[37] And Martina Cole's crime novel, *Maura's Game*, suggested that the Square was an ideal place to locate a criminal gang's safe house.[38]

The complex and its amenities have also been featured in film. The earliest seems to have been a British Pathé News item in 1938 entitled '[Dolphin Square] Should Auld Acquaintance . . .', which focused mainly on a display of synchronised swimming in the pool.[39] In the following year there was a fictional depiction in the thriller *A Window in London* (1939), directed by Herbert Mason. Here a young Michael Redgrave observes a murder in a block of flats as he passes by on a train. His wife, played by Sally Gray, is a switchboard operator. The Square appears briefly.[40] Later, the swimming pool was used in *The Sorcerers* (1967), a Boris Karloff horror film directed by Michael Reeves. The Square is also said to have been one of the locations in *Victim* (1961), directed by Basil Deardon and starring Dirk Bogarde and Sylvia Sims, which raised issues concerning homosexuality; and in *The Man Who Haunted Himself* (1970), another Basil Deardon film starring Roger Moore and Hildegard Neil.[41]

Several actors and other 'celebrities' may be added to those tenants whom we noted earlier in Chapter 3. Some of them were mentioned by Morris in his earlier history of Dolphin Square; others were referred to in newspaper and journal articles. The following certainly lived in the Square. Bebe Daniels and Ben Lyon enjoyed fame in Britain with their radio work, first with Vic Oliver in *Hi Gang!* (1940–9), and then with the sitcom *Life with the Lyons*, which ran from 1950 to 1961, transferring to television in 1955–60. They lived together in Keyes House from 1966 until Bebe died in 1971; Ben stayed on until the following year.[42] Another 'husband and wife team', Vanessa Lee and Peter Graves, were also residents. Lee appeared with Ivor Novello in several musicals; Graves was an actor specialising in musicals and comedy. He became the 8th Lord Graves, Baron of Gravesend, Co. Londonderry, in 1963. The couple lived in Nelson House.[43] Then there was Ian Bannen, the character actor, who is said to have rehearsed his lines in the basement;[44] and Katie Boyle, former film actress and television personality, who was popular with the staff and allowed to keep a small dog, contrary to her tenancy agreement.[45] (In fact, Katie had two dogs.) She was briefly a tenant while waiting to move into a new house in 1977, shortly after the death of her second husband, Greville Baylis, following an accident. As she recalled in her autobiography:

> Teresa, two dogs and I took refuge in Dolphin Square. How I ever managed to look tidy for personal appearances I'll never know. The wardrobe was too small, an ironing-board was propped up in one

> corner, and I dragged clothes, as I needed them, from suitcases piled high in another. It was during those hot summer months of total upheaval in 1977 that I decided to write my book.[46]

Morris also refers to several others living at the Square: the actress, Jill Bennett, who had an extensive career in both theatre and films, but was plagued by a stormy marriage to John Osborne;[47] Peter Finch, the film star who won a posthumous Academy Award for his role in *Network* (1976);[48] Valerie Hobson, the actress who enjoyed a successful career in films before retiring after her marriage to John Profumo in 1954;[49] Raymond Huntley, a character actor who appeared in numerous films and television programmes;[50] Stewart MacPherson, the radio presenter who enjoyed success with *Down Your Way* and *Twenty Questions*;[51] the character actor, Basil Radford;[52] and Rodney Lovick, the TV actor best known for his role in *Edward and Mrs Simpson* (1978).[53] Others had a more tenuous relationship with the Square. In her two autobiographies Barbara Windsor notes that, in the course of her somewhat tortured affair with fellow *Carry On* actor Sid James, the relationship was conducted there for a short time. Barbara and Sid were simultaneously filming *Carry On Dick* at Pinewood studios and playing in *Carry on London* at the Victoria Theatre. This gave Sid an excuse to arrange a convenient 'love-nest':

> In April 1974 Sid bought an apartment in the South of France. While his wife Val went off to set up home, he looked for a flat in London. He found what he wanted in Dolphin Square, an exclusive block of flats in Pimlico, not too far from the theatre. He said it was to save him commuting every day from Iver . . .[54] It was the perfect love-nest and I'd often stay the night there with Sid after dinner.[55]

However, the flat was given up when *Carry on London* closed in the autumn.[56] Windsor also revealed that two years earlier she had looked at the possibility of renting a flat while conducting an affair with a young lover, Thomas Powell:

> I found the most wonderful flat, in Dolphin Square, a prestigious block in Pimlico, but, even as we looked over it, I knew in my heart

> that if I found an excuse not to go ahead, I wouldn't. As fate would have it, I was given one: tenants, I was told, were not allowed dogs. That was it as far as I was concerned. If I could not have my poodle, Freddie, I did not want the flat.[57]

The list of celebrities is probably much longer, and the following have also been linked with the Square, either as tenants, or as customers of the restaurant, swimming pool and gymnasium, though corroborative evidence is elusive: the Shakespearean and popular actress Suzanne Bertish; Sir John Clements, the film actor and theatre manager, who was artistic director of the Chichester Festival Theatre, 1966–73; the *Blue Peter* presenter Christopher Trace; the TV sports presenter Dickie Davies;[58] and more tenuously, Shirley Bassey, Julie Christie, and John Cleese.[59] Very few sports stars were mentioned, but in addition to the Marquess of Exeter, mentioned earlier, in 1969 the *Observer* revealed that the tennis player Rod Laver stayed in Dolphin Square, presumably in Rodney House, while competing at Wimbledon, and a number of athletes made use of the sports facilities and the pool, including the swimmer Linda Ludgrove, who was the daughter of the Square's swimming instructor, Bill Ludgrove.[60] What is certain is that the residents included Denis Kavanagh, a film director and producer who lived in Duncan House in the early 1950s. His films included *Starlight Serenade* (1944), *Return to the Desert* (1956) and *Rock You Sinners* (1958).[61] And there was Sean Mathias, the actor, who moved into Raleigh House when a young man in 1978. He went on to forge a successful career as a theatre and film director, notably in collaboration with Sir Ian McKellen. He produced and directed the film *Bent* (1997), and his theatre work has included National Theatre productions of *Uncle Vanya* (1992), *A Little Night Music* (1995) and *Anthony and Cleopatra* (1998).[62] And the oldest of the old stagers was Ray Rockman, real name Ray Braham, who celebrated her 100th birthday in Hawkins House in 1965. Ray, an American, had a brief acting career at the turn of the 20th century. She went to Paris to act with Sarah Bernhardt, and later returned to London to join Sir Henry Irving's theatre company.[63]

Royal personages and aristocrats have also figured in the life of the Square. According to Morris, Princess Margrethe, Queen Margrethe II of Denmark since 1972, stayed in the Square before her marriage to Henri,

Comte de Laborde de Monpezat in 1967. Two nieces of the Duke of Edinburgh, were also briefly and discreetly residents.[64] We have already referred to Princess Anne's arrival in 1993 (Chapter 6). Contrary to media speculation, it seems she was perfectly happy with her flat in Dolphin Square and moved only when her husband, Captain (later Vice Admiral) Timothy Laurence, left his job at the Admiralty to take command of the frigate HMS Cumberland in 1995. Notable among the sprinkling of aristocrats resident in the Square was Victor Hervey, the 6th Marquess of Bristol (Nelson House), who abandoned a wild and sometimes criminal way of life when young - he was known as 'Mayfair Playboy No.1' - to become a broker and businessman with interests in East Anglia and Dominica. His son John, the Earl Jermyn, also resided in Dolphin Square for a brief time. In the early 1970s he rented a flat in Hood House while still a teenager. One of his business associates recalled that it was 'utilitarian and non-palatial . . . [with] a white plastic framed mirror and white Lucite drinks trays'.[65] His subsequent profligacy, alcoholism and drug addiction eventually led him to give up the final lease on the family estate at Ickworth to the National Trust in 1998.[66] Other aristocrats included the 3rd Lord Greenway, the left-wing 5th Lord Monkswell, and the 4th Lord Mottistone, last Governor of the Isle of Wight.[67] There have also been a number of hereditary peers engaged in political work, such as Lord Belhaven and Stenton, Baron Glenarthur, a minister in the Scottish and Foreign offices, 1986-9, and Viscount Ullswater, an environment minister in 1994-5.[68] Finally, two Nigerian chiefs were once residents: Godfrey Amachree, a lawyer and former under-secretary at the United Nations, and Shafi Lawal Edu, a prominent businessman.[69]

'Commoner'-tenants attracting our attention include Charlotte Hurst, who in the late 1960s led a vigorous campaign for the restoration of the death penalty from her flat in Collingwood House, in association with Athlene O'Connell and Jane Hitchcock. The three women responded to the murder of three policemen in Shepherd's Bush in 1966 by obtaining more than a million signatures to a petition presented to the Commons by former cabinet minister Duncan Sandys in December 1969. But the attempt to reintroduce capital punishment failed, and on a free vote the two Houses voted for its permanent abolition.[70] In 1963, it was announced that Princess Anne was to be sent to Benenden School, the prestigious public school for girls. Two of its founders, Miss Christine

Sheldon and Miss Kathleen Bird, were then photographed in their Collingwood House flat for the *Observer*. The occasion coincided with the school's 40th anniversary. Started in 1923 by three teachers from Wycombe Abbey School, the new institution moved to Hemstead Park in Kent in 1924 and was renamed Benenden. The founders retired in 1954.[71] Penelope Turing, like Ida Cook (above, p.115) was an expert on opera and lived in 411 Beatty House from 1966. She had the distinction of having attended every Bayreuth Wagner festival from 1952 until 2008, a year before her death. She wrote a number of books, including the influential *New Bayreuth* (1969), and a biography of the German opera singer Hans Hotter (1983).[72] Robert Musel was an American journalist for United Press who spent most of his life in London. He was also a successful popular songwriter, well known for *Pappa Piccolino* and *Band of Gold*. He lived in the Square from 1949 to 1999.[73] Edward (Michael) Seymour-Rouse first lived in Keyes House in 1972, when working for the RSPCA as its Publicity and Appeals Officer. He went on to have a distinguished career as a campaigner for animal welfare, winning the Albert Schweitzer Medal in 1999 for securing a ban on leghold traps in the European Union.[74] Finally, one of the enduring tenants is Dicky Rutnagur, the distinguished Indian cricket correspondent, who wrote for the *Daily Telegraph* for many years. He has lived in Dolphin Square since 1966.[75]

THE POLITICAL CONNECTION

Since the letting policy of Dolphin Square was aimed at persons of working age without London homes who were employed full-time in central London, MPs and active members of the House of Lords were obvious candidates. The evidence suggests that as the life of parliamentarians became more arduous, and, after the select committee reforms of 1979, more professional – though there was still some distance to go[76] – it became more important than ever to be close to Westminster. Those members with seats which were a considerable distance from London, for example, in Scotland, predominated. Improved parliamentary allowances also encouraged more MPs to obtain a second home in London. Thus, increasing numbers took up flats, though the turnover rate was often high, given the vicissitudes of the electoral process. The Westminster rate book for 1980/1 indicates that 38 MPs were then in residence, together with a handful of working peers. The Dolphin Square listings are more complete. That for 1987 identifies 53 MPs, 18 peers, and a Conservative MEP. The highest number of MPs recorded was 63 in 1998, though by 2005 this had fallen to 45. The reason for this decline is not clear. Changes in the treatment of expenses, which allowed MPs to claim for mortgage payments on properties they were buying, may have been one factor. Uncertainty over the future of Dolphin Square is another possible explanation. The political composition of these tenants also changed over time. In 1987 and 1993 the number of Labour and Conservative MPs was roughly equal; in 1998, however, following Blair's landslide victory in 1997, there were 41 Labour MPs to only 11 Conservative. The disparity was still evident in 2005 (Table 7.1).

Table 7.1 Parliamentarians with Dolphin Square flats, 1987–2005

Date	*MPs*				*MEP*	*Lords*			
	Lab	Con	Lib/Lib Dem/ SNP	Total	Con	Lab	Con	Lib/ SDP/ Indep	Total
1987	24	23	6	53	1	8	6	3	18
1993	26	24	6	56	/	11	8	2	21
1998	41	11*	11	63	/	/	/	/	/
2005	30	7*	8	45	/	/	/	/	/

Source: DST listings of MPs, etc., n.d. [1987], 13 July 1993, 13 March 1998, 6 April 2005, DST.

* Includes Deputy Speaker

The early politician-tenants were said to include Harold Wilson, Labour Prime Minister, 1964–70 and 1974–6, and Iain Macleod, Conservative Leader of the House of Commons, 1961–3 and briefly Chancellor of the Exchequer until his death in 1970. However, substantive evidence of their residency has not been found.[77] We do know that in the 1970s Dolphin Square housed a number of MPs, some already of ministerial rank, others soon to have distinguished careers. They included the long-serving Liberal/Liberal Democrat Alan Beith (Berwick), deputy leader of the Liberals, 1985–8;[78] Gordon Campbell, Scottish Secretary, 1970–4;[79] Mark Carlisle, Education Secretary, 1979–81;[80] Dr Jack Cunningham, Labour MP for Whitehaven from 1970, and subsequently a minister;[81] Patrick Gordon Walker, Labour's Foreign Secretary, 1964–5;[82] Eric Heffer, the staunch left-wing Labour MP for Liverpool Walton and

Minister for Industry, 1974–5, who lived in Keyes House until his death in 1991;[83] Denis Howell, Labour MP for Small Heath, and a long-serving Minister for Sport;[84] Michael Mates, Conservative MP for Hampshire East since 1974, and a minister in 1992–3;[85] Sir David Steel, Liberal MP since 1965, and leader of his party from 1976 until its merger (which he orchestrated) with the Social Democrats in 1988;[86] and Dr Gavin Strang, another long-serving Labour MP and former junior minister, who represented Edinburgh East from 1970.[87] There were also three redoubtable backbenchers, Christopher Brocklebank-Fowler, Nicholas Fairbairn, and John Horam. Horam has the distinction of having sat in the Commons for three different parties.[88] Other MPs at this time included, on the Labour side, Neil Carmichael, Brynmor John, Home Office Minister, 1976–9; and for the Conservatives, Alick Buchanan-Smith. Energy Minister, 1983–7, Reginald Eyre, Neil Macfarlane, Sports Minister, 1981–5, James Scott-Hopkins, Vice-President of the European Parliament, 1976–9, Giles Shaw, and John Stradling Thomas, Minister for Wales, 1983–7.[89] Among the politicians coming into the Square in the 1980s were: Derek Foster, Labour MP for Bishop Auckland from 1979,[90] Sir George Gardiner, Conservative MP for Reigate and one of the 'Gang of Four' which secured Margaret Thatcher's election as leader;[91] Sir Russell Johnston, Liberal MP for Inverness since 1964, and soon to be deputy leader of the Liberal Democrats;[92] Bruce Millan, a Glasgow MP since 1959 and Labour's Secretary of State for Scotland, 1976–9;[93] Sir Hector Munro, Conservative MP for Dumfries since 1964, and a former junior minister;[94] and Malcolm Rifkind, Conservative MP for Edinburgh Pentlands from 1974, Secretary of State for Scotland, 1986–90, and subsequently Foreign Secretary.[95] In more recent times, the following have leased flats in the Square: Hazel Blears, Home Office Minister, 2003–6; Sir Menzies Campbell, Liberal Democrat leader, 2006–7; Alistair Darling, Chancellor of the Exchequer, 2007–10; William Hague, Leader of the Conservative Party, 1997–2001, and Foreign Secretary since 2010; Beverley Hughes, Minister for Immigration, 2002–4, and Minister for Children, 2005–9; Estelle Morris, Education Secretary, 2001–2; Dr Mo Mowlam, Labour MP for Redcar, and subsequently Secretary of State for Northern Ireland, where she oversaw the signing of the Good Friday Peace Agreement; and Sir George Young, Secretary of State for Transport, 1995–7.[96] The backbenchers included long-serving Labour MPs such as Sir Stuart Bell, David Clelland, Tom Pendry (Lord Pendry), Sir Ray Powell and Ted Rowlands (Lord Rowlands), and Conservatives such as Sir Patrick (subsequently Lord) Cormack, and another member who changed parties, Peter Temple-Morris (Lord Morris), who left the Conservatives for Labour in 1998.[97]

The Square's 'working peers' have included some notable figures, including Lords McFadzean and Shackleton. Francis Scott McFadzean was a successful businessman who transformed three great corporations – Royal Dutch Shell, British Airways, and Rolls Royce. He was managing director of Shell, 1964–76, then was knighted by Harold Wilson in 1975, and asked to take the chair of British Airways, where he presided over the integration of BEA and BOAC. Then in 1979, Margaret Thatcher persuaded him to take the helm at Rolls Royce, where he grappled with the challenging market for aircraft engines and began a much needed rationalisation drive. He was ennobled as Baron McFadzean of Kelvinside in 1980.[98] Edward Shackleton, the explorer and son of Sir Ernest, became an MP in 1946, and was Deputy Chairman of the John Lewis Partnership from 1975 to 1982. As Baron Shackleton he was a defence minister in 1964–7, Postmaster-General in 1968 and Leader of the Lords, 1968–70.[99] Another interesting peer was Michael Winstanley, a GP and Medical Officer, who combined political and sporting activity. He was Liberal MP for Cheadle, then Hazel Grove and he was also a television and radio broadcaster, cricket columnist, and Chairman of the Countryside Commission for a brief period. He attracted particular attention when, following his election in Hazel Grove in February 1974, it was discovered that his appointment as a sessional medical officer at the Royal Ordnance factory in Patricroft (Manchester) disqualified him from being elected as an MP. A bill had to be hastily introduced to retrospectively disregard this unwitting breach of the House of Commons Disqualification Act of 1957. However, Winstanley soon lost his seat at the second election in that year, in October. He was then elevated to the peerage.[100] Among their colleagues were Hamish Gray, a minister in the 1980s; Goronwy Roberts, a Labour MP who held several ministerial posts in the 1960s and 1970s; John Smith, Lord Kirkhill, a Scottish minister in the mid 1970s; Geoffrey Tordoff, an oil executive, President of the Liberal Party in 1983–4, chief whip for the Liberals and Liberal Democrats, 1984–94, and a Deputy Speaker, 1994–2008; and Ian Winterbottom, who held junior posts in the Wilson and Callaghan governments, became a founder member of the Social Democrats, and crossed the floor again to join the Conservatives in 1991.[101] More recent tenants include Julia Cumberlege, a Conservative junior health minister, 1992–7; Meghnad Desai, the LSE economist and Labour supporter who was caught up in LSE's Saif Gaddafi/Libya scandal in 2011; Jack Dormond, the hardworking Labour peer who was Chairman of the Parliamentary Party in the 1980s and when an MP cycled to the Commons from Dolphin Square; Ted Graham, a Labour Co-operative politician and the party's chief whip in the 1990s; Olive Nicol, also a Labour Co-operative politician, who was a Deputy Speaker, 1995–2002; and John Sewell, a Conservative minister for Scotland in 1997–9.[102]

At times, several floors of Dolphin Square resembled a political club such as the Carlton or the National Liberal. Often people lived adjacently, much as Julian Critchley had depicted in his novel *Hung Parliament*. Thus, there were pairings of Richard Banks (Conservative) and Jack Cunningham (Labour) on the 8th floor of Hood House, Alan Haselhurst (Conservative) and Alan Beith (Liberal) and Brynmor John (Labour) on the 3rd floor of Duncan, and Anthony Steen (Conservative) and Jack Dormond (Labour) on the 6th floor of Grenville. Labour MPs Martin Flannery and Michael McGuire were in adjacent flats in Frobisher, while on the 8th floor of Duncan House there were representatives of all three major parties: David Alton (Liberal), Tony Durrant (Conservative) and Lord Dean (Labour), and on the 7th floor of Howard three peers – Lords Belhaven, Campbell of Croy and Jenkin.[103] Mo Mowlam recalled in her autobiography that she once held a dinner party for Tony Blair and Sir Howard Davies, then Director-General of the CBI, in her 'wee', two-bedroom flat: 'There was a long discussion with Tony and Howard having different views and Jon [Norton, her husband] disagreeing with both. We were a bit short on furniture and the Blairs offered us their old kitchen table. It fitted perfectly . . .'[104]

Press coverage in relation to political residencies in the Square has been mostly silly or intrusive, or both. While some politicians such as William Hague and Mo Mowlam have been happy to admit to living there, others have not publicised the fact, either not thinking it important, or, being aware of media interest, valuing the privacy the Square may afford.[105] Inevitably, perhaps, some of the politicians have attracted gossip about their private lives. William Hague was a particular target when leader of the Conservative Party in 1997–2001. In 2000, for example, the *Evening Standard* made much of the fact that he and the recently ennobled Sebastian Coe, who was then Hague's chief of staff, were practising judo in the gym. 'This has not gone down well with Dolphin Square residents', the Londoner's diarist claimed, 'because they have recently taken to jousting without their jackets on. According to people trying to play squash nearby this week, their heaving sweaty torsos are not a pretty sight.'[106] And when Hague revealed that as a young man he had once drunk 14 pints of beer a day while working as a drayman's mate in Rotherham, the *Daily Sport* sent a 'sporty' young woman to Dolphin Square to challenge Hague to drink a yard of ale. After being ejected by security, she was photographed in rather suggestive poses outside the main entrance.[107] Notwithstanding this somewhat intrusive and unfair coverage, Hague and his wife Ffion 'thoroughly enjoyed' their time living in the Square.[108] More seriously, the unfortunate death of the backbencher Iain Mills in January 1997 produced a raft of articles about his lonely decline into alcoholism. The Conservative MP for Meriden was found dead in his flat on the ground floor of Duncan House by Derek Conway, a government whip. He had been an unobtrusive backbencher, who had entered the Commons in 1979 after working as a marketing manager for Dunlop. He was Norman Tebbit's PPS for six years, but had made no further progress up the parliamentary ladder. His death had the effect of turning John Major's Government into a minority administration and the subsequent inquest, which found that he had died of acute alcohol poisoning, raised questions in some journalists' minds as to whether Dolphin Square, with its penchant for anonymity, had in some way been partly responsible for his death. This was ridiculous, of course. The plain truth was that after he had been arrested when drunk in Great Smith Street in the previous April, none of his colleagues had done anything to try and help him.[109] Later, when MPs were placed under the microscope for their expense claims, some Dolphinites were caught up in the expenses scandal and its aftermath from 2009, including Sir Nicholas Winterton and Hazel Blears, while others who were in residence when the Square was sold to Westbrook were given the choice of either taking cash or moving to an Option B lease. Some of those who opted for the former attracted press attention, including

Andy Burnham, Beverley Hughes and Michael Mates.[110] And personal transgressions, whether silly or minor, were another area for press coverage, as many a public figure has found.

THE PROFESSIONS

If increasing numbers of politicians served to alter the 'feel' of Dolphin Square, then the numbers of military or ex-military personnel seemed to dominate the representation of the professions among the tenants. At any one time over the last 50 years, there were as many captains, majors, lieutenant-colonels, colonels and brigadiers, commanders and commodores, and rear admirals, major-generals and vice-admirals, as there were parliamentarians. For example, 84 are listed in the rate book for 1980/1.[111] Among the most senior officers there were several with distinguished war records. At the very top, the navy was represented by Admiral Sir Raymond Lygo, a pilot with the Fleet Air Arm during the war who was later commander of the aircraft carrier *Ark Royal* when it collided with a Russian destroyer in 1970. He became Vice-Chief of the Naval Staff and briefly, Acting First Sea Lord. After retirement from the navy he joined British Aerospace, and was its chief executive at the time of the Westland helicopter affair in 1986, when he was outmanoeuvred in the battle between BAe and the American firm Sikorsky for ownership of the company. Living next door to him on the 4th floor of Frobisher House in the early 1980s was Admiral Sir Peter White, a naval paymaster whose administrative skills were such that he attained the position of Chief of Fleet Support.[112] Admiral Sir James Eberle was also a tenant. He was Commander-in-Chief of Naval Home Command, and after retirement in 1983 became Director of the Royal Institute for International Affairs (Chatham House), and later Vice-Admiral of the UK.[113] The army was represented by General Sir Noel Thomas, a Royal Engineer who was awarded both the DSO and the Military Cross during the war, and became Master-General of the Ordnance; General Sir Peter Hunt, who received the DSO when commanding officer of the Seaforth Highlanders during the war and became Chief of General Staff; General Sir James Glover, Commander-in Chief of UK Land Forces, who while in Northern Ireland challenged existing perceptions about the capabilities of the IRA; and General Sir Garry Johnson, who served in Malaya and Borneo and later became Commander-in-Chief of Allied Forces Northern Europe.[114] Finally, the air force was represented by Air Chief Marshal Sir Thomas Prickett, a wartime pilot who was awarded both the DFC and the DSO, and later became Air Member for Supply and Organisation, Air Chief Marshal Sir John Barraclough, who was awarded a DFC in 1943 for his operations in the Indian Ocean, and later became Vice-Chief of the Defence Staff, and Air Secretary, and Air Chief Marshal Sir John Stacey, another fighter pilot who died prematurely while Deputy Commander-in-Chief of Allied Air Forces Central Europe.[115] Two colonels worthy of mention are John Blashford-Snell, the explorer, and Colin Mitchell. Blashford-Snell was a veteran of over 100 expeditions, including those to the Blue Nile, Darien Gap, and the Congo River; he was also a founder of the Scientific Exploration Society.[116] Mitchell enjoyed a distinguished military career in Italy, Palestine, Korea and Cyprus, but it was cut short after controversial action in Aden, where he was given the soubriquet 'Mad Mitch'; he was later Conservative MP for West Aberdeenshire.[117] In this male-dominated world, a few exceptional women may be found. One such was Commandant Elizabeth Craig-McFeely, Director of the Women's Royal Naval Service, who lived in Keyes House. Another is a current resident: Mary Ames, who was a Chief Officer in the same service.[118]

Some civil servants also elected to take a flat close to their place of work, particularly if they were engaged in onerous tasks. In the 1970s two came from the transport section of the Department of the Environment: Sir Idwal Pugh, Second Permanent Secretary, and later the Parliamentary and Health Service Ombudsman, lived in Raleigh House from 1974,[119] and Susan Fogarty, an Under-Secretary. Both were involved in the ill-fated Channel Tunnel project, on which construction had started when it was abandoned by the British Government in 1975. Fogarty, in particular, worked strenuously on the project. She rented a flat in Howard House from November 1973, and remained a resident until her death in 1983.[120] Other noted civil servants included Jean Nunn, the first woman to become a Deputy Secretary in the Cabinet Office, and whose career was cut short by illness;[121] Sir Hugh Foot, governor of Jamaica in the 1950s and the last governor of Cyprus, before becoming Lord Caradon and acting as a Junior Foreign Office Minister of Foreign Affairs and British Ambassador to the United Nations in Harold Wilson's governments;[122] Sir Anthony Parsons, ambassador to Iran in the 1970s, who played a critical role during the Falklands war while the UK's representative to the United Nations, and then acted as Margaret Thatcher's special adviser.[123] Sir William Cook was a civil servant and scientist specialising in rocket and submarine warfare, who led the nuclear programme at Aldermaston, presiding over the tests at Christmas Island in 1957. He subsequently became a member of the Atomic Energy Authority then returned to the Ministry of Defence as deputy chief scientific adviser, advising the Defence Secretary on the Tornado aircraft in the late 1960s. In retirement he was a director of Rolls Royce at a critical time, following its bankruptcy and reconstitution in 1971.[124] Sir Henry Wilson Smith was Permanent Secretary in the Ministry of Defence after the Second World War, and head of the overseas finance division of the Treasury during the convertibility and devaluation crises of 1947 and 1949. In 1951, he resigned as Second Secretary to join the board of the shipping and coal firm, Powell Duffryn. He served as its chairman from 1956 to 1969 and was also a director of the Bank of England, 1964–70, Deputy Chairman of GKN, and a part-time member of the National Coal Board.[125] Baron Upjohn was a lawyer who became a brigadier during the war, serving as legal adviser then vice president of the allied control commission in Italy. As a Law Lord he gave judgment on a number of important cases affecting property and contract law in the 1960s.[126]

Among the many other tenants from the professions and business, the following also catch the eye: Roland Bird, long-serving editor and sometime managing director of the *Economist*; Jane Bown, the celebrated photographer; Sir Charles Carter, an economist with an interest in Irish affairs, who was editor of the economic journal in the 1960s and founding Vice-Chancellor of the University of Lancaster; Dr Ian Churchill-Davidson, a distinguished radiotherapist at St. Thomas's Hospital and Richard Dimbleby's doctor; Sir Lionel Denny, a Lord Mayor of London and holder of the Military Cross and the Légion d'Honneur; Sir Roger Falk, chairman of management consultants Production-Engineering and long-serving member of the Monopolies and Mergers Commission; Sir John Lomax, Ambassador to Bolivia; Sir Ronald Mason, professor of chemistry at Sussex University and Chief Scientific Adviser to the Ministry of Defence; Sir Percy Rugg, leader of the GLC's Conservative opposition in the early 1960s; Sir Edmund Sargant, President of the Law Society; Sir Frederick Snow, a civil engineer who had worked for Cubitts, built Gatwick Airport, and fittingly for the first President of the Concrete Society, lived in a concrete building; Sir Frederick Warner, the engineer and expert on chemical risk management and nuclear safety; and Lord Wynne-Jones, Professor of physical chemistry at Newcastle University, a spokesman on scientific issues during the Wilson administrations, and active member of the North Atlantic Assembly in the 1970s.[127] The great and the good, indeed.

The Square was also home to diplomats who were housed there as a result of arrangements with specific ministries or embassies, though this practice was discontinued by the Trust. Thus, in the rate book for 1968/9, it is recorded that there were 14 'Treasury' flats, occupied by embassy officials from countries such as France, Germany, Czechoslovakia and Jordan.[128] They seem to have been given up in the early 1970s. For example, 310 Duncan House, occupied by someone from the Czechoslovak Embassy, was vacated at the end of 1972.[129] As we have seen, 'corporate lets' were prohibited by the Trust's sub-lease, and it may be that these arrangements were held on longer leases which expired.

GOOD AND BAD PUBLICITY

Whether tenants lacking celebrity status approved or disapproved of the relatively large numbers of 'famous' people living in the Square is a matter for debate. For much of the period their presence gave the flats a cachet. On the other hand, they also brought with them unwelcome attention at times, and we know that privacy and (for some) anonymity were valued features of living there. Some of the less well-known professionals were keen to play down the importance of the famous. For example, Andrew Probert, a transport policy adviser and tenant activist, who was interviewed by *The Times* in October 2004, said that while he thought the Square was 'posh' before he moved in, he felt there was in fact 'a real mix'.[130] As we have seen, the Square could attract approval and opprobrium in equal measure. The large number of 'celebrities' living there encouraged both good and bad publicity, and the increasing intrusiveness of tabloid journalism, exemplified by the success of the *Sun* and *News of the World* newspapers under Rupert Murdoch's ownership from 1969, intensified the process. The vicarious interest in the lives of celebrities and those in public life produced coverage which was both favourable and unfavourable, affecting by association public perceptions of Dolphin Square. Some examples will make this clear. Arthur Skeffington, the Labour MP for Hayes and Harlington from 1953 to 1971, was a man with a long and fairly distinguished record in the Commons. An economist and barrister, he had worked in both the Board of Trade and the Ministry of Supply during the war, and was parliamentary private secretary to two ministers in Clement Attlee's post-war government. Later he was Chairman of both the Fabian Society and the Labour Party, and a parliamentary secretary in the ministries of Land and Natural Resources and Housing and Local Government during the Wilson years. He led an inquiry into public participation in planning, which produced the Skeffington report on *People and Planning*. But in 1970 he attracted attention only when, having dined in the restaurant with friends, he was robbed while walking through the Square's gardens on his way back to his flat in Howard House.[131] Similar incidents were also faithfully reported in the press. Sexual impropriety was often hinted at, and sometimes rose to the surface. Some incidents were harmless fun, but some were more serious. For example, in 1965 three young women decided to swim naked in the pool. The police were called, and this somewhat innocuous affair led to an appearance at Bow Street Court and a £2 fine with 21s. costs for each of the swimmers on account of their 'insulting behaviour'. The critic Bernard Levin was moved to condemn this 'absurd' conviction.[132] More serious was the discovery of a brothel in the Square. In 1971, considerable newspaper coverage was given to the revelation that a Duncan House tenant, Sybil Benson, was using her flat for 'immoral purposes'. Mrs Benson had taken a three-year lease on the flat in May 1969.[133] According to the *People*, the services she offered were often sadomasochistic in nature, and the newspaper made sure its coverage was extensive, taking photographs of the madam and 'Rene' in the flat in a 'sting' operation [see Illustration 35]. It was pointed out that while Mrs Benson was paying £13 7s. 6d. a week plus £3 in rates, she was making an average of £1,260 a week from her business. Mrs Benson said that she limited the number of clients to six a day, and 'had to be careful not to annoy the neighbours – such as the "senior official of the Czech Embassy next door"'.[134] The article provoked a complaint from Sir Lionel Denny to the Dolphin Square management. Garrard, the general manager, explained that the newspaper's facts were broadly true and that the tenant had been evicted. In mitigation, he pointed out that Mrs

Benson's references had been 'impeccable', and that the nature of the property, with its many entrances and exits, made 'security virtually impossible'.[135] Sadomasochism also featured in further tabloid revelations, this time in 1990. The *Sunday Mirror* revealed that Sir Anthony Meyer, MP for Clwyd North West, had had a long-standing affair with the model and blues singer, Simone Washington. Meyer, a former Secretary of State for Employment, was already well known as an archetypal Tory 'wet', a pro-European and the 'stalking horse' who challenged Margaret Thatcher for the party leadership in 1989. The revelations about his affair followed Meyer's bid for the leadership, which resulted in Thatcher's subsequent resignation in 1990, and in Meyer's ostracism and deselection as an MP. Ms Washington, it seems, had produced a diary, which she showed to the notorious socialite and satirical writer, Willie Donaldson. Her story then appeared under the headline 'I bathed my spanking MP in champagne'.[136] It was suggested in some quarters that a flat in Dolphin Square was, as with Windsor and James, the location for some of their assignations.[137] Finally, in 2003, the press had much fun with the unfortunate experience of a peer of the realm, who met a barmaid at the Commons Sports and Social Club, showed her round the Lords and then foolishly agreed to her visiting him at his flat in Dolphin Square. A story duly appeared in the *News of the World*, which sought to hide its salacious interest in the encounter by expressing concern about parliamentary security. In a multi-page article it was alleged that the barmaid was in fact a drug-dealing prostitute. Impropriety was strongly denied by the victim, but the publicity remained a considerable embarrassment.[138]

Notoriety of a different sort came with the recent allegation that Father Michael Seed, a Franciscan friar and former ecumenical adviser to the Archbishop of Westminster, had been prepared to sell papal knighthoods to businessmen in return for charitable donations. Seed was a flamboyant figure, who had celebrated mass for the Blairs during their time in Downing Street and had been instrumental in the conversion of Conservative politicians Ann Widdecombe and John Gummer to Catholicism. The *Mail on Sunday* claimed that Seed was living rent free in a Dolphin Square flat owned by one of the papal knights whose honour he had helped to secure.[139] A much darker tale with Catholic overtones was the brief connexion between Dolphin Square and the Provisional

IRA. Feathers were clearly ruffled in Pimlico when it emerged that the IRA had used Dolphin Square as a temporary base for their first strike in England. In March 1973, four cars carrying the bombs which were used in an attack on targets in central London were parked in its garage on the night before they were planted. (This was revealed during the trial of the perpetrators in Winchester in September.) Two of the bombs, placed in cars parked at New Scotland Yard and outside the BBC's armed forces radio studio, failed to detonate and were defused. But two exploded, at the Old Bailey and outside the Army Recruiting Office in Whitehall. One man was killed and over 200 people were injured.[140]

LIFE IN THE SQUARE

For most tenants, Dolphin Square offered a pleasant and convenient home in central London. Over time many of them shared a sense of camaraderie or community spirit, which, we may suggest, attracted a 'Peter Dolphin' to rent a flat in Grenville House, or Kathleen Bird of Benenden School to call her second home in Benenden 'Dolphin Cottage'.[141] Of course, there were residents who were uninterested in their surroundings, and others who were distinctly troublesome to the Trust, as we have already noted. The management's more professional approach to letting and the fixing of rents brought with it a greater attention to the observance of the restrictive covenants attached to the three-year leases. Subletting was generally prohibited, except in limited circumstances for brief periods, and since the flats were designed for those working in central London, the existence of absentee tenants was treated more seriously as time passed (see above, p.187). Unreasonable behaviour and indebtedness provided other headaches for the management, and some tenants got into difficulties in a rather spectacular manner. One of these was Captain Leonard Plugge, whom we referred to in Chapter 3 (p.107). He is mentioned in Julian Critchley's autobiography, *Westminster Blues*, which pointed out that Captain Plugge, 'who had started Radio Luxembourg and was remembered for his lavish parties at the Dorchester', had lost his Chatham seat to Arthur Bottomley at the 1945 election.[142] This tenant, who preferred his name to be pronounced 'Plooje', attracted the attention of Dolphin Square's general manager, Garrard, in 1967, and was given notice to quit 701 Beatty House in February 1968. He was also required to vacate three basement rooms he was using in Beatty and Keyes House. It had been discovered that he had sublet 702 Beatty House, the flat next door to his and once occupied by his wife. She remained the leaseholder, but her husband was charging a married couple £25 a week. Antisocial behaviour was also cited, including numerous complaints of noise and no fewer than three incidents of causing a flood by leaving a bath unattended with the taps running. However, after receiving assurances from Captain Plugge, the Committee of Management decided to withdraw the proceedings for eviction subject to suitable undertakings being given by the tenant. But the behaviour of the Plugge family continued to give the management concern, and three flats - and three basement rooms - continued to be used, sporadically and confusingly, by Plugge, his wife, and their two sons, until matters came to a head at the end of 1970. A report from Garrard set out the management's view of events. In March of that year Captain Plugge's flat, 701 Beatty House, had been rendered uninhabitable by a serious fire, whereupon it was discovered that the electricity supply had been disconnected by the London Electricity Board for non-payment of bills. As Garrard explained, 'on about 10th April 1970 Captain Plugge left England for Mexico. He is now believed to be in California'. Mrs Plugge's tenancy of 702 Beatty House expired in March 1970, but was renewed for a further three years, notwithstanding evidence of subletting. The tenancy of the third flat, 902 Hood House, which was held in the name of Captain Plugge's eldest son Frank, expired in October 1970, but the flat was being occupied by Plugge's youngest son Greville, who had endeavoured to enter into a new lease in the summer of 1970. Matters had then been clouded by his brother's demand that *he* be granted a new lease, which in turn was affected by the revelation that he was the subject of bankruptcy proceedings. The bailiffs were also looking for Captain Plugge in relation to a debt of £475, and Garrard was certain that as soon as he returned to England he would be arrested and taken to Pentonville Prison. Further misdemeanours included a summons for a speeding offence for Frank Plugge, which was intercepted at 902 Hood House in November by his brother Greville, who claimed he was the lessee. Plugge senior made a final attempt to retain his Dolphin Square fiefdom, cabling Garrard from Beverley Hills to the effect that 'Am not under whatever circumstances breaking up my dear little family neither relinquishing any of my three family flats'. His son Greville appealed to the trustees in a letter in November 1970, in which he contended that the management was nursing a personal animosity against his father. The web of intrigue which was being spun round the several tenancies was finally broken in January 1971 when the Management Committee decided to instigate legal proceedings to regain possession of 701 Beatty and 902 Hood House and the three basement rooms, and to refuse a further renewal of the lease on 702 Beatty House when it expired in 1973.[143]

Less complex and certainly more distressing, was the plight of the actress Chili Bouchier and her husband 'Bluey' Hill, whom we also met in Chapter 3. By no means all of Dolphin Square's 'celebrities' were affluent, and acting was often a precarious profession and not necessarily well-paid over the long term. A good example is provided by the experiences of Ms Bouchier. She and Hill had pooled their resources in the Square and taken a lease on 807 Howard House in 1951. This was to be their home for 23 years, she recalled.[144] However, by the early 1970s her own sporadic work and Hill's heavy drinking, the product in part of a long period of unemployment as a film director, created a financial crisis for the couple. Her plight is documented in her autobiography and diary. After a period of rent arrears the Dolphin Square management requested the couple to vacate their flat at the end of their next three-year tenancy, in 1973. The flat was in Hill's name, but the rent was paid by Bouchier. According to her:

> I continued to send the rent, but they said that they could not accept it was rent but would keep the money all the same. This rather suggested that they no longer considered Bluey as a tenant, and it was a disquieting situation. Dolphin Square is like a great village and everybody knows everybody's business. It was obvious that the management knew that Bluey had been out of work for over three years and that I was no longer in 'The Mousetrap'. Therefore we were deemed no hopers with no future.[145]

The treatment of the Hills may appear harsh, though it was consonant with the Trust's policy towards tenants in arrears. And by this time the Hills were no longer model tenants. Chili's diary for 1972 indicates that Bluey was becoming more difficult to live with, and his drunkenness led to unpleasant incidents within Dolphin Square and to court appearances. Rent payments appear to have been sporadic and hand-to-mouth.[146]

The management offered a renewal of the lease, but at a substantially increased rent, and on condition that the rental payments were guaranteed. This could not be done, and the couple were evicted.[147] In Chili's words they were 'both over sixty and homeless'. One of Hill's friends found them a room in the Irish Club in Eaton Square as a temporary measure, whereupon Chili was offered another year in 'The Mousetrap'. But they did not return to Dolphin Square, and were soon living in a council flat.[148]

In such a large complex of flats, it was the exceptional and the unusual that interested the residents. Thus, murders and suicides, burglaries, muggings, fires and floods certainly attracted attention from time to time. In February 1979, for example, a married couple were found dead in their flat in Keyes House. It seems that the wife had murdered her husband and then committed suicide.[149] Chili Bouchier's diary for 1972 contains a fascinating account of an arson attack on an adjoining flat. She wrote that, one evening,

> 'Arrived back from theatre at night to find fire engines outside Howard House. Terrified that it might be us. When got to 8th floor found 809 gutted out. Place crawling with firemen police & detectives. Arson suspected. Policeman outside flat all night. Could hear police radio. Couldn't sleep. Gave Bobby tea and biscuits.

The following morning she wrote: 'Detectives round again. Asked to use our phone. Many calls from Scotland Yard . . . Man sought for arson. I wonder if it was the sinister-looking character I saw knocking on door of 809 at 3.30 one morning. Very thin, very pale – dressed all in black – with black fur hat.' And the next day: 'Couldn't eat – very nervous . . . Girl in 809 found – a do-gooder – try's [sic] to help ex-prisoners. Had life threatened a few times.'[150] Rather puzzlingly, there is no reference to this incident in the minutes of the Committee of Management, although the trustees were informed at about the same time that a woman had been attacked in the garden, the telephone box screwed to the wall in a kiosk in Rodney House had been stolen, and that an unauthorised subtenant in Collingwood House had been arrested for being in possession of cannabis.[151] The trustees were also told about a serious fire in 01 Grenville House in February 1973. Garrard reported that 'the tenants of the flat were not the most desirable tenants but after taking legal advice it was considered that the fire should not be used as a reason for terminating the tenancy. The Tenant's wife, who works for the *Daily Mirror*, is exerting pressure through the newspaper's solicitor, for restitution to be effected as quickly as possible'.[152] There was also a serious fire on the 5th floor of Collingwood House in January 1997. In this incident two young men died, and the Trust was moved to re-examine its fire safety procedures. The principal lesson was that tenants should be instructed to remain in their flats unless directly affected by the fire. The Trust also took steps to improve fire safety, including the provision of smoke doors, dry risers, and smoke detectors in each flat.[153]

There was also considerable interest in any changes to the amenities, including the several changes to the restaurant, shops, sports facilities, and so on. The fountain pond in the centre of the garden regularly attracted nesting ducks, but the phenomenon attracted a considerable correspondence in the period 1996–2002. For some residents, the establishment of a duck-feeding roster inspired a 'sense of community and communication' in the Square, and they sought to encourage the management to share their sense of responsibility.[154] On the other hand, decisions as to what to do about them attracted differing strategies, even among the more enthusiastic tenants, such as Julie Ronald, Marjorie Ferris and Rudolph Bissolotti, known as the 'Honorary Duck Master'.[155] This was a more complex matter than might have appeared at first sight, ranging from control of the number of breeding pairs and transporting the ducklings to water, to the need for extreme care when cleaning the fountain. The vocal minority were keen to take advice from experts at Kew Gardens, the Wildlife Trust at Slimbridge in Gloucestershire, and the RSPCA. Successive general managers showed considerable patience with the problem, but they could not please everyone. The DSTA was divided in its opinion, though one committee member felt that 'The Square will not be the same English eccentricity without them'.[156] Sometimes feelings ran high. In 1998 the cleaning of the fountain led to the chemical burning of ducklings' feet, and the attempt of the RSPCA to move the brood did not go well. An anonymous card sent to Wray was particularly unpleasant: 'TO WHO IS RESPONSIBLE FOR THE ABOMINABLE WAY you TREATED the DUCKS', it read. 'LETS [sic] HOPE FOR YOUR SAKES that there is NO REINCARNATION, AND if THERE IS BE SURE TO

STAY WELL AWAY FROM DOLPHIN SQUARE FOUNTAIN! YOU INHUMANE lot'.[157] On the other hand, another vocal minority were equally hostile to the ducks, or at least to the ramshackle contraptions erected to assist them, and in 2000 they obtained legal opinion that feeding them was a direct contravention of the Dolphin Square tenants' regulations. By 2002, this veritable 'can of worms' was resolved when the management took a firmer position, discouraging the feeding of ducks and ducklings and indicating that the RSPCA would be asked to deal with any brood which found its way to the fountain.[158]

What also gave the Square its distinctive character was in part the product of a determination on the part of the tenants' association, the DSTA, and others to provide events designed to foster a community spirit. For tenants who wished to join in there was a full programme of activities organised by the management and others based around the Square's various amenities: croquet, tennis, cricket, bridge, dinner dances, keep fit classes, a children's room, and an artists' group. The DSTA itself attempted to be inclusive, appointing representatives for each of the 12 houses (Rodney House was naturally excluded). It arranged a series of social events - cocktail and tea parties, parties for summer, Christmas and new tenants' 'meet and greet', lectures, and visits to places of interest. Each of the Square's anniversaries - 50th (1987), 60th (1997) and so on - was marked by a fête or garden party. However, the DSTA's primary purpose was to act as a conduit for tenants' concerns and complaints. And when the DSTA and SOS (Save Our Square) became embroiled in the battle for ownership of the Square (Chapter 6, pp.252-3) social events took something of a back seat. For this reason, and to counter a feeling of isolation experienced by some of the Square's older residents, the Blue Dolphin Club was founded by two trustees, Jan Prebble and Deirdre Marshall, and others in March 2000.[159] The Club organised an impressive number of events - 25 in the first year - including a fête in the Spanish garden. Among the numerous activities arranged over the next six years were visits to Clarence House and Highgrove, a trip to Calais and sails on Warwick Bergin's motor yacht from the River Hamble. The only discordant note was provided by an invitation to speak extended to Jeffrey Archer in 2003, which proved a contentious choice.[160] A 'good neighbour' scheme, Caring Dolphins, was also part of the Club's activities from 2003, and in 2006 it published *Hotchpotch*, a lavishly-illustrated historical memoir of the Square.[161] The Club's apogee was a summer fête in 2004, held in the Spanish garden and opened by former tenant, the Princess Royal.[162]

It is not clear how much this considerable effort was appreciated. An attitudinal survey, conducted by the DSTA in 1996, before the Blue Dolphin Club was founded, was completed, in the main, by the more senior residents. While the results should not be taken too seriously – this was in no sense a scientific sociological exercise – the respondents listed rent levels, security, maintenance and the gardens as the most important considerations (identified by over 90 per cent of respondents). These were followed by security of tenure, noise, guest rooms and shops (76–89 per cent). Only 55 per cent mentioned the swimming pool, 48 per cent the restaurant, and social activities, tennis croquet, bridge and squash came way down the list.[163] No doubt the Blue Dolphin Club made a difference later on, but the conclusion seems to be that while there those for whom Dolphin Square was a home and who were more inclined to join in its social life, for others, increasingly the majority, it was a more temporary pied-à-terre to be used while working in central London.[164] Looking around the gardens today, there is no shortage of dedicated benches to the memory of long-standing residents who clearly loved the place. In 2004, Princess Anne unveiled a memorial bench to Marjorie Lyall, who had died aged 93 in the previous year.[165] Mention must also be made of 'Victor and Squirrel', i.e. Victor Mollo, the noted bridge player, and his wife Jeanne, who lived in the Square from 1950;[166] Bud Flanagan; Irene Hicks, the 'Bird Lady', a resident from 1937 to 1999;[167] Heather Harding and Florence Hookway, residents from the 1970s; Ada Dunning, a tenant of Keyes House from 1938 to 1982; and the politician Lord Patrick Gordon-Walker and his wife, Audrey, who are commemorated on two benches. Finally, there was a young woman, Alexandra Arnold, who spent her entire life in the Square until she was killed in a car crash.[168] On the other hand, there is now a more transient population, and until the existing tenancy arrangements are altered, this is likely to persist, working against the inclusive, all-embracing life which the Square has tried to provide since the late 1930s.

NOTES

1 708 Hawkins House from 16 March 1960: WCC Rate Book, 1959-60, WCA.

2 April Ashley MBE (b. 1935), pioneering transsexual.

3 Sarah Churchill (1914-82). See her *Keep On Dancing: An Autobiography* (1981), p.181.

4 *The Times*, 6 June 1961, p.7, 28 July 1961, p.6, 7 September 1961, p.17, 14 September 1961, p.17; WCC Rate Book 1961-2, WCA.

5 David Profumo, *Bringing the House Down: A Family Memoir* (2006), p.206.

6 Christine Keeler, *Scandal!* (1989), *The Truth at Last: My Story* (2001), and with Douglas Thompson, *Secrets and Lies* (2012).

7 Keeler, *Scandal!*, p.114, *The Truth at Last*, p.126, *Secrets and Lies*, p.134. Dolphin Square is not mentioned in Rice-Davies's autobiography with Shirley Flack, *Mandy* (1980).

8 The fullest account is in Keeler, *Secrets and Lies*, pp.134-5, 137-9. See also *The Times*, 6 June 1963, p.6.

9 Ibid. pp.209-10, 217-19, 240-2, and see *The Times* and *Guardian*, 20 April-7 December 1963, *passim*.

10 Profumo later told his son that he had met Keeler prior to Cliveden in Murray's Club, but there is some doubt about this: Profumo, *Bringing the House Down*, pp.158-9.

11 Profumo was also in many ways a victim of the annoyance that political leaders experienced over the revelation of Vassall's spying. For further insights, see the recent book by Richard Davenport-Hines, *An English Affair: Sex, Class and Power in the Age of Profumo* (2013).

12 It is by no means certain that Keeler had an affair with Ivanov, who was nicknamed 'The Playboy of the Eastern World'. Cf. Profumo, *Bringing the House Down*, pp.160-1.

13 *Parl. Deb. (Commons)*, 5th ser. (Session 1962-3), vol.674, George Wigg, 21 March 1963, c. 725, and see also Lord Wigg, *George Wigg* (1972), p.263ff. On Wigg (1900-83), Labour MP for Dudley, 1945-67; Baron Wigg, 1967, see *Who's Who of British Members of Parliament*, IV, and Woodrow Wyatt, 'George Edward Cecil Wigg', *OxDNB*. Wigg's attack on Profumo was 'as much personal as political': cf. Julian Critchley, *Westminster Blues* (1985), p.33.

14 *Parl. Deb. (Commons)*, 5th ser. (Session 1962-3), vol.674, Barbara Castle, 21 March 1963, c.740. Keeler had attracted media attention when she fled the UK after having been called as the principal witness in the trial of John Edgecombe, a rival for her affections, who had shot at her. *The Times*, 15 March 1963, p.12, 2 April 1963, p.6. See also Lord Denning's account of 16 September 1963, reprinted in *John Profumo and Christine Keeler, 1963* (HMSO, 1999 edn), p.16ff.

15 Charles J.L. Elwell (Security Service), memo. on interview with Capt. G.M. Bennett, 24 August 1962, 29 August 1962, TNA TS58/639, and see also Law Officers' Department, Royal Courts of Justice, file on Vassall, TNA LO2/1169.

16 Edwyn Sherwood (Security Service), affidavit, 30 November 1962, TNA TS58/639.

17 See affidavits of Gerald Rhodes and Evelyn Parsons, n.d. [1962], and Eve Parsons (Lettings Manager, Dolphin Square Ltd)-Dr G. Lang, 16 February 1959 and reply, Fladgate & Son-Parsons, 18 February 1959, Lloyds Bank-Dolphin Square Ltd, 20 February 1959, Treasury Solicitor files: Lord Radcliffe, Vassall Tribunal of Inquiry reports, papers, etc., TNA 58/639; Parsons, evidence to Tribunal, 17 January 1963, TNA ADM116/6385.

18 Memo. on 'Vassall's Finances and Standard of Living', 22 November 1962, TNA TS58/639.

19 John Vassall, *Vassall: The autobiography of a spy* (1975), p.126.

20 Law Officers' Department, Royal Courts of Justice, file on Vassall, TNA LO2/1169; Sir Clifford Jarrett (Permanent Secretary, Admiralty), Memo. on 'Implications of Vassall', 17 September 1962, TNA ADM1/28028; T.G.D. Galbraith (Civil Lord of the Admiralty), statement, 30 September 1962, TNA DEFE13/261.

21 Sir Roger Hollis, affidavit, 5 December 1962, TNA TS58/639 and see also Roger Wilkes, *Daily Telegraph*, 19 January 2002, property p.6.

22 David Leitch, 'The spy who rocked a world of privilege', *Sunday Independent*, 8 December 1996, p.21. Vassall later served as a volunteer for the British Records Association. My thanks to Alex Ritchie for this information.

23 Cdr T.D. Galbraith (1891–1985), Baron Strathclyde, 1955, 505 Frobisher, 507 Nelson, 602 Rodney. See e.g. WCC Rate Book No.5 for year ending 31 March 1948, No. 25 for 1968–9, WCA; Appendix 2.

24 Galbraith-Peter Thorneycroft (Minister of Defence), 30 October 1962, TNA DEFE13/261. Tam Galbraith (1917–82) was MP for Glasgow Hillhead, 1948–82, PUSS, Scotland, 1959–62, PS, Transport, 1963–4, KBE 1982: see *Who's Who of British Members of Parliament*, IV.

25 David Leigh, 'MI5 and the Minister's Wife', *Observer*, 23 October 1988, p.33; Tam Dalyell, obituary of Niall MacDermot (1916–96), Labour MP for Derby North, 1962–70, in *Independent*, 27 February 1996, p.12, and see also *The Times*, 26 February 1996, p.19. The Macdermots lived in 607 Beatty.

26 Leopold Raymond Fletcher 1921–91). See *Independent*, 13 September 1999, pp.1, 3; DST, Occupation/vacation list, July 1974, DST.

27 Christopher Andrew and Vasili Mitrokhin, *The Mitrokhin Archive: The KGB in Europe and the West* (2000 edn), pp.526–7.

28 *Observer*, 20 February 1983, pp.1–2.

29 Joan Morgan (1905–2004); Morgan, *Citizen of Westminster* (1940): *Independent*, 24 July 2005, p.45.

30 A.N. Wilson, *The Sweets of Pimlico* (1977), pp.15, 19, 21, 53–4.

31 Drabble, *Angus Wilson*, p.144.

32 Wilson, *Sweets of Pimlico*, p.92. Mantilla, a scarf worn over the head and shoulders, was used by Westbrook as the name of its property management company.

33 A.N. Wilson, *Betjeman* (2006), p.304. I am grateful to John Webber of Grenville House for this reference. Canon Hood lived in 606 Rodney. Betjeman read the lesson at Hood's memorial service: Candida Lycett Green (ed.), *John Betjeman Letters. Vol.2: 1951 to 1984* (1995), p.449.

34 Julian Critchley, *Hung Parliament* (1991), pp.9–10. On Julian Critchley (1930–2000), Conservative MP for Rochester and Chatham, 1959–64, Aldershot, 1970–97, Kt, 1995, see Mark Garnett, 'Sir Julian Michael Gordon Critchley', *OxDNB*.

35 A substantial underestimate!

36 Critchley, *Hung Parliament*, p.88, and see also pp.56–7, 86–7.

37 A.L. Kennedy, *The Blue Book* (2011), p.311.

38 'Vic [Joliff, gangster] was in another safe house. This time it was a flat in Dolphin Square.' Martina Cole, *Maura's Game* (2002), p.272.

39 http://www.britishpathe.com/video/dolphin-square-issue-title-should-auld-acquaint-anc/query/Dolphin+square. There was another Pathé feature in 1964 entitled 'Dolphin Square: In the Swim Next Year'.

40 http://www.britmovie.co.uk/films/A-Window-in-London_1939/. My thanks to Jan Prebble for drawing my attention to the film.

41 http://www.britmovie.co.uk/films/The-Sorcerers_1967/ and . . . films/Victim/1961 and www.movie-locations.com/movies/s/Sorcerers.html.

42 Bebe Daniels (1901–71) and Ben Lyon (1901–79) were American film actors with substantial careers before their work in the UK. See Phil Watson, 'Life with the Lyons', http://www.otrarchive.blogspot.co.uk/2009/04/life-with-Lyon-bbc.html. They occupied 710 and 711 Keyes: *London Evening News*, 6 July 1966; DST, Occupation/vacation list, July 1972, DST.

43 Vanessa Lee (1920–92), appeared in *King's Rhapsody*, 1949 and *After the Ball*, 1954. Peter Graves (1911–94), 8th Baron Graves, 1963, appeared in films such as *Mrs Fitzherbert*, 1947, *The Admirable Crichton*, 1957 and *Alfie*. 1966. The couple, who married in 1960, lived in 505 Nelson.

44 Ian Bannen (1928–99), appeared in several films, including *Flight of the Phoenix*, 1965, and in TV dramas, including *Tinker Tailor Soldier Spy*, 1979. He was a tenant of 807 Keyes for many years.

45 Katie Boyle (b.1928), appeared in *What's My Line?*, and presented the Eurovision Song Contest four times from 1960 to 1974.

46 Katie Boyle, *What This Katie Did: An Autobiography* (1980), p.185.

47 Nora Noel (Jill) Bennett (1929?–90), 507 Howard.

48 Peter Finch (1916–77), also received BAFTA awards for *A Town Like Alice*, 1956, *The Trials of Oscar Wilde*, 1960, and *Sunday Bloody Sunday*, 1971. His flat was 902 Grenville.

49 Valerie Hobson (1917–98), appeared in *Werewolf* and *Bride of Frankenstein* in 1935, *Great Expectations*, 1946, and *Kind Hearts and Coronets*, 1949. See Profumo, *Bringing the House Down*. Unfortunately, I have been unable to verify her residence.

50 Raymond Huntley (1904–90), appeared in the TV drama series *Upstairs Downstairs*, 1971–5, and in films such as *Can You Hear Me, Mother?*, 1935, *Passport to Pimlico*, 1949, *The Dam Busters*, 1955, and *Room At The Top*, 1959. His flat was 209 Howard.

51 Stewart MacPherson (1908–95), enjoyed success as a radio reporter during the war, then presented the quiz *Ignorance is Bliss*, 1946. He returned to Canada in 1949. See Paul Fox, 'Stewart Myles MacPherson', *OxDNB*. Evidence of his residence has not been found.

52 Basil Radford (1897–1952), appeared in numerous films, including *The Lady Vanishes*, 1938, *Millions Like Us*, 1943, and *Passport to Pimlico*, 1949. Evidence of his residence has not been found.

53 Rodney Lovick also appeared in films, including *Charlie Muffin* (1979) and *The Great Muppet Caper* (1981). He lived in 711 Collingwood.

54 Barbara Windsor, with the assistance of Joan Flory and Damien Walne, *Barbara: The Laughter and Tears of a Cockney Sparrow* (1990), pp.102–3.

55 Barbara Windsor and Robin McGibbon, *All of Me: My Extraordinary Life* (2000), p.213, and see also Robert Ross. *Smasher! The Life of Sid James* (2009), p.214. The Dolphin Square flat had been mentioned earlier in Cliff Goodman, *Sid James: a biography* (1995), p.196.

56 Windsor and McGibbon, *All of Me*, p.220.

57 Ibid. p.188.

58 Suzanne Bertish (b.1971); John Selby Clements (1910–88), CBE, 1956, Kt, 1968; Christopher Trace (1933–92); Dickie Davies (b.1933).

59 These names figure in gossip columns about the Square, e.g. in *Estates Gazette*.

60 *Observer*, 29 June 1969, p.20, and see also *Playboy*, June 1971; *Westminster & Pimlico News*, 19 August 1966, cuttings, DST.

61 Denis Leo Kavanagh (1906–84), 202 Duncan. See *Manchester Guardian*, 16 November 1954, p.3; http://www.imdb.com/name/nm0442546/.

62 Sean Mathias (b. 1956), 05 Raleigh, DST, Occupation/vacation list, January 1978, DST; www.imdb.com/name/nm0558773.

63 *Westminster and Pimlico News*, 15 January 1965, p.1. Her 101st birthday was marked by the *Evening Standard*, 15 January 1966, p.6; Ms Braham lived in 506 Hawkins until 1968.

64 Morris, *Dolphin Square*, p.107; material for the Square's Golden Jubilee, 1987, DST.

65 Peter Geiger, quoted in Marcus Scriven, *Splendour & Squalor: The Disgrace and Disintegration of Three Aristocratic Dynasties* (2009), p.248. Scriven, *Splendour & Squalor*, p.248.

66 Victor Hervey, 6th Marquess of Bristol (1915–85), Chancellor of the International Monarchist League, 1976–85, 307 Nelson; John Hervey, Earl Jermyn (1954–99), 7th Marquess of Bristol, 1985, 601 Hood, 1972–5. See Peter Mandler, 'Frederick William John Augustus Harvey', *OxDNB*, Michael De-La-Noy, *The House of Hervey: A History of Tainted Talent* (2001), p.184ff., Marcus Scriven, *Splendour & Squalor*, p.112ff.

67 Charles, 3rd Baron Greenway (1917–75), 703 Collingwood, 1971–5 [his widow, Cordelia, remained in the Square until her death in 2010]; Gerard, 5th Baron Monkswell (b. 1947), 01 Keyes; David Seely, 4th Baron Mottistone (1920–2011), former naval captain, Lord Lieutenant, IOW, 1986–95 and last Governor, IOW, 1992–5, 308 Nelson, 103 Collingwood.

68 Robert Hamilton, 13th Lord Belhaven and Stenton (b. 1927), committee activist, 710 Howard; Nicholas Lowther, 2nd Viscount Ullswater (b. 1942), PUSS, Employment, 1990–3, Minister, Environment, 1994–5, 104 Frobisher; Simon, 4th Baron Glenarthur (b. 1944), Minister, Scottish Office, 1986–7, Foreign & Commonwealth Office, 1987–9, 201 Nelson.

69 Shafi Lawal Edu (1911–2002), 303 Howard, 201 Grenville; Godfrey Kio Amachree, 101/2 Raleigh, 806 Beatty.

70 *Guardian*, 10 December 1969, p.11, *The Times*, 16 August 1966, p.1, 17 December 1969, pp.1, 8, 19 December 1969, p.1. The Commons vote was 343–185.

71 Misses Sheldon and Bird lived in 703 Collingwood. They died in 1969 and 1982 respectively. The third founder was Miss Hindle. *Observer*, 21 July 1963, p.10. See http://www.benenden.kent.sch.uk/2309/overview/history-of-benenden.

72 Penelope Ann Tryon Turing (1925–2010): <wagneropera.blogspot.co.uk>. Entry, 31 July 2010.

73 Robert Saul Musel (1909–99), 703 Collingwood, 109 Frobisher, 304 Raleigh, 302 Drake. See *Daily Telegraph*, 17 September 1999, p.31.

74 (Michael) Edward F. Seymour-Rouse (1920–99), Publicity and Appeals Officer, RSPCA, 1970–7, Publicity and Public Relations Officer, 1977–9, Director of European Liaison, RSPCA, 1979–88, Director of European Affairs, the International Fund for Animal Welfare, 1988–98; founder, with Richard Ryder, of the Eurogroup for Animal Welfare, 1980, and its Director, 1986–8; 511 Keyes. *Animal Welfare*, May 1999, p.22, and information provided by Dr Richard Ryder, 2012.

75 Dicky Jamshed [Ramshed in 1968/9] Rutnagur (b.1931), 708 Grenville, cricket correspondent, *Hindustan Times*, 1958–66.

76 Cf. Hennessy, *Whitehall*, pp.329–336, 730ff.

77 Both are referred to in Morris, *Dolphin Square*, p.107, and DSTA, Newsletter, November 1976, p.17. Sir Alan Dawtry confirms that Macleod was never a tenant.

78 Alan Beith (b. 1943), Liberal/Liberal Democrat MP for Berwick since 1973, Liberal Democrat Leader of the House, 1999–2003, Kt, 2008, 304 Duncan, 702 Hood. *Who's Who*.

79 Gordon Campbell (1921–2005), Conservative MP for Moray and Nairn, 1959–74, Secretary of State for Scotland, 1970–4, Lord Campbell of Croy, 1974, 501 Grenville, 704 and 907 Howard. David Torrance, 'Gordon Thomas Calthrop Campbell', *OxDNB*.

80 Mark Carlisle (1929-2005), Conservative MP for Runcorn, 1964-83, Warrington South, 1983-7, Lord Carlisle, 1987, Minister, Home Office, 1972-4, Secretary of State for Education, 1979-81, 409 Keyes.

81 Dr John Cunningham (b. 1939), Labour MP for Whitehaven, 1970-83, Copeland, 1983-2005; PUSS, Energy, 1976-9, Minister of Agriculture, 1997-8, Cabinet Office Minister, 1998-9, Lord Cunningham, 2005, 806 Hood. *Who's Who.*

82 Patrick Gordon Walker (1907-80), Labour MP for Smethwick, 1945-64, Leyton, 1966-74, Lord Gordon-Walker, 1974, Secretary of State for Commonwealth Relations, 1950-1, Foreign Secretary, 1964-5, 105/6 Frobisher. Robert Pearce, 'Patrick Chrestien Gordon Walker', *OxDNB.*

83 Eric Heffer (1922-91), Labour MP for Liverpool Walton, 1964-91, Minister of State for Industry, 1974-5, 704 Keyes. See Andrew Roth, 'Eric Samuel Heffer', *OxDNB.*

84 Denis Howell (1923-98), Labour MP for Birmingham All Saints, 1955-9, Birmingham Small Heath, 1961-92; Minister for Sport, 1964-70, Minister of State for Housing & Local Government, 1969-70, Minister for Sport, 1974-9, also Minister for Water Resources, 1976, Minister for Snow, 1978-9, Lord Howell, 1992, 607 Beatty. See Tam Dalyell, 'Denis Herbert Howell', *OxDNB.*

85 Michael Mates (b. 1934), Conservative MP for Hampshire East, 1974-2010; Minister of State for Northern Ireland, 1992-3 (he resigned after the discovery of his links with the fugitive businessman Asil Nadir, of Polly Peck), 02 Howard, 03 and 902/3 Hawkins. *Who's Who.*

86 David Steel (b. 1938), Liberal/Liberal Democrat MP for Roxburgh. Selkirk & Peebles, 1965-83, Tweedale, Ettrick & Lauderdale, 1983-97, Member for Lothians, Scottish Parliament, 1999-2003, KBE, 1990, Lord Steel, 1997, 707 Beatty, 703 Nelson, 902 Beatty. *Who's Who.*

87 Dr Gavin Strang (b. 1943), MP for Edinburgh East, 1970-2010; PUSS for Energy, 1974; PS, MAFF, 1974-9; Minister for Transport, 1997-8, 06 Grenvillle. *Who's Who.*

88 Christopher Brocklebank-Fowler (b. 1934), MP for King's Lynn, 1970-4, North West Norfolk, 1974-83, a Conservative, but joined SDP, 1981, then Labour Party, 1996, 801 Raleigh; Nicholas Fairbairn (1933-95), Conservative MP for Kinross and Western Perthshire, 1974-83, Perth and Kinross, 1983-95, Solicitor-General for Scotland, 1979-82, Kt, 1988, 705 Hawkins; John Horam (b. 1939), Labour MP for Gateshead West, 1979-83, joined SDP, 1981, joined Conservatives, 1987, and became Conservative MP for Orpington, 1992-2010, 02 Howard. See Michael Fry, 'Sir Nicholas Hardwick Fairbairn', *OxDNB; Who's Who of British Members of Parliament,* IV.

89 Neil Carmichael (1921-2001), PUSS, Transport, 1967-9, Environment, 1974-5, Lord Carmichael, 1983; Brynmor John (1934-88), PUSS, Defence, 1974-6, Minister, Home Office, 1976-9; Alick Buchanan-Smith (1932-91), PUSS, Scotland, 1970-4, Minister, MAFF, 1979-83, Energy 1983-7; Reginald Eyre (b. 1924), PUSS, Environment, 1972-4, Trade, 1979-82, Kt., 1983; Neil Macfarlane (b. 1936), PUSS, Education, 1979-81, Minister for Sport, 1981-5; James Scott-Hopkins (1921-95), PUSS, MAFF, 1962-4, Vice -President, European Parliament, 1976-9, Kt., 1981; Sir Giles Shaw (1931-2000), PUSS, NI, 1979-81, DOE, 1981-3, Energy, 1983-4, Minister, Home Office, 1984-6, DTI, 1986-7; and John Stradling Thomas (1925-91), Treasurer of HM Household, 1979-83, Minister, Wales, 1983-7, Kt., 1985.

90 Derek Foster (b. 1937), Labour MP for Bishop Auckland, 1979-2005, Opposition Chief Whip, 1985-95, Lord Foster, 2005, 609 Collingwood.

91 George Gardiner (1935-2002), Conservative MP for Reigate, 1974-97, Kt, 1990, defected to Referendum Party, March-June 1997, 707 Hood, 601 Frobisher. See Mark Garnett, 'Sir George Arthur Gardiner', *OxDNB*, George Gardiner, *A Bastard's Tale: The Political Memoirs of George Gardiner* (1999).

92 David Russell Russell-Johnston (1932–2008), Liberal MP for Inverness, 1964–83, Inverness, Nairn & Lochaber, 1983–97; deputy leader, Liberal Democrats, 1988–92, President of the Parliamentary Assembly of the Council of Europe, 1999–2002, Kt. 1985, Lord Russell-Johnston, 1997, 611 Keyes. See Mark Stuart, 'David Russell Russell-Johnston', *OxDNB*.

93 Bruce Millan (b. 1927), Labour MP for Glasgow Craigton, 1959–83, Glasgow Govan, 1983–8, European Commissioner for Regional Policy,1989–95, 801 Beatty.

94 Sir Hector Munro (1922–2006), Lord Munro from 1997, Conservative MP for Dumfries, 1964–97; PUSS, Scottish Office, 1971–4, PUSS, DoE (Sport), 1979–81, PUSS, Scottish Office, 1992–5, 301 Keyes, 303 Hood.

95 Sir Malcolm Rifkind (b. 1946), Conservative MP for Edinburgh Pentlands, 1974–97, Kensington & Chelsea, 2005–; Scottish Secretary, 1986–90, Transport Secretary, 1990–2, Defence Secretary, 1992–5, Foreign Secretary, 1995–7, currently [2012] Chairman of the Intelligence and Security Committee; 201 and 304 Howard. *Who's Who.*

96 Hazel Blears (b.1956), Labour MP for Salford, 1997–2010, Salford & Eccles, 2010–, Minister, Home Office, 2003–6, SoS for Communities and Local Government, 2007–9; Sir Menzies Campbell (b. 1941), Liberal /Liberal Democrat MP for North East Fife, 1987–, leader, Liberal Democrat Party, 2006–7; William Hague (b. 1961), Conservative MP for Richmond (Yorks), 1989–, SoS Wales, 1995–7, Leader, Conservative Party, 1997–2011, SoS, FCA, 2010–; Beverley Hughes, (b. 1950), Labour MP for Stretford and Urmston, 1997–2010, Minister, Immigration &c., 2002–4, Children &c., 2005–9, Baroness Hughes, 2010; Estelle Morris (b. 1952), Labour MP for Birmingham Yardley, 1992–2005, SoS, Education & Skills, 2001–2; Mo Mowlam (1949–2005), Labour MP for Redcar, 1987–2001; Secretary of State for Northern Ireland, 1997–9, Cabinet Office Minister and Chancellor of the Duchy of Lancaster, 1999–2001; Sir George Young (b. 1941), Conservative MP for Acton, 1974–83, Ealing and Acton, 1983–97, North West Hampshire, 1997–, Financial Secretary, Treasury, 1994–5, SoS, Transport, 1995–7, leader, House of Commons, 2010–12.

97 Sir Stuart Bell (1938–2012), Labour MP for Middlesborough, 1983–2012, Second Church Estates Commissioner, 1997–2010, Kt, 2004, David Clelland (b. 1943), Labour MP for Tyne Bridge, 1985–2010, Whip 2001–2; Tom Pendry (b. 1934), Labour MP for Stalybridge and Hyde, 1970–2001, Lord Pendry, 2001; Ray Powell (1928–2001), Labour MP for Ogmore, 1979–2001, Kt, 1996; Edward Rowlands (b. 1940), Labour MP for Cardiff North, 1966–70, 1972–83, Merthyr Tydfil and Rhymney, 1983–2001, PUSS, Wles, 1969–70, 1974–5, Foreign Office, 1975–6, Minister, Foreign Office, 1976–9, Lord Rowlands, 2004; Sir Patrick Cormack (b. 1939), Conservative MP for Cannock, 1970–4, South West Staffordshire, 1974–83, Staffordshire South, 1983–2010, Kt, 1995, Lord Cormack, 2010; Peter Temple-Morris (b. 1938), Conservative MP for Leominster, 1974–2001, PPS, Transport, 1979–81, Lord Temple-Morris, 2001.

98 Francis Scott McFadzean (1915–92), Managing Director, Shell T&T, 1964–76, Chairman, British Airways, 1976–9, Chairman, Rolls Royce, 1980–3, Baron McFadzean of Kelvinside, 1980, 510/11 Howard. See Bob Reid, 'Francis Scott McFadzean', *OxDNB*. He is not to be confused with William McFadzean (1903–96), Baron McFadzean of Woldingham, Chairman and Managing Director, BICC, 1954–61, Chairman, 1961–73, Chairman, FBI, 1959–61, director, Midland Bank, 1959–81, deputy chairman, 1968–77.

99 Edward, Lord Shackleton (1911–94), explorer, Labour MP for Preston, 1946–50, Preston South, 1950–5, Chief Registrar, JLP, 1955–64, 304 Hawkins. See Andrew Roth, 'Edward Alexander Arthur Shackleton', *OxDNB*, and information from Judy Faraday (JLP).

100 Michael, Lord Winstanley (1918–93), GP, Medical Officer, Royal Ordnance Factory, Patricroft, 1950–74, Liberal MP for Cheadle, 1966–70, Hazel Grove, 1974, presenter, Granada TV's *This is Your Right*, 1970–4, Baron Winstanley, 1975, Chairman, Countryside

Commission, 1978–80, 905 Howard, 805 Raleigh. See Robert Ingham, 'Michael Platt Winstanley', *OxDNB; The Times*, 2 April 1974, p.16.

101 James Hector, Lord Gray of Contin (1927–2006), Conservative MP for Ross & Cromarty, 1970–83, Baron Gray, 1983, Minister, Energy, 1979–83, Scottish Office, 1983–6; Lord Goronwy-Roberts (1913–81), Labour MP for Caernarvon, 1945–74, Minister of State for Wales, Education & Science, Foreign & Commonwealth Affairs, and Trade, 1964–70, Minister of State, Foreign & Commonwealth Affairs, 1978–9; John Farquharson Smith, Lord Kirkhill (b. 1930), Minister, Scotland, 1975–8; Geoffrey, Lord Tordoff (b. 1928), marketing executive, then public affairs manager (chemicals), Shell UK, 1950–83; Baron Tordoff, 1981, President, Liberal Party, 1983/4, Liberal chief whip, 1984–8, Liberal Democrat chief whip, 1988–94, deputy speaker, 1994–2008; Ian, Lord Winterbottom (1913–92), Labour MP for Nottingham Central, 1950–5, Lord Winterbottom, 1965, PUSS, MoD, 1966–7, 1968–70.

102 Julia, Baroness Cumberlege (b. 1943), Baroness Cumberlege, 1990, PUSS, Health, 1992–7; Meghnad, Lord Desai (b. 1940), professor of economics, LSE, 1983–2003, Baron Desai, 1991[on Gaddafi, see Desai, *Guardian*, 5 March 2011, p.32]; John, Lord Dormand (1919–2003), Labour MP for Easington, 1970–87, Baron Dormand, 1987; Edward, Lord Graham (b. 1925), Labour MP for Edmonton, 1974–83, Baron Graham, 1983, Labour Chief Whip, 1990–7; Olive, Baroness Nicol (b. 1923), president, CWS, 1981–5, Baroness Nicol, 1983, Deputy Speaker, 1995–2002; John, Lord Sewell (b. 1946), Baron Sewell, 1996, PUSS, Scotland, 1997–9.

103 Information from DST listings, plus WCC rate books. Other MPs living on the same floor included: Lewis Carter-Jones (Lab) and Russell Johnston (Lib), David Marshall (Lab) and Nicholas Winterton (Con), David Howell (Lab) and Richard Shepherd (Con), Derek Foster (Lab) and Sir Michael Shaw (Con), and David Alton (Lib) and Peter Temple-Morris (Con), Ernest Armstrong (Lab) and Sir Michael Thornton (Con). There were 6 pairs of MPs on the same floor in 2005.

104 Mowlam, *Momentum*, p.17, and see also Paul Murphy, 'Marjorie [Mo] Mowlam', *OxDNB*. The flat was 04 Collingwood.

105 Cf. Jo-Anne Nadler, *William Hague: In His Own Right* (2000), pp.11–12, Mo Mowlam, *Momentum: The Struggle for Peace, Politics and the People* (2002), pp.16–17, and Julia Langdon, *Mo Mowlam* (2000), pp.207, 309, which mention Dolphin Square, and Alan Beith, *A View from the North: life, politics and faith seen from England's northernmost constituency* (Newcastle, 2008), Eric Heffer, *Never a Yes Man: The Life and Politics of an Adopted Liverpudlian* (1991), David Steel, *Against Goliath: David Steel's Story* (1989), and Alistair Darling, *Back from the Brink* (2011), which do not. This does not imply that the latter were hiding anything. For example, Heffer, in common with others, was happy to record his residency on the electoral register, while Beith referred to renting a flat 'when the allowances improved', though he found his 'comfortable London base . . . never really feels like home': *View from the North*, p.72.

106 *Evening Standard*, 26 May 2000, p.12.

107 *Daily Sport*, 11 August 2000, p.11.

108 Cf. William Hague–Jan Prebble, 20 October 2003, DST.

109 *The Times*, 17 January 1997, pp.1, 21, *Daily Mail*, 17 January 1997, pp.1, 25, *Observer*, 19 January 1997, p.5, *Guardian*, 27 February 1997, p.3, *Independent*, 28 February 1997, p.7, *Daily Mail*, 28 February 1997, p.27, *Sunday Telegraph*, 2 March 1997, p.20.

110 See *Daily Express*, 5 April 2004, p.6, *Private Eye*, 14 May 2004, p.6, 19 October 2012, p.8, *Daily Telegraph*, 8 and 30 May 2009, *Independent*, 18 October 2012, p.22.

111 The number had fallen to 70 by 1988: WCC Rate Book (fiche), 1980–1, 1988–9, WCA.

112 Admiral Sir Raymond Lygo, KCB (1924–2012), Cdr, Ark Royal, 1969–71, Vice-Chief of the Naval Staff , 1975–8, Acting First Sea Lord, 1977, joined BAe, 1978, was Group MD,

1983-6, Chief Executive, 1986-9, Chairman, TNT Express, 1992-7, 301 Duncan, then 202 and 409 Frobisher. See Lygo, *Collision Course* (Lewes, 2002). Admiral Sir Peter White, GBE (1919-2010), Director of Fleet Services, 1969-71, Port Admiral, Rosyth, 1971-4, Chief of Fleet Support, 1974-7, 410 Frobisher, 809 Hood.

113 Admiral Sir James Eberle GCB (b. 1927), C-in-C, Fleet, 1979-81, C-in-C, Naval Home Command, 1981-2, Director, RIIA (Chatham House), 1984-90, Vice-Admiral of the UK, 1994-7, 504 Howard, 208 Nelson, 902 Collingwood. See James Eberle, *Life on the Ocean Wave, From Greenland's Icy Shore* and *Wider Horizons* (Durham, 2007).

114 General Sir Noel Thomas KCB DSO MC (1915-83), Master-General of the Ordnance, 1971-4, 608 Hood; General Sir Peter Hunt KCB DSO DL (1916-88), Chief of Staff, Scottish Command, 1962-4, Commandant of Sandhurst, 1966-8, Chief of General Staff, 1973-6, 608 and 907 Howard; General Sir James Glover, KCB, DL (1929-2000), Cdr, Land Forces, N. Ireland, 1979-80, Deputy Chief of Defence Staff (Intelligence), 1981-3, Vice-Chief of Imperial General Staff, 1983-5, Cdr-in-Chief, UK Land Forces, 1985-7, director, British Petroleum, 1987-98, Chairman, Royal Armouries Int., 1993-, 605 Drake. See Frank Kitson, 'Sir James Malcolm Glover' *OxDNB*; General Sir Garry Johnson KCB MC (b. 1937), C-in-C Allied Forces Northern Europe, 1992-4, Chairman, International Security Advisory Board, 1995-.

115 Air Chief Marshal Sir Thomas Öther Prickett, KCB DSO DFC (1913-2010), Air Member for Supply and Organisation, 1968-70, 405 Hood; Air-Chief-Marshal Sir John Barraclough, KCB CBE DFC AFC (1918-2008), 209 Squadron, 1942-4, Station Cdr, Biggin Hill, 1954-6, Senior Operations and Training Officer, Singapore, 1958-61, Vice-Chief of the Defence Staff, 1970, Air Secretary, 1972-4, underwriter, Lloyds, 1979-85, 505 Howard (see Alex May, 'Sir John Barraclough', *OxDNB*); Air Chief Marshal Sir William John Stacey KCB (1924-81), Deputy Commander-in-Chief of Allied Air Forces Central Europe, 1979-81, 02 Beatty. There were also four Vice Admirals, three Lieutenant-Generals and three Air Marshals, the most notable being Vice-Admiral Sir Louis Le Bailly, Director General of Intelligence at the Admiralty, 1972-5 (during which time he lived in the flat previously occupied by the Admiralty spy John Vassall); and two Vice-Admirals who subsequently became Admirals - Sir William Pillar, Chief of Naval Support, 1979-82, and Sir Peter Herbert, who played a significant part in the Falklands campaign as Flag Officer Submarines, and was subsequently Vice-Chief of the Defence Staff, 1983-4.

116 Col. John Blashford-Snell FRSGS (b. 1936), 807 Keyes.

117 Lt Col. Colin Mitchell (1925-96), MP for West Aberdeenshire, 1970-4, 901 Nelson, 804 Drake. See Tam Dalyell, 'Colin Campbell Mitchell', *OxDNB*.

118 Cmdt. Elizabeth Craig-McFeely, CB (b. 1927), MOD (Navy), 1969-74, Director, WRNS, 1979-82, 304 Keyes (in 1995 she married Rear Admiral Colin Dunlop); Mary Ames, Chief Officer, WRNS, 803 Raleigh.

119 Sir Idwal Pugh KCB (1918-2010), 2nd Permanent Secretary, DOE, 1971-6, Parliamentary and Health Service Ombudsman, 1976-9, 201, then 801 Raleigh. See DST Occupation/vacation list, January 1974 and April 1976, DST.

120 Susan Winthrop Fogarty (1930-83), Under-Secretary, DOE, 1973-8, Transport, 1978-83, 401/2 Howard, 1973-83. See DST Occupation/vacation list, November 1973, WCC Rate book (fiche), 1983-4, WCA, and Terry Gourvish, *The Official History of Britain and the Channel Tunnel* (Abingdon, 2006), p.107ff.

121 Jean Nunn CB (1916-82), Deputy Secretary, Cabinet Office, 1967-70, 806 Nelson. See Lord Allen of Abbeydale, 'Jean Josephine Nunn', *OxDNB*.

122 Hugh Mackintosh Foot (1907-90), GCMG, Governor, Jamaica, 1951-7, Governor, Cyprus, 1957-60, Lord Caradon, 1964, Minister, Foreign Office, 1964-70, British Ambassador to United Nations, 1964-70, 203 Drake. See Lena M. Jeger, 'Hugh Mackintosh Foot', *OxDNB*.

123 Sir Anthony Parsons GCMG LVO MC (1922-96), Ambassador to Iran 1974-9, Permanent UK representative to United Nations, 1979-82, special adviser to Thatcher, 1982-3, author, *The Pride and the Fall: Iran 1974-9* (1984), lecturer and research fellow, Exeter University, 1984-96, 309 Howard. See Glencairn Balfour-Paul, 'Sir Anthony Derrick Parsons', *OxDNB* and *Independent*, 14 August 1996, p.24.

124 Sir William Cook KCB FRS (1905-87), Director, Physical Research, Admiralty, 1947-50, Deputy Chief Scientific Adviser, MOD, 1950-4, Deputy Director, Aldermaston, 1954-8, Member. Engineering and Development, Atomic Energy Authority, 1958-64, Deputy Chief Scientific Adviser, MOD, 1964-70, Chief Adviser (Projects) to Defence Secretary, 1967-70, director, Rolls Royce, 1971-6, 601 Howard. See John Challens, 'Sir William Richard Joseph Cook', *OxDNB*.

125 Sir Henry Wilson Smith KCB KBE (1904-78), Permanent Secretary, MOD, 1947-8, Second Secretary, Treasury, 1948-51, director, Powell Duffryn, 1951-69 (Chairman, 1956-69), director, GKN, 1951-72 (Deputy Chairman, 1962-72). Member, National Coal Board, 1956-60. *The Times*, 4 April 1978, p.16, 703 Keyes.

126 Lord Upjohn CBE (1903-71), Allied Control Commission, Italy (Chief Legal Adviser, 1943-4, Vice President, 1944-5), Chancery Judge, 1951-60, Lord Justice of Appeal, 1960-3, Baron Upjohn, 1963, Lord of Appeal in Ordinary, 1963-71, Chairman, St. George's Hospital Medical School, 1954-64, 309 Hawkins. See Hilary Magnus and H.M. Cretney, 'Gerald Ritchie Upjohn', *OxDNB*.

127 Roland Bird (1908-2003), joined *Economist*, 1933, deputy editor, 1946-63, contributing editor, 1963-78, managing director, 1969-71, finance director, 1971-8, married Ann Geraldine St. Pierre Bunbury of 505 Duncan in 1978; Jane Bown CBE (b. 1925), photographer, *Observer*, from 1950 (see *Guardian*, 19 December 1990, p.30); Sir Charles Carter FBA (1919-2002), economist, Vice-Chancellor, Lancaster University, 1963-79 (see Roger Middleton, 'Sir Charles Frederick Carter', *OxDNB*); Dr Ian Churchill-Davidson (1920-80), Physician in charge of radiotherapy and oncology, St. Thomas's Hospital, 1969-79; Sir Lionel Denny GBE MC (1897-1985), Lord Mayor of London, 1965-6, Chevalier, Légion d'Honneur, 1967; Sir Roger Falk (1910-97), Chairman, P-E International, 1973-6, member, Monopolies Commission, 1965-73, Monopolies and Mergers Commission, 1973-80; Sir John Garnett Lomax, KBE CMG MC (1896-1987), Ambassador to Bolivia, 1949-56; Sir Ronald Mason KCB FRS (b.1930), Professor of Chemistry, Sussex University, 1971-88, Chief Scientific Adviser, MOD, 1977-83, Chairman, University College London Hospitals NHS Trust; Sir Percy Rugg (1906-86), Conservative party leader, GLC, 1959-65; Sir Edmund Sargant (1906-98), President, Law Society 1968-9; Sir Frederick Snow (1899-1976), Frederick Snow & Partners, President, Concrete Society, 1966/7 (see F.A. Sherman and Robert Shaw, 'Sir Frederick Sidney Snow', *OxDNB*); Sir Frederick Warner FRS (1910-2010), senior partner, Cremer and Warner, 1963-80, President, Institution of Chemical Engineers, 1966-7, and several other bodies, technical adviser to Flixborough and Windscale inquiries, 1974-8; William Francis Kenrick Wynne-Jones (1930-82), professor of physical chemistry, King's College Newcastle/Newcastle University, 1947-68, Lord Wynne-Jones, 1964, Chairman, Scientific and Technical Committee, North Atlantic Assembly, 1973-7.

128 The following flats were held to be 'Treasury' ones: 106 and 711 Beatty (South Africa), 211 Collingwood (Germany), 202 Drake (France), 310, 405, 605 and 807 Duncan (Czechoslovakia, Denmark, Germany), 104 Frobisher (Jordan), 402 Hawkins (Iraq), 601 Hood (Jordan), 106 and 403 Howard (Finland, Czechoslovakia), and 701 Raleigh (Germany). WCC Rate Book, 1968-9, WCC.

129 DST Occupation/vacation list, December 1972, DST.

130 *The Times*, 22 October 2004, bricks and mortar, p.4.

131 *Guardian*, 4 September 1970, p.8. On Skeffington (1909-71) see *Who's Who of British Members of Parliament*, IV, *The Times*, 30 July 1969, p.7, 20 February 1971, p.7. Skeffington

was a tenant of 809 Howard. The tenancy was held by his wife, Sheila, and the fact of his being an MP was not advertised.

132 *Daily Express*, 15 June 1965, p.1, *South London Press*, 18 June 1965, p.13; Bernard Levin, in *Daily Mail*, 16 June 1965, p.8.

133 Morris-Mrs S. Benson, 7 May 1969, DST. The letter began 'Dear Madam . . .'

134 *People*, 17 January 1971, p.17, *Westminster and Pimlico News*, 22 January 1971, p.1. The flat was 309 Duncan, rent £58 a month. The Czech Embassy flat was 310 Duncan.

135 Garrard-Sir Lionel Denny (901 Grenville), 25 January 1971, DST. Mrs Benson, who previously rented a flat in Pont Street, came with favourable references from her former landlord, a firm of London solicitors, and Lloyds Bank: DST.

136 See Terence Blacker, *You Cannot Live as I Have Lived and Not End Up Like This: The Thoroughly Disgraceful Life and Times of Willie Donaldson* (2007?), p.245.

137 Sir Anthony Meyer (1920–2004), MP for Eton and Slough, 1964–6, West Flintshire, 1970–83, Clwyd North West, 1983–92, Chief Secretary, Treasury, 1970–2, SoS for Employment, 1972–4. See Mark Stuart, 'Sir Anthony John Charles Meyer', *OxDNB*, *Sunday Mirror*, 23 September 1990, pp.1, 4–5; *Guardian*, 24 September 1990, p.20. Mark Edmonds, writing in the Evening Standard magazine, claimed that Washington was a resident: *ES*, April 1992, p.9.

138 *News of the World*, 16 March, 2003, pp.1, 4–7; *Mail on Sunday*, 16 March 2003, p.11, *Daily Mirror*, 17 March 2003, p.15, and see also *Sunday Times*, 15 January 2012, p.9.

139 *Mail on Sunday*, 27 March and 3 April 2011.

140 *The Times*, 9 March 1973, pp.1 and 4, 11 September 1973, p.5; *Guardian*, 9 March 1973, p.1, 11 September 1973, p.1.

141 WCC Rate Book, 1968–9, 1971–2, WCA.

142 Critchley, *Westminster Blues*, p.27. In fact, Plugge created the International Broadcasting Company in 1931, which worked indirectly with Radio Luxembourg until 1936. See also *Daily Express*, 2 March 1966.

143 Garrard, reports, 18 March 1968 and 7 December 1970, DST Committee of Management Minutes, 21 March 1968, 19 January 1971, DST. Mrs Plugge left 702 Beatty in July 1973: DST Occupation/vacation list, July 1974, DST.

144 Bouchier, *Shooting Star*, p.192.

145 Ibid. p.214.

146 Chili Bouchier, Diary, 20 January–24 April 1972, Bouchier papers, Women's Library, London, 7/CHB/1/1/6.

147 In July 1973: DST Occupations/vacation list, 20 July 1973, DST.

148 Bouchier, *Shooting Star*, pp.215–16, 223–4.

149 DST, incident book, 12 February 1979, DST.

150 Chili Bouchier, Diary, entries for 30 and 31 March and 1 April 1972, Bouchier papers, Women's Library, London, 7/CHB/1/1/6.

151 DST Committee of Management Minutes, 12 July 1972, DST.

152 DST Committee of Management Minutes, 14 March 1973, DST.

153 DST Committee of Management Minutes, 21 January, 25 March and 22 July 1997, DST.

154 Julie Ronald (Duncan)-Rudolph Bissolotti (Beatty), 25 June 1996, DST.

155 Cf. Crawford-Bissolotti, 26 June 1996, DST.

156 Nicholas Morse (DSTA)-Crawford, 28 June 1996, DST.

157 Anonymous card, and see Wray-Bissolotti, 30 July 1998, DST.

158 Helen Johnston (Portrait solicitors)-Genevieve Beverley-Hole (Hood), 22 May 2000, Wray-Bissolotti, 7 March 2001, 23 April 2002, DST.

159 By July 2000 the Club was constituted as follows. Chairman: Deirdre Marshall; Vice Chairman: Rita Henry (launderette manager); Treasurer: Gillis Burgess; Committee: Doreen Alberts, Marjorie Lyall, Diana Molen and Dame Shirley Oxenbury.

160 *The Times*, 5 September 2003, p.6, *Private Eye*, 5 September 2003, p.11.

161 *A Hotchpotch of Tales from Dolphin Square* (January 2006 edn).

162 Blue Dolphin Club Newsletters, 2000–6, DST file on Blue Dolphin Club, DST.

163 DSTA Questionnaire results, in Patricia McVicar (DSTA)-Crawford, 28 March 1996; DSTA, Dolphin News, Spring 1996, p.4.

164 Interview with Evelyn, Lady Sargant (Keyes), 14 March 2012. The current long-standing residents include Rachel 'Ricky' Rees, who was a driver for MI6 during the war, and Violet Harrison.

165 *Westminster and Pimlico News*, 24 June 2004, p.2. Miss Lyall (1909–2003) lived in 507 Nelson from 1966, and was Secretary, then Chairman, of the DSTA in the early 1970s.

166 Victor Mollo (1909–87), contract bridge player and author of *Bridge in the Menagerie* (1965) and other books on the subject, 204 Duncan, 1950–71, 302 Drake, 1971–4, 801 Grenville, 1974–87. His wife Jeanne lived in the Square until 2009.

167 Irene Hicks, 207 Nelson, 904 Keyes.

168 Alexandra Arnold, 204/5 Drake, Heather Harding, 102 Drake, Florence Hookway, 802 Beatty, Ada Dunning, 402 Keyes, Lord and Lady Gordon-Walker, 105/6 Frobisher. Shorter stays are also sometimes commemorated, notably Gordon and Marjorie Langley, who lived in 302 Howard, 'the scene of their short happiness together', from 1938 until Flight Lt. Langley was killed in service in 1943.

CHAPTER 8

CONCLUSION

DOLPHIN SQUARE AFTER THE SALE, 2006–2012

The most recent change of ownership at Dolphin Square, the fifth in 70 years, involved somewhat labyrinthine corporate arrangements, which sometimes obscured where responsibility actually lay. Eventually, an organisational chart clarified the position. It indicated that Westbrook Partners were the owners of the lease, though in fact the ownership had been effected through a subsidiary company, Westbrook Dolphin Square Ltd. Below them was Brookhouse Capital Ltd., a real estate management company established in July 2005 and charged with the task of giving strategic direction to a third entity, Mantilla Holdings Ltd., from 2006 Mantilla Ltd., the management company which employed the Dolphin Square staff. The new owners did not introduce dramatic changes to the letting environment in 2006. After all, about a third of the residents were Option B tenants, and some of the remaining residents had elected to give up their existing rights in return for a cash sum, yet had remained in the Square. This was particularly true of a number of the relatively new entrants who were, in any case, more accustomed to a rent closer to the market rate in Westminster. As to the amenities, there were some adjustments, but the basic provision of gardens, shops, restaurant, bars, sports centre and swimming pool, remained intact. Nevertheless, as time passed, significant change was evident. In April 2006, the Rodney House hotel and the fine dining restaurant, Allium, were closed. Space was taken for a more imposing entrance hall fronting Chichester Street, leaving the restaurant as a more modest, brasserie-style affair located around the swimming pool. At the same time, and in accordance with the settlement of the Section 146 proceedings (see Chapter 6, p.254), Mantilla closed the hotel, making 85 employees redundant.[1] However, in the following year the facilities quickly reverted to 'serviced apartments', on the basis under which they had operated before Rodney House was marketed aggressively as a hotel in the early 2000s.

The new owners then took stock of the flats they had acquired. Nearly 400 of the eligible tenants had elected to accept a cash offer from Westbrook. As for the flats which were not part of the offer to tenants, there were about 600 flats which could be refurbished and let at higher rents. An expenditure of about £25 million was made, and by the summer of 2007 most of the flats had been relet. The rent roll, which had amounted to £12 million before the sale, quickly doubled.[2] In the process, the new landlords were now appealing to a somewhat different clientele. In place of the retired colonels, diplomats and civil servants favoured in the past, there was a more transient population of thirty-something professionals. Brookhouse's asset manager, Amos Barber, suggested that this meant that Dolphin Square had come full circle, appealing to the same kind of middle-class people it had sought to attract in the late 1930s.[3] At the same time, Mantilla took steps to reduce costs, and in 2008 a major staff rationalisation exercise resulted in 48 redundancies, with maintenance, security and portering being targeted. Some new posts were created, it is true, but with a further round of redundancies in April 2009, the number of staff fell by about a third.[4]

There is always a tension between the profit motive, the search for efficiency, and quality of service, and at Dolphin Square economies on this scale did not go unnoticed, especially among the older residents. In March 2008, readers of the Blue Dolphin Club's newsletter were offered a balance sheet of change by an anonymous Option B tenant in March 2008. Ten 'gains' under Westbrook's management were counterbalanced by ten 'losses'. There were, for example, new carpets, a remodelled entrance hall, refurbished lettings and accounts departments, and a newly designed bar/restaurant and swimming pool, but reductions in portering had been introduced, charges for car parking and guest rooms were higher, catering facilities had been rationalised, common spaces such as the Chichester and Anson rooms had been closed, the swimming pool had become a members-only club, and economies in the maintenance of the garden were evident in the neglected flower beds.[5] Subsequent debate revealed serious problems in 2008–10 with the 'building management scheme', a new electronic system of regulating the provision of heating and hot water, and concerns about the level of security.[6] Of course, the newsletter provided a forum that tended to attract more complaints than praise, and some of the criticisms of the new management may appear rather trivial to outsiders. However, they may be taken as indicative of a less sympathetic approach to the needs of older tenants in a housing complex where a 'younger demographic' was now regarded as the principal market.[7] Recent evidence suggests that the maintenance of an ageing building may be compromised by an over-zealous cut in staffing levels and a reliance on outside contractors. This is a development that will affect all tenants.[8]

At the top of the corporate pyramid, Westbrook Partners were keen on acquiring further iconic properties in central London, and in 2007 Shell-Mex House, the art deco block in the Strand, was bought for about £490 million. The partnership also acquired 123 Buckingham Palace Road, a mixed development of offices and retail colonnade.[9] At the same time, the senior managers, having largely completed the refurbishment programme, turned their attention to acquiring the freehold of Dolphin Square. In September 2007 Westbrook Dolphin Square Ltd offered Friends Provident Life & Pensions Ltd £97.8 million for this under the terms of a notice asserting Westbrook's right to collective enfranchisement. Under the Leasehold Reform, Housing and Urban Development Act of 1993, the owners of leases of over 21 years in length had the right to act together to purchase the freehold of their building, subject to the restriction that no leaseholder should own more than two flats. An important amendment in 2002 removed the requirement for the leaseholder to occupy the flat for which the freehold was sought.[10] An unintended consequence of the reform was that it opened the way for investing landlords such as Westbrook to seek to gain freehold status. Having taken expert advice, including that of Knight Frank, the company then created 612 Jersey-registered companies and sold each of them one or two of the 1,223 flats on 27-year leases, which it contended allowed it to serve notice of its right to the freehold.[11]

Friends Provident were unwilling to part with a valuable freehold when the outstanding lease had less than 30 years to run. They challenged Westbrook's device and in November 2007 served a counter notice on Westbrook. Simon Lacey, who, as we have seen, had been closely involved in the battle for the Dolphin Square leases since 1997, and was now head of central London residential and commercial property at F&C Investments, which managed Friends Provident funds, was quoted as saying: 'it is debateable whether [the] law was intended to allow non-domiciled private equity investors to compulsorily acquire on the cheap a major asset of a British life insurance company.'[12] Over the next 18 months an expensive legal battle was mounted, with Friends Provident claiming that it was costing them £13,000 a day. But in February 2009, with the dispute about to be heard in the high court, Westbrook withdrew its action and were required to pay the freeholder's costs. The company gave as a reason the fact that market conditions were now 'unfavourable'.[13] This was not the end of the matter, however. A second attempt to force the issue was started in May 2010. Westbrook served another notice on Friends Provident, and offered a larger sum – £111.6 million – for the freehold. This offer was also rejected by Friends Provident, who served a counter notice in July. Westbrook went to court to obtain a declaration that it could use the Jersey-company device to obtain the freehold, but Lacey made it clear that his company would 'fight tooth and nail' to oppose the American landlords.[14] Property experts were divided on the merits of the case. John Stephenson, a senior partner at Bircham Dyson Bell, was quoted as saying that

> As a matter of the general principles of English law, it is not wrong to order and structure your affairs so as to achieve a specific legal result. It may be that these companies have been formed for this specific purposes, but to say that the structure therefore isn't real and is a sham is a high bar to get over.

On the other hand, Stan Gallagher, barrister at Tanfield chambers, argued the opposite:

> The broad purpose of collective enfranchisement legislation is to allow groups of individual flat owners to club together to buy the freeholds of their blocks. So it would be an anomalous and surprising outcome if an investment company, holding the headlease of what is reputedly the largest residential block in Western Europe, has managed to find a bulletproof way of orchestrating a collective enfranchisement in order to compulsorily acquire the freehold . . . The decisive issue will be whether

> Westbrook can establish that the 600-odd firms to whom it has granted long sub-leases of the pairs of flats are not 'associated companies' within the meaning of the Companies Acts.[15]

The legal proceedings have reflected this dubiety. Thus, in September 2011 Mr Justice Arnold ruled that Westbrook had no right to bring a second claim, and the claim was 'an abuse of process'. This supported the position of Friends Provident, which by this time had merged with the life assurance businesses acquired from BUPA and AXA to become the more substantial Friends Life.[16] However, in May 2012 the Court of Appeal judges overturned the ruling.[17] Westbrook now appeared to have gained the initiative, but at the time of writing [April 2013] the outcome remains to be decided. What is clear is that the future of Dolphin Square rests on the result. Whoever gains the unfettered freehold will be in a position to introduce more radical changes. They may even be tempted to knock the flats down and redevelop the site.

Meanwhile the Dolphin Square Foundation began its task of providing key worker and social housing, using the Trust's proceeds from the sale. Launched in 2007, the Foundation set out to spend approximately £27 million in the first instance on a variety of projects in partnership with both 'not for profit' and 'for profit' partners. The intention was to allocate 70 per cent of its resources to key worker housing, with the remainder invested in social housing. It completed its first affordable homes project in July 2011, with the refurbishment of seven properties in Queen's Park for occupation by people with learning disabilities. Its first major project was the construction of 39 flats for 100 people in Moreton Street, north of Dolphin Square. Work began in 2011 on the £14.5 million development, which will open as One Church Square in July 2013. In 2012, six further sites had been acquired or earmarked for development, and £5 million was allocated to a project in Churchill Gardens, for the refurbishment of former Council apartments to use as temporary accommodation. The sums received from the Dolphin Square Trust amounted to £95 million in 2012.[18]

Dolphin Square 2005 Ltd. was also operational. This company had been set up to safeguard the interests of the Option B tenants, who numbered 376 in November 2010. It also assumed the Trust's right to nominate a governor of the Dolphin Square Foundation. One of its more important actions was to take up the several complaints arising from problems with the heating and hot water systems in 2008–10. It therefore decided to employ a permanent member of staff to liaise with both the tenants and Mantilla, and Richard Tovey was subsequently appointed.[19] With Dolphin Square 2005 Ltd. operating in effect as a 'super tenants' association', the need for two other bodies diminished. The DSTA declined to the point where it was happy to allow the Blue Dolphin Club to take over its responsibilities. In 2010, the amalgamated body became the Blue Dolphin Tenants' Association.[20]

THE APPEAL OF DOLPHIN SQUARE

What was the enduring appeal of Dolphin Square? As we saw in the previous chapter, writers such as Margaret Drabble and A.N. Wilson were able to convey a sense of diversity, edginess and excitement that attracted writers and actors. At the same time, the rather different attributes of comfort, service, privacy and value for money clearly appealed to many middle-class residents. Some of whom we may call the 'rich and famous' continue to be drawn to the place.[21] Of course, the Square was not immune from the more general changes in housing and society which were apparent in the later twentieth and early twenty-first centuries: the declining appeal of the rented sector for the more affluent, the persistence of housing shortages in London, and the challenge offered by commercial development in the inner-London boroughs. As time went on the Square began to reveal its age. In spite of the considerable sums spent on maintenance and repair, this immense building was showing signs of wear, especially to the basic fabric. Thus, Sebastian Faulks, writing in the 1990s at the time of Princess Anne's tenancy, suggested that its 'cachet' and 'fizz' had given way to something more seedy. 'The radios installed in each sitting room no longer work: the Bakelite control on the wall, that once switched to Home, Light or Third, is reminiscent of an NHS hospital in need of a refit.' Faulks also observed a preponderance of older residents: instead of 'rising businessmen' and 'debutantes', there were 'elderly women with heavy face powder, small dogs and the tottering walk made famous by the late Dick Emery'.[22] This assessment was a trifle unfair, and, of course, was made before £46 million was spent on repairs and refurbishment in the 12 years to 2005 (Appendix 11).

Discussions about the general value of Dolphin Square do not usually extend to its architectural appeal or singularity. This is evident, for example, in the standard work on the modern flat, by Yorke and Gibberd, which lists several private schemes in the mid-late 1930s, including Lawn Road, Hampstead, High Point in Highgate, Pullman Court in Streatham, and Roehampton Lane, but not Dolphin Square.[23] The same is true of Hilary French's *Key Urban Housing of the Twentieth Century*, which selects local authority projects such as Churchill Gardens, the Byker Wall in Newcastle, and, elsewhere in London, Robin Hood Gardens in Poplar, and Ernö Goldfinger's Balfron and Trellick Towers, but makes no mention of the Square.[24] The same omission was noted by A.N. Wilson, when reviewing Todd Longstaffe-Gowan's book on London's Squares. This, he felt, was a pity, since Dolphin Square was an 'innovative development', which became 'an enclave for the professional classes or for non-Londoners who wished for an anonymous pied-à-terre'. However, Wilson finds the building 'uninspiring', and repeats Pevsner's rather bleak assessment, although he does observe that the architects Leslie Martin and Patrick Hodgkinson drew some inspiration from it when designing the Brunswick Centre in Bloomsbury.[25] But while the Brunswick achieved Grade II listing status in 2000, the Trust's application for the listing of Dolphin Square in 2004 was unsuccessful. The Square had already been designated as a Conservation Area by Westminster Council in 1990. The intention behind the listing application was clearly to strengthen the protection of its architectural features and amenities after the sale to Westbrook. The response of the listing inspector was negative, however, and his verdict was confirmed by the Department for Culture, Media and Sport in October 2005. Dolphin Square was not considered to 'possess sufficient special interest, either architecturally or historically, to merit listing'.[26] The English Heritage inspector's report concluded that the building was

> clearly a vast and imposing development that cannot be ignored, but this prominence also dilutes the impact of the fairly standard Neo-Classical styling. Furthermore, many of the interior

> spaces of note have been quite altered. Dolphin Court [sic] certainly has claims to historic importance for its scale, for its method of construction in the context of it as an early pre-war response to the threat of bombing, and for the remarkable concept of self-sufficiency in its overall planning.

However,

> Dolphin Square's significance is recognised in its designation in 1990 as a Conservation Area that neatly includes the whole complex, its thirteen houses, the commercial range, and even the tennis courts complex in the south side of Grosvenor Road, extending into the River Thames. The main strength of the building is its impressive scale and presence along the river-front and its monumental planning with integrally designed gardens and non-residential services. These merits, however, are duly recognised and protected by its designation as a conservation area, which after a full assessment, does indeed seem to be the most appropriate designation to recognise its level of interest, while the claims to historic importance and striking scale and plan are noted, there is insufficient overall special architectural interest to this enormous 1930s complex to recommend it for listing.[27]

The Trust's efforts in its application to link the Square to the operations of De Gaulle and the Free French during the war backfired somewhat, since the English Heritage protection team was unable to find any evidence to support the view that the Square played a significant role in the activities of the Free French, in comparison with, for example, their headquarters in Carlton Gardens.[28] Westminster Council's Conservation Area Audit of 2008 corrected the record, pointing out that Grenville House had been occupied by De Gaulle's staff.[29] The audit was the final stage in the conservation review process, building on the Council's decision in 1990 to designate the site as a Conservation Area. It concluded that the Square was 'generally well-maintained' and expected a Conservation Area to be effectively managed via existing development control and enforcement powers. The audit identified both positive and negative features. The negative elements, which invited attention, were the riverside buildings, which 'failed to acknowledge and enhance the riverside location', and some small-scale alterations and additions to the building itself, notably the use of uPVC casement windows on the ground floor of Rodney House, the location of plant and air conditioning units in the basement light well on Chichester Street, and the 'unsympathetic' placing of security cameras on Beatty House. However, these were outweighed by the positive elements. The building was 'monumental', and a 'highly visible landmark on this part of the Thames', though from the outside it appeared 'monolithic and impenetrable'. Architecturally, it possessed a 'strong sense of uniformity', with the absence of external pipework, etc. contributing to the 'simplicity of the design'. The shopping arcade and the garden drew praise. Dolphin Square was held to be 'of significant historical and architectural interest as an example of high-density 1930s housing, being the largest example of self contained flats in Europe when built'. Although unlisted, it was clearly a 'building of merit'.[30] Whether it really was the largest block of flats in Europe is an open question which demands investigation. The Social Democrats in Vienna built several large apartment buildings with over 1,000 flats for working-class occupation in the period 1919–34. The best known is the iconic Karl-Marx-Hof in Vienna, designed by Karl Ehn and constructed in 1926–30. Rightly described as 'monumental', it comprised 1,382 apartments, with shops, schools, laundries, bathing facilities, youth hostel, dental and maternity clinics, library and post office, and covered an area – about 38.5 acres – which made it five times larger than Dolphin Square. On the other hand, its continuity is broken on one side of the central garden, and thus it is not a continuous single building as Dolphin Square is. Furthermore, Karl-Marx-Hof was an example of municipal housing, and not a speculative housing project built by the private sector.[31] Continental builders also inspired emulation in the United Kingdom, though few developments were larger than Dolphin Square. One of the largest was Quarry Hill, a 938-flat estate built on 26 acres built by Leeds City Council in 1935–41. Constrained by wartime pressures, it was never completed, and was demolished in 1976–8 after flaws in its steel and concrete construction made refurbishment prohibitively expensive.[32] Also affected by the war was Aberdeen's Rosemount Square, a small but impressive four-storey, horseshoe-shaped block with 104 flats, approved in 1939 and finally completed in 1945. Inspired by the Karl Marx-Hof and schemes in Rotterdam, it nonetheless invites comparison with Dolphin Square, even though it enjoys a Scottish Grade A listing.[33] One thing is clear. As a private sector development, Dolphin Square had few if any equals in Europe when it was built.

AN EXPERIMENT IN HOUSING?

We must conclude by considering the Dolphin Square development within the broader context of housing provision for the middle class in central London. This unusual example of apartment living, with its self-contained features and comparatively high density, was first of all promoted and built by the private sector firm, Costain, as a speculative venture. However, after the reduction in government rent control it attracted speculators during the property boom of the mid–late 1950s. Tenant activism encouraged Westminster City Council to buy the property from Maxwell Joseph, its action supported by a mortgage sanctioned by the Ministry of Housing and Local Government. After a brief period of direct management in 1964 the Square became the responsibility of a housing trust. For 40 years it was run as a unique example of non-profit-making housing for largely middle-income families in London. The Council retained the right to approve rent levels and nominate Trust members, but the flats were managed by the Dolphin Square Trust for those working in central London with longer-term residents enjoying subsidised rents thanks to the proceeds from the hotel apartments in Rodney House. No money was required from the public purse, because following the 'back-to-back' arrangement between the parties in 1964 the cost to the Council of borrowing the money to buy the Square was fully reimbursed by the Trust.[34] More recently, ownership and management came full circle. Dolphin Square returned to the private sector in 2006 when the outstanding leases were sold to Westbrook.

As we have seen, critics have been divided about the significance of Dolphin Square as a not-for-profit operation. For much of its life the Trust operated as an Industrial and Provident Society, its initial object being to 'carry on the business or trade of providing housing for letting . . . and any associated amenities . . .'.[35] However, it did not have a duty to house people on low incomes, and the extent to which it provided a mixed tenancy group became a matter for debate. When the Trust operated as a housing association, from 1976 to 1992, it eventually provoked criticism for its lack of diversity, contributing to the decision to deregister (see Chapter 5, pp.202–6). Over time, the balance certainly shifted. In the 1960s the majority of tenants regarded Dolphin Square as their home, but new tenants increasingly had a more transient relationship with the place: for example, military officers on three-year contracts, MPs subject to the vicissitudes of the ballot box, and civil servants or managers moving to posts in central London while retaining a family home in the provinces. The interest of the media in celebrity tenants tended to encourage negative reactions, and notably criticisms of the Square as a bastion of privilege,[36] but these neglected the fact that the property was providing an extremely useful base for those with more modest means who needed to work in central London. This group undoubtedly benefited from the facility, enabling them to make a more effective contribution to London's economy. As we have seen, some journalists made much of the disparity between the rents paid by long-standing Dolphin Square tenants and those paid by Westminster's council house tenants in nearby Churchill Square. These criticisms gathered momentum when the prospect of a sale emerged from the late 1990s. And yet, aside from the fact that the rents quoted were often in error,[37] there was a collective failure to present the data in context. Simple rental comparisons ignored the transformation of the council housing sector since 1979. There was the 'right to buy' introduced by the Thatcher governments; a change in the method of providing subsidies, which instead of being paid to the local authority to support its housing went directly to families in need in the form of housing benefit; and pressure to increase council house rents because the housing stock could no longer be valued at historic cost, but had to be valued and serviced at current value. And in the comparison with Dolphin Square, few commentators made the point that below market rentals were not available to new entrants, but only to those who remained in the Square for successive three-year tenancy periods, or that these same tenants, by remaining in the rented sector instead of moving to the increasingly popular owner-occupier sector, had forgone the advantage of lower housing costs based on the historic purchase of a property subject to substantial capital gains in the longer run.[38]

Of course, the current housing crisis, with its accompanying evidence of gentrification and social segregation in central London,[39] has had a severe impact on the capital's poorer families, and in this context revelations of privileges for a segment of largely middle-class people in Westminster began to appear somewhat distasteful, as did the fact that the local authority, which in Shirley Porter's time had sought to manipulate housing for electoral gain, was party to the operations of the Trust.[40] Here, the anxiety of Westminster's Conservative majority to dispose of the lease was driven by the expectations of realising a significant sum while at the same time removing a relationship complained of by the Labour minority. In fact, the sale of Dolphin Square will surely lead to a positive housing outcome in that the bulk of the proceeds from the sale have been vested in the new Dolphin Square Foundation, whose prime duty is to build affordable housing in central London. At the same time, the interests of those tenants who wished to remain in the Square have been protected for the lifetime of the original lease.

In 2006, Dolphin Square returned to the private sector management which had been in place from 1936 to 1963. But during Westminster Council's brief stewardship, 1963–4, and the period of the Trust's management, 1965–2006, it served as an instructive example of what could be done creatively in a high-cost housing area to provide accommodation where employment locally was a principal consideration.

NOTES

1 DST Committee of Management Minutes, 26 January 2006, DST; *Evening Standard*, 13 April 2006, p.15.

2 Information from Amos Barber of Brookhouse Capital.

3 *Estates Gazette*, 9 June 2007, pp.72–4.

4 *Estates Gazette*, 2 August 2008, p.22; *Blue Dolphin Club Newsletter*, July 2008, April 2009. My thanks to Jan Prebble for this source.

5 *Blue Dolphin Club Newsletter*, March 2008, and see also November 2007 and April 2008.

6 Ibid. May 2008, January–December 2009.

7 Note, in particular, arguments over the provision of a heavy door offering access to the main lobby from the arcade end of the Square on Chichester Street. The more elderly tenants regarded it as a way of dissuading them from crossing to the other side of the square via the new reception area. Ibid. November 2007, January 2009.

8 Information from Dolphin Square 2005 Ltd., 2013.

9 *Financial Times*, 5 July 2007, p.19; *Estates Gazette*, 13 October 2007, p.37; information from Barber.

10 Leasehold Reform, Housing and Urban Development Act 1993, 1993 c.28; Commonhold and Leasehold Reform Act 2002, 2002 c.15.

11 See preamble in *Westbrook Dolphin Square Ltd v Friends Provident Life & Pensions Ltd*, EWCA Civ 666.

12 Lacey, quoted in *Estates Gazette*, 13 October 2007, pp.37, 48.

13 *Estates Gazette*, 18 September 2010, pp.74–7. With the case set to be heard on 23 February 2009, Westbrook abandoned its action on the 16th.

14 Lacey, quoted in *Estates Gazette*, 18 September 2010, p.77.

15 John Stephenson, and Stan Gallagher, quoted in *Estates Gazette*, 18 September 2010, p.77.

16 *Estates Gazette*, 17 September 2011, p.51; *Evening Standard*, 6 January 2012, p.54.

17 Judgment in *Westbrook Dolphin Square Ltd v Friends Provident Life & Pensions Ltd*, EWCA Civ 666, and see *Evening Standard*, 8 May 2012, p.42; *Estates Gazette*, 2 June 2012, p.85, 11 August 2012, pp.42–7.

18 Dolphin Square Foundation, *R & A 2011/12*, pp.6–7; DST Committee of Management Minutes, 20 June and 21 November 2007, DST; *Evening Standard*, 6 January 2012, p.54; information from Steve Logie, Operations Manager, Dolphin Square Foundation.

19 DST Committee of Management Minutes, 11 November and 9 December 2010, DST.

20 DST Committee of Management Minutes, 9 December 2010, DST; Blue Dolphin Club Newsletter, March 2010.

21 Recent media accounts have referred to senior policemen such as John Stevens (Baron Stevens of Kirkwhelpington) and Sir Ronnie Flanagan, First Minister of Scotland and SNP leader Alex Salmond, and Prince William. *Daily Telegraph*, 9 February 2007, p.27, *Sunday Express*, 27 May 2007, p.12, *The Times*, 27 March 2008, p.4.

22 Faulks in *Guardian*, 6 February 1993, p.25.

23 F.R.S. Yorke and Frederick Gibberd, *The Modern Flat* (3rd edn, 1950).

24 Hilary French, *Key Urban Housing of the Twentieth Century: Plans, Sections and Elevations* (2008).

25 A.N. Wilson, review of Todd Longstaffe-Gowan, *The London Square: Gardens in the Midst of Town* (New Haven, 2012), in *Times Literary Supplement*, 14 September 2012, pp.10–11.

26 Chris Fosten (Historic Environment Case Officer, Department for Culture, Media & Sport)-Wray, 4 October 2005, DST. The verdict also applied to a subsequent application for listing by SOS.

27 Inspector's Advice Print, 24 January 2005, DST.

28 Philip Seely (Heritage Protection Team, English Heritage)-Fosten, 23 March 2005, DST. Seely did not consult Westminster's records, which indicate that the Free French occupied Grenville House from 1942 (see Chapter 3, p.99).

29 City of Westminster Department of Planning & City Development, *Conservation Area Audit and Management Proposals 45: Dolphin Square* (October 2008), p.14. My thanks to Drummond Robson for referring me to this report.

30 Ibid. pp.15, 20, 25, 31–4, 37–9.

31 Kenneth Frampton and Yukio Futagawa, *Modern Architecture 1851–1945* (New York, 1983), p.302; Helmut Gruber, *Red Vienna: Experiment in Working-Class Culture 1919–1934* (Oxford, 1991), pp.46, 207; Eve Blau, *The Architecture of Red Vienna 1919–1934* (Cambridge, MA, 1998), esp. pp.320–30, 366–8; French, *Key Urban Housing*, p.42. The smaller Sandleitenhof complex had more flats - 1,587 - but it was not a single building.

32 Alison Ravetz, *Model Estate: Planned housing at Quarry Hill, Leeds* (1974), p.50ff.; Peter Mitchell, *Memento Mori: The Flats at Quarry Hill* (Otley, 1990).

33 Mark Chalmers, 'Rosemount Square, Aberdeen: Modernism in Granite', *Urban Realm* (2011), http://www.urbanrealm.com/blogs/index.php/2011/07/06/rosemount-square-aberdeen-modernism-in-granite?blog=16.

34 Brooke, 'The die is cast', Chairman's note for DSTA Newsletter, October 2005, DST; Interview with Sir Rodney Brooke, 25 October 2012.

35 Rule 2, Dolphin Square Trust Ltd Rules, 4 June 1964, DST.

36 Cf. Andrew Perloff, Chairman and Chief Executive of Panther Securities, in address to Panther Securities plc, *R & A 2009*. Perloff was an office boy at Marcus Leaver, the agents instructed to sell Dolphin Square in 1963. He later approached Westminster Council to find out whether they would sell their lease. He criticised the Square as 'subsidised accommodation for the rich or well connected', Westminster's role in its purchase as a 'dreadful mistake', and the Trust as 'accountable only to itself'.

37 See, in particular, Mira Bar-Hillel and Sara Salman, in *Evening Standard*, 3 November 2000, pp.10–11. For example, the weekly rent of Alistair Darling's flat was given as £77 (actual: £215), William and Ffion Hague's flat £114 (actual: £268).

38 Stonefrost, 'Dolphin Square Trust', 2008, pp.15–16; Interview with Brooke, 2012. One of the few balanced newspapers articles on the Square was Patrick Kidd's 'The Square Deal', *The Times*, 22 October 2004, bricks and mortar, p.4.

39 Cf. Chris Hamnett, 'Gentrification and the Middle-class Remaking of Inner London, 1961–2001', *Urban Studies*, 40:12 (2003), 2401–26, and Rowland Atkinson, 'Padding the Bunker: Strategies of Middle-class Disaffiliation and Colonisation in the City', *Urban Studies*, 43:4 (2006), 819–32.

40 Rodney Brooke has noted that Porter was an admirer of Dolphin Square, and she commissioned a study to see if it could be emulated. Interview with Brooke, 2012.

APPENDIX 1

DOLPHIN SQUARE TENANTS, SOUTH BLOCK, 1937

Flat no.	1st tenancy Month/ year	Name	Date occupied MMYY	Electoral Register 1937	Rent £	**D** Discount **F** Furnished
A01						
A02	6.37	Silverman, ES			140	D
A03	7.37	Louis, Sir C			130	D
A04		Staff				
A05		Staff				
A06	3.37	Darlington, AV	4.37		105	D
A07	11.36	Tait, Dorothy M Miss	12.36	R	90	
A08	5.37	Sheridan, PC Miss	7.37		100	D
A101	2.37	Colgan, William A	5.37	R	145	
A102						
A103						
A104	6.37	Machin, GM			175	
A105	3.37	Thompson, EV	6.37		95	
A106	12.36	Hancock, Kenneth S	2.37	R	115	
A107						
A108	5.37	St Clair Sergant, HF			328	F
A109	3.37	Fenner, Beatrice Mrs	3.37	R	85	
A201	12.36	Harris, V Edith Hon	2.37	R	145	
A202	11.36	Ferriman, David G	12.36	R	145	
A203	4.37	Berger, O	4.37		145	
A204	3.37	Josephs, Elizabeth	3.37	R	175	
A205	10.36	Sibthorp, Eliz A Miss	1.37	R	95	
A206	11.36	Duncan-Clay, Robert Dr	12.36	R	115	
A207	7.37	Trapman, LA			130	D
A208	3.37	Nangle, HJ			145	
A209	1.37	Dejan, W Mrs	2.37		85	
A301	4.37	Hunt, MA Mrs			145	
A302	6.37	Coke, R Mrs			145	
A303	3.37	Hornstein, R Baroness	4.37		145	
A304	3.37	Wigan, DG	4.37		175	
A305	12.36	Jordain, Betty Miss + Welch	1.37		95	
A306	11.36	Forbes, Hilda Mrs	11.36	R	115	
A307	4.37	Sedgwick, LST	6.37		130	D
A308	7.37	Bunwell, RHC			125	
A309	3.37	John, Norma Miss	5.37	R	85	
A401	3.37	Lyon, Geoffrey M	5.37	R	145	
A402	12.36	Bruce, John	1.37	R	145	
A403	2.37	Owen, James R	2.37	R	145	
A404	11.36	Shires, Ida CK	11.36	R	175	
A405	10.36	Rourke, Francis LA	12.36	R	95	

A406	1.37	Harlow, Nora M	2.37	R	115	
A407	2.37	Cammiade, Philip F	3.37	R	130	D
A408						
A409	10.36	Simson, Eliz M	11.36	R	85	
A501	10.36	Haines, Arthur DC	11.36	R	145	
A502	11.36	LeQuesne, Charlotte L Mrs	12.36	R	145	
A503	10.36	Weatherall, Helena Mrs	11.36	R	145	
A504	11.36	Witherington, Kenelm	11.36	R	175	
A505	10.36	Martinuzzi, IF Dr	11.36		95	
A506	11.36	Murray, Ronald O	11.36	R	115	
A507	4.37	Kemper & Orsky	5.37		130	D
A508						
A509	10.36	Arnold, Daisy E	11.36	R	85	
A601	6.37	Clark, GBH			150	D
A602	10.36	Scott-Rutherford, Ivan	12.36	R	145	
A603	10.36	Dawson, Florence M Mrs	11.36	R	145	
A604	10.36	Colquhoun, Emma MM	12.36	R	175	
A605	12.36	Stobart, Phyllis C Miss		R	100	
A606	2.37	Doyle, Elaine L Miss	3.37	R	115	
A607	7.37	Bateman, DE			130	D
A608						
A609	1.37	Davies, GM Miss	4.37		85	
A701	4.37	Hunt, MA Mrs			150	
A702	2.37	Feldman, Robert A	6.37	R	145	
A703	10.36	Anderson, Alfred B	1.37	R	145	
A704	1.37	Bourn, Thomas A	2.37	R	175	
A705	3.37	Bourn, Thomas A	2.37	R	100	
A706	10.36	Hayman, William GE Fl-Lt	11.36	R	115	
A707						
A708						
A709	10.36	Edwardes, Norman	12.36	R	85	
A801	3.37	Summerskill, William H Dr	4.37	R	455	
A802	2.37	Anson, F Mrs Rt Hon	5.37		260	
A803	12.36	Lingley, Loris Gale	1.37	R	115	
A804	6.37	Bird, DFS Mrs	7.37		130	D
A805						
A806	11.36	Cameron, Jessie Miss	12.36	R	80	
A901	4.37	Apsley, VEM Rt Hon Lady	5.37	R	400	
A902	3.37	Savory, Agnes R	4.37	R	300	
A903						
B01	1.37	Lycett, Douglas L	2.37	R	100	
B02		general manager HJ Castle		R		
B03		'stores'				
B101	11.36	Kamm, Amy Mrs	12.36	R	100	
B102	5.37	Clark, Sarah E	7.37		310	
B103	5.37	Clark, Sarah E	7.37		210	
B201	10.36	Meyer, Joan B Miss	11.36	R	100	
B202						
B203	3.37	Bridgman, Leonard	4.37	R	220	
B204	5.37	Gordon, Isabella Mrs			155	

B205	5.37	Gordon, Isabella Mrs			155	
B301	11.36	Torres, LMJ	12.36		100	
B302	4.37	Crossman, Vera	6.37	R	310	
B303	4.37	Crossman, Vera	6.37	R	220	
B304	2.37	Knight, Lilian Mrs	3.37	R	155	
B305	6.37	Fyffe, W			145	D
B401	10.36	Deakin, Thea N	11.36	R	100	
B402						
B403	11.36	Soley, Ivy Eleanor	12.36	R	220	
B404	2.37	Berryman, ML	3.37		155	
B405	6.37	Bright, JHG			145	D
B501	5.37	Penhale, Nancy			100	
B502	4.37	Pyemont, W	4.37		310	
B503	2.37	McPherson, Gilbert	3.37	R	220	
B504	2.37	Wood, Lynda Mrs	3.37	R	155	
B505						
B601	12.36	Kalisch, H	1.37		100	
B602	12.36	Sellers, CH	5.37		310	
B603	3.37	Costain, MM Mrs	4.37		220	
B604	4.37	Thornton, JR	5.37		155	
B605						
B701	10.36	Le Fontaine, Donald	12.36		100	
B702	12.36	Curtis, Raphael	12.36	R	295	
B703	1.37	Fellows, Ernest	4.37	R	190	
B704	2.37	Hildesley, Anthony G	2.37	R	145	
B705	7.37	Wright, EAH			145	D
B801	3.37	Grimes, Mollie E Mrs	3.37	R	80	
B802	3.37	Treglown, WM	5.37		260	D
B803	6.37	Catchpole, FE			210	
B804	2.37	Abram, C + Macdonald PK Misses	3.37	R	145	
B805	7.37	Bulteel, JC			140	D
B901	11.36	Bailey, Maud Miss	1.37	R	75	
B902	12.36	Willett, Guy W	2.37	R	255	
B903	4.37	Damnhorn, AJ			165	
B904						
C01		guest room				
C02						
C03		Housekeeper's office				
C101						
C102						
C103	10.36	Dawes, Howard H	2.37	R	100	
C201						
C202						
C203	6.37	Briggs, A	7.37		220	
C204						
C205	1.37	Thomas, Stephen K	1.37	R	100	
C301	6.37	Judd, EL Capt			150	D
C302	6.37	Judd, EL Capt			150	D
C303	6.37	Mornington, CE Mrs			220	

C304						
C305	11.36	Bloomfield, Joan DA	12.36	R	100	
C401	5.37	Dewez, Guy			145	D
C402	2.37	Marsden, Audrey Dr	3.37	R	155	
C403	2.37	Quinton, EW Miss			220	
C404	3.37	Halliday, J			310	
C405	3.37	Alcock, PM			100	
C501	6.37	Hill, RJ Mrs	7.37			
C502	5.37	Young, GAG Capt	5.37			
C503	3.37	Hill, Lilian J + Knowles, Norah J Misses	5.37	R	220	
C504	12.36	Clifton, Charles F	1.37	R	310	
C505	11.36	Gray, Dorothy Miss	11.36	R	100	
C601	7.37	Lidbury, C			145	D
C602	4.37	Byrte, AJ	6.37		155	
C603	2.37	Gifford, Lord	5.37	R	220	
C604	12.36	Ramsay, Bertha L	12.36	R	310	
C605	11.36	Fryer, Stanley TJ	12.36	R	100	
C701	6.37	Winckler, FNV			145	D
C702	12.36	Scott, Margaret Mrs	1.37	R	145	
C703	1.37	Corbett, FM	2.37		190	
C704	12.36	Chettle, FW	1.37	R	295	
C705	12.36	Pickard, Huia M	12.36	R	100	
C801	7.37	George, E Mrs			140	D
C802	3.37	Salisbury, CR	4.37		145	
C803	5.37	Phillips, Hugh			210	
C804	1.37	Welch, Eric S	3.37	R	275	
C805	3.37	Bell, WH	4.37	R	80	
C901						
C902	10.36	Brooke, Philip Capt	12.36	R	165	
C903	3.37	Beech-Elliot, V	6.37		255	
C904	5.37	Brooke, PR	6.37		75	
D01						
D02						
D03						
D04						
D05		Management Office				
D06						
D07						
D08						
D101	11.36	Brown, George H	11.36	R	85	
D102						
D103	6.37	Lowther, OP			130	D
D104	9.36	Live, R	12.36		115	
D105	12.36	MacGuire	12.36		95	
D106	6.37	Ormsby, N			175	
D107						
D108						
D109	2.37	Skeen, Dorothy M	3.37	R	145	
D201	4.37	Roberton, Alan B	4.37	R	85	

D202	3.37	Jones, Lydia A	4.37	R	125	D
D203	12.36	Jones, George R	12.36	R	130	D
D204	10.36	Morris, Marion M Mrs	11.36	R	115	
D205	2.37	Ollard, Edith Mrs	3.37	R	95	
D206	3.37	Clancy, Vernon Y + Cantley, Denis F	4.37	R	175	
D207	4.37	Evans, J Mrs			145	
D208						
D209	1.37	Kiar, KS	2.37		145	
D301	12.36	Mitchell, David M	12.36	R	85	
D302	1.37	Gain, Winifred Mrs	3.37	R	125	D
D303	5.37	Kitchen, CB	5.37		130	D
D304	11.36	Anderson, George W	11.36	R	115	
D305	1.37	Evans, Dylan P	2.37	R	95	
D306	5.37	Thellusson, CAH			175	
D307	11.36	Newgass, Mary	12.36	R	145	
D308	4.37	Drummond Hay, JWEH	7.37		145	
D309	11.36	Lambert, Thomas E Major	12.36	R	145	
D401	1.37	Sawyer, DM	3.37		85	
D402	1.37	Sloan, John R	3.37	R	135	D
D403	6.37	Seppala, AR			130	D
D404	2.37	Winning, Robert C	3.37	R	115	
D405	11.36	Hart, Francis C	1.37	R	95	
D406	1.37	Bolwell, Harry	3.37	R	175	
D407	2.37	Ranns, Charles W	2.37	R	145	
D408	1.37	Bruère, H	2.37	R	145	
D409	10.36	Hewison, Robert JP	11.36	R	145	
D501	10.36	White, Amy	11.36	R	85	
D502	2.37	Goodban, PD	6.37		135	D
D503	4.37	Kahn, S	5.37		130	D
D504	12.36	Oram, Frederick S	2.37	R	115	
D505	12.36	Bell, Edward ND	2.37	R	95	
D506	11.36	Naylor, Gordon St George	12.36	R	175	
D507	11.36	Macy, Peter	12.36	R	145	
D508	4.37	Edwards Glass Co Ltd			145	
D509	10.36	Hales, Frederick	12.36	R	145	
D601	10.36	Turpitz, Marjorie E Miss	11.36	R	85	
D602						
D603	6.37	Knowles, SJ	6.37		130	D
D604	12.36	Kennedy, Ethel G Miss	1.37	R	115	
D605	1.37	Bullock, CP Capt	2.37		100	
D606	2.37	Harvey, Eveline Mrs	4.37	R	175	
D607	11.36	Nissen, E	1.37		145	
D608	4.37	Westbrooke, BA	5.37		145	
D609	2.37	Dexter, George	3.37	R	165	
D701	12.36	Gabriel, John P	1.37	R	85	
D702						
D703	5.37	Kirkpatrick, Charlotte Mrs		R	130	D
D704	10.36	Nunnenmacher, KA	11.36		115	
D705	12.36	Chettle, FW	1.37		100	

D706	3.37	Mellor, Una Sara Maxwell Mrs	4.37	R	175	
D707	11.36	Mackay, Lilias Urquhart Mrs	11.36	R	145	
D708	12.36	Brindley, Beavis	3.37	R	145	
D709	2.37	Queble, O Miss	2.37		165	
D801	11.36	Pace, Ethel Miss	12.36	R	80	
D802	10.36	Lutyens, Ernest Francis	11.36	R	145	
D803						
D804	10.36	Paterson, Reginald S	11.36	R	115	
D805	11.36	Anson, Thomas G	12.36	R	260	
D806	1.37	Mayo, Thorva Eyres	3.37	R	455	
D901						
D902						
D903						
E01		'tenant's maid'				
E02	7.37	Finningley, EL			110	D
E03	12.36	Jago, Irene	1.37		85	
E04	2.37	Hordern, Charles Lt Col	4.37	R	165	
E05	2.37	Mayfield, Rowena L	3.37	R	165	
E06	5.37	Belfrage, J Mrs	6.37		130	D
E07		'male staff room'				
E08		'female staff room'				
E09	6.37	Tabor, GJH			85	
E101	12.36	Hutton, Thomas B	12.36	R	85	
E102	12.36	Boulton, TC	12.36		165	
E103	1.37	Wittusen, A	3.37		165	
E104						
E105						
E106		'furnished'				F
E107						
E108						
E109						
E110	7.37	Rougemont, MJ de			130	D
E201	10.36	Arthur, Evelyn V Mrs	12.36	R	85	
E202	3.37	Balcomb, Alfred W	4.37	R	165	
E203	1.37	Porte, Mynnie Mrs	2.37	R	165	
E204	11.36	Coppock, Harry S	12.36	R	120	
E205						
E206	3.37	Smith, S Heckstall	5.37	R	125	D
E207	4.37	Hicks, FN	6.37		120	D
E208	3.37	Bowker, Joyce Mrs	3.37	R	120	D
E209	3.37	Vise, Jack Raymond	3.37	R	125	D
E210	6.37	Grigg, DL Mrs	7.37		130	D
E301	10.36	Turner, Patricia B Miss	1.37	R	85	
E302	4.37	Roberton, I	7.37		165	
E303	1.37	Fleming-Gibson, Harry	2.37	R	165	
E304	10.36	Pengelly, Percy W	12.36	R	120	
E305	7.37	Allan, WAR Capt			130	
E306	3.37	Errington, Eric	3.37	R	125	D
E307	3.37	Johnstone, Rupert DC	4.37	R	120	D

E308	3.37	Foote Foster, Kenneth E	5.37	R	120	D
E309	2.37	Potter, John D	3.37	R	125	D
E310	4.37	Barton, HJO			130	D
E401	4.37	Handley-Davies, Annie H Mrs	4.37	R	85	
E402	4.37	Blount, WH	7.37		165	
E403	12.36	Purtell, Amy K	12.36	R	165	
E404	4.37	Tebbutt, Eliz Mrs	4.37	R	120	
E405	6.37	Warburton, P			130	D
E406	6.37	Warburton, P			135	D
E407	12.36	Lambert, Lucy Mary	12.36	R	125	D
E408						
E409	4.37	Seymour, AH	5.37		135	D
E410	4.37	Rutter, RH	7.37		130	D
E501	4.37	Rideout, HD			85	
E502	3.37	Wareham, Frederick C	4.37	R	165	
E503	11.36	Whitelaw, Elsie L + Sybil L Misses	1.37	R	165	
E504	11.36	Young, George S	2.37	R	120	
E505	11.36	Moss, Robt Fred	12.36	R	130	D
E506	4.37	South, EF	6.37		135	D
E507	1.37	Frost, Agnes Miss	3.37	R	125	D
E508	4.37	Sloan, IH [crossed out]			125	D
E509	3.37	Harrison, EF	4.37		135	D
E510	4.37	Prince, OJP	6.37		130	D
E601	9.36	Austin-Potter, C	11.36		85	
E602	9.36	Walker, G	11.36	R	165	
E603	5.37	Paterson, James G	6.37	R	165	
E604	11.36	Edmonds, Ella Mrs	12.36	R	120	
E605						
E606						
E607						
E608						
E609						
E610						
E701	11.36	Doel, LL	1.37		85	
E702	12.36	Pullen, George A	2.37		165	
E703	3.37	Berry, PC	4.37		165	
E704	10.36	Hart, Ida F Miss	12.36		120	
E705						
E706	7.37	Burke, EP			140	D
E707	12.36	Anderson, I ['Mona']	3.37	R	145	
E708	6.37	Mitford, CMKF			135	D
E709						
E710	6.37	Bruce Norton, GJF			130	D
E801	10.36	Kirkpatrick, William R	12.36	R	80	
E802						
E803	11.36	Yates, Harold	1.37	R	150	
E804	11.36	Burghley, Rt Hon Lord	12.36	R	120	
E805	7.37	Pattinson, AV			130	D

E806						
E807						
E808						
E901						
E902	11.36	Lambert, Marjorie C Miss	12.36	R	115	
E903		matron Pantin, E	12.36			
E904	11.36	Brownstone, Kate	2.37	R	200	
E905						
E906	5.37	Wood, TP	6.37		120	D
F01	4.37	Shepherd, FW	5.37		120	D
F02	5.37	Logan, ME Miss	6.37		120	D
F03						
F04						
F05	5.37	Gaze, HC	6.37		85	
F06	3.37	O'Neill, H O'Hagan			165	
F07	3.37	O'Neill, H O'Hagan			165	
F08	11.36	Gathercole, AM Mrs	12.36	R	85	
F09	4.37	Goodban, GHC	6.37		120	
F10						
F11	2.37	Kenyon, J	3.37	R	85	
F101						
F102	4.37	Poulter, L 'furnished'	5.37	R	328	F
F103						
F104	6.37	Collins, JW	7.37		120	D
F105	4.37	Baker, Matthew	5.37	R	120	D
F106	6.37	Jones, G	5.37		120	D
F107						
F108	12.36	Sneath, RAS	2.37	R	85	
F109	12.36	Barrington, EL	1.37	R	120	
F110	3.37	Carpenter, F	4.37	R	165	
F111	2.37	Board, TFA	3.37	R	165	
F112	1.37	Hurst, HS	2.37	R	85	
F201	4.37	Wade, E Miss	5.37	R	140	
F202	6.37	Sayer, CE			125	D
F203	3.37	Ferrer, JR	4.37		120	D
F204	3.37	Mort, ER	4.37	R	120	D
F205	4.37	Gardiner, CGR	6.37		120	D
F206	4.37	Flint, VMC Miss			120	D
F207	6.37	Jacques, EV Mrs			195	
F208	10.36	Umney, E	12.36	R	85	
F209						
F210	1.37	Collins, JAS	4.37		165	
F211	1.37	Henry, JM	3.37	R	165	
F212	10.36	McCarthy, IR	11.36	R	85	
F301	5.37	Cliff, ND			130	D
F302	3.37	Norman, NE Mrs	4.37	R	125	D
F303	4.37	Mange, SM	7.37		120	D
F304	3.37	Castang, P			120	D
F305	3.37	Patterson, MS Mrs	6.37		120	D

F306	3.37	Clarke, C	4.37	R	120	D
F307						
F308	1.37	Schulhof, FJ	2.37		85	
F309	11.36	Gibson, F Mrs	12.36	R	120	
F310	2.37	Newcombe, RD	5.37	R	165	
F311	12.36	Cook, Ida Miss	3.37		165	
F312	12.36	Casson, BV	2.37		85	
F401	5.37	Farquharson, ME	6.37	R	130	D
F402	5.37	Farquharson, ME	6.37	R	135	D
F403	4.37	Oldham, DLE Miss	6.37		125	D
F404						
F405						
F406						
F407	5.37	Harries, DG			195	
F408	12.36	Clark, FW	12.36	R	85	
F409						
F410	1.37	Rome, GF	2.37	R	165	
F411	1.37	Betts-Brown, DIMW	3.37	R	165	
F412	3.37	Ashworth, D Miss	4.37	R	85	
F501	3.37	McLauchlin, JC			130	D
F502	4.37	Ward, W		R	135	D
F503	3.37	Alcock, PM			125	D
F504						
F505	7.37	Mann, M Miss			125	D
F506						
F507	7.37	Blomfield, C Mrs			195	
F508	10.36	Twigge-Molecy, CEJ	11.36	R	85	
F509	10.36	Hoskins, JS	12.36	R	120	
F510	4.37	Kimber, CD	4.37		165	
F511	4.37	Kimber, CD	4.37		165	
F512	2.37	Hingorani, R	3.37		85	
F601						
F602						
F603						
F604						
F605						
F606						
F607						
F608	10.36	D'Antal, AL	11.36	R	85	
F609	12.36	Swinburn, LM Miss	1.37	R	120	
F610	4.37	Knapp, AM Mrs			165	
F611	3.37	Woods, OFGB + Leichten-stein, C	3.37	R	165	
F612	12.36	Salgo, P	2.37		80	
F701						
F702						
F703	5.37	Rowe, HR	5.37	R	135	D
F704						
F705						

F706						
F707	5.37	Mackenzie, E Lady			195	
F708	5.37	Mackenzie, E Lady			85	
F709	11.36	Foster, RH	2.37	R	120	
F710	12.36	Campbell-Staples, P	1.37	R	165	
F711	2.37	Clayton, EH	3.37	R	165	
F712	5.37	Brown, C Miss			85	
F801	5.37	Davey, DW	6.37		130	D
F802						
F803						
F804	4.37	Bax, REV	5.37		350	
F805	11.36	Pott, MV Miss	11.36	R	80	
F806	5.37	Cotterill, D May	6.37		120	
F807						
F808						
F809	11.36	Alesbury, EM	12.36	R	80	
F901	6.37	Scrimgour, D			120	D
F902	6.37	Scrimgour, D			175	D
F903	1.37	Wedgwood, Josiah Rt Hon	1.37	R	165	
F904	10.36	Gladstone, IOJ	3.37	R	280	
F905	12.36	Wade, AM Miss	3.37	R	75	
F906	11.36	Armstrong, AV			115	
F907						
O01	3.37	Rigby, John C Dr	4.37	R	125	D
O02	4.37	Ellis, Harold J	7.37		110	D
O03	11.36	Wakeman, Isobel F	12.36	R	85	
O04	12.36	Bullock, PC Capt	1.37		165	
O05	3.37	Pollock, David T	6.37	R	165	
O06	12.36	Wolf, JC Miss	1.37		85	
O07		'staff foreman flat'				
O08						
O09						
O10						
O11	5.37	Gamlen, MCL Miss			85	
O101	2.37	Burton, CJ	3.37		85	
O102	1.37	Carlton, Charles H	3.37	R	85	
O103	2.37	Kinsman, Gerald RV Col	3.37	R	165	
O104	11.36	Crutchett, Charles A	3.37	R	120	
O105	11.36	Williams, DM Miss	12.36		85	
O106						
O107	7.37	Swain, CD			120	D
O108	7.37	Yellen, EE			120	D
O109	4.37	Lawford, ME			120	D
O110	7.37	Jenkins, E Mrs			120	D
O111						
O112	2.37	Crosleigh, F Mrs	6.37		130	D
O201	12.36	Campbell, A Miss	1.37		85	
O202	2.37	Herbert, Dennis Sir Rt Hon	2.37	R	165	
O203	1.37	Wright, Elspeth Mrs	2.37	R	165	

O204	10.36	Noble, Thomas G	11.36	R	120	
O205	10.36	Barrow, Clariss M	11.36	R	85	
O206						
O207	3.37	Sillitoe, AM	6.37		120	D
O208	5.37	Booth, ED Mrs			120	D
O209	5.37	Ritchie, W	7.37		120	D
O210						
O211						
O212	5.37	Mabey, GE	6.37		130	D
O301	11.36	Cochrane, John P	12.36	R	85	
O302	12.36	Watts, Joyce L	3.37	R	165	
O303	1.37	Doyle, Helen Mrs	2.37	R	165	
O304	10.36	Plomer, Alice S Mrs	12.36	R	120	
O305	11.36	Morgan, Evelyn Mrs	3.37	R	85	
O306	12.36	Brownhill, Alice Mrs	3.37	R	235	
O307	5.37	Bonser			95	D
O308	3.37	Salmon, SM	4.37		120	D
O309	6.37	Johnson, L Mrs			120	D
O310	3.37	Rich, David	6.37	R	120	D
O311	3.37	Marriner, John S	4.37	R	125	D
O312	4.37	Eweiss, EM Dr	4.37		130	D
O401	11.36	Nightingale, Manners Percy	12.36	R	85	
O402	10.36	Henderson, Arthur	12.36	R	165	
O403	12.36	Long, Annie Miss	1.37	R	165	
O404	10.36	Palmer, Winifred L Miss	11.36	R	120	
O405	11.36	Neilson, Christopher BV	12.36	R	85	
O406						
O407						
O408						
O409						
O410						
O411						
O412	1.37	Cates, Conyers Seeley	3.37	R	130	D
O501	10.36	Sweetlove, Marg Miss	11.36	R	85	
O502	10.36	Henderson, E Mrs	12.36		165	
O503	5.37	Woolam, Leslie J	6.37	R	165	
O504	12.36	Friedman, Jessie	1.37	R	120	
O505	1.37	Huggett, Dorothy L	2.37	R	85	
O506	6.37	Auerbach, P	7.37		195	
O507						
O508						
O509						
O510	7.37	Jones, MS Miss			125	D
O511	3.37	Stuart, EJ OBE	6.37		135	D
O512	11.36	Wallace	11.36		140	
O601	2.37	Gross	2.37		85	
O602	12.36	Neville, Norman J	12.36	R	165	
O603		Minto ['N/C']	11.36			
O604	12.36	Pearson, A	1.37		120	

O605	11.36	Couck, M	12.36		85	
O606	1.37	Hankinson, Hilda M	2.37	R	195	
O607						
O608						
O609						
O610						
O611						
O612	1.37	Taylor, George L	3.37	R	140	
O701	10.36	Steer, Phyllis Miss	11.36	R	85	
O702	1.37	Hurst, BD + Gordon, G	2.37	R	165	
O703	4.37	Manley, GEL	7.37		165	
O704	7.37	Leask, CR			120	
O705	3.37	Henzell, Mabel Miss	4.37	R	85	
O706	12.36	Hamlyn, Andrew D	3.37	R	195	
O707						
O708						
O709						
O710						
O711						
O712	7.37	Bellinger, WM Mrs			130	D
O801	3.37	Burley, Reginald T	5.37	R	80	
O802	2.37	Norman, DM Mrs	6.37		150	
O803						
O804						
O805	11.36	Smith-Ross, Mary Miss	12.36	R	80	
O806						
O807						
O808						
O809	4.37	Brandt, I	6.37		140	
O810						
O901						
O902	11.36	Clapham, HN	2.37		115	
O903	12.36	Parker, RM	1.37		75	
O904						
O905	2.37	Wallace, EB	4.37		165	
O906						
O907						
P01		housekeeper Borcherds, Mrs				
P02		laundry centre + tradesman				
P03	6.37	Goldring, T Mrs			130	D
P04	9.36	Murphy, Denis V Dr	11.36	R	165	
P05	9.36	Murphy, Denis V Dr	11.36	R	165	
P06	12.36	Siddall, Winifred M	1.37	R	85	
P07	4.37	Greenwood, Charles	5.37	R	110	D
P08	6.37	McLavy, R 'cancelled'			125	D
P09	1.37	Aickman, Dorothy J	2.37	R	85	
P101	6.37	Warner, RO			130	D
P102						
P103						
P104		'furnished'				F

P105						
P106	5.37	Hammond, AE Mrs	6.37		130	D
P107	2.37	D'Oyly John, Cecil R	2.37	R	120	
P108	2.37	Giddy, Osman CH Lt Cdr	2.37	R	165	
P109	2.37	Smith-Skene, R Miss	4.37		165	
P110	11.36	Wilkinson, Percival SM	12.36	R	85	
P201	4.37	Steele, TS	6.37		130	
P202	3.37	Preston, CP	4.37		125	D
P203	3.37	Rissik, SA	6.37		120	D
P204	3.37	White, Paul J	4.37	R	120	D
P205	5.37	Collier, AC	6.37		130	D
P206	1.37	Collier, AC	6.37		125	D
P207	12.36	Graham, Ruby G	3.37	R	120	
P208	12.36	Paterson, Adeline	12.36	R	165	
P209	4.37	Pasterfield, Ernest	5.37	R	165	
P210	12.36	Clarke, Frank L	1.37	R	85	
P301	12.36	Mellar Smith, Philip HC	3.37	R	130	D
P302	5.37	Renwick, EW	7.37		125	D
P303	4.37	Park, James A	5.37		120	D
P304	4.37	Newton, Pamela M Miss	4.37	R	120	D
P305	3.37	Clarke, Thomas	3.37		130	D
P306	3.37	Clarke, Thomas	4.37		125	D
P307	10.36	Winchester, Charles P				
P308	12.36	Hunt, George W Carew	4.37	R	165	
P309	12.36	Hunt, George W Carew	4.37	R	165	
P310	10.36	Robinson, Frank K	11.36	R	85	
P401	4.37	Melville, J	6.37		130	D
P402						
P403						
P404						
P405						
P406	3.37	Francis, HF			130	D
P407	10.36	Taylor, Dorothy M Dr	11.36	R	120	D
P408	2.37	Merrylees, KW	4.37		165	
P409	2.37	Shields, Garnet W	4.37	R	165	
P410	1.37	Day, Florence G	2.37	R	85	
P501	3.37	Johnson, Edwin	5.37	R	130	D
P502						
P503	7.37	Powell, AO			125	D
P504						
P505						
P506	11.36	Bell-Wright, Adnah Geo	11.36	R	130	D
P507	3.37	Langbehn, Cecil TWL	3.37	R	120	
P508	11.36	Clifford, Alexander G	12.36	R	165	
P509	3.37	Klein, EAW	3.37		165	
P510	11.36	Tebbutt, Mrs ['cancelled']	12.36		85	
P510	5.37	Forester Agar, N Mrs	5.37		85	
P601	7.37	Gribble, M Mrs			130	D
P602						
P603						

P604	7.37	Cleminson, JAS			125	D
P605						
P606	12.36	Boulter, RB	1.37	R	140	
P607	4.37	Hollely, ON	5.37	R	120	
P608	10.36	Haldane, AM Mrs	12.36	R	165	
P609	11.36	Armstrong-Jones, ROL	12.36	R	165	
P610	2.37	Hooker, AE Miss	2.37	R	85	
P701	6.37	Lawton, WE	7.37		130	D
P702						
P703						
P704						
P705						
P706						
P707	2.37	Wall, Elsa	5.37	R	120	
P708	11.36	Isdell-Carpenter, RIH	12.36	R	165	
P709	2.37	Donald, NA	3.37	R	165	
P710	11.36	Godfrey, EB Miss	11.36	R	85	
P801	6.37	Hoskins, JS	7.37		130	D
P802						
P803						
P804	5.37	Lorant, S			130	D
P805	7.37	McKernan, PE			120	D
P806	12.36	Findlay-Wilson, AC	2.37	R	150	
P807	4.37	Mitchell, MRM	5.37		150	
P808	10.36	Hare, ML	11.36	R	80	
P901	12.36	Lacon, PH	2.37		130	
P902						
P903	6.37	Isserlis, L			175	D
P904	1.37	Whitaker, FJ	3.37	R	130	
P905	11.36	Linney, P Mrs	12.36	R	115	
P906						

Source: Dolphin Square Ltd. register of leases, southern section, 1936–7, DST.

Key:
A Grenville House
B Drake House
C Raleigh House
D Hawkins House
E Nelson House
F Howard House
O Collingwood House
P Frobisher House

APPENDIX 2

DOLPHIN SQUARE TENANTS, 1963

Flat no.	Name	RC	Co
A01	Hellier, LA		
A02	Russell, PH		
A03	Winston, Sol & Sylvia		
A04	Mellier Smith, PHC		
A05	Gall, PA Miss	RC	
A06	Richardson, A		
A07	Dickson, KAJ		
A08	Symonds, AI Mrs	RC	
A101	Laming, JH		
A102	Herring, PS Mrs		
A103			Co
A104			Co
A105	Holmes, G	RC	
A106	Quennell, JM Mrs		
A107	Smith, CN		
A108	Dewar, D		
A109	Moseley, L		
A201	Taylor, FE Mrs		
A202	Moore, YL Mrs		
A203	Beaton, MW Mrs		
A204	Stevenson, OM Mrs		
A205	Snell, PM Miss	RC	
A206			
A207	Barclay, AE Mrs		
A208	Brown, SC		
A209	Kolendo, W Major	RC	
A301	Bazarte, AF		
A302	Carton, EM Mrs		
A303	Neilson, EL		
A304	Miller, J		
A305	Smythe, WB Mrs		
A306	Limmer, C Miss		
A307	Mackenzie, J Mrs		
A308	Alford, FR		
A309	Welsh, E Mrs	RC	
A401	Brimble, LJF		
A402	Pitt, VJ Miss		
A403	Maynard, FG		
A404	Sarkies, MR		
A405	Swain, S	RC	
A406	Lloyd-Thomas, JI Miss		
A407	Renwick-Abbs, AP Miss		
A408	Gillies, JB Col		

A409	Regan, M Mrs	RC	
A501	Fourie, WC		
A502	Archer, JD Capt		
A503	Merritt, P		
A504	Parker, B		
A505	Cameron, MM Miss	RC	
A506	Johns, FA Mrs		
A507	Storch, B		
A508			
A509	Aller, W Miss	RC	
A601			
A602	Gordon, H		
A603	Clare, J Mrs		
A604	Grunis, S		
A605	Umney, DE Mrs		
A606	Mazzoletti, R		
A607	Braddon, R		
A608	Parsons, RA		
A609	Cronhelm, MH Mrs	RC	
A701			
A702			
A703	Clark, K		
A704	Tunney, K & Synge, JM		
A705	Spring, WH		
A706	Emerson, Sir Ralf		
A707	Wakeman, IJ Miss		
A708	Watt, Katherine Dame		
A709	Whiteman, LW	RC	
A801	Bingen, EA		
A802	Curtis, AB		
A803			
A804	Viking Holdings		Co
A805	Alsop, R Mrs		
A806			
A901	Berker, LM		
A902	Ingman, DS		
A903	Liebig's Extract		Co
B01	Holt, I Mrs		
B02	Jack Hylton Ltd		Co
B03	Gibson, RFW		
B101	Cromwell-Knox, AE		
B102	Fraser, JC		
B103	Fraser, JC		
B201	Bradley, ME Miss	RC	
B202	Lago, C Capt		
B203	Kanna, K		
B204	Batchelor, JS		
B205	as 204		
B301	Taylor, E Miss		
B302	R Costain		Co

B303	as 302		
B304	Whithair, L Mrs		
B305	Pritchard, AE		
B401	Aviss, E Mrs		
B402	Markus, E		
B403			
B404	Mowbray, HM Miss		
B405	Mattocks, RM		
B501	Gadd, A		
B502	Adams, J Mrs		
B503	Stewart, SM Mrs		
B504	Bally, MAN Lt-Col		
B505	De Pass, RD		
B601	Sidebotham, HM Miss		
B602	Watson, MA Mrs		
B603	Seligman, FJ Mrs		
B604	Baker, WROG Major		
B605	Burns, DI		
B701	Paton, P Mrs	RC	
B702	Grewcock, RJG		
B703	Grant, HB		
B704	Nicolaeff, A Miss		
B705	Cox, CB		
B801	Steck, ES Miss	RC	
B802	Hazlehurst, HE Col		
B803	Perks, B Mrs		
B804	R Costain		
B805	Wadlow, GA		
B901	Robson, S Miss		
B902	Rewane, AO		
B903	Hill, CB		
B904	R Costain		Co
C01	Maxwell, O Mrs		
C02	Edwards, K.H.		
C03	Whatmore, FM Miss		
C04	Fourie, PJW		
C05	Lucas, CG Mrs		
C101	Farnsworth, C		
C102	as 101		
C103	Byre, B	RC	
C201	Sherman, A		
C202	Cufley, CA & MH Mrs		
C203	Olden, HG		
C204	Woods, L Dr		
C205	Whyte, WM Mrs	RC	
C301	Alston (Long Melford) Ltd		Co
C302	as 301		
C303	Clayton, HTH		
C304	Phillips, S		
C305	Taylor, BVL Mrs		

C401	Clayton, A		
C402	AG Linfield		Co
C403	Rees, JL		
C404	Yapp, RPH		
C405	Kerr, BJ Miss		
C501	Wharton, HD		
C502	Matthews, EWR		
C503	Flanagan, Bud		
C504			
C505	Morrison, MEO Mrs	RC	
C601	Lewkowicz, RH Mrs		
C602	Craggs, R Mrs		
C603	Harden, E Mrs		
C604	Butterfield Ltd		Co
C605	Wiley, I Mrs	RC	
C701	Genzmer, I Miss		
C702	Winchester, DC		
C703	Forster, KE		
C704	McLaughlin, JC		
C705	Antoniou, A	RC	
C801	Mitchell, J		
C802	Sykes, D		
C803	Ingram, G		
C804	Scott-Farnie, GR		
C805	Walker, DA	RC	
C901	Miles, EC Capt OBE		
C902	Latham, MW Mrs		
C903	Hampshire, JM Mrs		
C904	Barron, AK Mrs	RC	
D01	Nettleton, C		
D02	Dunfield, EKA Miss	RC	
D03	Shepherd, CG	RC	
D04	Filschstein, E Miss	RC	
D05	Bliss, HT		
D06	Wagner, K Miss		
D07	Kidman, MM Mrs	RC	
D08	Bracewell, E Mrs		
D101	Schrijvers, A Miss		
D102	Hornsby, IE Mrs		
D103	Curtis, K Mrs		
D104	Caseley, R Miss		
D105	Bailey, MF Miss	RC	
D106	Nesbitt, M Dr		
D107	Rukeyser, WS		
D108	Nunn, THE Capt		
D109	Clay, IN Miss		
D201	Powers, SG		
D202	Young, KG		
D203	Levy, SI		
D204			

D205	Murray, EF Miss	RC	
D206	Rix, AH		
D207	Callaway, HSK		
D208	Harrison, CF		
D209	Morris, J Mrs		
D301	Harvey, R Miss		
D302	Daroux, WG		
D303	Berners Lee, H Mrs		
D304	Weller, NJ		
D305	Smith, A Miss		
D306	Hampshire, WP		
D307	Dundon, HC Dr		
D308	Blackman, H		
D309	Arnold, RD Mrs		
D401	Hartog, J Mrs	RC	
D402	Sheridan-Taylor, H		
D403	Thompson, RS Miss		
D404	Riddell, HJ Miss		
D405	Forbes, EF Mrs	RC	
D406	Tadman, Y Mrs		
D407	R Costain Ltd staff		Co
D408	Bartley, C Lady		
D409	Rena, EM Mrs		
D501	staff housekeeper		
D502	Crawter, B Miss		
D503	Taylor, D Mrs		
D504	Barnard, BM Mrs		
D505	Arthur, HC Miss		
D506	Braham, RR Mrs		
D507	Peebles, ACC CVO		
D508	Christopherson, HO		
D509	Bailey, EG Mrs		
D601	Steven, SG		
D602	Lee, DL Miss		
D603	Falconer, JI Mrs		
D604	Woolman, L Miss		
D605	Higgs, RD		
D606	Higgs, RD		
D607	Bufton, LM Miss		
D608	Mulqueen, MM Mrs		
D609	Goldberg, L		
D701	Bevan, I	RC	
D702	Patten, JR Brig		
D703	Holdsworth, D		
D704	Morris, ME Miss		
D705	Morrah, DRM Miss	RC	
D706	Lord, G Mrs		
D707	Rushmore, FH Brig		
D708	Ellis, HL Mrs		
D709	Wheeler, TC		

D801	Van Stokkum, ETM		
D802	Dick, RT		
D803	Davis, SGH		
D804	Delgado, MW Mrs		
D805	R Costain Ltd staff		Co
D806	Keribiriou & Co		Co
D807	as 806		
D901	Adeline, J		
D902	Roe, RD Col		
D903	as 903		
D904	Nordale		Co
E01	Kenney, DEA Mrs		
E02	North, DE Miss	RC	
E03	Birch, GM Mrs		
E04	St John White, W		
E05	Spencer, OM Mrs		
E06	R Costain Ltd		Co
E07			
E08	Nicholson, DV Mrs		
E09	Eilers, GM Miss	RC	
E101	Anderson, WJ		
E102	Sammut, F Mrs		
E103	Oliver, Vic		
E104	Norveil, P		
E105	Garle, KJ		
E106	Simson, PR Mrs		
E107	Coleman, BH		
E108	De Geynst, REL		
E109	Aitken, LR		
E110	Davies, AM Mrs		
E201	Dawn, RP		
E202	International Invisible Zipper		Co
E203	as 202		Co
E204	as 202		Co
E205	Eggar, JTK		
E206	Fuller, K Mrs		
E207	Weiss, C		
E208	Gordon, LW Mrs		
E209	Horsfield, FI Mrs		
E210	Anthony Worham Ltd		Co
E301	Summerell, AP Miss		
E302	Peacock, HJ		
E303	Dunnage, LA		
E304			
E305	Howard, BM Mrs		
E306	Caplin, L		
E307	Gyenes, PI		
E308	Wray, CF		
E309	Winterbottom, I		

E310	Carnaby, LM Miss		
E401	Dowson, PM		
E402	as 401	401	402
E403	Woodard, AEL		
E404	McCormick, J		
E405			
E406			
E407	Lambert, M Mrs		
E408	Goring, HAO		
E409	Jones, H Wynn		
E410	Orme, EA		
E501	Baugh, ME Miss	RC	
E502	Whitehouse, CM Mrs		
E503	Soley, IE Miss		
E504	Tremlett, EBM		
E505	Barratt, MJ Miss		
E506	Sandilands, E Miss		
E507	Lord Strathclyde		
E508	Barnes, DE Miss		
E509	Poole, AJ Dr		
E510	Thompson-Smith, MR Mrs		
E601	Griffiths, ME Miss	RC	
E602	Levine, L		
E603	Hawley, G Mrs		
E604	Pepper, CS		
E605	Lord Sinclair		
E606	Stewart, JR		
E607	Hawkins, P Mrs		
E608	Elmer, LP	RC	
E609	Mann, M Miss		
E610	Auld, EBF		
E701	Dobson, E Mrs	RC	
E702	Sworder, ERD Cmdr		
E703	De Rougemont, MJ Miss		
E704	Marsh, CDJ		
E705	Cleaton, AC Mrs		
E706			
E707	Berwick, EC Miss		
E708	Humble, E Mrs		
E709	Gallop, MDC Mrs		
E710	Mallett, CG		
E801	Paine, RM Miss	RC	
E802	Dawtry, AG		
E803	Lomax, John Sir		
E804	Allerhand, G Miss		
E805	Gardiner, KJ		
E806	Nunn, JJ Miss + Gibson, A Dr		
E807	Smyth. John, Brig Sir VC MC MP		
E808	as 808		

E901	Sanderson, V		
E902			
E903	Lund, DL Mrs		
E904	Birdwell, MI Mrs		
E905	Hobson, H		
E906	as 905		
F01	Linton, V Miss		
F02	Logan, ME Miss		
F03	Messulam, R		
F04	Lawrence, F Mrs		
F05	Sarson, RD Miss	RC	
F06	O'Neill, CM Mrs		
F07	Asprey, PJD		
F08	Askey, ID Miss [Arthur]		
F09	Warwick, NE		
F10	Jacksons Australian Meats		Co
F11	Coles, GS	RC	
F101	Gordon, WHLG Col MC CBE		
F102	Bate, MS Miss		
F103	Champion, JAC		
F104	Catto, E Miss		
F105	Lovick, AW		
F106	Jones, G Miss		
F107	Miles, NJ		
F108	Beatts, MI Mrs	RC	
F109	Podmore, WE		
F110	Livingstone, G Mrs		
F111	Sidwell, DA		
F112	Madeley, DV Miss	RC	
F201	Ward, V Mrs		
F202	Meade-Miller, EC Mrs		
F203	Pearce, D		
F204	Gadd, NM Mrs		
F205	Curran, ME Mrs		
F206	Glidewell, AM + Gibbons, AL Ms		
F207	Wickstead, I Mrs		
F208	Mills, AK Miss	RC	
F209	Penman, AT		
F210	Hambidge, GE Mrs		
F211	Bloye, RE		
F212	Collins, GY Miss		
F301	Nicholls, THL Grp-Capt		
F302	Baines, ANH		
F303	Davis, PJ Miss		
F304	Wilde, MY		
F305	Green, A		
F306			
F307	Kehely, CG Sq-Ldr		
F308	Brodie, AM Miss		

F309	Marks, GP		
F310	Gould, B Mrs		
F311	Cook, I Miss		
F312	Armstrong, FZ Miss	RC	
F401	Christopher, COE Mrs		
F402	as 401		
F403	Czechoslovak Embassy		Co
F404	Burbury, PVH Miss		
F405	Schulze-Boing, JKH		
F406	Palmer, M Mrs		
F407	Hunt, FG Surgeon Rear-Admrl		
F408	Adams, AM Miss	RC	
F409			
F410	Cuckney, EJ Air Vice-M		
F411	Simmonds, EJ Mrs		
F412	Fleming, RF Mrs		
F501	Thomas, M Mrs		
F502	Birks, JBW		
F503	Sherwood, R Mrs		
F504	Day, M Wing-Cmdr		
F505	Schulte, AFH		
F506	Thomas, WK Miss		
F507	Bennett, M Mrs		
F508	Davis, GM Miss	RC	
F509	Hacking, MJ Miss		
F510	McFadzean, FS		
F511	as 510		
F512	Sikes, AFS Miss		
F601	Button, JC		
F602	Pickles, F		
F603	Bolt, S Miss	RC	
F604	Parker, TR Major		
F605	Adams, J		
F606			
F607	Staniland, JB		
F608	Curtis, PS Miss		
F609	Butler, ME Mrs		
F610	Skelton, GFA Air-Comdre		
F611	Van Thal, H		
F612	Lowe, N Miss	RC	
F701	Calafatis, JD Mrs		
F702	Morriss, JR		
F703	Walter, RO Miss		
F704	Niewiarowski, PF Mrs		
F705	Penhale, N Miss		
F706	Fisk, A Dr		
F707	Wilson, P Mrs		
F708	Ali, SM		
F709	Walters, M Miss		

F710	Briggs, JN		
F711	Errington, Eric Sir JP MP		
F712	Philipps, SF Miss		
F801	Walton, JR		
F802	Humphreys, RS		
F803	Sim, AC		
F804	R Costain Ltd		Co
F805	De la Motte, E Mrs		
F806	Grantham, B		
F807	Hill, B		
F808	Duggan, TG		
F809	Skeffington, S Mrs	RC	
F901	Hewett, FS		
F902	Stephens, SA Mrs		
F903	Wedgwood, the Dowager Lady		
F904	Cumberlage, CF CBE		
F905			
F906	Mullooly, VM Mrs		
F907	Simon, Rt Hon Viscount CMG		
F908	Meanteath, J Miss	RC	
G01	Smith-Barnett, E Mrs		
G02	Wheatley, PE Miss		
G03	Keogh, HC Miss		
G04	Taylor, J		
G05	Selected Hotels Ltd		Co
G06	as 05		Co
G07	R Costain Ltd		Co
G08	Kitson, JP		
G09	Evans, HE Miss	RC	
G10	Dalmahoy, PH		
G101	Howard, D Miss		
G102	Moore, FE		
G103	Norman, DCJ		
G104	Norris, HJ		
G105	Bellerby, VL		
G106	Stanton, M Mrs		
G107	Morley-Fletcher, C Mrs		
G108	Ogle, PA Mrs		
G109	Lavadinovic, D AMSE		
G110	Pears, SJ		
G111			
G112	Brebner, J Dr		
G201	Baxter, FM Miss		
G202	Crawford-Price, AJ Mr/Mrs		
G203	Staroszczuk, TJ		
G204	Haffar, LH Miss		
G205	Adams, REFM Mrs	RC	
G206	Raphael, D Mrs		
G207	Woodham-Smith, GI		

G208	Culhane, DM		
G209	Noble, PR		
G210	Stevenson, JRW		
G211	Tarpaz, N		
G212	Hickling, GE Mrs		
G301	Newell, MAM Mrs		
G302	Bangkok Bank Ltd		Co
G303	Shohet, A		
G304	R Costain Ltd		Co
G305	MacIntyre, JM		
G306	Greene, RW		
G307	Jackson, JH		
G308	Parker, SMG Mrs		
G309	Harwood Trust		Co
G310	Watling, DB		
G311	JLP Denny Ltd		Co
G312	as 311		Co
G401	Green, D Miss		
G402	Vargas, AL		
G403	Blackwood, DJ Miss		
G404	Wilson, FA Mrs		
G405	Thompson, ASG	RC	
G406	Moore, WW		
G407	Stallard, RJ		
G408	Chalaud, FDA		
G409	Quinn, DM Mrs		
G410	Bennett, PS + Davies, AM		
G411	Khan, AW		
G412	Dalton, ME Miss		
G501	Robinson, NM Miss	RC	
G502	Dunn, CI Miss		
G503	J Kimbell & Co Ltd		Co
G504	Whittome, DEC Dr		
G505	Gray, S Miss	RC	
G506	Pearson, EE Hon Mrs		
G507			
G508	Jenkinson, AM Mrs		
G509	Smith, GA		
G510	Foggie, RJ		
G511	Luck, GE		
G512	Greenwell, WE		
G601	Barrington, HMV Mrs	RC	
G602	Shepherd, H Mrs		
G603	Findlater, Mrs		
G604	Mole, EL Group-Capt BSc		
G605	Eddowes, MJ Mrs	RC	
G606	Boyle, RP		
G607	Sherjan, MA Mrs		
G608	Richardson, ECL Sqdn-Ldr		

G609	Green, TEB		
G610	Little, G Mrs		
G611	Foster, AM Mrs		
G612	Hamilton, DAW		
G701	Plugge, L Capt	RC	
G702	Couch, EC Mrs		
G703	Furniss, DI Mrs		
G704	Thornton, M Miss		
G705	Mallinson, NI Miss	RC	
G706	Lewington, WE Dr		
G707	McCarthy, TJ		
G708	Logan, DM Miss		
G709	Wilkie, NM Mrs		
G710	Walker, SP		
G711	Duncan Stratton & Co (UK) Ltd		Co
G712	Bettley, JND		
G801	Shepherd. DM Miss		
G802	Bearder, J Mrs		
G803	Lowe, JCE Mrs		
G804	Jackson, M Miss		
G805	Campbell, M Mrs	RC	
G806	Anderson, MA Mrs		
G807	Wood Hall Trust Ltd		Co
G808	Van Den Bergh, SJ Mrs		
G809	Bolton, George Sir KCMG		
G901	Boutle, BW	RC	
G902	Shaw, DJS		
G903	Williams, EM Mrs		
G904	Sutton, OP Cmdr		
G905	Russell-Hay, G Lt.-Col OBE		
G906	Foster, L Miss		
G907	Greene, RW		
G908	Shaw, GW		
H01	Donnet, EC Miss		
H02	Cantlay, LF		
H03	Varvill, MH		
H04			
H101	Taylor-Carroll, AR Miss		
H102	Norman, RB		
H103	King, RW		
H104	Periera, EC Miss		
H105	Easton, T		
H106	Thompson, MI Mrs		
H107	De Luxe Films [Asst]		Co
H108			
H109	Aarons, N		
H110	Dowding, TW		
H111	Wodehouse, DC	RC	
H201	Featherstone, JW		

H202	Verdi, AS		
H203	Wearing, KR Mrs		
H204	Mollo, V		
H205	Alcock, LF Mrs		
H206	Bensusan, EN Mrs		
H207	Leonard, S		
H208	Farmer, K Miss		
H209	Ball, G		
H210	as 209		
H211	Morris, M Miss	RC	
H301	Manning, B		
H302	Brookes, S		
H303	McLeod, NCD		
H304	Brookes, P		
H305	Gregson, AG Miss		
H306	N F Ramsay & Co		Co
H307	Fraser, JA		
H308	Napier, K Mrs		
H309	Denny, VW		
H310	Johanes, J		
H311	housekeeper		
H401	Schmeidler, GA		
H402	Beardshaw, JE		
H403	Richards, LW		
H404	Botibol, L		
H405	Thind-Clausen, E Mrs		
H406	Bussey, L		
H407			
H408	Clover, GR		
H409	Lewis, JW		
H410	Thursby-Pelham, A Mrs		
H411	Spears, MMJ Miss	RC	
H501	Morris, CTH		
H502	Donaldson, CEM Cmdr MP		
H503	Cashman, B Miss		
H504			
H505	Moxey, DE		
H506	Edwards, APJ		
H507	Arthur, HM Mrs		
H508	McWilliam, PM Miss		
H509	Rutherford, IT Lady		
H510	Philip Horton & Co Ltd		Co
H511	Seymour-Rouse, EF		
H601	Sheehan, M Miss		
H602	Tomlinson, GE		
H603	Tyndall, WE Maj-Gen		
H604	Bond, MW		
H605	Sailer, AM Miss		
H606	Roe, EL		

H607	Blackwell, GB		
H608	R Costain Ltd		Co
H609	Worth, GAB		
H610	Tennant, G Mrs		
H611	Heath, OC Miss	RC	
H701	Porter, JR		
H702	Connaught Rooms Ltd		Co
H703			
H704	Scott, WP		
H705	Kellie, WT		
H706	R Costain Ltd		Co
H707	National Fire Protection Co Ltd		Co
H708	Gordon-Brown, DS Capt		
H709	Hoare, VJ		
H710	Murray, TB		
H711	Lardner, EF Miss		
H801	Wenham, GM		
H802	Thursby-Pelham, VAG		
H803	Jawor, T Col		
H804	Forbes, EH Miss		
H805	not shown		
H806	Konig, CA		
H807	Pedersen, PA		
H808	Watson, GJ		
H809			
H810	Purvis, JH Mrs	RC	
H811	Thirkell, R		
I102	R Costain Ltd		Co
I104	R Costain Ltd		Co
I105	R Costain Ltd		Co
I110	Ward, CE Capt		
I117	R Costain Ltd		Co
I202	R Costain Ltd		Co
I210	R Costain Ltd		Co
I213	R Costain Ltd		Co
I308	Whitley, FM Lady	RC	
I312	R Costain Ltd		Co
I320	R Costain Ltd		Co
I324	R Costain Ltd		Co
I405	R Costain Ltd		Co
I408	Hope, MM Mrs	RC	
I410	McGee, AB	RC	
I423	Marquis, EE Mrs	RC	
I426	R Costain Ltd		Co
I502	R Costain Ltd		Co
I509	Crowe, AW	RC	
I511	Sciver, A water surveyor		Co
I512	R Costain Ltd		Co
I521	R Costain Ltd		Co

I601	Butler, EE Mrs		
I604	R Costain Ltd		Co
I607	R Costain Ltd		Co
I610	R Costain Ltd		Co
I620	R Costain Ltd		Co
I626	R Costain Ltd		Co
M01	Wilkinson, KLM Miss	RC	
M02	Young, J		
M03	as 02		
M04	Diacre, K		
M101	Donaldson, A Miss		
M102	Whitworth, R		
M103	Wissler, AF Mrs		
M104	Corsan, ED Mrs		
M105	Hartman, DD		
M106	Shafto, VJ Miss		
M107	Leslie-Whittaker, AJ Miss		
M108			
M109	Calder, MI Mrs		
M110	Beaumont, FN		
M111	as 110		
M201	Russell, DJ Miss	RC	
M202	Hayman, A Dr		
M203	Wadsworth, G		
M204			
M205	?		Co
M206	Ward, JM Miss		
M207	Croxford, EJ Mrs		
M208	Panter, PM Miss		
M209	Nesbit, SEM Miss		
M210	H Pye & Sons Ltd		Co
M211	Mishcon, V		
M301	Sobotka, EMM Mrs	RC	
M302	Gifford King, JK		
M303	Edwards, CL Lt-Col		
M304	Gerahty, ED Mrs		
M305	Henderson, AJ		
M306	Henderson-Begg, L Mrs		
M307			
M308	Mitchell, HF		
M309	Kaye, S		
M310			
M311	Ryder, Frances Lady CBE		
M401	Wallaker, EW		
M402	Dunning, A Miss		
M403	Robinson, JF		
M404	Faviell, IA Miss		
M405	Donnelly, F Mrs		
M406	Innis, JF Mrs		

M407	Lee, R Mrs		
M408	Elgood, FE		
M409	R Costain Ltd		Co
M410	Juanals, RM Sqdr-Ldr		
M411	Valentine, R		
M501	Ludecke, M Miss	RC	
M502	Cantlay, DF		
M503	Latham, B		
M504	Wakeling, ME Mrs		
M505	Kerr, D		
M506	Harrison, EC + M Misses		
M507	Ross, IA		
M508	Godfrey-Isaacs, M		
M509			
M510			
M511	Gilmore, BT		
M601	Sweeney, IM Miss	RC	
M602	Handel, C		
M603	Fry, CG		
M604	Knight, HM + DE Misses		
M605	Andrews, VG Miss		
M606	Drummond, JW		
M607	Caris Carter, DA Mrs		
M608	Corp, JJ Mrs		
M609	Stevens, G Mrs		
M610	Boyton, E Dr		
M611	Pacheco, O Miss		
M701	Bass, VE Miss		
M702	Al-Rawi, Fouad		
M703	Lewington, WJ		
M704	Seeley, FJBF Prof		
M705	Sheffield, J		
M706	as 705		
M707	Smith-Ross, J		
M708	Houghton, MM Miss		
M709	Weinberg, H Miss		
M710	Henderson, A Rt Hon Major MP		
M711	as 710		
M801	Taylor, FM Mrs		
M802	Coyle, LE Mrs		
M803	Byre, L Mrs		
M804	as 803		
M805	Greenfield, RS	RC	
M806	Paterson, R		
M807	Bannen, IE		
M808	Walters, Thorley		
M809	Feldman, R		
M810	Levin, L		
M901	McPherson, WD		

M902	Adams, F		
M903	Howe, HG		
M904	Hicks, RM Mrs		
M905	Maudsley, GB		
M906	Howard, EA Miss		
M907	Anson, EM Mrs	RC	
M908	Von Bulow, E Mrs		
N01	Allen, EA Miss		
N02	White, EM Mrs		
N03	Simpson, MA Sqdr-Ldr	RC	
N04	Van Bergen, SE Miss		
N05	Feinsilber, J Dr		
N06	as 05	RC	
N07	Georgeson, FH		
N08	Gill-Davies, DG		
N09	staff newsshop manager		
N101	Barclays Bank DCO		Co
N102	Redburn, KF		
N103	Price, MB Miss		
N104	Stewart, DE		
N105	Doyle-Davidson, JAH		
N106	Dane, PMHW		
N107	Lindsey, CS		
N108	Cuthbertson, JF		
N109	Minardi, C		
N110	Chamberlyne, PT		
N111	Dumaresq, LC Mrs		
N112	Jones, DE	RC	
N201	Boldero, AJ		
N202	Stowe & Bowden Ltd		Co
N203	Conway-Cross, B Mrs		
N204	Welch, E Mrs		
N205	Harper-Nelson, M Miss		
N206	Panter, AG Miss		
N207	Hunter, AE		
N208	Newman, LJ Major	RC	
N209	Warby, F		
N210	Herbertson, MJ Mrs		
N211	Burt, HA Dr FRCP		
N212	Cook, MJ Miss	RC	
N301	Swinden, RCB		
N302			
N303	White, MG Mrs		
N304	Gurney, AH		
N305	Levy, MI		
N306			
N307	Landucci, FE Miss		
N308	Dymsza, L Mde	RC	
N309	Wreford, RJ		

N310	Thomas, DH		
N311	Lewis RHP the Hon		
N312	Beddall, EM Mrs	RC	
N401	Crampton, GP Brig		
N402	Plazzotta, R Mrs		
N403	Harding, PJ		
N404	Price, DJ		
N405	Windle, E Mrs		
N406	Agnew, DE Miss		
N407	Cousins, EG		
N408			
N409	Cayley, VD Miss		
N410	Browne, CB		
N411	Onslow, Mary Lady		
N412	Shingles, R	RC	
N501	Anderson, F McB Mrs		
N502	Lewis, HM Dr		
N503			
N504	Brand, JM		
N505	Harvey, F		
N506	Ireland, JCH		
N507	Kugele, GC		
N508			
N509	Nervo, J		
N510	Boardman, TV		
N511	Clark, GBH Capt		
N512	Macdonald, PK Miss		
N601	McQuillin, VO		
N602	Hepburn, R Miss		
N603	Hinds, EM Miss		
N604	R Costain Ltd		Co
N605	Singer, CN Mrs		
N606	Moskin, L		
N607	Tower, HB Rev		
N608	Jacob, AM Miss	RC	
N609	Redman, JJ		
N610	Bullough, EG		
N611	Pye, LF Mrs		
N612	Maxwell Knight, CH Major	RC	
N701	Curry, KR		
N702	Maury, M Mde		
N703	Whytock, AH		
N704	Hill, W		
N705	Elder, D Mrs		
N706	Wojtczak, J Mrs		
N707	Winter, PM Mrs		
N708	Waugh, MA Mrs	RC	
N709	Dacomo, S		
N710	Gover, CC		
N711	D'Oyly, Mrs		

N712	Napier, E Mrs		
N801	Richards, WE Miss		
N802	Peek, GW		
N803	Mayo, TE Mrs		
N804	Baker, EE		
N805	as 804		
N806	Loewy, H		
N807	Massey-Dawson, WG Mrs		
N808	Kitchin, CB		
N809	May, MO Miss	RC	
N901	Williams, AN Maj-Gen		
N902	Plugge, LF		
N903	Wade, B Mrs		
N904	Davidson, J Miss		
N905	Hillyard, PCH		
N906	Se Foods Ltd		Co
N907	Tingey, N Mrs		
N908	Bell, WED		
N909	Gates, AW	RC	
O01	Wagstaff, R Mrs		
O02	Eke, DM Miss		
O03	Von Hofmannsthal, R		
O04	Bottrill, FR		
O05	Rimington-Wilson, HL		
O06	Havinden, JR		
O07	Torney, DS		
O08	Jones, E Mrs		
O09	Wade, CW		
O10	Pollard, M		
O11	Paton, I Miss		
O101	Tobias, RJ Miss		
O102	Fletcher, NSJ		
O103	Foxton Ferguson, I		
O104	Crutchett, CA		
O105	May, IJ Mrs	RC	
O106	Birks, HL Maj-Gen CB DSO		
O107	Richards, B Mrs		
O108	Miller, PR Miss		
O109	Hadfield, MG Miss		
O110	Cheeseman, RGL		
O111	Green, D		
O112	Pontifex, D Mrs		
O201	Rowell, J Miss		
O202	Alexander, JRW		
O203	Currie, N Dr		
O204	Noble, TG Major, RE		
O205	Davy, RM Miss	RC	
O206	Holford, BA Miss		
O207	Moskwa, PJ		
O208	Booth, ED Mrs		

O209	Turner, JHW		
O210	Morgan, A		
O211	Whibley, GH		
O212	Munson, BJ		
O301	Steer, PN Miss	RC	
O302	Halliday, RTW		
O303	Dykes, GM		
O304	Thompson, DC		
O305	Chambers, K Mrs	RC	
O306	Sharman, M		
O307	Hurll, JM Mrs		
O308	Stille, CE		
O309	Ashley, R Mrs		
O310	Wills, GM Mrs		
O311	Page, JA Major		
O312	Tratman, RE Mrs		
O401	Ward, D	RC	
O402	O'Connor, FR Capt		
O403	Brecknell, M St.J		
O404	Hortop, BAK		
O405	Bramley, J Miss		
O406	Field, E St.J Mrs		
O407	Faesler, A Dr		
O408	Major, AJ		
O409	Harris, E		
O410	Nelles, C Miss		
O411	Bull, PJF + Carrell, CH		
O412	Wallace, SGB		
O501	Greenlees, RCC Capt		
O502	Smith, P Mrs		
O503	Borland, IH		
O504	Duckett, S		
O505	Booth, CR Sqdr-Ldr	RC	
O506	R Costain Ltd		Co
O507			
O508	Wright, AE		
O509	Breze, ME Miss		
O510	Stone, DA		
O511	Englemann & Buckham Ltd		Co
O512	as 511		
O601	Elliott, AM Miss	RC	
O602	Owen, GMB Miss		
O603	Bostock, CMC Brig		
O604	Fine, GJ		
O605	Bolter, AC		
O606	Johns, DM		
O607	Edward Lumley & Sons Ltd		Co
O608	Markus, MH Mrs		
O609	Choppin, FH		
O610	Fussell, KM Dr		

O611	Hurst, JL		
O612	Orange, W		
O701	Ratzer, JH		
O702	Campbell, NS		
O703	Sheldon CM + Bird, KE Misses		
O704	Bishop, DW		
O705	Burroughs, GD Miss	RC	
O706	East, SI		
O707	Henderson, Lord		
O708	Dieltiens, VMC Miss		
O709	Parsons, CR Mrs		
O710	G.M. Wenham & Co Ltd		Co
O711	Rumbold, GR		
O712	Arnold, PH		
O801	Bass, H Miss		
O802	Paddison, WJ		
O803	Webb, DG		
O804	Tempros, H		
O805	Kirkwood, OAE Miss	RC	
O806	Matthews, L		
O807	Van Stokkum, ETM		
O808	Vaughan, E Miss		
O809	Westbury, MA		
O810	Tinson, EHM Miss		
O901	Hurst, J		
O902	Redfern, JC Miss		
O903	Giles, LA Miss		
O904	Dalkemps Ltd		Co
O905	Schlageter, M Miss		
O906	Fielding, AC		
O907	Douglas, EC		
P01	Lloyd-Williams, A Miss		
P02	McGregor, JG		
P03	Browne, AWH		
P04	Ferris, MM Dr		
P05	as 04		
P06	Saias, IM Mrs	RC	
P07	Bertram, EJ Miss		
P08	Macalester, A Mrs		
P09	Wells, GW		
P101	McLaughlin EE + Howard, N Ms/rs		
P102	Lewis, A		
P103			
P104			
P105	Crick, T Very Rev		
P106	as 105		
P107	Butterworth, PK		
P108	Webster, ML Mrs		
P109	Musel, R		
P110	Anderson, M Mrs		

P201	Booth, DG Mrs		
P202	Simmonds, JP Miss		
P203	Devine, PH		
P204	Fraser, BMA Mrs		
P205	Wood, EP Miss		
P206	as 205		
P207	Law, GS		
P208	Graham, K Mrs		
P209	Bissolotti, S Mrs		
P210	Bowen, DW Miss	RC	
P301	Ramsey Moon, E Mrs		
P302	Links, E Mrs		
P303	Hayes, GHD Miss		
P304	Rayner, R		
P305	Wood, HI		
P306	as 306		
P307	Mitchell, HK		
P308	Spicer, EE Miss		
P309	as 308		
P310			
P401	Travers, WA		
P402	Wynter, TM Dr		
P403	Smith, EE Mrs	RC	
P404	Beaumont, GC Mrs	RC	
P405	Rayner, JA		
P406	Burwood, MI Mrs		
P407	Alalouff, M		
P408	Marouf, T		
P409	Reynolds, G Miss		
P410	Young, GMU		
P501	R Costain Ltd		Co
P502	Traverse-Healy, TH		
P503	Nash, R Mrs		
P504	Jones, SHJ Miss		
P505			
P506	Steer-Webster, VC Col OBE		
P507	Young, VG Miss		
P508	White-Smith, RH		
P509	as 508		
P510	Rea, JA Mrs		
P601	Draper, IR		
P602	Lincoln, GP		
P603	Sexton, BN		
P604	Stevenson, NM		
P605	Gibbons, EJ Brig		
P606	as 605		
P607	McDonald, AF		
P608	Sweeney, JC		
P609	Rainsford-Hannay, RW		
P610			

P701	Robson, AT		
P702	Rangel, G		
P703	Tarkowski, ZMT		
P704			
P705	Brassey, Lady		
P706	Roberts, AE		
P707	Lane, J Miss		
P708	Hole, CEMB		
P709	Mount, GR		
P710	Branch, GE Miss	RC	
P801	Williams, E Miss		
P802	SAF Sampson Ltd		Co
P803	Swayne, MB Mrs		
P804	Harrison, CA		
P805	Edwards, WA		
P806	Reed, FET		
P807	as 806		
P808	Train, RW		
P901	Secretan, REP		
P902	Richmond, EL		
P903	Rogers, PP Mrs		
P904	O'Brien, A Miss		
P905	Myers, PSF		
P906	Gerard, E Mrs		
P907	White, A	RC	

Source: Schedule of Tenants Eligible to Vote in the Referendum relating to the Transfer of Dolphin Square to an Housing Association, 23 October 1963, DST.

Key:
A Grenville House
B Drake House
C Raleigh House
D Hawkins House
E Nelson House
F Howard House
G Beatty House
H Duncan House
I Rodney House
M Keyes House
N Hood House
O Collingwood House
P Frobisher House

RC rent controlled
Co corporate let

APPENDIX 3

DOLPHIN SQUARE TRUST INCOME AND EXPENDITURE, NET INCOME AND ACCUMULATED SURPLUS/DEFICIT, 1965–92/3

Year ending 30 Sept	*Income [£m]*	*Constant 1993 prices [£m]*	*Expenditure before tax [£m]*	*Constant 1993 prices [£m]*	*Net income after tax before special provisions [£'000s]*	*Reported surplus/ (deficit) [£'000s]*	*Reported accumulated surplus/ (deficit) [£'000s]*
1965†	0.47	4.45	0.46	4.36	10.0	0	0
1966	0.67	6.11	0.70	6.38	(32.2)	(33.2)	(33.2)
1967	0.70	6.23	0.81	7.21	(101.1)	(102.1)	(135.3)
1968	0.73	6.20	0.76	6.46	(31.3)	(33.3)	(168.7)
1969	0.80	6.46	0.74	5.98	61.1	25.1	(143.5)
1970	0.88	6.68	0.78	5.92	97.5	61.5	(82.0)
1971	0.93	6.46	0.89	6.18	26.7	25.7	(56.3)
1972	1.01	6.53	0.94	6.08	35.4	34.4	(21.8)
1973	1.09	6.46	1.16	6.87	(47.7)	(28.7)	(50.5)
1974	1.20	6.13	1.22	6.23	(17.6)	(18.6)	(69.2)
1975	1.31	5.40	1.35	5.56	(34.4)	(36.6)	(35.8)[a]
1976	1.49	5.26	1.41	4.98	53.8	51.5	0.6[b]
1977	1.71	5.21	1.38	4.20	188.9	186.6	7.2[b]
1978	1.93	5.43	1.71	4.81	129.3	126.4	3.6[b]
1979	2.15	5.34	1.90	4.72	140.7	137.3	66.0[b]
1980	2.38	5.00	2.27	4.77	60.8	55.9	1.98[b]
1981	2.53	4.76	2.32	4.36	117.1	112.2	4.1[b]
1982	2.81	4.86	2.60	4.50	114.8	109.3	13.4[b]
1982[r]	***2.78***	***4.81***	***2.68***	***4.64***	***14.8***	***9.3***	***13.4***
1983	3.08	5.10	2.97	4.92	12.0	5.9	19.3
1984	3.49	5.50	3.30	5.20	23.2	16.9	36.2
1985	3.80	5.65	3.62	5.38	18.6	12.3	48.5
1986	4.14	5.95	4.00	5.75	112.4	105.1	153.6
1987	4.56	6.29	4.47	6.17	18.0	9.4	163.0
1988	4.57	6.01	4.63	6.09	(127.6)	(136.5)	26.5
1989	4.87	5.94	4.76	5.81	21.0	12.9	39.4
1990	5.67	6.32	5.21	5.81	234.5	10.6[c]	50.1
1991	5.22	5.50	5.01	5.28	258.5	199.1[c]	249.2
1992[rc]	5.74	5.75	6.11	6.12	(292.8)	(292.8)	1,360.8[d]
1993[rc]	7.65	7.65	7.09	7.09	543.5	543.5	1,904.3
1965–93	77.58	168.63	74.57	163.19	1,593.1	950.1	

Source: DST, ***R & A 1965–92/3***; Wood, report, 1 November 1983, DST Committee of Management Minutes, 8 November 1983, DST.

Key:
† 1st 9 months.
r Accounts restated from 1982/3, in accordance with the requirements of the Registered Housing Associations (Accounting Requirements) Order of 1982. In the revised format transfers to repairs equalisation account are included in the income and expenditure account. The restated accounts for 1981/2 [1982r] are not included in the summations (the difference in net income is explained by provision of £100,000 for irrecoverable VAT).
rc From 1991/2 the accounts were revised, following the Trust's decision to deregister as a housing corporation. I have reworked the new accounts to establish comparability with earlier years. Income therefore includes investment income, and expenditure is stated after provision for depreciation, but before appropriations to repairs and dilapidations to 1982, and subsequently where shown. In 1992/3 restaurant income and costs were incorporated into the income and expenditure accounts.
a after £70,000 transferred ***from*** repairs equalisation account.
b after sums transferred ***to*** repairs equalisation account: £15,000 (1976), £180,000 (1977), £130,000 (1978), £75,000 (1979), £120,000 (1980), £110,000 (1981), and £100,000 (1982).
c after provision for catering co. losses [£215,128 1989/90, £51,299 1990/1 and dilapidations. £33,223 was provided for catering co. losses in 1991/2].
d after writing back £1.43m. previously in reserve as a provision for cyclical repairs and maintenance.

APPENDIX 4

COMPONENTS OF DOLPHIN SQUARE INCOME, 1965–2004/5

Year (1 October – 30 September)	*1. Unfurnished Flats [£m]*	*2. Rodney House flats [£m]*	*3. Guest rooms [£m]*	*4. Rodney House flats +guest rooms# [£m]*	*1. Constant 1993 prices [£m]*	*4.Constant 1993 prices [£m]*	*1. % total income*	*4. % total income*
1965†	0.32	0.10	0.01	0.11	3.03	1.04	68	23
1965/6	0.44	0.15	0.02	0.17	4.01	1.55	66	25
1966/7	0.46	0.17	0.02	0.19	4.09	1.69	66	27
1967/8	0.47	0.17	0.02	0.19	3.99	1.61	64	26
1968/9	0.50	0.21	0.02	0.23	4.04	1.86	62	29
1969/70	0.54	0.24	0.02	0.26	4.10	1.97	61	29
1970/1	0.56	0.27	0.02	0.29	3.89	2.02	60	31
1971/2	0.58	0.31	0.03	0.34	3.75	2.20	57	34
1972/3	0.59	0.37	0.03	0.40	3.49	2.37	54	37
1973/4	0.62	0.43	0.03	0.46	3.17	2.35	52	36
1974/5	0.66	0.49	0.03	0.52	2.72	2.14	50	40
1975/6	0.70	0.61	0.04	0.65	2.47	2.30	47	44
1976/7	0.74	0.75	0.05	0.80	2.25	2.44	43	47
1977/8	0.79	0.89	0.05	0.94	2.22	2.65	41	49
1978/9	0.81	1.03	0.07	1.10	2.01	2.73	38	51
1979/80	0.90	1.11	0.08	1.19	1.89	2.50	38	50
1980/1	0.98	1.19	0.09	1.28	1.84	2.41	39	50
1981/2	1.05	1.34	0.09	1.43	1.82	2.47	37	51
1982/3r	1.23	1.48	0.10	1.58	2.04	2.62	40	48
1983/4	1.43	1.69	0.10	1.79	2.25	2.82	41	49
1984/5	1.57	1.91	0.10	2.01	2.33	2.99	41	50
1985/6	1.74	2.01	0.12	2.13	2.50	3.06	42	51
1986/7	1.87	2.19	0.13	2.32	2.58	3.20	41	51
1987/8	1.95	2.32	0.12	2.44	2.57	3.21	43	53
1988/9	2.09	2.32	0.14	2.46	2.55	3.00	43	50
1989/90	2.35	2.85	0.15	3.00	2.62	3.35	41	53
1990/1	2.48	1.93	0.14	2.05	2.61	2.16	47	39
1991/2	3.07	2.03	0.13	2.10	3.12	2.13	53	37
1992/3	4.02	2.10	0.13	2.22	4.02	2.22	53	29
Total 1965–92/3	35.51			34.65	83.97	69.06	50	41
					1. Constant 2005 prices	*4. Constant 2005 prices*	*1. % total income*	*4. % total income*
1993/4	4.58			2.53	6.10	3.37	52	29
1994/5	5.18			2.78	6.67	3.58	53	29
1995/6	5.63			3.26	7.08	4.10	55	32

1996/7	6.22			3.77	7.58	4.59	53	32
1997/8	6.75			3.99	7.95	4.70	53	32
1998/9	7.25			3.85	8.41	4.47	54	29
1999/ 2000	7.73			4.89	8.71	5.51	52	33
2000/1	8.44			4.86	9.35	5.38	54	31
2001/2	8.80			4.47	9.58	4.87	57	29
2002/3	9.34			4.98	9.86	5.27	55	28
2003/4	9.48			4.89	9.74	5.03	56	29
2004/5*	9.63			4.77	9.63	4.77	59	29
Total 1993/ 4-2004/5	89.03			49.04	100.66	55.64	55	30

Source: DST, ***R & A 1965–2004/5***.

Key:
† 1st 9 months.
* 11 months to 31 August 2005.
# Conference Centre income from 1988/9 is excluded here (£6,172 in 1988/9, rising to £57,553 in 1991/2, £50,830 in 1992/3)
r accounts restated from 1982/3.

APPENDIX 5

UNFURNISHED FLAT RENT SCALES, 1965–2005 (£)

Flat type	*1965*	*1971*	*Flat type*	*1974 fair rent*	*1982 fair rent*	*Flat type*	*1988 fair rent*	*Flat type*	*1993 fair rent*	*Full Rent Bands*	*1988*	*1993*	*1999*	*2001*	*2005*	*2005 Bands*
1C	325	408	1C	480	984	1C	2281	1C	3400		3200-				8100	
1B	350	432	1C(M)	528	1104	1C(M)	2583	1CU	3900						8835	
1A	375	480	1B	516	1068	1B	2490	1B	3750	1	2800-4100	5050-6950	6063-9370	6681-10325	9572	8100-12518
2C	425	540	1B(M)	564	1200	1B(M)	2792	1BU	4200						10308	
2B	475	612	1A	564	1200	1A	2779	1A	4200						11045	
2A	525	672	1A(M)	612	1284	1A(M)	2995	1AU	4500						11780	
								1A+	-						12148	
								1AU+	-						12518	
2A+	575	744	2C	636	1392	2C	3236	2C	4850						11605	
3B	550	696	2C(M)	696	1512	2C(M)	3524	2CU	5250						12895	
3A	600	768	2B	732	1608	2B	3733	2B	5600						12895	
3A+	650	828	2B(M)	792	1716	2B(M)	4007	2BU	6050	2	4500-6000	7350-10000	9370-12402	10530-15479	14184	11605-17060
4B	700	900	2A	816	1764	2A	4125	2A	6200						12895	
4A	750	960	2A(M)	876	1884	2A(M)	4405	2AU	6600						14184	

4A+	800	1032	2A+	888	1920	2A+	4509	2A+	6750						15651	
5A	850	1092	2A+(M)	984	2064	2A+(M)	4818	2AU+	7200						17060	
5A+	900	1164	3B	828	1764	3B	4082	3B	6100						15474	
6B	900	1164	3B(M)	924	1896	3B(M)	4414	3BU	6600						16763	
6A	950	1212	3A	924	1992	3A	4625	3A	6900	3	6000-7500	8950-11350	12677-15433	14040-19361	16763	15474-21337
6A+	1000	1284	3A(M)	996	2148	3A(M)	5014	3AU	7500						18053	
7A	1000	1284	3A+	984	2124	3A+	4923	3A+	7400						19875	
7A+	1200	1496	3A+(M)	1080	2292	3A+(M)	5341	3AU+	8000						21337	
			4B	1068	2316	4B	5504	4B	8250						-	
			4A	1140	2448	4B(M)	5724	4BU	8600						25539	
			4A+	1224	2664	4A	5816	4A	8700	4	8000-9500	11900-14300	16536-19292	23400-28354	25539	25539-30946
			4A+(M)	1320	2832	4A(M)	6148	4AU	9200						26816	
			5A	1296	2796	4A+	6326	4A+	9450						28144	
			5A+	1380	2952	4A+(M)	6758	4AU+	10100						30946	
			5A+(M)	1512	3000	5A	6796	5A	10100						-	
			6B	1368	3060	5A+	7181	5A+	10800	5	9500-11000	14300-16600	20670-23426	26100-30958	32393	28486-33788
			6A	1416	3252	5A+(M)	7296	5AU	-						28486	
								5AU+	10950						33788	
			6A+	1512	#	6A	7439	6BU	11250						34139	
			7A	1512	#	6A+	7895	6A	11100							
			7A+	#	#	6A+(M)	8309	6A+	11800	6	11000-12000	15250-18200	24000-28514	31590-33750	35502	34139-36474

			7A+	#	#	6A+(M)	8309	6A+	11800	6	11000-12000	15250-18200	24000-28514	31590-33750	35502	34139-36474
			7A+(M)	#	#	7A	7895	6AU+	12450						36474	
						7A+	9275	7A	11800						37155	
						7A+(M)	10225	7A+	13800	7	12000-13500	18200-20400	29998-35510	34380-37395	40365	37155-40850
								7AU+	15200						40850	

Source: DST.

Key:
not found

APPENDIX 6

RODNEY HOUSE CHARGES, 1965–2005 (£)

At April	*Single room, per day*	*Lounge and twin bed-room, per week (4 weeks rate)*	*Single constant 1993 prices*	*Lounge/twin, constant 1993 prices*	*Single Index 1965 = 100*	*Lounge/twin Index 1965 = 100*
1965	3.5	26.75	33.15	253.36	100	100
1966	4	/	36.49	/	110	/
1967	4.25	/	37.84	/	114	/
1968*	4.5	32.50	38.24	276.16	115	109
1969	4.75	/	38.63	/	116	/
1970	5	37.50	37.93	284.50	114	112
1971	5.25	41	36.48	284.89	110	112
1972	6	45	38.79	290.93	117	115
1973	7	55	41.47	325.84	125	129
1974	7.5	60	38.32	306.60	116	121
1975	8.5	75	35.01	308.93	106	122
1976	10	90	35.32	317.89	107	125
1977	12	110	36.57	335.18	110	132
1978	17	130	47.88	366.12	144	145
1979**	22	170	54.61	422.02	165	167
1980	24	224	50.48	471.13	152	186
1981	27	245	50.76	460.58	153	182
1982	30	270	51.93	468.48	157	185
1983	33	300	54.64	496.77	165	196
1984	35	318	55.19	501.45	166	198
1985	38	348	56.50	517.48	170	204
1986	42	384	60.40	552.33	182	218
1987	46	420	63.51	579.89	192	229
1988	49	441	64.48	580.32	195	229
1989	65	570	79.36	695.89	239	275
1990	80***p***	/	89.24	/	236	/
1991	88***p***	774	92.74	815.69	280	322
1992	88***p***	774	89.38	786.16	270	310
1993	92***p***	810	92	810	278	320
1994	96***p***	850 140***d***	93.67	829.36 136.60	283	327
1995	99***p***	888***w***148***d***	93.41	837.85 139.64	282	331
1996	99***p***	155***d***	91.21	142.80	275	338
1997	99***p***	170***d***	88.42	151.82	267	359
1998	100***p***	180***d***	86.35	155.43	260	368
1999	130	175***d***	110.59	148.87	334	352
2000	130	165***d***	107.39	136.31	324	323
2001	140	175***d***	113.63	142.04	343	336
2002	/	/	/	/	/	/

2003	165	195*d*	127.99	151.26	386	358
2004	175	195*d*	131.83	146.89	398	348
2005	185	205*d*	135.58	150.24	409	356

Source: Folder of Rodney House charges, and reports to DST Committee of Management Minutes, 1965–2005.

Key:
d daily rate
p premium rates quoted here. Standard rates (for 1st and 2nd floors) were £70 in 1990, and approx. 85% of premium rates, until 1999, when the distinction was abolished
w 4-week rate not shown after 1995 [index spliced from 1996]
* August
** July after VAT increase
/ not found

APPENDIX 7

COMPONENTS OF DOLPHIN SQUARE EXPENDITURE, 1965–92/3

Year (1 October-30 September)	*1. Wages and salaries* [£m]*	*2. Repairs and maintenance [£m]*	*3. Loan interest [£m]*	*1. % Total exp.*	*2. % Total exp.*	*3. % Total exp.*
1965†	0.09	0.05	0.21	20	11	46
1965/6	0.14	0.13	0.29	20	19	41
1966/7	0.15	0.21	0.29	19	26	36
1967/8	0.17	0.14	0.29	22	18	38
1968/9	0.18	0.10	0.29	24	13	39
1969/70	0.20	0.13	0.28	26	17	36
1970/1	0.24	0.19	0.30	27	21	34
1971/2	0.27	0.17	0.30	29	18	32
1972/3	0.33	0.34	0.29	28	29	25
1973/4	0.39	0.30	0.29	32	25	24
1974/5	0.47	0.29	0.29	35	21	21
1975/6	0.53	0.28	0.29	38	20	21
1976/7	0.59	0.17	0.29	38	12	21
1977/8	0.68	0.37	0.29	40	22	17
1978/9	0.74	0.49	0.28	39	26	15
1979/80	0.88	0.66	0.28	39	29	12
1980/1	0.97	0.55	0.28	42	24	12
1981/2	1.09	0.63	0.28	42	24	11
1982/3r	1.16	0.71	0.27	39	24	9
1983/4	1.30	0.92	0.27	39	28	8
1984/5	1.39	1.13	0.27	38	31	7
1985/6	1.51	1.20	0.27	38	30	7
1986/7	1.64	1.48	0.27	37	33	6
1987/8	1.72	1.37	0.26	37	30	6
1988/9	1.79	1.41	0.26	38	30	6
1989/90	2.06	1.57	0.26	40	30	5
1990/1	2.22	1.15	0.25	44	23	5
1991/2	2.42	1.57	0.25	40	26	4
1992/3	2.97	1.29	0.25	44	19	4
Total 1965–1992/3	28.29	19.00	7.99	38	25	11

Source: DST, ***R & A 1965–92/3***.

Key:
† 1st 9 months
* including maintenance labour
r accounts restated from 1982/3

APPENDIX 8

DOLPHIN SQUARE CATERERS LTD. PROFIT AND LOSS ACCOUNT, 1965/6–91/2 (£)

Year (1 October–30 September)	*Income: Restaurant*	*Swimming pool*	*Squash*	*Sauna*	*Sunbed*	*Total income**	*Expenditure*	*Operating profit/(loss) before tax*	*Profit/(loss) after tax*	*% of income: Restaurant*	*S-pool*	*Squash*	*Sauna/sunbed*
1965/6†	17,629	7,629	11,168	-		36,793	40,232	(3,439)	(3,439)	48	21	30	-
1966/7	6,271	4,380	11,222	-		22,615	22,141	474	474	28	19	50	-
1967/8	8,142	6,078	13,197	-		27,702	24,107	3,595	4,957*a*	29	22	48	-
1968/9	8,905	6,344	15,690	-		31,194	26,189	5,005	4,966	28	20	50	-
1969/70	10,309	7,172	20,411	6,918		45,083	38,569	6,514	6,514	23	16	45	15
1970/1	10,651	10,249	25,028	19,840		65,834	55,341	10,493	10,393	16	16	38	30
1971/2	10,338	11,599	27,575	23,063		73,232	59,915	13,317	7,217	14	16	38	31
1972/3	10,207	13,158	28,098	23,338		76,642	67,777	8,865	9,183*b*	13	17	37	30
1973/4	9,973	14,062	29,929	20,511		78,156	70,215	7,941	4,235	13	18	38	26
1974/5	11,555	17,882	33,169	23,969		90,125	83,332	6,793	6,814*c*	13	20	37	27
1975/6	14,922	21,094	45,440	24,721		108,510	99,727	8,783	4,883*c*	14	19	42	23
1976/7	16,485	19,997	47,630	32,543		117,718	114,476	3,242	1,521	14	17	40	28
1977/8	19,513	29,839	61,554	30,297		144,829	117,600	27,229	15,748*c*	13	21	43	21
1978/9	20,290	30,597	60,486	26,857		143,578	146,652	(3,074)	(2,349)	14	21	42	19
1979/80	21,087	35,156	75,075	34,907		171,839	163,939	7,900	4,604	12	20	44	20
1980/1	17,110	41,022	78,817	51,069		195,022	191,133	3,889	2,581	9	21	40	26

1980/1	17,110	41,022	78,817	51,069		195,022	191,133	3,889	2,581	9	21	40	26
1981/2	(1,250)	38,975	73,645	55,892		174,402	178,529	(4,127)	(2,661)	-	22	42	32
1982/3	5,000	45,179	68,441	66,556		190,809	186,716	4,093	1,583	3	24	36	35
1983/4	5,000	43,402	67,018	62,556		179,144	192,254	(13,110)	(13,110)	3	24	37	35
1984/5	5,000	48,781	64,922	80,156		209,498	208,692	806	(19)	2	23	31	38
1985/6	12,366	56,110	65,450	71,884	26,515	246,316	243,776	2,540	3,589	5	23	27	40
1986/7	3,951	61,905	65,936	86,050	36,700	269,834	276,642	(6,808)	(6,808)	1.5	23	24	45
1987/8	0	54,405	66,273	75,784	36,945	244,517	302,053	(57,536)	(57,536)	-	22	27	46
1988/9	3,164	85,653	77,790	41,982	11,832	228,532	312,909	(84,377)	(84,377)	1.4	37	34	23
1989/90	18,517	85,587	78,066	84,584	20,329	301,091	391,040	(89,949)	(89,949)	6	28	26	35
1990/1	31,250	77,605	76,888	91,973	23,410	322,410	379,685	(57,275)	(57,275)	10	24	24	36
1991/2	31,250	100,681	86,878	106,784	23,827	373,913	407,136	(33,223)	(33,233)	8	27	23	35
Total 1965/6-1991/2	327,635	974,541	1,375,796	1,142,234	179,558	4,169,338	4,400,777			8	23	33	32

Source: DSCL and DST accounts, 1965/6-1991/2.

Key:
† 18 months to 30 September 1966
* including interest received
a rates overprovision in 1964/7 credited to account
b dividend of £20,000 declared
c dividend of £10,000 declared

APPENDIX 9

DOLPHIN SQUARE TRUST INCOME AND EXPENDITURE, NET INCOME AND ACCUMULATED SURPLUS/DEFICIT, 1993/4–2004/5

Year (1 October–30 September)	*Income [£m]*	*Constant 2005 prices [£m]*	*Expenditure before tax [£m]*	*Constant 2005 Prices [£m]*	*Net income after tax before special provisions [£'000s]*	*Reported surplus/ (deficit) [£'000s]*	*Reported accumulated surplus/ (deficit) [£'000s]*
1994	8.75	11.65	7.93	10.56	591.8	591.8	2,496.1
1995	9.70	12.49	9.19	11.83	219.6	219.6	2,715.7
1996	10.28	12.92	9.71	12.21	273.8	273.8	2,989.5
1997	11.75	14.32	10.30	12.55	985.0	985.0	3,974.5
1998	12.63	14.88	11.36	13.38	823.1	774.2t	4,748.7
1999	13.48	15.65	12.82	14.88	521.3	521.3	5,270.0
2000	14.82	16.70	13.11*	14.78	683.7	(316.3)t	4,953.8
2001re	15.60	17.28	13.79	15.27	860.6	293.9t	5,599.2
2002	15.49	16.87	15.72*	17.12	-393.2	(461.0)t	5,138.2
2003	16.88	17.87	15.85	16.78	417.7	417.7	5,555.9
2004	16.82	17.29	16.72	17.19	-153.2	(296.4)t	5,259.5
2005†	16.31	16.31	16.64	16.64	-1082.2	(1082.2)	4,177.2
1994–2005	162.51	184.23	153.14	173.19	3,748.0	1,921.4	-
1982–93	55.60	96.34	53.77	93.07	936.1	595.7	-
1981–92	50.48	92.39	49.00	89.35	509.7	164.4	
1993–2005	170.16	194.67	160.23	182.86	4291.5	2,464.9	-

Source: DST, ***R & A 1993/4-2004/5*** (reworked, with income including 'other operating income' and income from investments; and expenditure including interest payable); Appendix 3.

Key:

† 11 months to 31 August 2005
* after provision made for fall in value of investments
t after transfers to reserves
re accounts restated

APPENDIX 10

DOLPHIN SQUARE AMENITIES: INCOME AND OPERATING PROFIT/LOSS, 1993/4–2004/5 (£'000S)

INCOME

Year (1 October–30 September)	*Rodney House apartments/ guest rooms*	*Sports Centre/ Health Spa [Zest!]*	*Restaurants/ bars*	*Conference centre*	*Garage/car bays*	*Shops/ offices*
1993/4	2,480.1	429.2	596.7	45.7	129.3	250.3
1994/5	2,747.7	500.8	671.6	94.6	229.3	203.4
1995/6	3,176.7	507.3	641.8	74.8	210.8	111.1
1996/7	3,719.6	559.4	/	88.3	238.2	113.0
1997/8	3,948.8	545.4	/	77.6	254.6	108.7
1998/9	3,710.9	444.8	1,788.6	116.2	244.3	114.3
1999/2000	4,670.8	498.2	1,660.9	159.3	256.4	113.9
2000/1	4,635.0	560.7	1,791.6	172.3	259.1	161.6
2001/2	4,096.1	617.0	1,742.9	245.3	273.3	165.7
2002/3	4,624.4	679.2	1,753.9	353.9	260.6	134.1
2003/4	4,534.5	722.5	1,481.1	260.7	256.5	140.7
2004/5*	4,374.6	614.3	/	203.8	236.1	119.2
2004/5	/	673.2	1,501.2	216.8	/	/

OPERATING PROFIT/(LOSS)

Year (1 October-30 September)	Rodney House	Sports Centre/ Health spa	Restaurant deficits before costs	Restaurant costs 'landlord'/ refurbishment[††]	Restaurant total	Garage/ car bays	Shops/ offices
1993/4	557.7**	(27.9)	(40.4)	134.0	(174.4)	/	/
1994/5	90.7	(61.6)	(38.0)	74.1	(112.1)	0.3	118.9
1995/6	459.3	(105.7)	(140.7)	84.6	(225.3)	61.4	46.2
1996/7	956.9	(137.9)	(160.7)	100.1	(260.8)	90.0	43.3
1997/8	787.5	(73.5)	(309.1)	141.2	(450.3)	87.9	43.8
1998/9	320.2	(424.4)	(269.1)[†]	184.8	(453.9)	68.6	55.4
1999/2000	714.4	(331.5)	(243.0)[†]	277.7	(520.7)	83.4	54.8
2000/1	431.4	(251.8)	(250.2)[†]	315.8	(566.0)	59.8	118.2
2001/2	(1,198.7)	(241.8)	(183.4)[†]	265.1	(448.5)	64.7	117.8
2002/3	(162.2)	(179.2)	(137.1)[†]	161.3	(298.4)	84.4	75.8
2003/4	(360.5)	(43.4)	(234.6)[†]	142.9	(377.5)	76.5	77.5
2004/5*	/	/	(183.3)[†]	123.5	(306.8)	/	/
2004/5	/	/	(199.0)[†]	/	/	/	/

Source: DST.

Key:
* 11 months to 31 August 2005
** includes Conference and Business Centres (otherwise excluded)
† In 1998/9 Sodexho made a contribution of £250,000 towards operating losses; thereafter it met half of the excess loss over the agreed budget loss
†† approximations only in some years
/ not found

APPENDIX 11

COMPONENTS OF DOLPHIN SQUARE EXPENDITURE, 1993/4–2004/5 (£M)

Year (1 October –30 September)	*1. Staffing costs*	*2. Repairs and maintenance [revenue account]*†	*3. Restaurant costs [operating and landlord]*	*4. Depreciation*	*5. Legal and professional fees*	*1. % Total exp.*	*2. % Total exp.*	*3. % Total exp.*	*4. % Total exp.*	*5. % Total exp.*
1993/4	3.14	1.87	0.57	0.15	0.11	40	24	7	2	1
1994/5	3.35	2.43	0.59	0.18	0.10	36	26	6	2	1
1995/6	3.59	2.44	0.63	0.23	0.15	37	25	6	2	1
1996/7	3.93	2.64	0.65	0.34	0.19	38	26	6	3	2
1997/8	3.95	2.85	0.84	0.68	0.17	35	25	7	6	1
1998/9	4.24	2.76	1.74	1.26	0.15	33	22	10	10	1
1999/2000	4.42	2.17	1.54	1.75	0.27	34	17	12	13	2
2000/1	4.59	2.48	1.65	2.08	0.37	33	18	12	15	3
2001/2	4.67	2.91	1.53	2.42	0.38	30	18	10	15	2
2002/3	4.63	3.56	1.52	2.18	0.68	30	19	9	14	4
2003/4	4.67	3.70	1.62	1.69	0.90	28	22	10	7	6
2004/5*	4.37	2.70	1.31	1.15	2.87	26	16	8	7	17
Total	49.55	32.51	14.19	14.11	6.34	32	21	9	9	4

Source: DST, ***R & A 1993/4–2004/5.***

Key:

† spending on maintenance charged to capital account: £0.38m, 1995/6; £0.60m, 1996/7; £1.88m, 1997/8; £2.74m, 1998/9; £2.42m, 1999/2000; £2.02m, 2000/1; £2.28m, 2001/2; £0.72m, 2002/3; £0.46m, 2003/4; £0.21m, 2004/5 Total: £13.71m; Total (capital and revenue): £46.22m.

* 11 months to 31 August 2005

APPENDIX 12

CORRESPONDENCE BETWEEN TENANT ACTIVISTS AND RODNEY BROOKE, 2005

1. Rosemary Henley–Rodney Brooke (Chairman, DST), 17 April 2005

Dear Mr Brooke,

I am in receipt of your letter dated 14 April 2005.

It appears to be all about your 'duty' to the Community at large and your concerns about the end of the lease. I contend that your duty is to protect the tenants of Dolphin Square, which the Trust was created to protect. It has no responsibility to housing in Westminster, this is the Council's responsibility and not yours. Although the Minister's letter has unaccountably gone missing, there is plenty of evidence indicating that the building was bought by Westminster city council ON BEHALF OF THE TENANTS and the lease was to run until 2034 ie 60 years to pay off the mortgage and 10 years to build up a dilapidations fund.

. . .

I do not understand why, at this late stage, you should claim you have a responsibility to the wider community. It is not a claim you have ever made prior to last October's meeting and I suspect it is a figleaf to cover your embarrassment at selling us down the river. You are Chairman of a Trust created solely to protect the tenants of Dolphin Square and if you cannot do something to rectify the present deplorable situation, you should resign . . . .

2. Brooke–Henley, 19 April 2005
Dear Miss Henley
Thank you for your letter of 17 April. I am distressed by its contents, since I value your opinion highly.

1. The Trust has a larger responsibility than to the present tenants. We have two leading Counsel's opinion on the point and ignore them at our peril.

2. While the Trust's lease extends to 2034, its ability to let new tenancies expires in 2024. Thereafter the Trust would become unviable and its bargaining power would be lost

. . .

9. I am sad that you call for my resignation. Believe me, I should love to resign a Procrustean bed which brings no pay, no plaudits and many unpleasant letters such as yours. However, I believe myself to have a higher moral duty which is to protect the tenants of Dolphin Square consistent with our overall duties as trustees. Should I resign, it would, of course, bring nearer the day when WCC can fill the Trustees with its own nominees – who might well have scant interest in the present tenants . . .

3. Brooke–Lord Russell-Johnston (Chairman, DSTA), 26 August 2005

Dear Lord Russell-Johnston
Thank you for your letter of 20th August. I note what you say, but neither the Committee or management of DSTL intend to call a halt to the proposed sale. Nor do we agree with the suggestion implicit in your letter that the proposed sale contravenes any rights or expectations arising from the answer to Question 9.[1]

Both before, during and after registration with the Housing Corporation, Dolphin Square Housing Trust has always existed as a body established for community advantage through the provision of housing facilities, and in that sense has always sought to profit the community. It still does so, and I am advised that it is required to do so by virtue of its constitution as a body registered as an Industrial and Provident Society ("IPS"). If it were not so registered it would plainly be unable to continue in

1 'Question 9', raised during deregistration as a housing association, asked: 'Would we still be a non-profit making housing association?' The answer was: 'Yes – just as we were before we registered with the Housing Corporation'. Prendergast-tenants, 15 July 1991, DST.

existence; even if it were allowed to de-register as an IPS, which is open to question, the result would be that it would lose its limited liability . . .

Thus deregistration as an IPS is therefore simply not an option. But so long as it is so registered DSTL has a dominant duty to the community, and that is what is intended to be fulfilled by the proposed sale.

The other side of the coin is of course that DSTL has never existed for private profit and does not so exist now. That means in particular that not only has it never sought nor can it seek to secure private profits to its members, it equally cannot exist simply to secure benefits to the residents of Dolphin Square otherwise than so far as is consistent with its community objective, for it is not a private trust for the benefit of residents.

The answer to Question 9 states no more than this: that DSTL neither had nor would after deregistration with the Housing Corporation exist for the making of private profit. It would continue to be an association dedicated to the provision of housing for the benefit of the community. This did not mean that it would never use its assets profitably. For example, charging rents as indicated in the answer to Question 4 might well over the years have been expected to throw up a profit to Dolphin Square Housing Trust [sic] which it would have been bound to use in accordance with its community objectives.

By the proposed sale DSTL seeks to use its main asset in such a way as will secure very substantial funding for its community housing objectives, but in a manner which will, in the view of the Committee fully respect the legitimate rights and expectations of its tenant body. It would plainly be for private profit now to disregard the opportunity to secure funding for community housing objectives in the interests of meeting the requirements of the present tenant body . . .

2. Russell-Johnston–Brooke, 29 August 2005

Dear Rodney,
I read your letter of 26th August with ever-increasing astonishment and, I'm afraid, the word "casuistry" sprang to my mind. Of course, it was a lawyer's letter of a certain kind, which I have got to know over the years.

It completely ignores the developments and changes which, from 1986 on, have led us to our present position.

It ignored also the circumstances which led to the founding of the Trust (the then take-over of the Square by a company only interested in profit: so we return to Square One!) and the principles upon which it was established set out by the then Westminster Council in 1965 and subsequently, unequivocally attested to, by Sir Alan Dawtry, Sir Gordon Pirie and Mr Jack Dribble [sic]: all persons of high repute.

Instead, it sets out a completely new scenario in which you state that, what is now being done, is the outcome of a careful evaluation by the Trust, of its responsibilities to the wider community.

As you put it: "Dolphin Trust has a dominant duty to the Community and that is what is intended by the proposed sale" and later: "The Trust seeks to use its main (should that not be 'only'?) asset in such a way as will secure substantial funding for its community housing projects."

If that was true, you would not have sought as, admirably, you did (twice!) to purchase the lease!

If that was true, you would not be acquiescing in the Square being taken over by a company only interested in maximizing profit.

If that was true, it would have been normal for tenants to be told long, long ago, that the Trust had been thinking about its "Community Housing Objectives" (I wasn't aware that it had any!) and had reached certain conclusions which it wished to air & discuss.

I understand of course, all too clearly, that you have decided to connive in Westminster Council's policy reversal but please don't try and dress this up as a considered moral decision.

It isn't . . .

Source: DST

INDEX